Small Screen, Big Picture

"**An amazingly in-depth and accurate look at just about every facet of the TV business,** *Small Screen, Big Picture* effectively and entertainingly illuminates the painstaking process by which television shows get made and what various industry professionals actually do. **If you're trying to break in, you'll learn a ton of essential information. If you're already in, you'll be surprised by how much you thought you knew but didn't.**"

—DAVID WALPERT, consulting producer (*Miss Guided, Will & Grace, Just Shoot Me!*)

"There isn't a class, seminar, or lecture that covers every aspect of the business as well as *Small Screen, Big Picture* does. Between Chad's own professional experience and the guidance of the many executives, writers, and other industry professionals, the book's insight is invaluable. **The only other way to gain such a thorough understanding of the television business is to have worked in it for years.**"

—DAVID WINDSOR, supervising producer (*Happy Hour; What I Like About You; Two Guys, a Girl and a Pizza Place; Do Over; Like Family*)

"The world of TV writing is much like the hell that is high school, only the nerds are nerdier, the jocks are jockier, and all the mean girls want to eat your young. With the help of Chad's book and breezy writing, one will be able to navigate the treacherous waters and dimly lit corridors and emerge overpaid and well fed, just like the rest of us."

—TOM KAPINOS, creator/executive producer (*Californication*)

"Chad Gervich's keenly written, inspiring book is a must-read not only for writers but anyone looking to obtain both a global and intimate understanding of how the craft and business of television works. *Small Screen, Big Picture* is **the Swiss Army knife of the TV industry, with every tool necessary to carve a productive career.**"

—FRANCESCA ORSI, director, drama series programming, HBO Entertainment

"Gervich's book has assembled information that normally takes upward of ten years of working in the business to learn. This book should be required reading for any college student who wants to pursue the craft and business of television writing. **A must-have!**"

—LIZ TIGELAAR, supervising producer (*Brothers & Sisters, Dirty Sexy Money, What About Brian, American Dreams*)

"Not just a showbiz primer, **but *the* comprehensive guide to the TV industry for any writer who's serious about making it.** This book covers everything from basic jargon to the anatomy of a successful show. Most important, it's full of advice on whom and how to impress. The only thing more useful to your writing career is . . . well . . . writing. But read this first. **If I'd had *Small Screen, Big Picture* when *I* was trying to break into the business, I'd have twelve Emmys by now!**"

—VIJAL PATEL, writer (*'Til Death*)

"This is very rare for a studio executive to say, but after reading *Small Screen, Big Picture*, I have no notes. **Undeniably the best guide to the business of TV ever written.**"

—BRYAN SEABURY, vice president, drama development, CBS Paramount Network Television

"Clear off your bookshelves and make sure *Small Screen, Big Picture* will always be in easy reach! Believe me, you'll use it! Chad Gervich has everything you'll ever need to break into television, catch a rising star, or stay ahead of the curve. It's all here—from the lingo and jargon to the rules of engagement to the reality of the TV business. **Chad's written the best must-have, must-read, must-consult book on television in ages! There's no better way to understand the ever-changing picture of television than by reading *Small Screen, Big Picture*.**"

—GARY GROSSMAN, executive producer, Weller/Grossman Productions (*Strictly Dr. Drew, Rachael Ray's Tasty Travels, Wolfgang Puck, Beyond the Da Vinci Code*)

"Finally, **a perfect road map for making it as a television writer.** I wish I had this book ten years ago."

—BRAD COPELAND, writer/producer (*Arrested Development, My Name Is Earl*) and screenwriter (*Wild Hogs*)

"Chad Gervich has written **an authoritative, highly entertaining insider's guide** to the American television industry. He shares his insights about every single aspect of the business and, in the end, manages to make the story of the process as fascinating as the shows themselves. They say that if you like sausage, you shouldn't ask how the sausage is made. But Chad takes us inside the sausage factory, and everyone who is interested in television will love his book. An invaluable guide for fans and professionals alike."

—DAVID TENZER, entertainment lawyer and former television packaging agent at Creative Artists Agency

"Whether you're a writer, director, executive, or actor, this book gives you **the full picture of what's happening in every area of a television show** . . . not just in the writers' room or onstage, but in the offices of the networks, studios, and agencies. It lets you know how all the pieces fit together, which goes a long way toward making you stronger in your own discipline."

—MARISSA JARET WINOKUR, actress and producer

"The in-depth information and insight Chad Gervich provides **acts as a compass to lead you through the labyrinth that is the television business.** He answers not only the 'who,' 'what,' 'where,' and 'how,' but also the 'why,' which is invaluable in understanding what steps need to be taken to be successful in the TV industry. I wish this resource had been available when I was starting out."

—DUPPY DEMETRIUS, co-producer (*The Closer*)

"This book **puts you into the mind and experience of people on both sides of the desk:** both the new writer—the trembling Dorothy/Tin Man/Lion—and also the Wizard. It guides you to find your own strength. I especially loved the chapter 'The Writers' Room.'"

—HAL ACKERMAN, screenwriting area head, UCLA Department of Film, Television and Digital Media

"Comprehensive, cleanly written, and incredibly well researched . . . this book should be **the bible for aspiring screenwriters** or anyone looking to traverse the raging waters and shifting tides of the television business."

—DAVID FURY, executive producer (*24, Angel*) and co-executive producer (*Lost, Buffy the Vampire Slayer*)

"If you're crazy enough to pursue a job in the entertainment industry, read Chad's book. **Solid and insightful info and advice coupled with wit and charm. It will give readers an edge in a business that is more competitive than ever.** Read it."

> —JOHN MILLER, executive vice president, The Weinstein Company (*The No. 1 Ladies' Detective Agency, Project Runway*)

"*Small Screen, Big Picture* is **required reading for anyone contemplating a career in television.** Even seasoned Hollywood professionals will complete Chad Gervich's exhaustively researched book much more knowledgeable than when they began it."

> —SETH HOFFMAN, executive story editor (*Prison Break*)

"This book is **packed with insight for aspiring TV writers.** Chad answers the questions you're asking, as well as ones you're not asking that maybe you should be."

> —SEAN WHITESELL, writer/producer (*Homicide: Life on the Street, Oz, Cold Case*)

"Gervich provides the reader with peerless insight into the always daunting task of understanding how writers, studios, networks, and multinational corporations work together (and sometimes against each other) to supply the audience with the TV shows they enjoy in the comfort of their own homes. **This book should be on the syllabus of every film school across the nation.**"

> —ANUPAM NIGAM, co-producer (*Psych*)

"There's a certain art to navigating the business of television. *Small Screen, Big Picture* gives you the numbers to paint by."

> —KIP KOENIG, executive producer/co-creator (*Welcome to Bedlam*) and supervising producer (*Grey's Anatomy*)

"**This book will help the uninitiated break into the fraternity of television . . . without the nasty pledge-night stuff.**"

> —ANDREW J. GOLDER, executive producer (*The Gong Show, Identity, Solitary, Win Ben Stein's Money*)

Small
Screen,
Big
Picture

Also from mediabistro.com

Get a Freelance Life   Margit Feury Ragland

mediabistro.com presents

Small
Screen,
Big
Picture

A Writer's Guide to the TV Business

CHAD GERVICH

Foreword by Howard Gordon, executive producer of *24*

THREE RIVERS PRESS · NEW YORK

Library of Congress Cataloging-in-Publication Data

Gervich, Chad.
Mediabistro.com presents
small screen, big picture: a writer's guide to the TV business / Chad Gervich;
foreword by Howard Gordon
Includes index.
1. Television authorship. 2. Television—Production and direction. 3. Television—
Vocational guidance. I. Title.
PN1992.7.G48 2008
791.4502'32—dc22   2008003093

ISBN 978-0-307-39531-3

Printed in the United States of America

Design by Lynne Amft

10 9 8 7 6 5 4 3 2 1

First Edition

For Kelly,

who put up with all the sleepless nights,
neurotic breakdowns, and panicked rewrites.
I love you. Don't go anywhere.

Contents

Somewhere out there in space,
there's a huge black ball of nothingness
racing toward every television set in America.

It's our job to stop it.

—WARREN LITTLEFIELD
Principal, The Littlefield Company

Small Screen, Big Picture

Foreword

by Howard Gordon

I remember being in a writers' room about ten years ago, and someone—a brilliant and famous writer whose name I'll keep to myself for now—rhapsodized about the exquisite ecstasy of the writing process. "Don't you love it when you get lost inside the story, and the characters start speaking for themselves, and you look up and realize eight hours have passed?" I nodded dumbly, and smiled. Because I had no idea what the fuck he was talking about.

I've never had that experience. Never. Me, I'm a grinder. And a second-guesser. Since I can remember, I have suffered from some undiagnosed combination of OCD and ADD that causes me to spend hours on a preposition. Which is a long-winded way to describe this simple truth: I hate writing. I really do. Even writing this foreword is excruciating. Every word weighs on me like a millstone. Every. Single. Word.

What makes the process even more excruciating is that I am my own worst critic. No one has more contempt for my work than me. So studio and network notes are usually a cakewalk. Whatever they dish out, chances are I've already dished out for myself and come back for seconds.

So why do I write? Because as much as I hate writing, I love having written. All the pain suddenly falls away when the dialogue turns from a bunch of words under a character name into the living voices of real people, and the plot becomes more than just a series of events but a story worth telling. However we get there, if we're lucky, eventually we get there. Word by word. Line by line.

I write because it's the only thing I've ever wanted to do. Not a day goes by that I don't appreciate what a privilege it is to be a member of this profession. I suppose in some way, being a writer is the buy-in that allows me to enjoy the company and respect of my fellow writers. To count so many professional writers as friends and colleagues is one of my proudest accomplishments. I may not enjoy the creative process as much as my unnamed colleague, but I'd wager my WGA pension that I get every bit as much pleasure from my final draft—which only makes me want to belly up to the laptop and do it all over again.

Writing and producing a television show is a mysterious craft, and we all bring to it our own unique energy and talent. But the business of making a television show is the common ground we all have to navigate. You'd think that after twenty-four years as a working writer, I'd have figured out pretty much everything there is to know about the television business. But after reading Chad Gervich's book, I found that wasn't the case at all. In fact, I didn't know how little I knew until I read *Small Screen, Big Picture*.

This isn't just an operating manual for aspiring writers and executives; it's for anyone who's ever wondered how television shows are born. Within these pages you'll find a map of the twisted and thorny path an idea must travel before it becomes a script, then a pilot, and finally a television series; one that, more likely than not, will be canceled before its first season is even finished shooting. You'll discover that even after a writer is lucky enough to have beaten back the demons of his own self-doubt and written a script he's satisfied with, that's when the real adventure begins. You'll learn how to navigate though the minefield known as the development process and how to defend yourself against that fickle species known as the creative executive, whose opinions are sometimes helpful but can often deal the death blow to a project. Chad sobers us with the truth of how difficult a process it is, but he also gets us drunk with the hope that comes from the promise of creating a show that works. He is a storyteller and an insider whose love for television practically vibrates in every sentence.

Had there been a book like this when I started my career, I would have saved myself a lot of time. And the business has only gotten more confusing—much more confusing—than when I started working as a writer. As the 2008 WGA strike demonstrated, the television business is changing faster than even the most forward-thinking pundits could have predicted.

With the explosive growth of digital recorders and broadband and wireless platforms, the revenue models are being reconfigured at a dizzying pace. But none of it has gotten ahead of Chad's understanding. He tells the reader exactly what to expect and when to expect it. Even if the craft of writing can't be learned, certain mistakes can be avoided with enough good information. And the information Gervich has gathered is as good as anything I've ever read on the subject.

I wish I'd written this book myself. It's the book I always told myself that I'd write one day. But the truth is that Chad wrote it much better than I could ever have written it. So ultimately I'm grateful to him—not just for educating me on a business I thought I understood, but for saving me so much time.

Enjoy *Small Screen, Big Picture*. If you love television, you'll have a hard time putting it down.

Author's Note

I showed up at my first day of work at the Littlefield Company's Beverly Hills offices—parking garage populated with Ferraris, walls covered with Lichtensteins—wearing a shirt so new it still smelled like the Van Heusen outlet. It was 1999, and no one in L.A. had worn Van Heusen since 1883, but I didn't care. Or, more accurately, didn't know. I had my first job, and while it wasn't exactly a writing or producing gig, I was naïvely determined to be Joss Whedon by the end of the year.

Fresh out of UCLA grad school, I was starting as a development assistant at former NBC Entertainment president Warren Littlefield's new TV production company. I had met Warren through an MFA mentoring program, but not only did I know nothing about how TV was bought, sold, produced, or distributed, I had no idea how to be an actual assistant.

As I learned to roll calls, write coverage, and keep my boss's calendar, one thing became painfully clear: there was a massive gulf between myself and the people around me. These people talked about "overalls" and "if-comes" and "franchises" and "license fees." I wanted to talk about last night's *Buffy* episode and brainstorm how to turn Christopher Durang plays into TV shows. They drove BMWs and ate at Mr. Chow's and had drinks at Sushi Roku. I wore Van Heusen shirts and drove a 1989 Plymouth Acclaim. It was like I had been invited to a dance with the popular kids—a dance I'd always wanted to go to—only to arrive and discover I had no idea how to dance.

As writers and artists, many of us grow up feeling out of place, like our families and friends never quite "get us," and for those of us longing to write movies or TV shows, Hollywood holds the allure not of glitz and glamour, but of a place where we'll *fit in*—where we'll find other writers who grew up loving *E.T.* and *Annie Hall* and *My So-Called Life.* Which is why it's a bitter wake-up call when you arrive and realize you don't necessarily belong.

It wasn't that people didn't share my passion for great writing and entertainment—I actually find most people in television, whether writers, directors, agents, or executives, appreciate good work and are incredibly passionate about their jobs. What made me an outsider was that people on the "inside"—working writers, producers, and executives—understood something I had never fully realized or digested: that television is, first and foremost, *a business.* And like all businesses, it comes with its own rules, processes, and pathways. Which means the writers, producers, directors, actors, agents, and execs who are most successful are those who know how to navigate those pathways.

Working at Littlefield, I began to understand how TV shows are bought and sold, developed and produced. When I became a director's assistant on *Malcolm in the Middle* and *Girls Club* two years later, I began learning the ins and outs of physical production. As a writer's assistant on *Septuplets,* an unaired FOX drama, I witnessed the politics and procedures of a writing staff. And as a showrunner's assistant on CBS's *Star Search,* I had my first taste of producing reality. Every day, at each of these jobs, I made innumerable mistakes—and with each mistake I learned something new: how networks differ from studios, why some shows outperform others, when it's appropriate (or not) to dispute a network's note. I began realizing that TV shows are more than just compelling stories and innovative concepts, but carefully crafted works designed to survive TV's intricate corporate clockworks. And the shows and writers that succeed are usually those that adhere to certain creative and commercial rules.

In 2003, I returned to the Littlefield Company as a development executive. I spent two years working with writers and producers, developing comedies, dramas, and reality shows. Then, in the spring of 2005, everything changed.

Warren and I had spent the last several months working on *Foody Call*, a reality project I'd conceived based on *Cook Your Way Into Her Pants*, a cookbook-slash-how-to-get-laid guide for men. We'd sold the concept to Style Network in the fall of 2004, shot the pilot in February of 2005, and were now waiting for Style's response. *Foody Call* had been a pet project of mine ever since some of my coworkers at Littlefield had laughed it off and said it couldn't be sold, so when Warren called to tell me Style had made their decision—my breath caught in my throat.

"They're picking up the show," he said, "for ten episodes."

Three months later, I left my job as an exec to become a producer on the show—which meant that after giving notes, monitoring deadlines, and steering producers' creative processes, I suddenly found myself on the other side. *I* was the one dealing with executives' notes. *I* was the one racing to meet deadlines. *I* was the one fighting for my creative choices. And while this was what I'd always wanted—to develop and produce my own TV show—I couldn't help but be *utterly petrified*.

Fortunately, being an executive had given me insights and relationships that helped me as a producer. I'd seen common missteps made by other producers, and I didn't want to repeat them. And that's when it hit me: If I had known earlier all the things I knew now, how much easier might my path have been? Could I have excelled quicker? Pitched smarter ideas? Developed better shows? While my bosses and co-workers had been hugely supportive and nurturing, how much faster would I have learned if I had had, years earlier, some kind of . . . of . . . *book*? Some kind of guide to walk me though TV's multifarious business structures and practices? A map to illustrate how the industry's disparate parts worked together as a whole, and how that whole affected TV's creative processes? If I had only had *that*, I thought, I could've begun my career with deeper stores of knowledge, stronger creative muscles, and sharper business savvy.

Thus the idea for this book began to percolate, and a few months later, when I began teaching at mediabistro.com, I knew I'd found the perfect partners. Mediabistro.com is one of those rare companies that maintains relationships with top-shelf professionals while still servicing the talented aspirants who are its lifeblood. So I began talking with Laurel Touby, the founder of the company, and Taffy Brodesser-Akner, then the head of the

L.A. office, about a book that would not only help young writers and producers learn the ropes of television, but also incorporate interviews, advice, and perspectives from working professionals. In other words, for all the people struggling to get into the TV business, we'd bring the TV business to them.

As of today, I've written, produced, or developed projects for nearly every network and studio. I've produced shows for both TV and the Internet. I've written countless articles for *Variety, Writers Digest, Fade In, Written By,* and *Moving Pictures.* And while I've learned a lot, I realize every day how much more I have to learn. Writing this book, in fact, has convinced me of two things: first, no matter how much I think I know, it's only the tip of the iceberg; and, second, *no one* in this industry knows everything. More than one hundred writers, producers, executives, directors, agents, managers, and assistants have been interviewed for this book, and each has his or her own stories, perspectives, methods, and processes. Many have completely differing opinions and suggestions.

Yet there's still one thing they all agree on: *television is a business.*

In the following pages you'll discover how that business works: how companies make money, how this affects shows' creative development, and how series are produced and programmed to give them their best chances of success. You'll journey from the top of TV's corporate food chain to the ground floor of pilot production. You'll hear firsthand how producers and executives design shows to negotiate media's corporate maze—and what *your* shows need to get on the air. You'll venture into the inner sanctum of a writers' room to watch a writing staff architect its stories, then uncover the truth about how new writers are hired and promoted.

You'll also explore how television is changing thanks to new technologies like the Internet, digital video recorders, and video-on-demand. Long-standing rules are collapsing. Traditional practices are evolving. New methods of production and distribution are popping up daily. And although no one's entirely sure where these innovations will lead us, there's never been a period more rife with opportunity and possibility.

Finally, this book will arm you with an arsenal of practical information about how to land that elusive first (or second) job, and even how to work your way up once you're there.

So think of this as your roadmap through the complex, ever-changing world of television. Like all maps, it's an interactive, hands-on guide, meant to be marked up, highlighted, and scribbled in wherever you feel the need. This book is also a snapshot—a photo of the industry at this particular time—to help you understand where the industry has been, why it's transforming, and how those transformations affect you and your career.

One last thing: *There's never one right answer to anything.* Television is a business of many exceptions and few rules, and even those are constantly being broken. Shonda Rhimes does things one way, Dick Wolf does them another. CBS has certain needs, FOX has others. Thus, all anyone can give you are insights and truths that, in their experience, have proven valid. But for the most part, the information here represents conventional systems and accepted rules of TV development and production.

So welcome to the first step of your long, fruitful television career. By the time you reach the last page, you'll know markedly more than your closest competitor. So settle in, grab a pencil, and start reading. And do me a favor: when you sell your first show, or your second, or your third . . . remember me in your Emmy speech.

Introduction

Octber 31, 2007, should've been a great day.

First of all, it was my birthday, which is *always* a great day (and just happens to fall on Halloween). It was also the day I was scheduled to give my publisher the manuscript for this book. Which means I had every reason in the world to celebrate that evening. Except for one thing . . .

October 31, 2007, was the *exact date* on which the Writers Guild of America's contract with Hollywood's networks and studios was set to expire, and the entire entertainment industry was bracing for a massive writers strike. A strike, people claimed, that would change *everything:* how TV shows were developed, how networks scheduled their air, how writers worked within the system. And none of that is what you want to hear the day you turn in a book about how television works.

Now that the WGA strike is over, we're still determining how far-reaching its effects will be. In some respects, the industry has returned to business as usual, but overall, the strike has revamped TV in three important ways:

- It gave writers unprecedented rights and compensation.
- It helped networks and studios break out of longstanding patterns of impracticality.
- It shined a spotlight on the exploding world of digital media, helping to pave the way for top-shelf TV and film writers to begin working in cyberspace.

So what caused this mini-revolution, and how did it play out?

Before the strike began, the WGA was aiming to renegotiate several main contract points with networks and studios. The WGA's contract is known as the Minimum Basic Agreement (MBA), or schedule of minimums, and it lays out the minimum payments union writers must receive for various work, from writing on sitcoms and dramas to selling or rewriting a movie. Every three years it's renegotiated, and in 2007, as everyone knew, the WGA was preparing to get bullish on several key points. These included greater residuals from home video revenue (to learn more about residuals, check out chapter 3) and jurisdiction over animation and reality TV (chapter 19). But the most important issue was getting fair compensation in digital media and the Internet. Under Hollywood's system at the time, writers were paid virtually nothing for content they created that was downloaded, streamed, or made otherwise available online. This was true not only for Internet-specific projects, like NBC's online spinoff of *The Office,* but also for online episodes of regular TV shows (like streaming or downloadable episodes of *Pushing Daisies* or *NCIS*). Writers feared that if they didn't fight for fair payment now, they'd be left in the dust as the Internet grew more pervasive and converged with traditional TV.

On July 16, 2007, three and a half months before the MBA expired, the Writers Guild began negotiations with the Alliance of Motion Picture and Television Producers (AMPTP), the trade organization representing more than 350 TV and film companies in collective bargaining agreements with Hollywood's trade unions (the Writers Guild, the Directors Guild, the Screen Actors Guild, etc.). While everyone in Hollywood knew a strike was a possibility, most expected writers to wait and strike until summer 2008, when a walkout could correspond with the June 30 expiration of directors' and actors' contracts. This would allow the three unions to strike together, giving them increased muscle.

But when negotiations reached a stalemate in October 2007, on the eve of the WGA's contract expiration, the industry rumbled with rumors of an immediate work stoppage. For one thing, writers figured striking in the fall would do more damage to TV shows currently in development and production. Secondly, writers feared the Directors Guild would step out and negotiate their own deal with studios before writers had a chance to finish their own. A DGA deal would provide a template for all other unions' negotiations, making it difficult for writers or actors to negotiate anything different. And because the DGA has a different membership from the WGA—about 40 percent of the DGA consists of technical workers who are compensated differently from writers—it would be an inappropriate template for writers.

On Wednesday, October 31—as I put the final touches on the first draft of this book—the WGA contract expired. Five days later, on Monday, November 5, the strike began. All over Los Angeles and New York, thousands of writers gathered at studio gates and, instead of heading in to their usual offices, formed picket lines, signs and banners in hand.

"It was surreal," says Craig Turk, a supervising producer on *Private Practice,* who spent the first day of the strike on picket lines outside FOX. "At that point . . . there didn't seem to be many people paying attention. There were a couple of cameras, but the reality of the strike hadn't settled in. Certainly the public at large wasn't sure why all these people in red shirts were marching around outside."

The effects of the strike were felt almost instantly. Talk shows like *Late Show with David Letterman, Late Night with Conan O'Brien,* and *The Tonight Show* went off the air immediately, followed by comedies like *The Big Bang Theory, Back to You, Two and a Half Men,* and *'Til Death.* Other shows like *CSI: NY* and *Grey's Anatomy* had stockpiled written scripts, and these remained in production as long as possible. Yet as weeks went on, more and more shows went off the air . . . until finally, all sixty-three scripted broadcast and cable programs went dark. (Movies weren't as impacted, since film productions don't need new scripts every week.)

But it wasn't just writers who felt the brunt of the strike. Thousands of crew members were out of work. So were prop houses, costume shops, florists, and caterers who serviced the industry, costing L.A.'s economy almost $20 million a day. Agencies and studios laid off employees and put hundreds on notice. As networks' ratings dropped over 20 percent, network salespeople were forced to refund millions of advertisers' dollars (barely a month into the strike, NBC alone had already refunded approximately $10 million).

Yet studios refused to give in to, or even negotiate, the writers' most important issues. Financial firm Bear Stearns issued a report saying that even if studios gave writers everything they asked for, it would reduce annual earnings per share no more than *one percent* for the seven major media conglomerates (Time Warner, Disney, Sony, NBC Universal, Viacom, News Corp., CBS). Time Warner would be hit hardest, paying $32.2 million over the next three years. (To put that in perspective, Time Warner's total 2007 revenue was almost $46.5 *billion*. If Time Warner averaged that same revenue for the next three years, it would take in $139.5 billion . . . over *4,300* times what it would need to pay the writers.)

Public opinion swelled in favor of the WGA, with over two-thirds of the public supporting writers and less than 5 percent backing studios. Major stars and directors like Steve Carell, Robin Williams, Woody Allen, James Brooks, and Ray Romano voiced their support. Still, the AMPTP refused to budge.

Finally, on December 7, the studios issued an ultimatum: either the WGA back off six major issues, including specific pay formulas for online content and jurisdiction over animation and reality, or they would end negotiations completely. Refusing to drop their core issues, the WGA stood their ground. That very night, the studios walked, leaving things in a seemingly interminable state of limbo.

"The point of the strike wasn't for us, it was for future writers," says Karine Rosenthal, a co-producer on FOX's *Bones*. "I owed it to writers who came before me . . . who sacrificed immensely to create the guild, to fight so credits were properly assigned, to fight for residuals and health care and a pension fund. That was all done for me . . . [but with] the issues being mainly jurisdiction over the Internet, the future of all media, those things were in jeopardy . . . [which meant] future generations would be losing all those things. *That* was what was worth fighting for."

Then, on Friday, January 11, 2008, the Directors Guild announced what writers had been dreading all along: directors were beginning negotiations for *their* contract with studios . . . six months early. Less than a week later, the directors emerged with a finalized AMPTP deal that included DGA jurisdiction over the Internet as well as compensation for both online downloads and streaming.

Although there was heated debate throughout Hollywood on whether or not these were big enough victories, one thing was clear: the directors had done what writers could not—in six days. Of course, they couldn't have done it without the pressure applied by the striking writers. Writers had pushed studios to the edge of the cliff, the directors had simply tapped them over the brink. And like it or not, there was now a template in place for the WGA.

With two de facto deadlines looming, the clock was now ticking. The first deadline was February 15, the date TV executives had pegged as the last date to save 2008's pilot season (we'll talk more about pilot season in chapters 5, 10, 11, and 12). The other was February 24: the Academy Awards, Hollywood's single biggest night of the year. Aside from its celebratory fanfare, the Oscars is typically TV's second-most watched annual telecast, just behind the Super Bowl, reaching over 40 million viewers and bringing in over $80 million in ad revenue for its host network (which, in 2008, was ABC). It also generates $130 million for L.A.'s local economy, as well as $100 million in promotion for clothing and jewelry designers donating wares to stars. Yet because the Academy Awards hires WGA writers, the show couldn't proceed with its usual writing staff until the strike was resolved. More important, SAG actors refused to cross writers' picket lines, meaning that unless the strike was over, the Oscars wouldn't have a single movie star. The strike had already KO'ed the January 13 Golden Globes telecast, costing NBC approximately $15 million in ad revenue and the city of L.A. an additional $80 million. But with the Oscars, the writers had a $300 million hostage. If the strike couldn't be ended in time, angry studios would have no incentive to continue negotiating. Something big had to happen.

On January 18, the WGA and AMPTP agreed to resume back-channel, off-the-record negotiations. The WGA also decided that to focus its battle on digital media, it would scrap its efforts to increase home-video residuals and unionize reality TV and animation.

Two weeks later, on February 2, rumors bubbled that the WGA and studios were close to an agreement. The following weekend, the Writers Guild announced it had a potentially acceptable contract proposal from the AMPTP, which the writers would then vote on. Finally, on February 12, after shutting down Hollywood for one hundred days, the Guild's 12,000 writers cast their ballots, and 92.5 percent voted to end the strike. Work resumed the next morning . . . a mere forty-eight hours before the networks and studios' February 15 deadline.

(On an interesting side note, it took another two weeks for the Writers Guild to ratify the new contract. On February 26, 2008, the AMPTP's contract became writ, and Hollywood was officially back in business.)

When all was said and done, the strike caused $2 billion in damage to the California economy. Over sixty shows were shut down. An estimated 35,000 people lost their jobs.

But the strike also won writers a foothold in the exploding world of digital media, allowing them to negotiate fair compensation for themselves and generations of writers to come. Even studios claimed they'd benefited from the strike. By being forced to shrink its pilot season, CBS saved almost $70 million in production costs. After refunding millions of dollars of advertisers' money for spots in canceled shows, NBC was able to sell those same ad spots to *other* advertisers at higher prices because as air dates drew closer, demand for ad time increased (we'll learn more about networks' ad-buying processes in chapter 13). The strike also gave cable networks a boost; with no scripted shows on broadcast networks, the top ten cable outlets saw audiences increase over 15 percent. (CNN, which was covering presidential primaries, watched audiences skyrocket 133 percent!)

Broadcast networks and studios began crowing that the strike had also been just the spark they'd needed to revamp longstanding business models. CBS vowed to reduce the amount of money spent on pilot production. NBC overhauled its ad-selling process. The CW demolished its comedy department to focus energies on its more successful dramas.

Most important, the strike illuminated the changing worlds of media and entertainment. It forced everyone to look at the seismic shifts transforming the industry, rebalancing powers, redirecting revenue streams, and siphoning off audiences.

"I don't know if the strike changed *everything*," says Jon Wax, FOX's vice president of drama development, "but it forced both sides to address the new reality we're all dealing with, which is an increasingly digital world. It was the first substantive step for everyone to discuss—albeit often in an acrimonious way—issues that both sides had been hiding from. Whether or not things that were decided will be in effect years down the line, I don't know. But it will always be remembered as the first time the business took the new reality seriously."

Throughout this book, we'll discuss how the strike affected certain parts of the industry (see the "Strike Zone" text boxes), the pros and cons of these effects, and how much of it is still changing. Of course, by the time you finish this book—or even this sentence—it will have changed again. Your job, as a writer, producer, or artist working in TV, digital media, or any related field, is to stay on top of it, keeping your finger on the pulse of how the industry evolves on a daily basis.

So what are you waiting for? Get reading!

May 5, 2008

PART I

From the Inside Out

How the Industry Is Structured

1

The Top of the Food Chain

In December of 1979, Warren Littlefield's career was plummeting downward.

Seven months earlier he had been living in New Jersey, working as vice president of development at Westfall Productions, a tiny independent production company in New York City. He had just finished producing *The Last Giraffe,* a TV movie for CBS about a married couple saving endangered animals in Africa. The movie had done well . . . so well, in fact, that Littlefield's boss had offered him the presidency of the company. Littlefield was only twenty-seven years old, and he'd been offered the presidency of an actual production company. Clearly, there was only one thing to do.

"I had to leave," he says, "because I didn't know enough to be president of *anything.*"

So Littlefield and his girlfriend packed their bags and moved to Los Angeles, where Littlefield landed a job as director of comedy development at Warner Bros. TV Studios. It was a step down from vice president, but he wasn't looking for advancement; he was looking for education. "Warner Bros. had more tools, strengths, and assets than anything I could work with in New York," Littlefield says. "They had series on the air, rosters of writers and producers, money, an organization. An established player."

Six months later, in January of 1979, Littlefield took another step down, accepting a job as manager of comedy at NBC, an actual network. At the time, NBC was "the fourth-place network in a three-network race" (CBS

and ABC were the only other broadcast networks), and was trying desper-
ately to recover from a programming strategy known as "The Big Event," in
which it had scrapped traditional series in favor of movies and specials. In
fact, NBC's only comedies were *Diff'rent Strokes* and *Hello, Larry;* ABC and
CBS together, meanwhile, offered more than twenty comedies, including
CBS's *WKRP in Cincinnati, The Jeffersons,* and *M*A*S*H,* and ABC's *Taxi,
Three's Company, Happy Days, Soap, Mork & Mindy, Benson, Laverne &
Shirley,* and *Barney Miller.*

Did Littlefield actually want to leave a gig at a successful studio for a
lower position at a last-place network?

"I said [to myself], 'I turned down being a president. I was a VP and
took a job as a director. Now I'm going to apply to be a manager. Wow, is
my career spiraling downward quickly.' But I wanted that job because I felt
my education would be even greater. There was nowhere to go but up."

So he took the job.

It turned out to be a smart move. Six months after joining NBC, Littlefield was promoted to director of comedy development. Six months after
that, he was promoted again. Over the next decade, Littlefield rose through
the ranks developing shows like *The Cosby Show, Cheers, Family Ties,* and
The Golden Girls, until finally, eleven years after turning down the presidency of Westfall Productions, Littlefield was ready to step into the presidency of NBC, the network he had helped bring to first place.

During the next nine years, as president of America's top-rated network,
Littlefield would develop and air such hits as *Seinfeld, Friends, Frasier, Will
& Grace,* and *ER.* He would guide NBC to 168 Emmy Awards and, in his
last three years, sell a record-breaking $6.5 billion in advertising. Yet despite
all his success, he would always look at his salad days as the foundation of
his career.

"As a developer and producer at Westfall, and then Warners, [I gained]
an understanding of how to develop and evaluate material," says Littlefield,
now a successful producer with his own production company, the
Littlefield Company, in partnership with ABC Studios. "NBC was twenty
years of learning. I learned strategically to know, as best as you can, what a
network wants and needs. I heard over a million pitches, developed and supervised thousands of pilots, and—while it's not a science—you learn from
your mistakes as well as your successes."

Television's a bit different now than when Littlefield started. Rather than a scant three networks, there are six broadcasters (ABC, CBS, NBC, FOX, CW, MyNetworkTV) and a host of cable networks, from heavyweights like ESPN and TBS to nascent channels like OWN and Plum. Innovative shows like *24, The Amazing Race,* and *Lost* populate the airwaves. And new technologies like downloads, streams, and iPods are changing the way TV is produced and distributed. Yet the basic structures, processes, and business models remain the same, and understanding them—and how they affect TV's creative processes—is essential to succeeding.

As we saw with Littlefield's career, there are three main tiers in the world of TV development, three types of companies that collaborate to make content and deliver it to your home:

- **Networks,** which distribute televisions shows, and include the six broadcasters (ABC, CBS, NBC, FOX, CW, MyNetworkTV) and a horde of cable channels (FX, BRAVO, HGTV, etc.).
- **Studios,** which finance shows and supply them to networks (ABC Television Studios, Warner Bros. Television, Sony Picture Television, etc.).
- **Production companies,** which develop and produce shows (Bad Robot, Grammnet, Dick Wolf, Rocket Science, etc.).

These three types of companies work together to make and distribute most of the shows you see on TV. So how many of them are there? How many companies are responsible for developing, financing, producing, and delivering the vast majority of the shows on your television right now? Hundreds? Thousands?

Nope.

Seven.

Yup, you read that right. *Seven.*

Okay, to be fair, that was a trick question. There are obviously more than seven places making and airing TV shows. But while there are indeed countless broadcast and cable networks, studios, and production companies, they're almost all owned or controlled by the same *seven parent companies.* CBS Corporation, General Electric, News Corporation, Time Warner, Walt Disney Co., Sony Corporation, and Viacom. These are the **media conglomerates,**

Television's Seven Primary Media Conglomerates

Conglomerate	Broadcast Networks	TV Studios
CBS Corp.	CBS, CW (shared with Time Warner)	CBS Paramount Television
General Electric	NBC	Universal Media Studios, NBC Universal Cable Studio
News Corp.	FOX, MyNetwork TV	20th Century Fox Television, Fox 21, Fox TV Studios
Time Warner	CW (shared with CBS)	Warner Bros. Studios
Walt Disney Co.	ABC	ABC Television Studios
Sony Corp.	N/A	Sony TV Studios
Viacom	N/A	N/A

massive corporations that own the six broadcast networks, all their studios, and most cable networks. Time Warner, for instance, is the same Time Warner that owns *Time* magazine and Warner Bros. Entertainment, which makes TV shows like *Smallville* and *Cold Case* and movies like *The Dark Knight* and *Harry Potter;* Time Warner also owns 50 percent of the CW (shared 50-50 with CBS), as well as TNT, TBS, CNN, HBO, DC Comics, Martha Stewart Books, and AOL. News Corporation owns FOX Broadcasting Company, 20th Century Fox Studios, and cable networks like FX, Fuel, and Speed, as well as Dow Jones, MySpace, and HarperCollins Publishing. Almost every show on television comes, in some way, from one of these seven conglomerates (and a handful of others, which we'll discuss in a moment).

There are actually two more main conglomerates, but because neither

Cable Networks	Other Holdings
Showtime	Simon & Schuster, CBS Films, CBS Radio, CBS Outdoor, etc.
USA, Bravo, SciFi, Oxygen, Chiller, Telemundo, A&E and History (w/ABC and Hearst Corp.), etc.	GE Healthcare, GE Money, Universal Parks & Resorts, etc.
FX, Fox News, Speed, Fuel, etc.	Dow Jones, HarperCollins Publishers, MySpace, News Outdoor, etc.
TBS, TNT, HBO, Cartoon Network, etc.	Time Inc., AOL, DC Comics, Warner Bros. Consumer Products, etc.
ESPN (w/Hearst Corp.), ABC Family, Disney Channel, SoapNet, A&E and History (w/NBC and Hearst Corp.), etc.	Disney Parks & Resorts, Disney Consumer Products, Hollywood Records, etc.
Game Show Network (50%, Liberty Media has 50%), etc.	Sony Pictures Ent., Sony Music Ent., Sony Electronics, etc.
MTV, BET, VH1, CMT, Comedy Central, Spike, Nickelodeon, etc.	Paramount Pictures, Atom Ent., Rhapsody, etc.

participates much in American television, they won't play a big role in this book. Germany's Bertelsmann AG owns RTL Group (Europe's biggest production and broadcasting company), Random House, and Gruner + Jahr (Europe's largest magazine publisher), and France's Vivendi owns Universal Music Group (Def Jam, Interscope Geffen A&M Records), Vivendi Games (*World of Warcraft, Diablo, Scarface: The World Is Yours*), 20 percent of NBC Universal (GE owns the controlling 80 percent), and several European TV companies.

There are also several "mini-conglomerates" that own many of the cable networks. Although there's nothing "mini" about these companies, they're not at the same level as Disney, GE, NewsCorp, and the big dogs. The main mini-congloms are Scripps Networks Interactive, Comcast, Discovery Networks, Hearst Corporation, and Liberty Media Corporation.

TV's "Smaller" Cable Conglomerates

Conglomerate	Broadcast Networks	TV Studios
Scripps Networks Interactive	N/A	N/A
Comcast	N/A	N/A
Discovery Communications	N/A	Discovery Studios
Hearst Corporation	N/A	N/A
Liberty Media Corp.	N/A	N/A

As you can see in the chart on pages 22–23, media conglomerates do many things besides television. GE, for instance, comprises six separate businesses— GE Industrial, GE Commercial Finance, GE Healthcare, GE Infrastructure, GE Money, and NBC Universal—that do everything from making light- bulbs to designing jet engines. Thus, each conglomerate is headed by a CEO responsible for managing its entire business portfolio, and while television is a hugely important piece of business, it's only one piece of a conglomerate's much larger pie. (In 2007, for example, NBC Universal generated $15.4 bil- lion of revenue—only 9 percent of GE's $172.7 billion. Of that $15.4 bil- lion, only about 25 percent came from the actual broadcast network of NBC; most came from cable channels, like USA and Bravo, and movies like *The Bourne Ultimatum.*) CEOs focus on mergers and acquisitions, evaluat- ing the profitability of each of the conglomerate's pieces, deciding what to keep, what to sell, what to improve, and what new properties to buy.

Reporting to each CEO are heads of each of the conglomerate's compa- nies. GE Industrial, GE Infrastructure, and NBC Universal all have their own CEOs who report to the head of GE. Like the CEOs of their parent conglomerates, these men and women often manage several different com-

Cable Networks	Other Holdings
Food Network, HGTV, Fine Living, DIY, Great American Country, etc.	Shopzilla, uSwitch, UpMyStreet, etc.
E!, Style, G4, Versus, Golf Channel, etc.	Comcast digital cable, Internet, digital voice, Comcast-Spectacor (Philadelphia 76ers, Flyers, Phantoms), etc.
Discovery Channel, TLC, Animal Planet, BBC America, Discovery Health, etc.	Over 100 channels in 170 nations
A&E and History Channel (with NBC and ABC), Lifetime, ESPN (w/ABC), etc.	King Features, 12 daily newspapers, 19 U.S. magazines, 29 TV stations, etc.
Starz, Encore, QVC, Game Show Network (50%, Sony has 50%), etc.	DirecTV, the Atlanta Braves, etc.

panies and divisions. NBC Universal is a GE company divided into several smaller branches: Universal Studios (movies), Universal Parks & Resorts (theme parks), Universal Media Studios (TV production), NBC (broadcast distribution), etc. Each of these divisions then has its own CEO or president who, in turn, reports to the CEO of NBC Universal, who reports to the CEO of GE.

Most conglomerates organize their TV operations into several units that work together to produce, finance, and distribute TV content. For instance, NBC Universal's television divisions are

- **NBC Entertainment**—the main network operation. NBC Entertainment develops and broadcasts scripted and unscripted series, specials, and movies. This is the company most people mean when they refer to NBC.
- **NBC News**—drives all the journalism on NBC, as well as MSNBC and the NBC News Network. Because news is an important and special part of a network's programming, news divisions operate independently of entertainment divisions, helping to maintain journalistic integrity.
- **NBC Sports & Olympics**—covers all network sports coverage. Like news, sports operates separately from entertainment.

- **NBC Universal Television Stations**—oversees the company's owned-and-operated stations (we'll discuss owned-and-operated more in the next chapter).
- **NBC Television Network**—governs all independently owned affiliate stations. (Even though this division is called the "NBC Television Network," it has nothing to do with the development of shows and entertainment. We'll talk more about affiliates in chapter 2.)
- **Universal Media Studios**—the studio responsible for financing, producing, and selling TV series to broadcast network buyers, including NBC.
- **NBC Universal Cable Studio**—the studio responsible for financing, producing, and selling series to cable networks like USA and SciFi Channel.
- **NBC Universal Television Distribution**—syndicates Universal Media Studios' series, as well as first-run programs, to both domestic and international distributors. We'll talk more about syndication in chapter 3.
- **NBC Universal Television Networks Distribution**—strategizes the growth of NBC Universal's cable and non-broadcast holdings, including Bravo, SciFi, and USA.

The branches we're looking at in this book are the two divisions most directly involved with the creation and development of mainstream TV content: the network, or entertainment division (NBC Entertainment), and the broadcast studio (Universal Media Studios). We'll also look at production companies, which play a unique role in the TV hierarchy.

2

Networks, Studios, and Production Companies

Harold Brook was seven or eight years old, standing in the Bronx Zoo, the first time he saw an octopus.

"I grew up in Manhattan," says Brook, "so I didn't see a lot of octopuses. It was the weirdest thing I ever saw. I was *scared.*"

Years later, after running business affairs departments for both NBC and CBS, Brook would recall that exact moment when thinking about the size and influence of each of the media conglomerates.

"You're talking about one entity controlling every part of the creation, every form of distribution, every income stream, every type of exploitation," says Brook, now the head of entertainment law firm The Point Media. "[It's] like an octopus with tentacles everywhere, all flowing through one entity."

Like the organs of an octopus, the insides of a conglomerate work together to keep the entire being alive. And although **networks, studios,** and **production companies** develop shows together, and often live under the same conglomerate's roof, they each have specific responsibilities. Networks deliver shows to your home, studios finance the shows networks air, and producers work most closely with creative production teams to bring those shows to life. But ultimately they all serve the health and vitality of a larger "entity": the conglomerate.

This chapter explores how networks, studios, and production companies collaborate to make this happen. To best understand how that collaboration works, let's begin with the most powerful of the three entities, the network itself.

NETWORKS

Networks, the distributors of televised content, make the ultimate decisions about what audiences will or won't see coming across their TV screens. This makes networks the most powerful players in television's corporate food chain, which is why Littlefield, climbing the corporate ladder, was willing to take a lesser title to work for one. As distributors, however, networks don't usually make or own their own shows. So the NBC network may air *My Name Is Earl* and *Medium,* but it doesn't actually make (or own) those shows. It acquires them from other companies, then distributes them over its air. (We'll discuss this more in a moment.)

We've already mentioned the six broadcast networks (ABC, NBC, CBS, FOX, CW, and MyNetworkTV), but there are also countless cable networks, from major outlets like USA and FX to niche distributors and start-ups like Fine Living and Reelz. Throughout this book, when referring to "networks," I usually mean **broadcast** networks, which remain the big guns of TV distribution and development. **Cable** networks are gaining ground, but broadcasters cover more of the country and claim most of TV's viewers. (As of September 2007, the National Cable and Telecommunications Association reported that about 58 percent of American households with television received cable service.)

Thus, to fully understand TV's development process, you must first understand how it works at the top: the broadcasters. This is where TV began and, for the most part, remains the most powerful.

Broadcast Networks

The defining characteristics of broadcast networks are the very definitions of the words *broadcast* and *network.*

Broadcasters literally "cast" their shows to as broad an audience as possible. Why? Because broadcast TV uses public airwaves to deliver its content, making it free to anyone with a TV set capable of receiving its signal. Viewers don't pay for content, so networks make money by selling ad space during shows. The bigger the audience, the more they can charge. In the fall of 2007, a thirty-second commercial on ABC's *Grey's Anatomy* cost about $419,000, an ad in *Desperate Housewives* cost $270,000, and *Two and a*

Half Men ads cost $231,000. (*Grey's Anatomy* boasted the 2007–2008 season's second-most-expensive ad space for a regularly scheduled series, just behind *American Idol,* which sold thirty-second spots for $750,000 . . . then upped the cost to almost $1 million. TV's most expensive ads go to the Super Bowl, which—in 2008—sold for $2.7 million.)

Broadcasters are also true "networks," organized systems of local stations linked to deliver the same creative content. ABC's network consists of all local ABC stations across the country like KGO in San Francisco (Channel 7); WTVO in Rockford (Channel 17); and K2TV in Casper, Wyoming (Channel 2). Each of these stations receives its shows via satellite from ABC's broadcast headquarters in New York, then transmits them via radio waves to antennae on viewers' TV sets. (Many viewers today, of course, get even their broadcast channels via cable or satellite. We'll discuss that process in a moment.)

Each of the more than 350 individual TV stations across America is located in a **market,** or **DMA (Designated Market Area)**, a geographical area whose population all receives the same TV signals. The country has approximately 210 DMAs, covering about 99.97 percent of the United States. (In 2007–2008 the largest market was New York City; the smallest was Glendive, Montana.) Most markets have one station of each major network: ABC, CBS, NBC, and FOX. Because MyNetworkTV and the CW are newer networks (both launched in 2006), they have fewer stations and reach fewer markets.

Most local stations can be broken into two types: **affiliates,** or privately owned stations, and **owned-and-operateds,** or stations actually owned by the network whose programs they air. Because the Federal Communications Commission (FCC) mandates that no broadcast network can own stations reaching more than 39 percent of the population, networks consist of both affiliate stations and owned-and-operateds.

Most affiliate stations are owned by **station groups,** companies holding multiple affiliates and having stakes in many kinds of media. Clear Channel, for example, owns nearly twenty stations across the country, as well as Premiere Radio Networks, Inside Radio, and Prophet Systems. Hearst-Argyle, a subsidiary of the Hearst Corporation, owns more than twenty-five local stations. Each individual station then contracts itself to air a particular network's programming. The Tribune Company, for instance, owns WGNO/

Channel 26, an ABC station in New Orleans, and WXIN/Channel 59, a FOX station in Indianapolis.

When a station aligns, or "affiliates," itself with a particular network, the network pays that station a fee, called **network compensation** (or "network comp"), to broadcast the network's programming. The network then keeps the ad revenue it makes from these shows' commercials, although it often allows affiliates to sell a few local spots on their own. CBS, for example, pays Montgomery, Alabama's WAKA/Channel 8 and Twin Falls, Idaho's KMVT/Channel 11 to air *Big Brother, Ghost Whisperer,* and *CSI:NY,* then keeps the money it makes from selling ad spots within those shows to companies like Hyundai, Chrysler, and Crest toothpaste.

REVERSING THE FLOW

Unlike most broadcasters, the CW actually *charges* local stations to air its programming. In other words, affiliate stations pay **reverse comp** in exchange for CW shows and ad spots. This arrangement evolved when the CW emerged from the ashes of failed networks UPN and the WB in 2006. The CW gave these networks' former stations a choice: either remain independent and find your own programming, or pay reverse comp for the CW's already-established shows like *Supernatural* and *Smallville*. Many stations signed up with the CW. Some remained independent. Others were snatched up by News Corp., which used the traditional network comp model to launch its own new network, MyNetworkTV.

It's also important to recognize that a network doesn't fill all of an affiliate's air time. It usually provides each station with a few hours of daily programming, with the exact amount varying by network, and the station itself fills the rest of its air with local programs, syndicated shows (which we'll discuss in chapters 3 and 26), and local news. Airtime can also be sold to "paid programmers," producers buying large chunks of time to air their own content. Sometimes this content is infomercials advertising products, other times it's actual TV shows, like when Media Rights Capital purchased the CW's 2008–2009 Sunday nights to program its own shows: *Easy Money, Valentine Inc., Surviving Suburbia,* and *In Harm's Way.*

So how is each station's air time filled? Each day's air is divided into **dayparts,** groups of hours based on demographics most likely to be watching television at that time. **Primetime,** for instance, is the three-hour daypart between 8:00 p.m. and 11:00 p.m. PST, when most viewers watch television. (See the sidebar below for a breakdown of dayparts.) ABC, CBS, and NBC, the oldest and biggest networks, provide stations with early morning programming (*Good Morning, America*), primetime (*Pushing Daisies, American Gladiators*), late night (*The Tonight Show, Jimmy Kimmel Live*), and a few hours of daytime (soap operas, *The View*). FOX has one morning show (*Fox & Friends*), two hours of primetime, and Saturday late night. The CW and MyNetworkTV have only two hours of primetime each weekday and two or three hours on Saturday or Sunday (as of fall 2008). Programming the remaining dayparts is up to each station.

On an interesting side note: a handful of privately owned stations, such as Boston's WSBK/Channel 38 and Jacksonville, Florida's, WJXT/Channel 4, choose to remain independent and not affiliate themselves with *any* major network. These stations are responsible for filling all their own dayparts using local news, syndicated shows, and locally produced programming.

THE DAYPARTS

Here's a breakdown of TV's main dayparts (ET and PST):

Early Morning (5:00–9:00 a.m.): Mostly news programs for adults getting ready for work and kids' programs. This is a highly profitable daypart because while **HUT levels** (**Homes Using Television**) may not reach primetime levels, audiences are constantly turning over as people race to work and school. Thus, advertisers continually reach millions of new viewers. Also, because news shows like *Good Morning, America* cost less than primetime series, networks pull in massive profits.

Daytime (9:00 a.m.–4:00 p.m.): Soap operas, court shows, and talk shows for homemakers and people at home during the day.

Early Fringe (4:00–7:00 p.m.): Local news and syndicated reruns as adults return from work.

Prime Access (7:00–8:00 p.m.): Game shows and reruns as families reconvene, prepare dinner, and start homework.

Primetime (8:00–11:00 p.m.): Sitcoms, dramas, high-concept reality shows, and specials for families relaxing. This is TV's biggest daily audience.

Late News (11:00–11:35 p.m.): News and local programming as adults get ready for bed.

continued

Late Fringe (11:35 p.m.–2:00 a.m.): Talk shows, reruns, and movies for liminal adults, late teens, and early twentysomethings.

Overnight (2:00–5:00 a.m.): Reruns, talk shows, movies, first-run syndication, and paid programming for liminal adults and night-owls.

Unlike affiliates, owned-and-operated stations (O&Os) are owned and managed by their network parents, so the networks act as station groups. For example, the NBC stations in New York (WNBC), Los Angeles (KNBC), Miami (WTVJ), and San Diego (KNSD) are all owned and operated by NBC proper. Although networks have more control over owned-and-operated stations than over affiliates, much of O&Os' business is still conducted at the local level, because this is one of the greatest sources of network revenue. Profit generated from ads during local newscasts is often larger than profit generated during primetime shows. After all, newscasts not only cost less to produce than primetime programs, but networks must pay affiliates to air their primetime shows. They also pay license fees to acquire most primetime shows, which we'll discuss in a moment. So networks have the expense of the show *plus* network comp. And since most O&Os are in large markets like New York and Chicago, thirty-second spots in local newscasts fetch their owners great sums. Remember, all ad revenue generated by owned-and-operated stations—whether from newscasts, daytime shows, late-night shows, or morning shows—goes right back to the parent networks, making owned-and-operated stations one of the most profitable parts of a network's operation.

FLASHBACK (AND FLASH-FORWARD): ANALOG VS. DIGITAL TV

Since the beginning of television, sounds and pictures have been broadcast on radio waves from television stations to TV sets as traditional **analog** signals. Until now. In 2006 the FCC decreed that as of February 17, 2009, all U.S. TV stations must broadcast only digital signals. But what does this mean for the future of television—and how will it affect you? Let's first look at the difference between analog and digital signals.

Analog signals transmit sounds and pictures by converting them to radio waves, then sending them to TV receivers by fluctuating those waves' amplitudes and frequencies. When a receiver picks up the signals, it translates the waves' fluctuations back into sounds and pictures.

Digital signals encode sounds and pictures as computerized bits of data, then transmit those bits to receivers, where they're decoded back into sounds and pictures.

Think of it this way: Analog signals are direct translations of the original sound and picture; digital signals are instructions telling a receiver how to re-create the picture itself. Thus, while digital signals aren't technically as accurate as analog signals, they preserve data much better. So as long as information is encoded properly, sounds and pictures appear better on your TV screen. Digital signals can also compress more data into less **bandwidth** (the amount of space into which a specific amount of information can be transmitted), allowing for more channels and more consumer-broadcaster interactivity.

Thus, in coming years, TV audiences will enjoy clearer, stronger sounds and images. We'll also have more channels to choose from, as well as the ability to interact with networks and local stations. TV viewers may soon be able to choose angles from which they watch sporting events, participate in game shows, and even control plots and characters of certain programs.

(*FYI:* Digital TV is not the same as **high-definition television,** which provides an even more detailed picture than regular digital TV. Standard TV sets can't receive high-def television, even with a converter box; in order to receive high-def TV, you need to purchase a television set that's HD-ready. Many people are already switching. In 2007, Americans hopping to high-def or digital TV discarded or recycled 68 million outdated TV sets!)

Cable Networks

Although we use the term freely, cable networks (MTV, USA, ESPN, etc.) aren't actual "networks" in the same sense as broadcasters because they lack an actual *network* of TV stations. Instead, cable networks send shows via satellite to separately owned **cable providers** or **cable operators** (Comcast, Time Warner, Charter Communications). Cable providers receive these satellite signals at their **headends,** regional clearinghouses in each area where an operator provides service. Each operator's headend collects programming from all the networks it carries, then converts that programming into a series of light pulses, which shoots out of the headend over fiberoptic wires to **nodes,** large metal boxes in customers' neighborhoods. Nodes convert the pulses to electronic signals, which are sent via coaxial cable connected directly to viewers' TV sets. Because cable provides a higher-quality picture without interference or static, operators charge their customers service fees and split the income with networks, making cable a subscription-based rather than an ad-based system. Most cable networks still sell advertising, however, as fees paid by providers are rarely enough to sustain networks' operations (more on this in chapter 18).

Cable's subscriber-based business model results in several differences when it comes to creating and developing content. First of all, since cable networks are available only to paying subscribers, they're not regulated by the FCC, meaning they can air riskier, racier material like *Rescue Me* and *Secret Diary of a Call Girl,* which would be too edgy for broadcast networks. Cablers can also focus on smaller, specialized niche audiences. There are networks geared exclusively to animal-lovers, decorators, teenagers, golfers . . . the list goes on, and the future will bring many more. Shows like *Flip That House* and *Good Eats* could never find large enough audiences on broadcast networks, which need many millions of viewers to survive, but they thrive in a subscription-based system where audiences pay for channels they want. For example, VH1's 2007 finale of *Scott Baio Is 45 . . . and Single* pulled in 1.6 million viewers. This was considered a success for VH1, but it would have been a dismal failure on NBC, where—only five days earlier—the finale of *America's Got Talent* garnered 13.9 million viewers. Similarly, MTV's 2008 season three return of *The Hills* was deemed a monstrous hit when it pulled in 4.7 million viewers, making it the year's most-watched cable telecast so far (and Monday, March 24's most-watched program on all of television for viewers aged twelve to thirty-four). But fifteen days later, when CBS's *Secret Talents of the Stars* premiered to 4.6 million viewers, only 100,000 viewers less, it was canceled after a single airing.

Cable "narrowcasters" are profitable because although audiences are small, so are budgets. TruTV or Fuel may never garner the ratings of ABC or FOX, but their shows cost a fraction of broadcasters'. Narrowcasters keep down costs by programming mostly reality content, which is often much cheaper than scripted fare. They're also more open to working with less-experienced (but still talented) writers and artists, making cable a great starting place for young aspirants trying to get their starts. It doesn't mean a newbie can simply waltz in and sell a show to TNT; it just means cable is rife with opportunities to break in, learn, and ascend through the ranks, often more quickly than at a broadcaster. We'll discuss this more in chapter 18.

STUDIOS

Now that we know that both cable and broadcast networks are content *distributors,* not content *makers,* where do they acquire much of their content? Who gives networks their shows?

This is where **studios** come in, the corporate moneybags that finance, own, and develop most of television's **scripted** entertainment (anything that's not reality). The six main TV studios—ABC Television Studios, Universal Media Studios, 20th Century Fox Television Studios, Warner Bros., CBS Paramount, and Sony Pictures Television—then sell the shows they've paid to create and develop to the networks that distribute them. 20th Century Fox Television, for example, produces and owns *Bones.* It funds the actors' fees, writers' salaries, physical costs, everything, then turns around and sells the show to FOX, the network that airs it.

To clarify, the word "sell" is a misnomer. Studios actually "license" shows, or lease them, to networks. Networks then pay per-episode **license fees** for exclusive rights to broadcast the first **run,** or airing, of a series. So 20th Century Fox never loses ownership of *Bones;* it just "rents" it to FOX (but in the world of television, where nothing's simple, we still say "sell").

So if networks don't technically own shows or their shows' studios, guess who does? That's right—the media conglomerates. That means while FOX network doesn't own 20th Century Fox, they're *both* part of News Corp., which means News Corp. reaps the profits of distributing *and* producing its programs, even when they're not distributed on News Corp.'s own networks.

TALK THE TALK: VERTICAL INTEGRATION

When one corporation owns the companies both supplying and buying its products, we say that that corporation has become **vertically integrated.** Media conglomerates like Time Warner and GE are perfect examples of **vertical integration.** Because they own both suppliers (studios) and buyers (networks), their buying/selling processes have become extremely insular; they like to own, sell, and buy their own products internally, often making it difficult for outside companies or producers (like yourself) to break in. As we continue through this book, we'll learn how vertical integration affects TV's creative processes—and how it helps and hurts your chances of selling a show or getting hired.

Because conglomerates are vertically integrated, each studio is charged with producing content for its parent network. ABC Television Studios is designed to create programming primarily for ABC network; Universal Media Studios develops shows chiefly for NBC. It doesn't always happen this way, but it's supposed to. Check out the sidebar below to see the six major broadcasters, their studio affiliation, and their conglomerate/owner.

CONGLOMERATES WITH BROADCAST NETWORKS AND STUDIOS

Conglomerate	Network	Studio
Walt Disney Company	ABC	ABC Television Studios
CBS Corp.	CBS, CW	CBS Paramount Television
GE	NBC	Universal Media Studios
News Corp.	FOX,	20th Century Fox Television,
	MyNetworkTV	FOX TV Studios
Time Warner	CW	Warner Bros. Television
Sony Corp.	—	Sony Pictures Television

But a studio isn't limited to selling shows only to its parent network; it can actually sell to *any* distributor. *House,* for example, is produced by GE's Universal Media Studios, yet airs on News Corp.'s network, FOX. Similarly, CBS Paramount produces *Medium,* which airs on NBC, and Warner Bros. produces *Two and a Half Men* on CBS. In this way, media conglomerates own and make money on programs airing on other conglomerates' networks as well as their own.

Still with me? Good. Because now things get even trickier.

As we know, broadcast networks make money by selling ad spots during programs they license, or lease, from studios. So, logic would dictate, studios make money by financing these shows, then licensing them to networks for more than it cost to make them . . . right?

Wrong.

The average cost of a first-season hour-long drama is about $2.5 million per episode. Yet the networks' average **license fee** for a first-season drama is about $1.8 million per episode. Likewise, the average cost of a first-year half-hour sitcom is about $1.2 million per episode, but networks pay studios about $775,000–$900,000. Yes, you read that right: the license fee is *less* than the production costs of the series. *Which means studios lose money on every episode they make.* And if a show has twenty-two episodes per season, its studio loses millions of dollars a year, often over $15 million for a first-year drama and about $8 million for a first-year comedy. Thus, by their second year, many dramas have lost close to $30 million, and comedies have lost close to $24 million. Which means if a studio gets four new dramas on the air this year, those shows alone will lose the studio about $60 million, and by the end of their second season, they will have lost $120 million.

No, the studios aren't crazy. They do this because by leasing shows to networks at low prices, they're able to retain ownership of their properties. In other words, if a network pays a small enough license fee that it makes a large enough profit by selling advertising, it doesn't need to own a show in perpetuity and it doesn't shoulder the financial burden if the series fails. So after a show's "broadcast run," distribution rights revert back to the owner, the studio, who can relicense the show to someone else and make more money. When that run ends, the studio relicenses the show again . . . and again . . . and again. Or: reruns. So a studio can continue "renting" the same show to various distributors, which means it may lose money up front, but if a show is a success, it stands to make money far into the future. This system is called **deficit financing,** because the studio covers each se-ries' financial loss, or deficit, in hopes of making its money back later.

The process of relicensing already-aired programs to other distributors is called **syndication,** and it usually involves selling second, third, or fourth runs to cable networks and individual stations across the country. Tradition-ally, studios have sold syndicated shows mainly to local broadcast stations, but now they syndicate shows to cable, the Internet, even cell phones. This is why you see reruns of *Scrubs* on local stations like WNYW/Channel 5 (New York's FOX station) and WLVI/Channel 56 (Boston's CW station) as well as Comedy Central. Each individual distributor, hungry for proven content that will attract large audiences, pays its own licensing fee. So the studio sell-ing the show doesn't collect a fee from just one buyer; it collects a fee from *every local station, cable network, or Internet company that buys the series.*

When Sony's *King of Queens* first sold into syndication, it sold to over half the local stations in the country for $2 million per episode—not counting DVDs and cable runs. This means *each station* paid $2 million per episode. The show's second round of syndication sold for $1.5 million per episode. So while Sony lost millions of dollars producing *King of Queens*'s first run for CBS, it made that money back in spades by reselling episodes across America. Analysts project that within the next decade, Sony could make over $1 billion reselling *King of Queens*.

FLASHBACK: WHY WE *REALLY* LOVE LUCY

Aside from being a comic masterpiece, *I Love Lucy* revolutionized TV creatively, technologically, and economically. In 1951, when the show was preparing for its first season of production, most TV programs were filmed in New York. But *Lucy*'s stars and producers, Lucille Ball and Desi Arnaz, lived in Hollywood. So Arnaz and director of photography Karl Freund concocted a way to record each episode before a live audience, like a play, with multiple cameras stationed around the perimeter of the stage.* The series could then be aired later on CBS's schedule. The method worked, but it raised production costs by several thousand dollars (at the time, a half-hour episode of TV cost about $19,500), prompting CBS to ask Arnaz and Ball to take pay cuts. Arnaz and Ball agreed to the cuts on one condition: their production company, Desilu, got to own the episodes of the show after their initial network broadcasts. CBS agreed. A few years later, Desilu sold the reruns of the series *back* to CBS for over $4 million—television's first syndication sale. And thus was born today's system of deficit financing.

---

* This is the **multicamera** method of shooting sitcoms, which we'll learn more about in chapter 6.

Of course, many shows never make it to syndication at all, and networks usually pay only for episodes that actually get produced. In the fall of 2007, for example, CBS ordered thirteen episodes of CBS Paramount's *Viva Laughlin,* then canceled it after airing only two episodes. But since nine episodes had been shot, CBS had to pay its studio, CBS Paramount, for those nine. Similarly, CBS canceled Warner Bros.' *Smith* in 2006 after three episodes (seven were shot). And FOX canned 20th's *Vanished* after nine (thirteen were shot). Which means if one episode of each show cost its studio $2.5 million (*Smith* reportedly cost over $3 million), and recouped only $1.8 million through its license fee, those shows lost their studios more than $6.3 million, $8.4 million, and $9.1 million respectively. Like many shows that don't make it to syndication, these programs never have the chance to make their money back, and they become permanent losses for their studios.

(In fact, studios lose more than just their per-episode deficits. While networks pay license fees only for episodes that get filmed, studios contract and pay actors and writers for each episode the network *orders*. So, if a network asks the studio to produce thirteen episodes of a particular series, then cancels it after eight episodes have been shot, the network only pays for eight episodes. But the studio pays actors and writers for all thirteen.)

That's why syndication is so important to studios. When one show sells into syndication, it not only recovers its own losses, it helps recover losses incurred by all the series that *don't* survive, which is most of them.

**WORDS OF WISDOM FROM JOE SCHLOSSER,
SENIOR VICE PRESIDENT OF COMMUNICATIONS,
NBC UNIVERSAL TELEVISION DISTRIBUTION**

"Syndication is the holy grail of the TV industry. Everyone who is producing for primetime is aiming to reach syndication, to get a backend. If you don't get to syndication, which is generally four seasons, or 100 episodes, then it's generally considered you weren't successful."

So put this in the front of your mind and don't forget it:

TV shows aren't just made to be hits today—they're made to be hits as reruns tomorrow.

This critical notion affects almost everything studios buy, sell, and develop. They aren't just looking for great stories with cool characters; they're looking for shows specifically designed to generate an endless number of episodes that can be re-aired run after run after run—and certain kinds of shows repeat better than others. In chapter 6 we'll discuss some techniques and devices writers and execs use to ensure shows can produce an infinite number of repeatable episodes.

FLASHBACK: FIN-SYN

Much of today's network-studio system stems from the institution and revocation of the FCC's landmark Financial Interest and Syndication Rules, more commonly known as "Fin-Syn." Enacted in 1970, Fin-Syn banned networks from two main functions: profiting from distributing TV series after their initial broadcast run, and

continued

operating in-house syndication divisions. The rules were intended to create diversity in the marketplace; the FCC figured if networks weren't financially invested in the long-term health of their series, independent studios and producers wouldn't be shackled to networks' creative and economic demands. Opponents of Fin-Syn argued that the rules worked against independent producers, because most small production companies couldn't afford to deficit finance their own shows. For over twenty years, Fin-Syn laws were hotly debated throughout Hollywood and Washington, until, in the eighties and mid-nineties, the FCC began to relax them. In 1996 the rules were abolished altogether, paving the way for the vertically integrated networks and studios of today.

The money made after, or in addition to, a series' network run is known as its **backend,** and it includes traditional syndication to local stations as well as to cable, the Internet, and mobile phones. It also includes home video (DVD, Blu-Ray, etc.) and download sales. Most of these methods aren't yet as profitable as traditional syndication to local stations, but they hold untapped potential, which we'll discuss more in chapters 3 and 20. Some shows are so successful they begin generating backend while still in their network runs. Early episodes of *My Name Is Earl, Will & Grace,* and *Two and a Half Men* were all sold into syndication while their first runs were still going strong.

PRODUCTION COMPANIES

If networks acquire and distribute shows, and studios finance, own, and develop shows, what does the third type of TV company, production companies, do?

Many people think production companies handle TV series' physical production, the actual "making" of the shows. But this isn't exactly right. The truth is, production companies, like studios, create and develop TV series.

The one major difference is that production companies don't have their own money, so unlike studios, they can't fund their own productions. They also don't usually have soundstages, equipment, or their own airtime.

Rather, production companies are organizations based around the talents and creative energies of a particular writer, director, actor, or producer. Bad Robot, for instance, was founded by J. J. Abrams, the writer/director who created *Alias, Felicity, Lost,* and *Fringe. Law & Order* creator Dick Wolf started Wolf Films. Kelsey Grammer, the actor-cum-producer behind *Girl-friends* and *Medium,* has Grammnet Productions.

Networks and studios partner with these companies because they consistently deliver high-quality, successful products. Wolf Films, for example, has proven it can provide compelling, provocative crime and mystery shows. The Mark Gordon Company routinely creates sexy, witty dramas like *Grey's Anatomy* and *Reaper.*

Thus, a studio agrees to pay a producer (or production company) a specific amount of money over a specific period of time in exchange for exclusive rights to anything that producer develops. The producer gets funding, the studio gets product and creativity: the marriage of money to creative skills.

This arrangement is usually called an **overall deal,** or **pod deal** (short for **production overall deal**), and it's the holy grail for most TV writers and producers. Although overalls and pods are essentially the same deal, overalls are made with individual writers or producers; pod deals are made with organizations, or actual companies. In 2006, for instance, Bad Robot signed a six-year pod deal with Warner Bros. Television. Warner agreed to pay Bad Robot founder J. J. Abrams $4 million a year, plus $2 million overhead, in exchange for ownership of anything he developed for TV during that period. So any television Bad Robot works on through 2012 will be in partnership with Warner Bros. Studios.

REALITY CHECK

Although most production companies are small shops devoted simply to developing shows—not physically producing them—there is one place where production companies work differently: reality TV.

While reality producers still work with networks to develop shows, they're frequently much more heavily equipped—literally—to deal with practical production.

"Reality budgets are so tiny compared to scripted," says reality showrunner Biagio Messina (*Beauty & the Geek, Scream Queens*), "[that] if you own your own equipment, you don't have to rent it from somewhere else."

It's not unusual for reality companies to have their own cameras, sound equipment, and edit bays. They're often production companies in the truest sense, both developing and physically producing their programs. We'll learn more about reality production in chapter 19.

When it comes to overall deals signed with individual writers or producers, some go to successful non-writing producers, like Neal Moritz (*Prison Break, Evan Almighty, I Am Legend*), who inked a two-year overall with Sony in 2006, or Jeffrey Kramer (former president of David E. Kelley Productions), who signed a two-year deal with CBS Paramount. But most are reserved for **showrunners,** high-level writers and producers with track records creating and running successful series: people like *The New Adventures of Old Christine* creator Kari Lizer, who has an overall with Warner Bros. until 2010, and *Bones* showrunner Hart Hanson, who inked a three-year, eight-figure overall with 20th Century Fox in 2007. A showrunner is a TV show's CEO. They're responsible for hiring, inspiring, and firing a show's staff and crew, from the lead actor to the head grip to the lowliest assistant. They deal with network and studio executives, publicists, marketers, agents, and managers. Most important, they organize a show's writing staff, known as the "writers' room," and flesh out the show's long-term and episodic stories. (While non-writing producers work closely with showrunners and their duties often overlap, the showrunner is still the head of the ship and makes most of the creative decisions. Non-writing producers give notes, help shows stay on schedule and under budget, and serve as liaisons between showrunners and network or studio executives.)

"Showrunners are conduits through which all decisions on a television show must flow," says Molly Newman, executive producer of ABC's *Brothers & Sisters*. "The buck stops there. The showrunner needs to know everything about what makes a show work, from directing to acting to postproduction, writing, handling writers, breaking stories. In addition to all that, they need a 'degree' in management and a 'degree' in psychology. They're the conduit through which network and studio concerns flow as well. It's a lot of pressure. It requires a lot of various skills, and it's nonstop: late nights, early mornings, weekends. It's difficult for one person to fill that position, so those people are rare who do it well."

Overall deals usually last one or two years and cost anywhere from $500,000 to $2 million per year, although huge showrunners like J. J. Abrams, David Kelley (*Boston Legal, Ally McBeal, The Practice*), or John Wells (*ER, The West Wing*) demand more. The producer or production company also receives a piece of the backend of any project they develop as part of their overall, which, as we'll learn in the next chapter, is where a

TALK THE TALK: EXECUTIVE PRODUCER

When you see the names of several producers flash across the screen at the beginning of a TV show, most of those are writers. "Producer," "co-producer," "supervising producer" . . . these are all titles for different levels of writers, or "writer/producers," who work on the show's writing staff. The highest possible title is **"executive producer,"** which usually indicates the showrunner. Other executive producers may be high-level writers on the staff, and still others may be non-writing producers overseeing the series. This is different from film, where "producer" is the highest credit. Check out chapter 14 to learn more about TV's hierarchy of writers and producers.

show's real money is made. In 2008, for example, 20th Century Fox signed with Seth MacFarlane (creator of *Family Guy* and *American Dad*) a four-year overall that incorporated financial benchmarks including DVD and merchandising sales for each of his series, placing the deal's latent value at over $100 million . . . potentially making MacFarlane the highest paid showrunner in television.

Traditionally, most studios have maintained about fifty to sixty overalls in all areas at any given time: comedy writers, drama writers, non-writing producers, reality producers, and even directors. This gives them a constant stable of go-to writers, producers, and pods. Studios work hand-in-hand with these producers and companies to create and develop shows, which they then pitch to the appropriate networks.

Studios don't just use overalls to generate new content; they also use them to staff existing shows. For instance, in 2007, 20th Century Fox Studios placed *Pepper Dennis* creators Gretchen Berg and Aaron Harberts on *Women's Murder Club,* which was airing on ABC, and Paul Redford (*The Unit, Vanished*) on *Journeyman* at NBC.

STRIKE ZONE: FORCED OUT

Although overalls bind a studio and writer/producer together for a specific period, most contain **force majeure** clauses, provisions saying that in the event of a major external force (like a fire that destroys the studio), the studio can terminate the deal. In January 2008, two months into the WGA strike, many studios enacted

continued

their force majeure clauses, axing almost seventy overalls with writers, producers, and directors. ABC jettisoned *Brothers & Sisters* creator Jon Robin Baitz and *Borat* director Larry Charles. 20th Century Fox booted *K-Ville* creator Jonathan Lisco and *Journeyman* creator Kevin Falls. CBS Paramount fired non-writing producer (and movie star) Hugh Jackman, whose deal had begun barely five months earlier. Studios claimed they were using the strike to usher in a new era of fewer and cheaper overalls, but less than a month after the strike ended, they once again began making multimillion-dollar deals. ABC Studios made two-year overalls with *Ugly Betty* creator Silvio Horta and best-selling chick-lit novelist Jennifer Weiner (*In Her Shoes, Good in Bed*). CBS Paramount renewed its deal with *CSI: Miami* co-executive producer Sunil Nayar. 20th Century Fox inked deals with *Dollhouse* writer Tim Minear, *How I Met Your Mother* showrunner Greg Malins, and *My Name Is Earl* producers John Hoberg, Kat Likkel, and Bobby Bowman. And Sony Pictures Television contracted over a dozen overalls with writers fired by other studios during the strike, including Graham Yost (*Boomtown, Raines*), Josh Berman (*Vanished, Killer Instinct*), and Will Gluck (*Luis, The Loop*).

Understanding studios' system of overalls is important because overall deals are the first place studios turn when they need new content or must hire writers for their shows (and we'll discuss them more in chapter 8). As a result, it has become increasingly difficult for new writers and producers to sell pitches or break into TV. Knowing this, your goal is to get into business or form relationships with people studios want to work with. Whether you're a first-time writer pitching a show or a staff writer hoping for a job, your best chance of success is to get the support or partnership of an established showrunner, preferably someone who already has an overall. In fact, when studios buy a show idea from a younger writer, they often pair him with one of their pods or overalls to supervise the project's development.

"Part of the reason really good executive producers and showrunners are at such a premium," says ABC development executive Brandon Riegg, "is that you can have a great idea, but if you have someone poorly executing it, the show's going to tank. On the flip side, you could have a mediocre or generic idea, but with the right creative vision, it could become a much bigger, broader show." Writers with overalls, presumably, have already proved they have this vision.

Of course, meeting showrunners and producers is easier said than done, and it's nearly impossible to persuade them to help you if you don't already know them. So part of your job as a writer is to put yourself in positions where you can meet people and form relationships. The best way to do this is to get a job in the industry, probably beginning as some kind of assistant. We'll discuss assistants more in chapter 24, but in a world where we're all six degrees of separation from everyone else, there are many ways of networking. In chapters 23 and 25, we'll talk about how to meet new contacts—and turn those contacts into jobs.

3

Syndication and Backend: How TV Shows Make Money

As we learned in the last chapter, a show's "backend" is money generated *after,* or in addition to, a series' first airing, its initial network run. Sometimes this means syndicating reruns to individual stations across the country. Other times it means home video sales, broadband distribution, and reselling episodes to cable outlets or international distributors. It can even include ancillary products like books, toys, and clothing. But regardless of *how* a show earns its backend, backend is responsible for the bulk of a show's profits.

In June 2007, for example, NBC Universal sold reruns of the first three seasons of *The Office* to TBS and ten local FOX stations for a combined deal valued at over $130 million. So if Universal Media Studios, the studio producing the show, spent approximately $1.4 million per episode and received a license fee of $900,000 per episode from NBC, the network airing the show's first run, each episode of *The Office* lost its studio about $500,000, or a total of almost $26.5 million. But with a $130-million syndication deal, Universal Media Studios suddenly found itself with a profit of approximately $103.5 million.

Although a series doesn't earn backend until after its initial broadcast run, backend and syndication are the ultimate goals of most TV shows. Thus, it's helpful to understand how backend works, why it's important, and how this affects series' architecture *before* you begin writing and creating actual shows. (Although studios retain the lion's share of their shows'

TALK THE TALK: RESIDUALS

Backend isn't the only way writers and producers make money on produced episodes of television. Writers, directors, and actors also receive **residuals,** payments for reuse of TV content. This is different from backend, which requires ownership in the show; residuals* are simply compensation for reusing material beyond its initial airing. In other words, every time a TV episode airs, its primary writers, directors, and actors receive a small payment. As the episode continues to re-air, those residual payments decrease.

Here's a quick breakdown of how residuals work (each rerun pays a specific percentage of the episode's original fee):

Run after initial broadcast	Primetime reruns on broadcast networks (excluding the CW and MyNetworkTV)	Non-primetime or non-broadcast reruns (including cable, the CW, and MyNetworkTV)
2nd run	50%	40%
3rd run	40%	30%
4–6th run	25%	25%
7–10th run	15%	15%
11–12th run	10%	10%
13th run (and beyond)	5%	5%

In an industry as unstable as entertainment, residuals are often an important part of writers' income. The Writers Guild, in fact, estimates that residuals account for almost half of its membership's income. This is why the most controversial issues during the 2007–2008 writers strike were the fights for better residuals from home video sales (DVD, Blu-Ray, etc.) and Internet downloads.

To learn more about residuals, check out the Writers Guild's Residual Survival Guide at www.wga.org.

---

* Residuals are often confused with "royalties," and it's easy to see why: they're virtually the same thing. Royalties are payments paid to copyright holders of original works, such as plays, songs, or novels. But TV writers (and screenwriters) sell their copyrights to TV (and movie studios), so they don't receive actual royalties. Yet they still deserve a portion of profits generated by their work, so networks and studios pay residuals, which are essentially the same thing as royalties—except with a different name.

backend, they do share a bit with shows' creators and producers. We'll explore this more in chapter 8.)

There are several main areas of a show's backend: domestic syndication on both broadcast and cable channels, distribution via home video and digital media (online streams and downloads), foreign sales, and ancillary materials (toys, books, clothing).

DOMESTIC SYNDICATION: BROADCAST AND CABLE

Although shows are now syndicated to broadcast networks, cable, or the Internet, when most people hear "syndication," they think of traditional broadcast syndication, so let's explore that first.

Broadcast Syndication

Traditional broadcast syndication, also known as "off-net" or "second-run" syndication, involves reselling hit shows to individual stations across the country. Although there are more than 350 local stations in over 200 markets, studios can usually only syndicate a show to one station per market. After all, when a station ponies up millions for a series' syndication rights, they want **exclusivity,** the sole right to air that run of that show in their market. That's why, in Phoenix, reruns of *Everybody Loves Raymond* are seen only on KASW/Channel 6, the local CW affiliate; in Albany, Georgia, the same show is seen only on FOX's WFXL/Channel 31. Studios aim to sell their reruns to one station in every market across the country.

Studios syndicate shows in two ways. Sometimes they persuade station groups to buy a show for all their affiliates, as when Tribune Broadcasting picked up *Two and a Half Men* and *Family Guy* for each of its twenty-six local stations. Other times, execs sell a show to only some of a group's stations, like when NBC Universal sold *Law & Order: Criminal Intent* to half of FOX's twenty-five O&Os.

Similar to a network buying a show from a studio, local stations don't buy the right to air a syndicated show indefinitely; they buy the right to air a specific run. A run usually lasts two years (and a station can air each episode only a certain number of times within those two years), although it changes on a case-by-case basis. When the deal expires, the studio resells the rights again. Some syndicated shows lose steam after a few runs. Others, like *I Love Lucy* and *Seinfeld,* run for decades and become multibillion-dollar industries. That's why, in the long run, the most successful shows are designed to be hits indefinitely, with the ability to rerun embedded in their architecture. In chapter 6 we'll talk about how studios and writers create shows that are inherently syndication-friendly.

Shows are sold into syndication for two kinds of payment: **license fees** and **barter time.**

A license fee is simply the amount of cash a station pays for its particular run. This varies from deal to deal, depending on the success of the show's last run. The first cycle of *Friends,* for instance, sold into syndication for $275,000 per episode. But a few years later, when Warner Bros. set out to sell a second cycle of syndication, *Friends* had saturated airwaves, dropping its license fee about 20 percent. Still, Warner Bros. sold the show into syndication through 2013, raking in $944 million in pure cash.

Barter time is commercial time within a show. Most of the time, when a local station buys syndication rights to a series, it pays the studio cash, then makes its own money by selling ad space within each airing (much like a network does). But sometimes, if a show wasn't a huge hit in its broadcast run, a local station isn't sure the show can make its money back. So instead of paying the studio upfront cash, the station offers the studio its own ad time to sell. 20th Century Fox's *Angel,* for instance, never had a massive following on the WB, so local stations were reticent to give the studio upfront dollars. Instead they allowed News Corp. to sell a portion of advertising time in each station's local *Angel* broadcast. Although this wasn't as desirable as dollars, it was the only option *Angel* had. (To be fair, *Angel* also ended up selling into cable syndication at TNT for almost $300,000 per episode. We'll discuss cable syndication in just a moment.) Although this is bigger a gamble for the studio, barter time can be much more lucrative than a license fee, and many syndication deals involve a combination of both. Sometimes, if a show has been extraordinarily successful, a studio demands cash *and* commercial time.

Because barter time is riskier, syndicators usually need to close a certain number of syndication deals in order to follow through on actually distributing repeats of a show. "If you don't have New York, L.A., Chicago, and at least 80 percent of the country," says Bill Carroll, VP and director of programming for Katz TV Group, a consultancy representing local stations across America, "there's no value to the barter time. And if there's no value to the barter time, you're not going to take that risk."

Also, when local stations buy reruns of a successful show, especially comedies (which tend to rerun better than dramas), they usually want to **strip** it, or air it every weekday. This makes shows easier to promote, since stations can simply say, *"The Simpsons,* Monday through Friday at seven o'clock." When stripping a show, local stations also often air episodes out of order, which is why it's important for shows to be repeatable without relying on audiences having seen every episode. And since there are 250 Monday–Friday telecasts per year, studios have traditionally needed about 100 episodes, or four or five seasons, before selling a show into syndication. But with the rise of cable networks and broadband, that number has fallen a bit. Here's why . . .

Cable Syndication

As cable networks have blossomed over the past few years, they've provided studios with whole new channels of syndication. Remember, broadcast networks, unlike cable outlets, only program a handful of hours of their own airtime; the rest is programmed by individual stations. But since cable networks don't have individual stations, they program all their own air—twenty-four hours a day, seven days a week. Thus, cablers are in more need of programming and have been actively snatching up broadcasters' reruns before local stations have a chance. (They especially like hour-long shows, which fill more air.) This is why you can see *Law & Order: SVU* on USA and *Cold Case* on TNT.

When it comes to reselling shows to cable, there are frequently two distinct components to the process: the **repurpose** deal and the syndication deal. Although they're separate windows, they're negotiated at the same time.

A repurpose deal allows cable outlets to air *weekly* episodes of a particular series (rather than daily), as Lifetime did with ABC Studios' *Grey's Anatomy* when it began airing reruns every Sunday at 11:00 p.m. Many cable networks strike deals to repurpose episodes immediately after their broadcast airings. SciFi, for instance, repurposes episodes of *Heroes* only days after they premiere on NBC. (This was an easy deal since NBC and SciFi are both owned by GE.) Because repurposed episodes air weekly rather than daily, cable outlets can stretch runs longer. This allows them to buy syndicated series long before broadcast stations can, since broadcast stations usually want enough episodes to strip. (*Grey's* was repurposed on Lifetime for $1.2 million per episode after only a year and a half on ABC.) This has forced broadcast stations to get more competitive and buy series before they've accumulated their hundred episodes, allowing syndicators to enter the marketplace with only sixty or seventy episodes. Thus, with more money chasing shows, more series have a chance of making *some* kind of backend.

When a repurpose deal expires, the second window kicks in. This is the actual syndication deal, where the cable channel begins airing stripped episodes of a show. (By this time, the series has usually accumulated enough episodes to be aired on a daily basis.) USA, for example, made a deal with Universal Media Studios to repurpose *House* twice a week until 2008, when the show's syndication deal would kick in and USA could program those same *House* episodes as a daily strip.

Syndicating a series to cable doesn't necessarily prevent a studio from selling it to local broadcasters as well. Sometimes, if a studio sells a show as strip to a cable network, it'll sell the same show to local stations for weekend airings—or vice versa. So USA repurposes *Law & Order* on weekends, while local stations strip it during the week. In a similar deal, Warner Bros.—after raking in almost a billion dollars (in both cash and barter time) from syndicating *Friends* to local broadcasters—collected another $200 million by selling the show in 2008 for $500,000 per episode to Nick at Nite (which was allowed to air the show after 6:00 p.m.) and for $275,000 per episode to TBS (which could only air the episodes before 7:00 p.m.).

HOME VIDEO, DIGITAL MEDIA, AND OTHER FORMS OF BACKEND DISTRIBUTION

As technology advances, new forms of distribution spring up every month, offering countless new outlets for syndication. Some shows are syndicated to airlines (CBS to American; NBC to United). Others, like Warner Bros.' *The Ellen Degeneres Show* and *Tyra,* are syndicated to XM satellite radio.

Today, one of the most popular forms of backend is home-video revenue (DVD, Blu-Ray, etc.). Although home-video sales don't come close to rivaling traditional syndication revenue, their numbers are rising. In 2003, FOX's canceled *Family Guy* sold a shocking 1.6 million units on DVD, persuading the network to resurrect the series in 2005. In 2007, when *Heroes'* second-season ratings began to wane, it was the show's whopping DVD sales—700,000 sales in six weeks—that convinced NBC Universal that the series was still worth its expensive price tag. And in 2006, when consumers spent $24 billion on home videos (both purchases and rentals), overall sales of DVDs began to slow—except for DVDs of TV shows, which made up 9 percent of all DVD sales and rose 7 percent from the previous year, primarily because of the success of **serialized** programs (series where stories stretch over many weeks or months) like *Heroes, Lost,* and *24.* Home video can be a huge boon to serialized shows, which often can't be viewed out of order, giving them little repeatability and, therefore, little syndication value. Conversely, **stand-alone** shows, like *Law & Order* or *CSI,* rarely do well on home video. We'll discuss the differences between serialized shows and stand-alones in chapter 6.

STRIKE ZONE: HOW THE 2007–2008 WRITERS STRIKE CHANGED HOME-VIDEO RESIDUALS

The truth is: it didn't . . . even though home-video residuals were one of the strike's hot-button issues. Home-video residuals have been a major sore spot with Hollywood's TV and film writers ever since 1985, when studios convinced the Writers Guild to settle for a residual rate of 1.5 to 1.8 percent of the studio's gross on DVD sales. This amounts to about four cents per DVD for the writer of that show or movie. (Yes, you read that right: *four cents.* To put this in perspective, the average price of a standard DVD is just under $20. In 2007, consumers spent approximately $23 billion buying and renting DVDs, Blu-Ray discs, and other home-video formats.)

During the 2007–2008 writers strike, the WGA fought hard to double the home-video residual rate to eight cents per DVD, but the studios wouldn't budge. Eventually, the writers agreed to stick with the current rate in order to make gains in digital media.

Of course, the most talked-about new form of syndication is digital media and **electronic sell-throughs** (**ESTs**), such as streaming, downloads, and **video-on-demand** (**VOD**). (In chapter 20 we'll talk about how digital media is providing opportunities for original content as well as backend.)

Audiences' preferred method of digital distribution seems to be watching **streams,** "live" data transmissions that can't be stored or recorded on a viewer's computer, a la YouTube or FunnyorDie. Because streams can't be kept, they're usually available for free and are advertiser-supported, making them an increasingly popular way to watch online video. According to a 2007 study by Deloitte and Touche, 38 percent of Americans stream TV shows online, and media buying firm Starcom USA estimates that in 2007, networks raked in $120 million in ad revenue from online streams. Although this is far behind the approximately $70 billion advertisers pump into actual broadcast and cable television (almost half of the $150 billion dollars spent each year on advertising across *all* media: TV, print, radio, etc.), it's a rapidly growing number. According to technology and market research firm Forrester Research, streams of online TV shows could be bringing in close to $1.7 billion by 2010. This prediction seems to be well on its way to coming true, as many studios are now generating income from online streams. In 2006, Twentieth Television syndicated *Arrested Development* to MSN, which made all fifty-three episodes available for streaming. (Twentieth Television, which is different from 20th Century Fox Television, handles News Corp.'s syndication operations.) That same year, ABC launched its ad-supported broadband player, which streamed over 140 million episodes of ABC's TV shows in its first year of operation.

Viewers can also download shows, or purchase electronic versions, from online retailers like iTunes and Xbox LIVE Marketplace, or VOD distributors like Comcast. Because downloads are actually purchased and kept, they're rarely ad-supported. Most online retailers charge about $0.99 or $1.99 for one episode of a television program, although some are experimenting with tiered systems where hotter, newer shows cost more than others. Retailers then split this, often about 30/70, with the show's network and studio (which get 70 percent). So for every $1.99 episode of FX's *Damages* distributed by an online distributor like iTunes, the network (FX) and studio (Sony) must share $1.39 (about the same profit generated per episode by a $30.00 DVD boxed set). From a percentage standpoint, this means downloads generate almost three times as much profit per viewer than ad revenue during an episode's initial network run, which usually brings in between forty and sixty cents per person.

While this seems like a strong argument for moving quickly toward online distribution, there are two main problems: First, the amount of money made via electronic sell-throughs is still fairly insignificant. In 2007, for instance, NBC Universal's movies and TV shows accounted for 30 to 40 percent of all of iTunes's video sales, and still generated only $15 million. (Fifteen million dollars may seem like a hefty chunk of change, but not compared with NBC-U's previous year's revenue of $16.2 billion. On an interesting side note, 2007 is the same year NBC-U and Apple squared off in a pricing dispute that eventually prompted NBC-U to move its content from iTunes to Amazon's Unbox.) Also in 2007, revenue from all TV and movie downloads was projected to reach $315 million—small potatoes compared with the over $70 billion raked in annually from TV advertising.

Second, no one's quite sure how to divvy up the EST money that *is* being made. After all, when a TV program airs for the first time on a network, the distributor (the network) keeps every penny of ad revenue. But when a show is bought online, the distributor (iTunes) keeps only 30 percent. So who gets the remaining 70 percent? The network? The studio? Deals are different for almost every program, and the split on EST profits depends on when an episode is downloaded during a show's life cycle. In 2007, ABC and Warner Bros. came to a groundbreaking two-year deal for all of Warner's shows at ABC: they decided that *Pushing Daisies, Men in Trees, Big Shots,* and *Notes from the Underbelly* could all be streamed on ABC.com for up to four weeks after their broadcast airing. Then, during the second year, Warner Bros. could *sell* these shows as ESTs or DVDs. When Warner sold J. J. Abrams's *Fringe* to FOX that same year, the network agreed to a similar deal, setting a revolutionary precedent.

Of course, deals like this become more complicated as other players, such as syndicated distributors, get involved. What if a show is downloaded from Amazon's Unbox while first-run episodes are airing on a broadcast network and repeats are airing in off-net syndication? Is the money split between the network, studio, and local distributor? Who gets what percentage? How do companies determine which airing—the network or the off-net—is driving more people to the download site? What if a show is downloaded from iTunes while episodes are on broadcast TV, broadcast syndication, *and* cable? And if cable networks and local stations buy a show's syndication rights, should they also get to stream those episodes on their home sites?

With "any new media deal . . . buyers ask for all rights," says Jerry Petry, executive vice president of administration at NBC Universal Television Group. "They want the ability to stream, to do downloads, VOD. So as a buyer, you're trying to get as many of those rights as you can; as a seller, you're trying to hold on to as many rights as you can. That's the flashpoint in basically every negotiation with every customer, whether it's international or domestic."

Thus the $1.39 generated from each download gets divided among many participants, and at the end of the day, most money generated by ESTs is fairly incremental—which is why TV execs often contend the main value of downloads and VOD is simply as a promotional tool driving audiences back to TV. Case in point: *Lost*'s TV viewership spiked 14 percent after ABC made episodes available over iTunes.

STRIKE ZONE: HOW THE 2007–2008 WRITERS STRIKE CHANGED ONLINE RESIDUALS

The truth is: before the 2007–2008 writers strike, there *were* no online residuals. So all those millions of dollars we talked about a moment ago (NBC's $15 million from iTunes, $250 million in ad revenue, etc.): writers saw almost *none* of it. While writers were paid traditional residuals for TV reruns and home-video sales, they received nothing for the profitable use of their products on the Internet.

Until the writers strike.

Writers gave up many valuable initiatives during the strike, simply to obtain online residuals. They sacrificed WGA jurisdiction over reality TV. They sacrificed WGA jurisdiction over animation. They even sacrificed efforts to raise home-video residuals from four to eight cents per DVD. Why? Because most evidence suggests that in a matter of years, *all* television—first runs and reruns alike—will migrate to the Internet, and writers knew now was the time to fight for fair compensation.

Here's a brief rundown of the Internet residuals won by the striking writers (keep in mind—writers can make up to about $16,000 the first time their show reruns on traditional television):

RESIDUALS FOR STREAMING TRADITIONAL TV SHOWS
Before paying writers residuals for streaming a particular TV episode, networks are allowed a seventeen- to twenty-four-day window, contiguous to the episode's

continued

initial network airing, to stream the show online *for free*. I know this doesn't seem great for writers, since this is the period when most viewers catch up on shows they've missed, but it's designed to help networks and studios compete against people watching shows on DVRs (digital video recorders). The idea is twofold:

A) Most viewers watching streams during that seventeen- to twenty-four-day window are people who would've watched the broadcast airing, but missed it, so networks don't consider those streams to be actual re-uses that should require payment. (It's analogous to someone watching an episode on DVR; it's not a rerun—it's just a delayed viewing of the first run . . . for which networks don't get paid.)

And B) Because most DVR-watchers fast-forward through commercials, any DVR-recorded commercials are devalued. This scares away advertisers, broadcasters' main revenue stream. So if networks can offer additional advertising through online streams, to make up for lost DVR viewers, it helps keep advertisers who may otherwise take their business elsewhere.

After this free window, writers get a fixed residual for the first two years: about $1400/year for unlimited streaming of a primetime broadcast one-hour drama, and $700–$800 for a half-hour. In the third year and beyond, they get 2 percent of whatever the distributor grosses, but that percentage is locked at a rate of about $800 per year for hour-long shows and $400 per year for half-hours. (If you think it's weird to have a percentage *and* a fixed rate, you're right—it's not fair. A writer taking 2 percent of the distributor's gross could be entitled to much more than $800 a year and never see a dime. But the WGA negotiators accepted this because they felt it established a decent framework for future negotiations.)

Writers of non-primetime or cable shows get much smaller residuals, based on a complicated formula. Residuals for streams of "library content," or older shows dating back to 1977, are payable at 2 percent of the distributor's gross.

RESIDUALS FOR DOWNLOADS OF TELEVISION SHOWS

For the first 100,000 downloads of a particular episode, the writer receives .36 percent of the distributor's gross. After 100,000 downloads, the writer receives .70 percent of the distributor's gross. (To put this in perspective: in the spring of 2007, most TV episodes averaged 200,000 downloads. This means for the first 100,000 downloads at $1.99, the writer of a particular episode would receive about $501 for the first 100,000 downloads and $975 for the second 100,000.)

RESIDUALS FOR ONLINE RENTALS OF TV SHOWS

The writer of the rented episode receives 1.2 percent of the distributor's gross.

FOREIGN SALES

One of the most important parts of a show's backend is its foreign sales. Sometimes this means selling actual produced episodes to other countries. Other times it means selling a **format,** or concept, so foreign producers can re-create the show with local actors and locations. In 2008, for instance, NBC Universal and Wolf Films sold the **format rights** of *Law & Order* to England's Kudos Film & Television, allowing Kudos to produce the British series *Law & Order: London.* That same year, China's Hunan TV acquired the format rights to *Ugly Betty,* developing their own version called *Invincible Ugly Woman.*

International sales rarely rival the money of domestic syndication. Comedies, especially, are worth less, since humor seldom translates abroad. An American comedy might garner a foreign license fee of only $150,000–$200,000 per episode. Dramas, serialized shows, and sci-fi series find more welcoming audiences overseas, sometimes selling for up to $1 million per episode, much more than they usually get from domestic stations. After airing the first season of *Heroes* at home, for instance, NBC Universal licensed the series to almost 150 international "territories" or overseas markets. It immediately premiered as the top show on Australia's Seven network and garnered the largest audience ever in the history of SciFi UK.

A major advantage of selling a program's foreign rights is it usually happens at the beginning of a series' life cycle, months or years ahead of a possible syndication sale. Like cable repurpose deals, foreign sales often bring studios up-front money that helps offset deficits accrued when producing the shows. Thus, studios often look to foreign sales to cover shows' deficits, and to syndication and home-video sales to bring in shows' profits. (However, many foreign sales require the studio to provide a certain number of episodes. A foreign buyer may agree to $850,000 per hour of a drama that delivers thirteen episodes. But if the show gets canceled or the studio fails to deliver thirteen hours, the buyer might pay only $150,000 per episode.)

Shows are usually sold internationally in two ways. In many cases, studios form **output deals,** or **volume deals,** where an international broadcaster agrees to "pre-buy" a certain volume of a studio's projects even before seeing them. Spain's Telecinco, for instance, has an output deal with CBS Paramount. In other cases, studios sell shows individually. A studio's international salespeople keep tabs on their company's development slate, and if foreign buyers learn of an interesting project, they can acquire it even before an American pilot has been shot. Most programs, however, are sold at the L.A. Screenings in late May, when studios invite foreign buyers, like French network M6 and Norway's TV2, to Los Angeles to screen pilots and pick up American series. During the Screenings, which usually last one to two weeks, studios ply foreign execs with parties, gifts, and meetings with TV stars in hopes of selling their shows overseas.

As TV has evolved, foreign sales have become more and more important to studios' revenue streams. In 2007, Fox TV Studios (a small News Corp. studio dedicated to lower-budget programming and new business models) produced *Persons Unknown,* a sci-fi thriller from screenwriter Christopher McQuarrie (*The Usual Suspects, Valkyrie*), exclusively for foreign distributors. Although the series had the look and feel of an American show, it was offered first to international buyers, *then* to American companies. While this model isn't the norm, it may indicate a future in which TV's primary landscape becomes much more global, with various companies producing shows for different countries and territories, or even premiering the same show simultaneously in multiple nations.

ANCILLARY PRODUCTS

Although certain shows like *Heroes, Alias,* and *Buffy the Vampire Slayer* have spawned large amounts of ancillary products like comic books, clothing, action figures, and video games, these products' incomes are rarely significant enough to be factored into a show's overall success. This income is so small, in fact, that unless a show is pitched in partnership with, say, Mattel, the possibility of ancillary material is never considered during a series' development process. The only exceptions are animated programs and children's shows, which are frequently developed to incorporate toys, books, and games. But when it comes to traditional live-action series, if a market for ancillary materials appears down the road, great—it's considered promotional icing on the cake.

As foreign sales and new forms of backend continue to grow, they allow development execs to take chances on riskier, less traditional projects. Shows like *24* or *Prison Break* may not be juggernauts in syndication, but if they can hold their own in foreign sales, downloads, and home video, studios have incentives to produce them.

"Five or ten years ago, the network license fee would cover eighty percent of the cost [of a TV drama] and you'd deficit finance the rest," says Petry, "but over the years, the cost of production . . . has increased at a much faster rate than networks have increased license fees. Studios have to figure out how they can bridge that gap, so there's now much more attention paid to international. Much more attention paid to 'how quickly can we get the DVDs?' "

In fact, as new technologies emerge, the concept of a traditional backend may become obsolete, and shows will simply have different distribution windows: a broadcast window, a cable window, a home-video window, etc., with no window being more important than another.

Of course, before a show can have *any* backend, it needs to be successful in its initial network run, or broadcast run. This is obviously easier said than done, and we've all seen brilliant shows get canceled before their time (*Freaks and Geeks,* anyone?). We've also seen horrible shows get on the air and—somehow—survive. In the next chapter we look at the various departments that work together to make or break a TV series—and how they keep networks and shows alive and kicking.

4

Inside a Television Network: A Lesson in Programming

In May 2006, ABC had just finished one of its best seasons in years. Sundays were going strong with returning shows like *Extreme Makeover: Home Edition, Desperate Housewives,* and *Grey's Anatomy,* as were Mondays with *Monday Night Football* and Wednesdays with *Lost.* ABC had also just rescheduled its summer reality juggernaut, *Dancing with the Stars,* to fall slots on Tuesday and Wednesday nights. There was only one thing ABC didn't have.

A Thursday-night hit.

And as ABC's execs knew, they would never be the number-one network without tackling Thursday night.

"ABC hadn't had a presence on Thursday in forever," says Kevin Plunkett, ABC's vice president of current comedy programming, "and Thursday is the most lucrative night."

Yet conquering Thursday was easier said than done. Thursday was dominated by CBS's *Survivor* at 8:00 p.m. and *CSI* at 9:00 p.m., a lethal one-two programming punch, and ABC wasn't sure what to program against it. It had a new show, *Ugly Betty,* which looked promising, but as every network scheduler knows, you don't launch a new show, especially an offbeat fashion-industry dramedy, alone in TV's most competitive time slot. You partner it with an established hit, something with loyal viewers (and lots of them), to clear the way.

So what to put there? *Lost* was anchoring Wednesdays—and had been losing its audience. That left ABC's powerful Sunday-night block: *Extreme*

> ### T.G.I.T.—"THANK GOD IT'S THURSDAY"
>
> Thursday has long been the night when broadcasters schedule their hottest shows—which seems odd, considering everyone knows Thursday is the unofficial beginning of the weekend and many people head out to bars and happy hours. Yet Thursday remains TV's biggest night: *ER, Seinfeld, CSI, Friends, The Cosby Show.* So why do networks place their most valuable properties on a night when many people are out socializing?
>
> "Some of the biggest advertising categories are retail (Wal-Mart, Target, etc.), automobiles, and movies," says Gaurav Misra, VP of programming for MTV and VH1, "and [these categories] have a massive spike in purchases on weekends. So advertisers attack weekend consumers on Thursday. They say [to networks], 'If you put your best shows on Thursday, we'll put most of our dollars on Thursday.' So viewers decide to stay in because the best shows are being aired on Thursday because the most money is put on Thursday. It's truly the tail wagging the dog."

Makeover: Home Edition, Desperate Housewives, and *Grey's Anatomy.* But moving one would mean dismantling the only night ABC had been winning handily.

"Every time you move a show, you lose members of your audience," says Lance Taylor, who was—at the time—ABC's senior vice president of current programming. "If it ain't broken, don't fix it. But if you don't begin to fix it, to blow it up, you never take a new night and expand your success."

So ABC looked to Sundays. While still top-twenty shows, both *Desperate Housewives* and *Extreme Makeover: Home Edition* had fallen off in the last year. But *Grey's Anatomy,* the capstone of the night, was growing. It wasn't beating *CSI,* TV's third-most-watched program of the previous season (behind *American Idol*'s Tuesday- and Wednesday-night episodes), but it had jumped from television's ninth-rated show to the fifth. And it was rivaling *CSI* in its share of adult viewers between the ages of eighteen and forty-nine, broadcast TV's most coveted demographic.

Moving *Grey's* seemed like a strong possibility, but if viewers didn't follow Seattle Grace's interns from Sunday to Thursday, ABC would have dismantled its most important night for nothing—and ruined its most promising property. Not to mention that ABC's sales department had been incredibly successful selling Sunday night ads in *Grey's Anatomy;* if the Thursday move failed, the network would lose millions of advertising dollars.

It was "hugely risky," says Plunkett, "because in a worst-case scenario, you've fucked yourself on Sunday *and* Thursday night. And ruined a great show."

But ABC decided to risk it. And to better their odds, they called on the talents of their in-house marketing and promotion departments.

"You couldn't go anywhere that summer without seeing 'Choose Thursday' billboards, 'Choose Thursday' ads in newspapers or magazines, online," Plunkett says. "The move was so effectively and thoroughly communicated, you couldn't help finding it on its new night and time."

The question, of course, was, while the audience might know where *Grey's Anatomy* was—would they follow? *CSI* had decimated every scripted show ABC had programmed against it in the last five years: *Life as We Know It, Kingdom Hospital, Push Nevada*. Would *Grey's Anatomy* be next?

ABC got their answer on Friday, September 22, the morning after *Grey's Anatomy* and *CSI* first went head-to-head. *CSI* pulled in almost 17,000,000 viewers and 18 percent of viewers aged 18–49. *Grey's* pulled in almost *20,000,000 viewers*—and *26 percent* of viewers aged 18–49. For the first time in years, thanks to the meticulous strategizing and coordination of its programming execs, ABC had won a Thursday.

Although programming is often a nebulous term, it's the heart and brain of all successful networks. Some people use it to refer to the process of developing shows; others use it in reference to the art of planning a network's schedule. Both are right. And while different networks organize programming departments differently, the *concept* of programming usually includes the same objectives:

- identifying and reaching target audiences
- scheduling and promoting actual shows
- determining and strengthening the network brand

There are six main divisions that cooperate in programming a network. At some companies, these are divisions of the actual programming department. At others, they're separate departments coordinated through the entertainment president. Either way, the six facets of programming are: development, current, research, scheduling, marketing, and promos.

DEVELOPMENT AND CURRENT

As we know, a broadcast network only schedules a limited number of day-parts of its own air. There are four divisions charged with programming those hours, and they're categorized according to daypart: Primetime Development, Current Programming, Late-Night Programming, and Daytime Programming.

Primetime Development

When people in television refer to "development," they usually mean the world of primetime development. Primetime is the daypart between 8:00 and 11:00 p.m., when **HUT levels** (Homes Using Television) are highest. As a result, this is where networks place their most expensive, highest-quality programming: sitcoms, dramas, mainstream reality. (Primetime is also important because it's the **lead-in** to late local news, one of local stations' most profitable dayparts.)

Most networks' primetime development departments are sectioned into five separate divisions: comedy, drama, **alternative**/reality, specials, and **longform** (TV movies and miniseries), and together they develop over a hundred scripted projects and ten or twenty alternative or reality projects each year. Most never see the light of day, but when execs find a project they like, they work with writers in taking the concept from pitch to script to pilot to series. We'll discuss this process more in parts II, III, and IV. We'll look at reality TV in chapter 19.

Current Programming

As a new primetime series gets up and running, it's handed from the development execs who shaped it to the **current department,** who maintains it. Because current execs oversee fewer shows than their development counterparts (usually four to six per current exec), they often oversee both comedy and drama (as opposed to development, where comedy execs cover only comedy and drama execs cover drama). Current's job is to supervise the general maintenance of each series (story arcs, casting, hiring directors), and to act as a liaison between the show and other departments at the network, studio, and production company (marketing, promotions, publicity, research).

Reality, specials, and longform do not have current departments. These projects remain under the domain of the execs who developed them. Interestingly enough, however, in 2008, in the wake of the writers strike, NBC, FOX, and CW attempted to streamline their network processes by eliminating or downsizing their current departments and folding those duties into their development departments.

Late-Night Programming

Late-night programming typically refers to the late fringe daypart between 11:35 p.m. and 2:00 a.m., when networks fill their air with light material like talk shows and sitcom reruns. Because people often have the same pre-bed rituals, "late-night programming is a massive profit center," says former NBC president Warren Littlefield, who orchestrated *The Tonight Show*'s Johnny Carson/Jay Leno handoff in 1992. "Once you lock in with the right format and the right talent, you can mark it down for decades at a time of massive income."

Daytime Programming

For local stations, daytime programming often consists of a mix of shows scheduled by each station's parent network, like CBS's long-running soap *The Young and the Restless,* and locally produced or **first-run syndicated** shows, like *The Oprah Winfrey Show.* At the networks, daytime executives cover only shows scheduled by the network itself—usually soaps, court shows, and talk shows—not shows each individual station acquires on its own. These shows often pull in large profit margins because production costs are so low. Most daytime soaps, for example, cost less than $250,000 per episode, less than one-sixth the cost of a primetime hour. And because they air daily, they can gather fiercely loyal audiences that watch for years at a time.

Unfortunately, many soap operas' fiercely loyal audiences seem to be drying up. Daytime soap ratings have been nose-diving for more than a decade as more women head to the workplace and home viewers are siphoned off by cable or the Internet. In the fall of 2007, ABC's *All My Children* audience dropped 14 percent from the previous year, and NBC's *Days of Our Lives* plummeted 19 percent, averaging a weak 2.4 million daily viewers. In fact, NBC eliminated its entire daytime programming department in 2008, handing its operations to the network's current execs. (We'll learn more about the inner workings of soap operas at the end of chapter 15.)

RESEARCH AND SCHEDULING

Although development and current departments manage networks' creative processes, they often take their cues from two other departments: Research and Scheduling.

Research

The research department's job is to pinpoint as precisely as possible who is watching what shows at what times. This information helps networks determine which shows are reaching their intended audiences, as well as each show's value to advertisers. This is important because advertisers aren't simply trying to reach the largest number of people possible; they're trying to reach the largest number of people in *certain demographics:* primarily, the demographics most interested in buying their products. Estée Lauder, for example, doesn't care about reaching the same audience as Ford Trucks; a Bratz commercial doesn't need the same viewers as Bud Light. Thus, advertisers don't just buy ad spots in *any* show, they buy spots in shows that reach their desired consumers.

Like the advertisers that keep them afloat, each network has its own identity and target audience, and networks program shows to keep those audiences happy and coming back. MTV aims for males and females, aged 12–24; ESPN shoots mostly for men. BET wants different viewers from CMT. Broadcasters, which aim for the widest audience of all, usually go for men and women between ages 18–49, traditionally the most sought-after demographic.

"Eighteen to forty-nine is a combination of disposable income and the perception that their buying choices aren't rigid," says Dan Harrison, NBC Cable's senior vice president of emerging networks. "Older audiences may have more disposable income, but they're not going try a new brand of toothpaste. In that eighteen-to-forty-nine sweet spot, you can probably get somebody to switch their car, try a different toothpaste, try a new beer, all those things."

That's why a show like *Heroes* is so valuable to NBC. Although *CSI,* *Ugly Betty,* and *Survivor* draw more total viewers each week, *Heroes* often passes them all in the valuable 18–49 demographic. Thus, in 2007, a thirty-second commercial in *CSI* cost about $248,000, and the same ad in *Heroes* cost about $296,000.

Yet how do networks make these determinations? How do they measure precisely who's watching? How do they gather audience data and make sense of millions of viewers across America? They do it through a ubiquitous, but often misunderstood, process called the Nielsen ratings.

INSIDE THE WORLD OF TV RESEARCH AND RATINGS

Researchers have traditionally learned who's watching shows by collecting data from Nielsen Media Research, America's top television research firm. In 2008, Nielsen was monitoring more than 35,000 people in about 14,000 households across the country; they hoped to expand to 100,000 people in 37,000 homes by 2011. Nielsen gathers its data from these randomly selected homes in three ways:

1. Local People Meters (LPMs) are electronic boxes that connect to TVs and track exactly *who's* watching a particular show at a particular time. The boxes come with remote controls that have separate buttons programmed for each member of the house. When a family's teenage son watches *Deal or No Deal,* he pushes his button on the remote. The people meter, already programmed with each person's demographic info, notes that a thirteen-year-old boy watched ten minutes of *Deal or No Deal.* When his forty-year-old mom starts watching *Breaking Bad* a few minutes later, the people meter catches the change. (Because LPMs are more expensive to create and install, and more complicated to use, Nielsen has traditionally placed them only in the largest ten or fifteen markets [New York, L.A., Chicago, Philadelphia, Houston, etc.]. By 2011, however, they hope to have them in fifty-six markets, measuring 70 percent of American TV households.)

2. Set meters are used primarily in midsized to large markets (Seattle, Memphis, etc.). Unlike people meters, they monitor what is being watched, minute by minute, but not by *whom.*

3. Handwritten paper diaries are also an important part of measuring viewers' habits, even in today's high-tech world. Viewers write down each program watched, the channel airing it, and the time it aired (diaries record info in fifteen-minute increments). At the end of each week they turn in their diaries, which are especially valuable in smaller markets where it's not economically viable to install more-expensive meters.

SWEPT AWAY!

Four times a year (November, February, May, July), Nielsen attempts to measure larger sections of the viewing public than it can through meters by distributing almost 2 million diaries to homes not measured electronically. Because these periods, known as **sweeps,** calculate a wider, supposedly more accurate section of the population, networks try to schedule splashier programming in hopes of luring eyeballs. Shows may kill off main characters, book popular guest stars, or incorporate sensational cliffhangers. As a result, sweeps are often criticized for being misleading about what the public's actually watching. But as audience-monitoring technology improves and advertisers experiment with new ways of reaching consumers, sweeps may soon fizzle out, replaced by more accurate, year-round measuring.

Early each morning, after collecting information from all its LPMs and set meters, Nielsen publishes three sets of reports. Metered market ratings, which come out at about 8:30 a.m. EST, measure the previous day's household and people meters in each market. At about 11:00 a.m. EST, Nielsen publishes fast affiliate ratings, which tally ratings for each network's local affiliates, based on national people-metered samples. Fast affiliates aren't "lineup verified," however, so if Miami's Wednesday-night broadcast of NBC's *Knight Rider* is preempted for local news, the fast affiliate ratings don't adjust for the change. Preliminary nationals, which arrive at 4:00 p.m. EST, *have* been lineup verified, making them more accurate than the fast affiliates.

In each report, Nielsen uses two kinds of calculations: **ratings** and **shares.**

Typically, these calculations measure entire households watching shows, but Nielsen also monitors individuals within those households. Thus, reading ratings can be a confusing business. When doing weekly or seasonal rankings of shows, Nielsen usually uses household ratings (HH ratings). But when tracking specific demographics (like adults 18–49), it usually uses individual measurements. What's most important is remembering that all measurements are percentage-based estimates of the larger population.

Ratings calculate the percentage of homes (or individuals within a specific demographic) watching a specific show out of all U.S. homes that *have TV sets,* whether those TV sets are turned on or not. So one ratings point equals 1 percent of all the television households in the "Nielsen universe," or all the households that *could* be watching television (each household is estimated to have about 2.6 viewers over the age of two). As of August 2007, that amounted to approximately 1,128,000 households per ratings point. This is based on a 2007–2008 Nielsen universe of about 286,000,000 individuals and 131,050,000 adults 18–49. (These numbers rise when they're recalculated each August as more people get television). So on Tuesday, April 29, 2008, when FOX's *Hell's Kitchen* pulled in 12.26 million viewers (according to Nielsen's fast affiliate ratings), it received a 5.5 rating among adults 18–49, meaning 5.5 percent of America's 131,050,000 adults 18–49 (who had television) were watching the show.

Shares measure the percentage of all homes (or individuals) *currently* watching TV that are tuned to a specific program. In other words, while ratings tally all TV households in the Nielsen universe, whether they're turned on or not, shares measure only TV households that are *turned on at that time.* So on April 29, 2008, when *Hell's Kitchen* garnered its 5.5 rating among adults 18–49, it also got a 14 share among adults 18–49, meaning the adults watching *Hell's Kitchen* comprised 14 percent of all adults 18–49 who were watching television *at that time.* So on Tuesday, April 29, 2008, 5.5 percent of all U.S. adults who *owned* TVs were watching *Hell's Kitchen,* and that equaled 14 percent of all adults 18–49 who were *watching* TV at the time. Combined, we say, "*Hell's Kitchen* had a 5.5/14 in adults 18–49."

Years ago, before broadcasters were competing with hundreds of cable and broadband channels for viewers' eyeballs, series were canceled if they didn't achieve a 30 share or more. Today, top shows bring in closer to a 20 share.

Ratings calculations are also changing as more people use **time-shifting** devices like **digital video recorders** (**DVRs**), iPods, and other machines allowing viewers to watch shows whenever or wherever they wish. Most networks now monitor live-plus-seven ratings, an estimate of audiences who watch the show during its original "live" airing, *plus* audiences who watch it on DVR up to seven days later. The third-season finale of *Grey's Anatomy,* for instance, pulled in around 22 million viewers on Thursday, May 17, 2007; but approximately 3 million *more* viewers recorded it on DVR, "time-shifting" it and watching it over the next week.

As tech companies develop new ways to make ratings systems more accurate, many are challenging Nielsen's dominance in the TV research arena. In 2007, TiVo introduced StopWatch, which tracks what TiVo users are watching, both live and recorded, down to the *exact second.* The following year, TNS Media Research and DirecTV announced the launch of DirectView, which mines viewing data from set-top boxes of over 100,000 DirecTV users.

Other companies are imagining whole new ways of monitoring audiences. IAG Research measures audience engagement, or how emotionally tied viewers are to specific shows. This is valuable in helping networks and advertisers determine how effective their programs and ads are. In spring 2008, for instance, CBS's *Welcome to the Captain* averaged a weak 2.2 rating and lasted a mere five episodes. But it tied with FOX's equally low-rated and short-lived *Unhitched* for third place behind *Heroes* and *Lost* in IAG's ranking of shows according to audiences' level of emotional engagement. So while not a lot of people may have watched those shows, those who did were passionate about them, and that can be valuable information for networks and advertisers eager to make an impression.

In a few years, *all* TV sets, DVRs, and cable boxes could include software that records precisely who's watching what when . . . and how much attention they're paying. We may also see software embedded in cell phones to pick up encoded TV signals so viewers can be monitored whether watching TV in a bar, on a friend's Xbox, or even on an iPod at a store's sales display. In fact, Nielsen itself has acquired BuzzMetrics, a company that monitors user-generated media online, and Telephia, which tracks data from cell phones and other mobile devices. As data get more accurate, programming execs will have a better sense of what shows to schedule when, and advertisers will have a better sense of where to put specific ads and how much to pay for them.

(For purposes of this book, however, we'll be sticking with TV's most common method of measurement: Nielsen's system of ratings and shares.)

SCHEDULING

The scheduling department decides how to slot shows into the network's calendar so they connect with the largest possible audience. Schedulers typically use three main scheduling **grids,** or special calendars, to do this: a yearly grid, a weekly grid, and a daily grid. Some schedulers create the grids on their computers; others use bulletin boards or wall-sized charts. Across the top of each grid is the timeline (months, days, etc.); down the side are hours, time slots, or dayparts. At any given time, the next day's grid is completely filled in, the weekly grid six months out is about 60 percent filled in, and next year's grid is often less than 40 percent filled in.

When new shows come in from the development department, schedulers categorize them according to theme and demographic: men's shows, women's shows, urban shows, action shows, etc. Each of these groups forms a **block** of programming to go on the grid, so a network may form a comedy block of all sitcoms or a crime block of all cop and legal dramas. (NBC usually has a comedy block on Thursday nights, which—in fall 2007— consisted of *My Name Is Earl, 30 Rock, The Office,* and *Scrubs.* CBS often has a Tuesday-night block of adult dramas, like fall 2007's *NCIS, The Unit,* and *Cane.*)

Blocks are smart scheduling tools because one show serves as the **lead-in** to the next, called the **lead-out.** "One of the most powerful and simple scheduling strategies in television is lead-in, lead-out," says Gaurav Misra, VP of programming for MTV and VH1. "[A viewer's momentum] is like a steam engine. When it's moving, it's hard to change direction. It's the same with viewers. Once they're on a channel—even in the age of the remote control, cable, and DVRs—it's surprising how glued they are. Less than they [once] were, but still glued."

When determining where to schedule blocks on the grid, schedulers first look at what their competition is scheduling and how audiences are responding. Does a rival network have a successful Wednesday block of female-driven comedies? Are men twenty-five to fifty-four looking for something to watch on Thursday nights? Networks' goal is to **counter-program,** or attract audiences not being serviced by other networks. For example, in 2007, ABC scheduled its new male-skewing comedies, *Cavemen* and *Carpoolers,* on Tuesdays at 8:00 and 8:30 p.m. to counter-program against FOX's light romantic mystery *Bones,* NBC's feel-good reality hit *The Biggest Loser,* CBS's military drama *NCIS,* and the CW's youth-skewing *Beauty and the Geek.* ABC wanted to be the obvious destination for male comedy fans with nowhere else to go. (Unfortunately, both *Cavemen* and *Carpoolers* tanked, and neither made it to its second season.)

Other networks like to "fish where the fish are," or program shows and blocks to compete with *similar* programs. Cable networks often do this because they need smaller audiences than broadcasters do. Perhaps a cable outlet has a new sci-fi series they want to schedule; they look at the grids and see that—as an example—NBC's *Heroes* ratings fluctuate about 10 percent each Monday, meaning 10 percent of *Heroes'* audience bounces in and out. This is about one or two million viewers, not a devastating amount for NBC, but a respectable audience for a small cable network. So the cable channel schedules its new sci-fi show *against Heroes* in hopes of snagging sci-fi fans who are watching, but aren't completely committed to NBC.

Networks also use *other* networks' shows as lead-ins and lead-outs, as when ABC moved *Grey's Anatomy* from Sundays to Thursdays. By doing this, *Grey's* occupied the 9:00 time slot just before NBC's hit medical soap, *ER.* As a result, all the medical-soap fans awaiting *ER* at 10:00 p.m. tuned in to *Grey's* an hour earlier. The move was brilliant: it not only boosted *Grey's* numbers, but *ER's* as well.

Similarly, when ABC debuted *Desperate Housewives* in September 2004, they scheduled it at 9:00 p.m. on Sundays, the former time slot of HBO's *Sex & the City. Sex* had finished its run a few months earlier, and ABC figured its audience of sophisticated, urban women needed a new home. They were right. *Desperate* premiered to 21 million viewers, immediately making it TV's most-watched new show in nearly ten years.

As their grids take shape, schedulers can identify holes in their net-work's calendar. Perhaps they need a third show to create a block of crime dramas several months down the road. Perhaps they predict they'll need a female-skewing comedic reality series, or a drama geared toward twenty-something men. They send this info to the development department, where execs begin searching for shows to fill the gaps.

Why is this important to understand? Because young writers often think selling a new TV show is simply about having a great idea. But a great idea is only half the battle; you need to have the great idea a particular network is looking for *right now.* And a network's needs can change on a weekly or even daily basis as shows succeed, fail, or get bought and sold. A network may have just bought a pitch for an exciting cop drama and want to find a companion. Or perhaps a network's new legal soap premiered unexpectedly well and they want more just like it. Or maybe they developed a teen comedy pilot that didn't make it to air, so they're now staying *away* from teen comedies. This is why writers, producers, and agents stay in constant contact with their friends at networks and studios.

GOING OFF THE GRID

As new technologies like DVRs, the Internet, and VOD services (Video-On-Demand) give consumers more control over what they watch and when, they're also diminishing the importance of traditional TV schedules. Many industry insiders and observers feel we're seeing the traditional schedule disintegrate. After all, what good are blocks, grids, and lead-ins if viewers can simply record, stream, or download shows whenever (and wherever) they want?

"With the advent of DVR and the accessibility of programming . . . the flow of particular nights is becoming less and less important . . . because you can cherry-pick what you want to see," says Jon Wax, FOX's VP of drama development. But does that mean scheduling isn't important? Hardly. "With reality and live sports programming, there's still plenty of day-and-date programming, 'watercooler programming' for the next day. For us, we have this behemoth . . . *American Idol* . . . [and] you need to watch it live if you don't want to be behind the times at the watercooler the next day. We think long and hard about what to have available to program and flow with *American Idol,* because we have a lot of people watching it live."

MARKETING AND PROMOTIONS

The final pieces of the programming puzzle are marketing and promotions, departments charged with attracting audiences to a network and its shows.

Marketing departments promote shows by purchasing advertising in other arenas: radio commercials, Internet ads, billboards, product tie-ins, etc. Promotions departments use *free* platforms, booking stars on talk shows like *The Tonight Show* or *The View,* sending casts on tours or to charity events, and creating trailers to broadcast on their own network's airtime. Promo departments also create a look, feel, and brand for the network as a whole—designing everything from **pop-up messaging snipes** and **bugs** (network and program logos you see in the corners of your TV screen) to network symbols and slogans (NBC's "Comedy Night Done Right," CBS's "We Are CBS," Oxygen's "Live Out Loud"). We'll talk more about marketing and promos in chapter 17.

These programming divisions are the central nervous systems of most networks. But this doesn't mean they don't have help, often working closely with a handful of other important departments, primarily talent and casting, business and legal affairs, and ad sales.

Talent and Casting

A network's talent and casting departments manage all interaction with **talent,** or actors and hosts, for the network's primetime shows. This includes scouting the country for fresh performers and overseeing casting processes for the network's comedies, dramas, and reality series. (For reality shows, most talent departments help find and book hosts. When it comes to finding "regular people" to be participants or contestants, the show hires independent, specially trained casting directors.)

Business and/or Legal Affairs

A network's business affairs department negotiates the license fees the network pays studios for their shows, as well as the network's repurposing rights. How many times can the network air episodes of a particular series? Can they stream them online? Legal affairs then executes the paperwork negotiated by business affairs: deals, contracts, product placement agreements. At some companies, legal affairs is part of the business affairs department; at others, they're separate teams. (Studios also have business and legal affairs departments, which work slightly differently. We'll look at that difference in a moment.)

Ultimately, of course, *all* the networks' departments work together to create the best shows possible in order to support one integral area of the network: ad sales.

Ad Sales

Networks' primary revenue stream is ad sales, making this one of the most important departments in the company. In 2006, almost $9.5 billion in network ad sales accounted for over one-third of CBS Corp.'s total revenue of $14.3 billion. As a result, ad sales departments often report to a level above the entertainment president, usually the CEO of the whole TV division, and the network's profit margin is how *that* CEO will be evaluated by *his* CEO.

Of course, one thing the sales department *doesn't* do is help develop shows or make final decisions on what gets picked up. But the better the development department's shows, the more people who watch the network and the higher the price tags ad salespeople can affix to spots. We'll discuss this process more in chapter 13.

HOW STUDIOS AND PRODUCTION COMPANIES ARE DIFFERENT

When it comes to finding and developing show ideas, studios don't work much differently than networks (even though they're guided by a different set of principles: networks look for shows they can program on current or near-future schedules; studios look for shows they can supply immediately to networks, then resell via other distribution channels in the future). Thus, studios have comedy, drama, current, and talent departments, which stay in constant contact with their counterparts at the networks, who keep them in the loop about networks' needs and holes. Interestingly, one area where studios *don't* have corresponding departments is in reality/alternative. Because most reality shows have little backend and are cheap enough not to need deficit financing, studios rarely bother developing them. Likewise, studios don't usually have daytime or late-night departments, as these shows are often owned by independent companies. CBS's *The Late Show with David Letterman* and *The Late Late Show with Craig Ferguson,* for instance, are both owned by Letterman's company, Worldwide Pants. CBS's *As the World Turns* and *Guiding Light* are both owned by Procter & Gamble Productions.

It's when it comes to money-making—remember: studios finance and own material; networks license and distribute material—that we see three main structural differences between studios and networks:

1. Because studios don't sell or share ad revenue, they don't have ad sales departments. They also don't have research or scheduling departments, which strategize network schedules in order to charge as much as possible for ad space. Studios instead work closely with their syndication arm, usually a separate company within the conglomerate's TV division, to reap as much backend value as possible from the shows they own. (ABC Television Studios, for example, resells its shows through Disney-ABC Domestic Television, Disney's syndication branch.)

2. Because studios finance and supervise the actual *making* of TV shows, most have production departments that oversee physical production. This involves everything from managing locations, such as studio-owned soundstages, to approving each show's shooting schedule and budget.

3. Studios also have their own business affairs departments, but whereas a network's business affairs department negotiates deals with studios, advertisers, and local stations, studios' business affairs departments handle **above-the-line** contracts for writers, directors, and actors on their shows. We'll examine how some of these contracts work in chapters 8 and 14.

Production companies are even smaller organizations than studios. Most employ fewer than ten people. Many have three or four. Some are simply a writer/producer and an assistant. Thus, production companies rarely have business affairs or marketing and promo departments. They're designed to deal only with their shows' creative aspects, so they simply function as development and current departments. Most production companies are so small, in fact, that everyone at the company works on both new *and* airing shows.

KEEPING YOUR OWN DEVELOPMENT REPORT

TV executives often monitor projects other networks and studios have in
helps them know what their competition is doing and track trends in the zeitgeist.
websites (see page 78). Here's how to organize your own development report

NBC

Project	Auspices	Studio/Prod. Co
Chuck	Writer/Exec. Prod: Josh Schwartz, Writer/Co-Exec. Prod: Chris Fedak, Director: McG	Warner Bros., Wonderland Sound & Vision
The Bionic Woman	Exec. Prod: David Eick, Writer/Exec. Prod: Laeta Kalogridis	Universal Media Studios
Fort Pit	Exec. Prods: Jim Serpico, Denis Leary; Writers/Exec. Prods: Michael Chernuchin, Peter Tolan	Sony Studios, Apostle
NoLa	Exec. Prod: Spike Lee, Writer: Sid Quashie	ABC Studios
The Anonymous Lawyer	Writer/Exec. Prod: Jeff Rake, Writer/Prod: Jeremy Blachman; Exec. Prod: Russ Krasnoff, Gary Foster	Sony Studios, Krasnoff/Foster Entertainment

development with a **development report,** or **competitive report.** This chart
You can keep your own report by reading trades and various entertainment
(this uses info from the 2006–2007 development season):

Logline	Status
A computer geek accidentally downloads secret CIA files into his head.	Put pilot, series pickup
Mangled in a car accident, a young woman is given new life by becoming part robot.	Cast contingent pilot, series pickup
An NYPD precinct where bad cops go to finish careers and young cops go to begin them.	Pilot pickup (never made it to series)
Character-driven drama about people in New Orleans trying to rebuild their lives.	Script commitment; not picked up to pilot
Based on blog (and book) written by Blachman while interning at NY law firm	Script commitment + penalty; not picked up to pilot

DEVELOPMENT RECON: WHERE TO LEARN WHAT NETWORKS AND STUDIOS ARE DEVELOPING

"If you want to be in this business, spend [$350], get yourself a subscription to Variety, and read it cover-to-cover every day. You'll learn everybody's name, who's important, and what's going on."

—Michael Valeo, talent and literary manager, Valeo Entertainment

Indeed, there's no better way to stay informed than by reading the trades and news sources that service the industry. Here's a quick list of some of the best, and you'll find more in the appendix.

TRADES AND PUBLICATIONS

Note: many of these trades are available for free, in their entirety, online. They also have free daily newsletters.

Daily Variety: www.variety.com

The Hollywood Reporter: www.hollywoodreporter.com

TV Week: www.tvweek.com

Broadcasting & Cable: www.broadcastingcable.com

Mediaweek: www.mediaweek.com

Multichannel News: www.multichannel.com

OTHER HELPFUL WEBSITES

Cynopsis: www.cynopsis.com

The Futon Critic: www.thefutoncritic.com

TVTracker: www.tvtracker.com

Studio System: www.studiosystem.com

Note: TVTracker and Studio System are higher-end services and may cost several hundred dollars a year.

THE CORPORATE LADDER

Executives in networks, studios, and production companies' development and current departments are organized in hierarchies, and—as a writer/producer—understanding those hierarchies can help you navigate the corporate system. Here's how companies arrange their ladders, from top to bottom:

Entertainment presidents coordinate their network's entertainment division, overseeing programming of all dayparts, including development, casting, marketing, scheduling, and promos. The entertainment president is often referred to as the network president, although there are several areas—news, sports, ad sales—he doesn't usually oversee.

Senior vice presidents head specific departments (primetime drama, marketing, talent and casting, etc.) and report directly to the president of entertainment. While they still remain involved in creative processes, they take on added responsibilities of administrative duties and managing execs beneath them.

Vice presidents have worked their way up over many years, so they often deal with higher-profile projects and showrunners. "You're not going to give a new show from David Kelley or Aaron Sorkin to someone in their first year as an executive," says Eric Kim, former VP of current at the CW. "You have to have the respect for the showrunner to give them someone more experienced. Stakes are higher for everyone involved."

Directors cover mid-level projects and serve as backups for VPs. They also bring in new projects and writers, which is how they get promoted. Thus, directors spend much time looking for fresh ideas and talented producers.

Managers shadow and learn from directors and VPs above them. Because these low-level execs are hungry to prove themselves, they're eager to bring in new writers and projects. Thus, managers are great people for writers to meet and form relationships with. (And to clarify: these are a different kind of "manager" from a talent or literary manager, which we'll talk about in chapter 22.)

Coordinators are halfway between assistant and executive. They no longer work "on a desk" as assistants, but they juggle both assistant duties (tracking information, distributing reports, organizing files) and executive duties (attending meetings, reading scripts, giving notes). Coordinators also work on low-level projects, such as online and mobile content.

Assistants are support for execs above them, and the number-one starting point for anyone wanting a career in entertainment. Although assistants do secretarial tasks—answering phones, organizing schedules, maintaining Rolodexes—they also give notes on projects, track competitive development, gather info from other assistants, and participate in meetings. We'll talk more about being an assistant in chapter 24.

Interns are unpaid employees who often get college credit instead of paychecks. Some interns are given actual job responsibilities, such as reading scripts and sitting in on meetings, while others simply observe how their company works. Internships are great ways to get your foot in the door, and many turn into paid positions. We'll discuss interns again in chapter 24.

5

The New Show Development Process: An Overview

Television has traditionally operated on a yearly cycle comprising three phases, or "seasons": development season, when new television concepts are created, pitched, sold, and developed; pilot season, when networks produce a select number of **pilots,** or test episodes, and decide which will go on to become series; and staffing season, when new and returning shows hire their writing staffs.

For most of TV's history, broadcast networks and studios have followed some version of this strict annual schedule, beginning with development season in the summer and ending with staffing the following spring. Many execs and producers, however, have long complained that the rigid, traditional schedule is financially draining, strategically limited, and creatively stifling. Thus, networks have begun experimenting with developing and premiering shows year-round. Plus, the 2007–2008 writers strike threw a major wrench into that season's development process, forcing companies to adapt the process even more. Today, TV is at a crossroads, still rooted in decades-long patterns while also trying to move into a more open, fluid future.

Still, the basic process and patterns of developing most scripted shows remain unchanged (development-pilot-staffing), regardless of the network timeline. This chapter gives you a bird's-eye view of the conventional schedule, then looks at how networks and studios are shattering old customs. We'll then dive into the nitty-gritty of each particular phase in chapters 10, 11, and 12.

DEVELOPMENT SEASON
(July–October/November)

As we know, most networks have five separate development departments: comedy, drama, alternative/reality, specials, and longform (TV movies and miniseries). Execs working in alternative/reality, specials, and longform hear pitches and develop projects year-round, but the bulk of a network's primetime drama and comedy **development slate**—its list of projects in development—is acquired and developed during development season, a four-to-five-month period when writers, producers, networks, studios, and production companies conceive, pitch, buy, and sell ideas for the following year. Because the development/production process often takes close to twelve months, projects bought during the fall of one development season usually don't premiere until the following fall, in the middle of the next year's development season. (The fall premiere tradition dates back to the 1960s, when ABC—the third-place network—devised it as a promotional gimmick. It caught on, and a few years later, all three networks—ABC, CBS, and NBC—were debuting shows in the fall.)

Development season usually kicks off with each of the studios and broadcast networks heading to a hotel or resort for a corporate retreat in June or July. There, they analyze last year's work, discuss needs and objectives for the upcoming season, and brainstorm new ideas. Some needs and objectives come from intel they've received from their research and scheduling departments. Research may tell them, "We're losing African American viewers. We need some shows to get them back." Scheduling may say, "We need a fourth show to fill a Monday-night comedy block geared toward women aged eighteen to thirty-four." Other times, execs simply want to find timely ideas that fit the network's brand. They discuss what's popular now, what will be popular in six months, what trends are fading out. Although pop culture is hard to predict, it's a development executive's job to know what books, movies, TV shows, video games, and albums are coming around the bend.

Good show ideas can come from virtually anywhere: newspaper articles, plays, short films, movies, songs, memoirs, documentaries. UPN's *Love, Inc.* was based on a *New York Times* article about a new dating service. NBC's *Kath and Kim* was based on a popular Australian show. *Ugly Betty* came from Colombia. *The Sarah Connor Chronicles* spun off the *Terminator* movies. ABC turned James Patterson's *Women's Murder Club* novels into a crime-solving drama series. *Medium* stems from true-life psychic Allison DuBois.

You have to be "able to pick cultural moments as quickly as possible and build a show around them," says Gaurav Misra, VP of programming at MTV. "*8 Mile* came out, and within weeks we had an emcee-battle show on the air. *Blue Crush* came out, and within weeks we had a surfer-girl show on the air."

Once networks figure out what kinds of shows they're looking for, they tell the studios, studios tell their pods, producers, and other writer/producer colleagues, and producers and writers brainstorm what they want to develop.

The selling process happens in reverse. Independent writers sell to pods and producers. Pods sell to studios. Studios sell to networks. This doesn't mean networks don't hear and generate concepts themselves, but when a network generates or acquires an idea that doesn't come through a studio, it usually "lays it off," or hands it to their studio to produce. The studio, in turn, may lay it off on a pod.

Networks, studios, and production companies also meet with the major **talent** and literary **agencies.** Maybe CAA (Creative Artists Agency) represents a writer who's perfect for writing Warner Bros.' new vampire idea. Perhaps Innovative Artists has a client with a soap-opera concept. Some meetings are pitches, where the writer tries to sell an actual show idea. Others are "generals," meet-and-greets that allow the parties to get to know each other.

As studios, networks, and production companies meet with writers and start buying pitches, they begin formulating development slates, their lists of current projects. It's important to understand that whether buying a pitch or hiring someone to write an internal idea, networks and studios rarely buy completed shows, scripts, or pilots; they buy pitches. In other words, when a studio or network buys a "show," even from one of their own overalls, they're usually buying just the *concept* for that show, not a written pilot script. This allows them to work with the writer and tailor the idea to their specific needs.

> ## THE ROAD LESS TRAVELED: SPEC PILOTS
>
> Occasionally a writer will write a **spec pilot,** a pilot he writes on his own, outside the network/studio system, in hopes of selling it once it's written. Traditionally, studios and networks have rarely bought spec pilots, preferring to buy pitches and concepts they can help mold to fit their company's brand and needs. Since 2004, however, when Marc Cherry's spec pilot *Desperate Housewives* became the season's blockbuster hit, networks and studios have been more open about buying specs. *Studio 60 on the Sunset Strip* came from *The West Wing* creator Aaron Sorkin. FOX's *The Oaks* came from David Schulner *(Desperate House-wives, Tell Me You Love Me)*. And *King of the Hill* writers Paul Corrigan and Brad Walsh sold *1321 Clover* to CBS. Like all pilots, many never make it to series (à la *1321 Clover*), but it's a trend that has given new hope to writers with show ideas. We'll talk more about spec pilots in chapter 21.

As a writer or producer, your job is to be one step ahead of development execs. If you're brainstorming how to make a show out of a movie or novel still six months away, you can rest assured that another insightful writer, exec, or forward-thinking agent has been thinking about it longer. That's why the best producers and executives keep extensive lists of entertainment projects in various stages of development at different companies around Hollywood; they're constantly tracking what will be popular and thinking of ways to capitalize on it.

A studio's first stop when looking for new projects is usually its stable of overalls. But studio execs also meet with showrunners and writers who *don't* have overalls, yet have proven themselves as talented TV writers or creators: mid-level writers, talented up-and-comers, even people who have sold pilots but haven't gotten on the air. Finally, execs meet with writers who have sold projects or found success in other mediums like features (movies), theater, or books. In 2006, NBC inked a development deal with YouTube sketch comedy stars Luke Barats and Joe Bereta, who went on to write NBC's half-hour comedy pilot *This Is Culdesac* (which was shot as a pilot, but never got on the air). That same year, CBS Paramount hired chick-lit novelist Emma Forrest to do a pilot adaptation of her best-selling *Cherries in the Snow* for the CW. (It also never made it to air.)

Studios rarely buy projects from first-time writers. This reticence doesn't come from stinginess or closed-mindedness, but from practicality. "The skill sets required to write a good script and to be a showrunner are radically different," says *Notes from the Underbelly* producer Lesley Wake-Webster. "An established writer usually has demonstrated that he or she has the ability to run a show or has been around people who have run shows. A new writer may have written an amazing script, but might be less tested. The network and studio might not know how this person is going to be as a manager of other people. How are they going to be when they're in charge of a hundred people on the cast and crew?"

When studios *do* buy projects from younger show creators, even those with some experience, they often pair them with experienced showrunners or overalls. Emma Forrest, a seasoned novelist, was paired with veteran showrunner Barbara Hall (*Joan of Arcadia, Judging Amy*) before embarking on CBS Paramount's *Cherries* pilot for the CW. Best-selling author Cecilia Ahern teamed with Donald Todd (*Life As We Know It, Brother's Keeper*) when creating *Samantha Who?* Thus, you can make your own projects even stronger by attaching a showrunner before you pitch.

Execs also come up with show ideas by looking to their **talent deals,** which are similar to overalls, except they're deals with actors, comedians, and performers the network or studio wants to use in their projects. Some are **holding deals,** where the network or studio simply takes the actor off the market in hopes of casting him or her into a show. In 2008, for example, FOX made a holding deal with *Battlestar Galactica* actress Tricia Helfer, then cast her into FOX TV Studios' *Burn Notice*. Others are **development deals,** where the company hopes to create a project especially for that performer, like when 20th Century Fox signed actress Eliza Dushku, then enlisted Joss Whedon to create *Dollhouse* specifically for her.

All this is to say that development season consists of hundreds of pitches coming together through various channels. Writers pitch to production companies. Actors pitch to overalls. Networks lay things off on studios. Sometimes rival studios even team up to create a co-production, or "copro," a show owned jointly by two different companies. It's a flurry of everyone putting together projects and scrambling to pitch the networks, TV's final arbiters of what gets bought and what doesn't.

In a single year, a network often hears over 1,000 pitches for new comedies and dramas. Of those 1,000 ideas, each network buys approximately 100 to 130 projects. Some buy more comedies, others buy more dramas, depending on their needs. By mid-October (of a traditional development season), most networks are "closed," meaning they've exhausted the year's development fund and aren't buying more pitches.

The networks, studios, and production companies then work together with their writers to develop the series concepts and pilots for each pitch they've bought. This involves everything from defining a show's characters and stories to writing a script for the pilot episode. Development often takes two or three months and involves constant communication between everyone involved. We'll explore this process in depth in part II.

Most pilot scripts are due to the network just before Christmas, and many network executives go home for the holidays with fifty or sixty scripts to read. Comedy execs take comedies, drama execs take dramas, and entertainment presidents take both (the head of each department usually gives him the most important, high-profile scripts from that department's genre).

When business resumes in early January, networks reconvene to discuss which scripts should move forward and which should get the ax. And so begins—*pilot season.*

PILOT SEASON (January–May)

Pilot season is when production companies and studios produce the pilots that have been ordered by the networks. Of their 100 to 130 scripts, each network usually selects twenty to thirty to be shot (which means, collectively, broadcasters often spend over $300 million per year in pilot production).

Which, of course, begs the question: What exactly *is* a pilot?

Many people think a pilot is simply the first episode of a series. But this is only partially true. A pilot is actually a prototype, a sample episode used to show a network how the series works and persuade execs to cough up millions of dollars for the full series. In other words, it's a selling tool designed to prove the show is a stronger investment than its competitors: creatively, commercially, financially. Thus, studios and networks often give pilots more time, money, and resources than they give to regular episodes. In 2004, *Lost,* one of the most expensive pilots in TV history, cost Disney nearly $14 million (the same budget as *Brokeback Mountain*). *Lost's* actual episodes cost about $10 million less.

STRIKE ZONE: TIMING IS EVERYTHING

The Writers Guild strike of 2007–2008 kicked off on Monday, November 5, five days after the expiration of the WGA's contract with the Alliance of Motion Picture and Television Producers. Initially the union had been planning its strike for the summer of 2008, to coincide with the June 30 expiration of the Directors Guild and Screen Actors Guild contracts. This would allow writers, directors, and actors to join forces, shutting down production on virtually all TV shows and movies. But as the WGA's October 31 contract expiration approached, Hollywood began rumbling with rumors that writers had changed their mind, instead wanting to strike as soon as possible. *Why?* Wouldn't they have been stronger with the added muscle of striking actors and movie stars?

While waiting would've indeed allowed actors to join the strike, the WGA figured that by striking in fall and winter, they could not only disrupt all TV shows currently shooting, they would threaten networks' entire pilot process, potentially costing conglomerates millions of dollars. They would also jeopardize May's upfront presentations, where networks sell close to $10 billion each year in TV advertising (more on this in chapter 13).

The writers' gambit paid off. Every scripted show in production shut down, and networks were forced to slash dozens of pilot scripts being developed. (This also meant those writers didn't get paid, but this was a sacrifice they were willing to make in order to win the strike.) Overall, over $700 million in production was lost, and another $1.3 billion was lost by auxiliary businesses such as restaurants, florists, caterers, and hotels who depended on TV production.

Of course, cutting pilot scripts also allowed networks to devote more energy and resources to projects they truly cared about, and many claimed that the writers strike helped them usher in a new age of development, where they would give more time and attention to smaller, more targeted development slates. Whether or not this holds true remains to be seen.

Deciding which scripts should go to pilot is "different at every network," says Dan Harrison, NBC Cable's senior vice president of emerging networks. "It really depends on the degree of collaboration at the network and where the strengths of the network president are. If the network president comes strong out of development, they're going to have a feel for it and may not involve everybody. There are other networks where you sit down with a template and say, 'We want [four] comedies on our schedule next fall, so we need to [shoot] fifty percent more than our desirable number.' So that involves scheduling. Research is usually involved a bit. Marketing, at some networks, is involved. It really depends on how collaborative [the network] is, and that starts from the top."

When a network "passes" on a project, or decides not to move forward, the studio can try to sell the project somewhere else. *My Name Is Earl* was originally bought by FOX, but when the network passed on the script, the studio (20th Century Fox) resold it to NBC, which turned it into one of the surprise hits of 2005.

Unfortunately, it's rare that rejected pilot scripts get resold. After spending gargantuan amounts of time, money, and energy developing their own projects, networks rarely pick up somebody else's hand-me-downs.

When a pilot *does* get picked up, the network commits to paying the pilot's license fee, usually about 60 to 70 percent of the pilot's budget (the remaining 30 to 40 percent comes from the studio; this is the deficit of "deficit financing"). The pilot then goes immediately into production, hiring its creative team, actors, and crew. This creates a mad race among projects to nab their first choices of performers, director, and designers. Many pilots *don't* get their first choices, which can hurt their chances of getting a series pickup in May. Of course, most pilots—even those that *do* get their first choices—don't get picked up to series anyway, meaning all those actors, directors, and designers are suddenly out of a job only a few months later. This is one of the great inefficiencies of pilot season: every network, studio, and show suffers because they all compete for the same resources at the same time. This is why year-round development is often so attractive; it would give networks and studios much larger talent pools from which to draw. Although the industry has begun moving toward year-round development, change comes slowly, and traditional pilot season hasn't completely dissolved.

Most finished pilots are due to networks in early May, just in time for **upfront announcements,** presentations where networks reveal fall schedules—both new shows and old—to advertisers and press (more on this in chapter 13). This gives producers about three months to make the pilot, and although that may seem like plenty of time, consider how long it takes to prep, shoot, and post a full-length movie: usually nine to twelve months, sometimes more. So three months isn't long, especially if you're making a one-hour drama, which is half the length of a movie, made in a quarter of the time (and for a quarter of the budget). It's even worse if you're making a ninety-minute or two-hour pilot like *Lost* or *Fringe.*

As producers deliver pilots in early May, each network looks at its choices and discusses which should become full series. They then announce the next season's schedule at the May upfronts in New York (more on this in chapter 13). Networks usually pick up four to eight new shows; so of the twenty to thirty pilots shot by each network, less than 30 percent make it to air. In 2007, NBC ordered eighteen scripted pilots and selected five to go to series (*Life, Chuck, Lipstick Jungle, The Bionic Woman, Journeyman*). ABC ordered twenty-eight pilots, picking up eight series for fall and three for midseason (for fall: *Samantha Who?, Cavemen, Dirty Sexy Money, Carpoolers, Pushing Daisies, Private Practice, Big Shots, Women's Murder Club;* for midseason: *Eli Stone, Miss Guided, Cashmere Mafia*).

So to recap: Networks hear over 1,000 pitches. They buy 100 to 130. Of those, twenty to thirty get shot as pilots. Of those, four to eight debut as series. Of those, half are usually canned before finishing their season. Of the remaining three to four, one or two *might* become hits. So if you're lucky enough to have your pitch heard, the odds of its success are less than one in a thousand.

When a network picks up a series, it orders a certain number of episodes. Most TV shows have twenty-two episodes per season, but few series get twenty-two-episode orders right out of the gate. Instead, most networks order thirteen episodes, including the pilot, so the show has twelve new episodes to shoot. If the series does well, the network orders the **back nine,** rounding out the twenty-two episodes. Some shows, like ABC's *October Road,* begin with six-episode orders. *Seinfeld* began with four.

THE INCREDIBLE SHRINKING TV SEASON

Since the beginning of television, networks have toyed with the appropriate number of episodes for a full TV season. In early days, most shows—which were transplants from radio—produced thirty-nine episodes per year. In the 1960s, as production costs increased, networks began ordering shorter seasons. The first season of *Gilligan's Island* (1964) produced thirty-six episodes. *Star Trek* (1966) shot twenty-nine.

Today, a typical TV season contains twenty-two episodes, although some networks have started giving larger orders to successful returning series, like when NBC ordered thirty episodes of both *Heroes* and *The Office* for its 2007–2008 season (the writers strike later prevented both shows from completing their orders). Others have returned to experimenting with *shorter* seasons. Like with *The Office* and *Heroes,* the 2007–2008 writers strike forced networks to air truncated seasons of shows. The CW's *The Game* produced only fifteen episodes before the strike. *Pushing Daisies* produced nine. *The Big Bang Theory* produced eight.

Yet to networks' surprise, they found advantages to shorter seasons. Fewer episodes mean lower production costs, but they also mean networks can yank failing shows sooner. Shorter seasons also allow networks to refresh schedules more often, allowing them to air *more* new series throughout the year. And because cable outlets have been airing shorter seasons for years, audiences are accustomed to it.

Shorter seasons can even help writers be more creative; if writers know they have a finite six or eight episodes (as opposed to a thirteen-episode order that could be axed halfway or stretched even longer), it allows them to flesh out more satisfying story arcs. (We'll learn more about how writers craft story arcs in chapter 15.)

"There has been a sentiment for years that if you didn't get a full twenty-two episodes, your show is not going to be viewed as a success," says Erin Gough-Wehrenberg, executive VP of Universal Media Studios, but "that sentiment is changing. The cable model has shown you can live in a world where—if people are hungry for your show—you can put on thirteen episodes every two years and people are going to watch. The key is being a hit show. The hard part, in those thirteen episodes, is getting enough people to watch the show, be hungry for it, then say, 'Okay, I'll come back.' But in success, it's a great model."

STAFFING SEASON (MAY–JUNE)

After the May upfront presentations, when networks announce their new and returning programs, staffing season begins and showrunners hire their series' writing staffs. Writing staffs usually consist of eight to twelve writers who do everything from conceiving and pitching episode ideas to writing, rewriting, and "punching up" each other's scripts. Thus, hiring the right writers is one of the most important decisions producers make. Producers find their perfect staffs by reading samples from hundreds of writers, which they receive from accredited agents, managers, and lawyers. Other samples come from co-workers, assistants, or friends.

Although hiring the staff is primarily the showrunner's decision, show-runners work closely with their network and studio, who have millions of dollars invested in each series. Execs must approve every person on staff, from the highest executive producer to the lowliest staff writer.

By the end of June, most shows have finished hiring and begun work-ing, outlining the season and writing episodes. Studios' and networks' cur-rent execs, those handling programs already on the air, take over the shows where development execs left off, and development departments start thinking about new shows for next year. The entire process begins again. (For a bird's-eye view of a traditional development year, and how it fits in with the rest of TV, check out the charts at the end of chapter 17.)

HOW IT'S ALL CHANGING

For years, networks have tried abandoning the annual development cycle. After all, if you're a network or studio, buying most of your year's projects in a three-month period—then shooting them at the *exact same time* as everyone else—hardly seems conducive to finding and creating the best material.

Unfortunately, networks and studios are deeply entrenched in habit, and while conglomerates may be powerful, they're not nimble. So while compa-nies *talk* about their desire to change, change itself has come slowly, and usually out of necessity. FOX, for instance, has long been attempting to do year-round development to avoid premiering shows in the midst of its fall Major League Baseball broadcasts. And in January 2008, two weeks before the end of the writers strike, NBC announced that the strike had catalyzed it to alter its business model and eradicate its traditional pilot season alto-gether. Instead of shooting the usual twenty to thirty pilots, NBC said it would cut back to around five per year. Thus, rather than spending millions of dollars on pilots that never air, it would use that money to greenlight cer-tain scripts right to series, a model that had worked for its sister cable net-works, USA and SciFi Channel. The next month, the network gave a six-episode order to writer Michelle Nader's adaptation of the hit Australian series *Kath and Kim.* It also picked up thirteen straight-to-series episodes of *Fear Itself,* a horror anthology, as well as thirteen episodes of *Crusoe,* a $35 million series cofinanced by NBC-U's Universal Media Studios and British production company Power, marking the first time a U.S. series was produced by a foreign company.

Other networks are changing their models as well. The strike prompted some to pick up pilots and series in the fall, months after the usual series pickup time, so they could start production *before* the impending strike. (Networks figured pilots could be produced and shot without writers, since actors and directors were still able to work.) ABC ordered six episodes of *Section 8* in September. NBC picked up *The Philanthropist.* And FOX gave a series order to *The Oaks,* which began shooting on November 5, the day the strike began.

Meanwhile, the strike prompted CBS to break the mold and acquire thirteen episodes of a Canadian series called *Flashpoint,* entirely written and produced for Canadian network CTV. NBC, ABC, and ABC Family followed suit with other Canadian series, sparking many to wonder if we'd entered a new era of international TV distribution. NBC also hired production company BermanBraun to develop an entire one-night block of thematically related programming, the first time a network had hired a single company to program a whole night.

Each of these developments has helped erode traditional schedules and processes. Of course, when the writers strike ended on February 13, 2008—in the middle of what would've been pilot season—networks immediately began picking up pilots to be shot, reverting back, at least somewhat, to a traditional schedule. This time, however, less money and a shorter calendar (upfronts were still scheduled for mid-May) compelled them to be smarter. CBS and the CW decided to pick up more presentations (low-budget, scaled-back pilots) than usual, and FOX scheduled table reads to help choose which scripts to pick up.

So will networks ever fully abandon traditional seasonal schedules and customs? Who knows? Year-round development and premieres have their own pitfalls. It's harder to promote shows airing at atypical times, because it's tougher to inform audiences, gather press for junkets and screenings, and amass viewers already ensconced in other shows.

"The strike certainly accelerated an erosion of the rigid process, the timetable as we knew it," says FOX VP of drama development Jon Wax.

"[But] I don't know that it'll ever go away entirely. For our network in particular, we seem to do better on balance when we premiere in the new calendar year. That's when—with *American Idol* and *24* launching—we seem to be clicking on all cylinders. So for years, we [have] wanted to have a more year-round schedule. Do I think [the old cycle] will ever completely go away? I don't know for sure, but it'll continue to erode for the foreseeable future."

Thus, while we continue to see networks getting inventive with how and when they acquire, produce, and premiere new programming, we may also see vestiges of traditional development-pilot-staffing seasons sticking around.

PART II

Development Season
From Pitch to Pilot Pickup

6

Recipe for a TV Show

Creating a successful TV show is a monumental task. As we learned, the percentage of pitches that become hit shows is about *one tenth of one percent*. So whether you're the world's most seasoned showrunner or a brilliantly talented upstart, creating a hit requires the perfect combination of talent, hard work, timing, contacts, industry understanding, and—most important—blind luck.

Hollywood, after all, is filled with talented writers who have never had a hit series. And I'm not talking about the thousands of writers pounding out spec scripts or taking their shots at pitch festivals. I'm talking about writers who have sold movies. Writers who have sold novels. Writers who have written on staff for *CSI, The Office,* and *24*. There are even writers who have created mega-hit, blockbuster TV shows—then followed them up with enormous flops. Steven Bochco, co-creator of *Hill Street Blues* and *NYPD Blue,* did *Cop Rock* and *Blind Justice*. David Kelley, of *Boston Legal* and *Ally McBeal,* did *Wedding Bells* and *Girls Club*. This doesn't tarnish their other brilliant achievements, it just proves there's no secret formula.

There *are*, however, certain building blocks and ingredients most good shows seem to have. In this chapter we discuss the mechanics and terminology of TV writing and development. But first, the obvious question:

WHAT MAKES A GREAT TV SHOW?

Compelling characters? Strong storylines? An interesting premise? Sure. But though each of those elements is necessary for a great *story*, there's a difference between a great story and great *television*. And by "great," I'm not just talking about the quality of an idea. I'm also talking about its marketability and salability. *Lost* may be an artful, innovative show, but it's a risky, almost unrepeatable model for a series (and it only makes it on the air when a power player like J. J. Abrams wants to do it). After all, what makes programs attractive to networks and studios is different from what makes them attractive to writers. The best ideas are a synthesis of both. And, while a storytelling medium, television is not the same as film. Or theater. Or novels.

In a novel or film, the story's over, well, when the story's over. Not so in TV, where characters come back every week and each episode is both a new story and a continuing saga. Thus, a good show, we often say, must have something very important: **legs,** or the ability to run, churning out stories, far into the future.

This doesn't mean there aren't successful shorter programs, or "one-offs" like movies and miniseries, designed to last a specific number of installments, but those aren't traditional series, and they're usually produced only as special events (TNT's *Into the West,* SciFi's *The Lost Room,* CBS's *Elvis*).

NICE LEGS!

"A television series needs to be an idea from which hundreds of stories can spring. A good TV show has a premise and characters that lend themselves to many stories . . . [unlike] a movie or a play, which is about one major story in a character's life."

—Adam Chase, executive producer (*Friends, Love, Inc., Clone*)

"A lot of people think writing a television show is like writing a movie. You tell this great story and you're done. But there's a lot more to a TV show. You have to think about the legs. Can this go on for three hundred episodes without us getting bored? A lot of people fail to remember that."

—Terri Lubaroff, senior VP, Humble Journey Productions

Legs are the first thing a buyer looks at when considering a TV project. But there's another essential ingredient as well. Back in part I, we discussed how TV shows aren't designed to run, they're designed to *rerun,* often out of order, without losing dramatic value. Remember: studios, the owners and financiers of most scripted television, lose money on almost every series they produce—until they sell it into syndication. Which means if your project can't be easily rerun, if it's too serialized or soapy, it can be unappetizing for a studio. So what's the second important ingredient of a sellable TV show?

Repeatability.

Those two fundamental qualities—legs and repeatability—account for most of TV's specific needs and nuances, rules and requirements.

In this section we'll discuss the five main storytelling components studios and networks also look for when gauging whether or not a series can go the distance: genre, premise, structure, characters, and voice.

GENRE

At its most basic level, there are two types of scripted television: comedy and drama. Though the obvious difference is that comedies are (presumably) funny and dramas are (presumably) dramatic, television uses an even more specific distinction: comedies last half an hour; dramas last an hour. Even in today's TV landscape—where shows like *Ugly Betty* and *The Office* blur the lines—hour-long shows are usually developed by drama execs and half-hours are developed by comedy. Thus, comedies are often referred to as half-hours, and dramas as hours.

Comedies, or Half-Hours

There are two types of comedies: **multicamera** and **single-camera.**

You'll recognize multicamera shows as traditional sitcoms like *Two and a Half Men, Rules of Engagement, Newhart, George Lopez,* and *Will & Grace.* Multicams are performed straight through, on a stage, before a live audience, and the action is recorded by cameras set up at the periphery of the stage. You can also identify them by their limited number of sets and their laugh track. **Single-camera** shows, on the other hand, are shot like movies, using only one main camera. (They often use more than one camera to cover other angles, but there's only one primary camera.) Single-cams utilize multiple sets and locations, and there's no laugh track or audience. Think *My Name Is Earl, Everybody Hates Chris, The Wonder Years,* and *Californication.*

Within these categories, there are many different genres: family comedies like *The Cosby Show* and *Everybody Loves Raymond,* office comedies like *Just Shoot Me* and *30 Rock,* ensemble (or "urban tribe") comedies like *Friends* and *Seinfeld,* romantic comedies like *Mad About You* and *How I Met Your Mother.*

(Pop Quiz: Who invented the multicamera set-up—and on what show? If you've been paying attention, this should be a no-brainer. If not, find the sidebar on page 38.)

Dramas, or Hours

Unlike comedies, all dramas are shot single-camera, but dramas also contain several of their own unique genres: **procedurals, soaps, character-driven,** and **event dramas.** And within these main genres are several subgenres: medical dramas like *ER,* legal shows like *Eli Stone,* action series like *Knight Rider,* family dramas like *Brothers & Sisters,* cop dramas like *Law & Order: SVU,* etc. Many shows even combine elements of different genres. *Boston Legal* is a character-driven "dramedy" (a show fusing both comedy and drama) that uses strong procedural elements. *Supernatural* tells procedural stories, but it also has character-driven elements that explore the family dynamics at its core. Here's a closer look at each genre.

Procedurals follow specific *procedures* to propel their characters through the story (*Without a Trace, The Closer, Law & Order*). Each week, *CSI*'s Gil Grissom, Brenda Johnson, and Anita Van Buren follow one clue to the next until they solve the episode's mystery. Although procedurals are often crime stories, not every procedural centers on cops and criminals. *House* is a medical procedural. *Shark* is a legal procedural. *Ghost Whisperer* and *Medium* put supernatural spins on their mysteries. *Monk* and *Psych* look at detective procedurals through lighter, more comic lenses.

Studios like procedurals because each story begins and ends in the same hour, allowing them to air out of order and repeat more easily, making them prime products for syndication. Networks like them because audiences don't have to catch every episode in order to understand what's going on.

On the other end of the spectrum come **soaps,** shows whose stories spring from character interaction and relationships: *Swingtown, One Tree Hill, Melrose Place.* Unlike procedurals, soaps are highly serialized, meaning stories play out over many episodes, sometimes even months or seasons. What brings audiences back is their emotional investment in the lives of the show's characters.

While a juicy soap can gather huge audiences and run for years (à la *ER,* which started in 1994 and passed *Dallas* as America's longest-running primetime soap), networks and studios are sometimes hesitant to develop and program them. Because they can't easily air out of order, soaps are hard to syndicate, and without a formula to each episode, it's difficult for audiences to tune in once and understand what's happening. The result: many soaps die prematurely. Remember FOX's *North Shore?* Or the CW's *Hidden Palms?* Or ABC's *Six Degrees?* Don't worry—neither does anyone else.

Like soaps, **character-driven dramas** (*Rescue Me, The West Wing, Kyle XY*) focus on characters and relationships, with one main distinction: character-driven shows tend to tell more-self-contained stories. This doesn't mean they don't use serialized elements; it simply means each episode is watchable on its own. Much of *Grey's Anatomy,* for instance, revolves around the soapy interactions of the Seattle Grace interns. But each episode is still buoyed by two things:

1. One or two patient-of-the-week stories. In every episode, the hospital admits a patient whose problem serves as that week's main story. Like a mini-procedural, it's begun, researched, and solved in the same hour.

2. Meredith Grey's thematic voice-over, which bookends each episode to give it shape and meaning.

Even if you've never seen another episode of *Grey's Anatomy,* these elements ensure that each hour will have its own beginning, middle, and end.

The last category, **event dramas,** is a relatively recent addition to the TV landscape. Event dramas (*Lost, Prison Break, 24*) tell one story, or deal with one *event,* over the course of an entire season or series. They often have high-concept premises, like *Threshold*'s alien invasion or *The Nine*'s multifaceted bank robbery. Sometimes the series begins with the event, as in *Jericho*, and sometimes it builds to the event, à la *Heist*.

Event dramas are usually highly serialized, and if viewers want to appreciate the whole story, they must tune in for every episode. This makes event dramas difficult for networks to program, and even more difficult for studios to syndicate—which, unfortunately, TV-makers have learned the hard way.

Between 2005 (one year after *Lost* became a TV phenomenon) and 2007, television exploded with no fewer than fourteen event dramas:

- *Surface*—NBC (2005)
- *Threshold*—CBS (2005)
- *Invasion*—ABC (2005)
- *Prison Break*—FOX (2005)
- *Reunion*—FOX (2005)
- *Kidnapped*—NBC (2006)
- *Heist*—NBC (2006)
- *Jericho*—CBS (2006)
- *The Nine*—ABC (2006)
- *Day Break*—ABC (2006)
- *Runaway*—CW (2006)
- *Vanished*—FOX (2006)
- *Drive*—FOX (2007)
- *Traveler*—ABC (2007)

Of the fourteen shows on that list, only one—*Prison Break*—wasn't canceled after its first season. And most—*Heist, Kidnapped, The Nine, Reunion, Day Break, Runaway, Vanished, Drive*—were canceled before finishing their initial orders. (*Jericho*, to be fair, *was* canceled, then resurrected for a seven-episode reprieve, which fared no better than its first run.)

The networks even toyed with "event comedies." ABC took a nosedive with *Big Day*, a 2006 half-hour about a young couple trying to survive their wedding. And it found only slightly more success with *The Knights of Prosperity*, which followed the hijinx of amateur criminals attempting to burgle Mick Jagger.

"Serialized stuff takes a lot more investment," says Gaurav Misra, vice president of programming for VH1 and MTV. "You have to give them a lot longer run to pick up an audience, [and] there's less repeat potential as you can't repeat stuff out of sequence, whereas you can air procedurals in any order you want."

So what does all this mean for TV creators and developers? It means studios and networks will be buying a lot fewer event dramas. The 2007 fall schedule didn't have a single one (not counting returning shows like *Prison Break*), and while networks picked up several high-concept programs (*Moonlight, The Bionic Woman, New Amsterdam, Reaper, Chuck*), each used self-contained episodes.

So what should creators and developers focus on instead? The bread and butter of television.

"We're always talking about finding the [next] great stand-alone show," says Dana Shelburne, a VP of development at 20th Century Fox. "Not necessarily procedural, but stand-alone episodes. It still has a life on DVD. It gives you an opportunity for syndication. And it works well for international."

PREMISE

A series' **premise** refers to a series' most basic overarching story. *Cheers* is a series about "a group of people held together by friendships formed at their neighborhood bar." *Heroes* "chronicles the lives of ordinary people who discover they possess extraordinary abilities" (according to its NBC website).

There are several elements that go into making and identifying a strong TV premise.

First of all, a premise should be easy to articulate quickly and succinctly, and it should be instantly understandable at its simplest level. The *Criminal Minds* website says the show "revolves around an elite team of FBI profilers who analyze the country's most twisted criminal minds, anticipating their next moves before they strike again." It's short, uncluttered, and you immediately grasp the series' story: good guys use special psychological skills to capture bad guys.

A great premise also sparks conflict. You know from the *Criminal Minds* premise that the show revolves around its good-guys-versus-bad-guys concept. On the other hand, simply describing "a small town of strange events, fantastical inventions, and off-kilter scientists" doesn't set up a strong premise, because it doesn't catalyze actual conflict. However, "an unorthodox sheriff attempts to rebuild his life in a small town of strange events, fantastical inventions, and off-kilter scientists" describes more than just the geography of SciFi's *Eureka.* It tells us there will be ongoing conflict as Eureka's sheriff, Jack Carter, attempts to maintain peace and put himself back together in a bizarre town full of unsettling incidents.

A good TV premise also doesn't define only one conflict; it generates an infinite number of *other* conflicts. It illustrates the series' legs. In *Criminal Minds,* each new criminal provides a new conflict. *Eureka* has as many stories as residents, ensuring it'll never exhaust its fodder.

Finally, a premise articulates how the show functions emotionally and thematically, how it taps in to its audience's larger issues and feelings.

"Friends," says *Friends* executive producer Adam Chase, "was about a specific time in your life when you're not a kid anymore, yet you're not quite an adult, either. You don't have your own family, so your friends are your family. It's very specific—and it's very universal. Everybody goes through it. If you're older, you remember going through it. If you're younger, you look forward to going through it. So that's your launching pad."

Thus, *Friends'* premise might read, "Six friends, just starting out in life, go through bad dates, horrible jobs, and crappy relationships, but no matter what life throws at them, they know the one thing they have to get them through . . . is each other."

STRUCTURE

Structurally, TV series fall into two categories: **serialized** or **stand-alone.**

Because the success of serialized shows depends on their ability to maintain audiences' interest in long-running storylines, their stories usually have rich backdrops and extensive histories. These are called the series' **mythology,** or **lore,** and writers slowly reveal bits and pieces to lure viewers along.

Sometimes a show's lore focuses on mysteries or secrets. Each season of *Desperate Housewives,* for example, introduces a new mystery for the housewives to solve (Mary Alice's suicide, the prisoner in Betty's basement, Dylan Mayfair's bizarre past). This is called the "season arc," because the story arcs over the entire season. Other mythologies are broad, intricate backstories. *Gilmore Girls*'s mythology involves the tempestuous relationship between Lorelai and her parents: how she got pregnant, ran away, and kept them from seeing their granddaughter.

Stand-alone shows are those in which each episode is a complete, self-contained story. Most shows operate this way, from comedies like *The Big Bang Theory* to procedurals like *Cold Case*. Although many shows incorporate serialized elements, like Jim and Pam's romance in *The Office*, stand-alones tend to be more emotionally satisfying and easier to syndicate.

So how do writers create a show that produces self-contained episodes? One way is to give the show a **franchise.** In fact, when you're pitching your series to network or studio execs, they'll often ask, "What's your franchise? Is there a franchise?" This is one of every executive's favorite questions. So . . . *what the hell is it?*

Franchises

First of all, let's talk about what a franchise is *not*. Many people think a franchise is a series that can be spun off into various incarnations, like *CSI, CSI: New York,* and *CSI: Miami.* While these are indeed types of franchises, a franchise—in the world of TV development—is something completely different.

A franchise is a literary device that allows new stories to be introduced organically, week after week. Most often it's a job or job setting that allows for endless parades of stories. Cops and detectives make great franchises because every case presents a new story. You never have to explain where stories come from on a cop show; the very nature of *being a cop* produces new cases, crooks, and victims, each with a new tale to tell. Hospitals work the same way; each patient presents a new problem or story. So do lawyers and legal shows.

"Hard" procedurals, shows driven completely by procedure rather than character, always have a franchise, but many non-procedurals use franchises as well. *Psych* and *Angel* use detective agencies, and because new clients bring new cases, executives and audiences never wonder how these shows will generate storylines in seasons six, seven, or twenty-nine. (Ironically, *Angel* switched its franchise in season five, when Angel, Gunn, Lorne, and Fred went to work for Wolfram & Hart, a law firm.)

Franchises not only generate endless stand-alone episodes, they help series survive architectural and cosmetic changes. Characters can leave, locations may change, but a good franchise ensures that a series will always have stories. *Law & Order* has survived a constantly kaleidoscoping cast thanks to its infallible crime-of-the-week franchise. And when actors George Eads and Jorja Fox threatened to leave *CSI* in 2004 if they weren't paid more money, CBS refused to negotiate. As the network knew, the star of *CSI* isn't an actor or character, but the format.

Think about franchises that could be appropriate for your shows. Not every idea needs one, but it makes projects more attractive to buyers. And a franchise doesn't have to be a doctor, lawyer, or cop. Writers and producers are constantly thinking up new jobs and setups to deliver compelling stories. *My Name Is Earl* has Earl's list. *Joan of Arcadia* receives missions from God. *Buffy the Vampire Slayer* faces off against weekly monsters and demons. The more creative you can be in inventing your own franchises, the better chances your shows have of selling—and surviving.

CHARACTERS

"The thing that sets shows apart," says Andy Bourne, senior vice president of development at the Littlefield Company, former NBC president Warren Littlefield's production company at ABC Studios, "is the people that live in that world. Everyone's done a spy show, everyone's done a medical show, everyone's done a cop show. [But] Vic Mackey on *The Shield* is a different kind of cop. You'd never seen that cop on television, and it's an interesting character to watch. *House* . . . there's never been a doctor on television like House. Ultimately it's that personality that affects how that [character] goes about solving a case or healing a patient. That's ultimately what makes the show new, interesting, and different."

Indeed, from *House*'s misanthropic doc to *CSI: Miami*'s swaggering Horatio Caine, it's a program's characters that allow us to relate to a show and view it as a reflection of our own lives. So creating honest, compelling characters (which doesn't necessarily mean they're likable, as Tony Soprano and *Nip/Tuck*'s Christian Troy can attest) is a vital part of developing a series.

TV shows have three types of characters: regulars, recurring, and guests.

Regulars are a show's main characters—or, more specifically, the actors who are contractually obligated to appear in a certain number of episodes.

Most regulars appear in every episode. Others appear in a limited number, so these are called seven-out-of-thirteens or ten-out-of-thirteens, referring to the number of episodes to which they're contracted. Most first-season shows have four to eight regulars. *Shark* began with Sebastian, Julie, Raina, Casey, Madeline, Isaac, Martin, and Jessica. *The Big Bang Theory* began with Leonard, Sheldon, Penny, Howard, and Raj.

Recurring characters don't appear in every show, and they don't usually have a series contract, but they continually reappear. In *The Office,* the lecherous Todd Packer isn't a main character, but he pops up from time to time to terrorize the folks at Dunder-Mifflin. This is different from someone who's a seven-out-of-thirteen, because the actor (David Koechner) has a separate contract for each episode. Recurring characters aren't integral parts of series; the writers simply like them and keep writing them in.

Guests appear in only one or two episodes, and they're usually tied directly to the **A-story,** which is the main story of an episode. When Steven Weber guest-starred on *Monk*'s season five premiere, "Mr. Monk Is On the Air," he played a DJ suspected of murdering his wife. He appeared in only one episode, but his character was the basis for the episode's A-story, or primary storyline.

As you're designing your series, focus on your regulars. Regulars are not only the main characters, they're the source of most of the show's stories. Thus, your job is to populate your world with compelling characters who—like a great premise—generate an endless number of conflicts between themselves and the world around them. In the first season of *Heroes,* most episodes didn't focus on Claire, Peter, and Hiro battling villains and outside forces; they focused on the arguments and confrontations that sprang up among the regulars themselves. Claire and Mr. Bennet went head-to-head about her social life, her birth parents, and how to protect her mom. Hiro and Ando debated how to work together. Nathan and Peter fought about their parents.

According to how its characters function, a show might be described as either an ensemble show or a **single-lead** show. Ensembles tell stories about an entire group. The A-story of an episode of *The Big Bang Theory,* for instance, could focus on Leonard, Sheldon, Wolowitz, or Koothrappali—or all four of them together.

Single-lead shows focus on one main character. *Saving Grace* is a "character-driven police drama with a female lead"; *24* is a "serialized action show with a male lead at the center." This doesn't mean there's only one regular; it just means each episode's A-story is seen from that lead's perspective. The cast of *Everybody Hates Chris* includes the entire Rock family, but the central character is still Chris. He drives the action of the episode, and everything that happens is seen from his point of view and concerns events surrounding his life.

Some single-lead shows are **talent-driven,** like *Seinfeld* or *The Bill Engvall Show,* where the series is developed around one particular performer. These shows have other characters, but their premises are designed to showcase the personalities of their stars. Like *Roseanne* and *George Lopez,* most talent-driven programs stem from the talent deals networks and studios make each development season.

As you're creating your show's cast of characters, it's essential to know how they function as a unit (are they an ensemble? is one person the main lead?), as well as how each person functions *within* that unit. Thus, approach your characters in two ways: defining who they are as individuals, and defining who they are in the context of their relationships.

Defining who they are as individuals. It's always fun—and necessary—to figure out the details of each character: where they were born, how they grew up, what their favorite ice cream is. But these aren't the pieces of information that truly bring your characters to life. They may help us form a mental picture, but in order to fully animate each person, it's important to give each of them his or her own unique perspective and worldview.

Friends' Ross, for instance, is a paleontologist who believes the world is constructed of science, math, and logic—making it difficult for him to navigate awkward emotional situations. Ross couldn't tell his first wife was a lesbian, he jumped out the window when his parents caught him smoking pot, and he blurted out Rachel's name at his wedding to Emily. Each of these examples illustrates how Ross's emotional ineptitude leads to uncomfortable situations and comic behavior, but the writers first had to understand how that character perceived the world.

Defining each character in the context of his/her relationships. People are rarely interesting in and of themselves; they become interesting when they begin interacting with those around them. Ross, in other words, may have an interesting worldview, but we don't start to understand how that worldview affects the show until we explain that the love of Ross's life is Rachel, a spoiled rich girl who—unlike thoughtful, pragmatic Ross— often acts impulsively, with little regard for consequences. Rachel represents everything Ross abhors; she's irresponsible, self-indulgent, irrational. Yet Ross can't resist her. He pursues her at every turn, not only causing him to constantly rethink his own perspective, but forcing him to act in embarrassing (and hilarious) ways. This relationship works because it generates conflict and mirrors many relationships in the real world. We see ourselves in Ross's actions as we watch him fumbling through relationships and dilemmas we've experienced ourselves.

WORDS OF WISDOM FROM JANE ESPENSON, CO-EXECUTIVE PRODUCER, *BATTLESTAR GALACTICA*

"Create characters and mesh them together in a way that their conflict isn't a matter of misunderstanding. Nothing Frasier and his dad can say to each other is going to make them go, 'Oh, I totally get you now!' They're two characters who just don't get each other and will never quite get each other, so every week there will be a new problem."

VOICE, OR POINT OF VIEW

Having said all this, there's one element of your show that's often more important than all the others, one element that sets it apart and makes it utterly unique and irresistible, that—no matter what happens, no matter how the project changes or who else comes aboard—can't be taken away. That element is . . .

You.

Or, as we like to say in television, your "voice," or point of view.

No matter what you've heard about projects being stolen or writers getting fired, if you've done your job correctly, your project will be completely undoable without you.

Why?

Because everyone on this planet has a story to tell, and no two stories are exactly the same. We've all had our own set of inimitable life experiences, so we all see the world a bit differently.

Your job, as an artist, is to figure out exactly how *you* see the world—then to articulate that to others. This is true whether you're a writer working in television, a sculptor working with clay, a painter working with oils. The great artists—from Magritte to The Clash to David Chase—see the world in unique, vibrant ways, and they know how to convey that vision to others. Through their work, we're able to experience—ever so briefly—life as someone else, and find the common bonds that make us human.

Think about some of your favorite TV writers. How do they see the world? How do their worldviews permeate their series?

To Chris Carter, creator of *The X-Files, The Lone Gunmen, Harsh Realm,* and *Millennium,* the world's a sinister place where free will is all but nonexistent. Everything we do is watched—and controlled—by omnipotent power brokers. Whether it's fighting *The X-Files*'s Syndicate or navigating the postapocalyptic *Harsh Realm,* we're all pawns in someone else's master plan.

How about comedian Bernie Mac and writer Larry Wilmore, the voices behind *The Bernie Mac Show?* Television had seen countless family comedies from a father's point of view, but to Mac and Wilmore, parenthood is neither the warm adventure of *Father Knows Best* nor the frustrating political struggle of *Everybody Loves Raymond.* To Mac and Wilmore, parenthood is an unwanted nuisance that's thrust upon us, and the best way to deal with it is forcefully and unwaveringly (which also reflects the show's narrative premise, since Bernie isn't actually his "kids' " father; he begrudgingly adopts them from his wayward sister).

Pinpointing your show's voice, or your own point of view, can take hard work and soul-searching. I think of it like this: "When you wake up in the morning and put on your glasses, what does the world look like?" And once you know this, how can you let other people see the same thing? There's no right or wrong answer. No blueprint. There are, however, exercises and tools you can use to strengthen your voice and find what makes you special as an artist.

"Finding your voice is figuring out what kinds of stories you want to tell," says Chase. "What are your favorite movies, TV shows, and books? What kinds of stories do you tell your friends? Are they essentially funny or essentially dramatic? That should tell you whether your interest is comedy or drama. And beyond that, what's your view of the world? Is there a part of your life that was particularly interesting or memorable? Often there will be an autobiographical element to a writer's work, but there doesn't need to be, and it doesn't always need to be obvious. Edgar Allan Poe was claustrophobic and made a living writing stories about being buried alive."

As you study movies, books, and pieces of art, scribble notes about how the work illuminates the creator's view of the world. How does J. K. Rowling see the world in *Harry Potter*? How about Edvard Munch in *The Scream*? Judd Apatow in *Knocked Up*? (And by the way—words like "scary" or "funny" do not explain the artist's vision; they explain your reaction to the art. Apatow doesn't see the world as "funny," he sees it as a place where—no matter how focused or unfocused you are—fate throws you horrific curveballs. Life, according to *Knocked Up*, is about how we navigate those curveballs—whether an unexpected baby, the discovery of a spouse's fantasy baseball league, or the realization that your business idea has already been done.)

Keep a journal, a private place where you can record your darkest, most dangerous thoughts. A writing teacher once told me, "When you're writing at your desk, and you're praying no one walks in and reads it—*that's* when you know you're doing your best work." Give yourself the luxury of having a place to do that. Have a notebook only you know exists, and fill it with all the things you'll never show anyone else. And don't just write in it; read your answers. How does the world look to the person who wrote them? What does this say about you?

Record conversations. Eavesdrop in public places. When you have a fight with your mother, your boyfriend, your wife—write it down. You'll not only start seeing natural rhythms of dialogue, you'll realize how you function and interact with other people. You'll also spot similarities in situations you pick up. Do you gravitate toward lovers' quarrels? Quirky flirtations? Frustrating, inarticulate diatribes? In other words, you'll start to notice *how you see the world.*

As you develop your voice, the more honest and articulate you can be, the more audiences will understand and relate to your life experience. The more they'll see the world through your eyes. This is the element that, if executed successfully, makes you virtually inextricable from the project. It's also why television, unlike film, is often referred to as a "writer-driven" medium, whereas film is usually a "director-driven" medium. Movies are finite experiences; each story last two hours and it's over, never to be repeated or continued again (sequels not withstanding). So film executives can hear an idea from a writer, love it, and bring in another writer to write the script. Since it only happens once, they just need the best possible writer for that particular idea. A director then brings the screenplay to life according to his own unique vision. But in television, the writer doesn't tell just one story; he tells a new story, with the same characters, *every week*. (TV directors, in fact, are rarely expected to bring unique visions to their work, since most episodes must be visually and stylistically consistent with the rest of the series.) Thus, if executives love a writer's vision for the show, they need—and expect—him to guide and inform every episode of the series. Which is why you need to make sure your vision is so specific and unique it can't be executed without you. If you're worried you may be expendable, then you haven't developed your vision enough to *keep* you from being expendable.

This is your goal as a storyteller, whether telling tales in the pages of a novel, in the acts of a teleplay, or in a series pitch to network executives. The more confident your voice as a writer, the more powerful your audience's experience—and the better your odds of selling a show.

Now, let's talk about how to beat those odds and get your show sold.

The Pitch

"What the network or studio really wants is a good story, well told, by a distinctive voice," says showrunner Adam Chase (*Friends, Love Inc., Clone*). "[So] for a pitch, you basically become a storyteller in the most old-fashioned sense. You sit with people in a room, generally in a circle, like people did thousands of years ago, and you tell them a story. If they like the story, they don't chop your head off. Or in this case, they pay you money to write it."

In this chapter, we'll discuss how to pitch your show with the skill of a master storyteller. I like constructing pitches in seven distinct sections, which, in the end, flow in and out of each other to introduce the series, engage listeners, and navigate the systemic needs of networks, studios, and production companies. You can change the order of sections, and you may not use every word you write, but feel free to use this seven-part paradigm to guide your audience through the world of your show.

1. INTRODUCTION

Your opening is one of the most important parts of your pitch. This is where you let your audience step into your skin, see the world through your eyes, and connect emotionally with the universe of your story. Accomplish this up front, allow listeners to see reflections of themselves in the world they're entering, and you're already halfway to a sale.

"Knowing somebody's inspiration and why they're passionate about this project is the most important thing," says Jen Chambers, a development executive who has worked at Maverick TV (*The Riches*), The Jim Henson Company (*Farscape*), and FOX. "[I want to hear] anecdotes, and somebody saying, 'I'm so sick of what's going on in the world today, of Michael Vick and George Bush, and I want to do a show where I, as a viewer, watch these guys get taken down. That's where my inspiration comes from.' [You want to] feel their passion for a project, to know they have a vision. If you don't have a vision, no one's going to trust you."

Many writers begin by talking about a universal experience, something everyone understands and relates to. If you were pitching *Friends,* for instance, you might use Adam Chase's description from the last chapter and begin like this:

"We've all been through that time just after college when we're no longer kids, we're not adults, and we're trying to figure out who we are and how we fit in the world. Where should we live? What should we do? What kinds of relationships do we want? The only way to figure it out is trial and error. We take shitty jobs, endure abusive bosses, rent crappy apartments. We have awkward dates, and our hearts get broken at every turn. We're not with our families, we're not in school, and nothing's the way it's supposed to be.

"But somehow we make it through. Because at the end of the day, there's one thing that keeps us going. One thing that gets us by. And no matter how awful our bosses or painful our dates, that one thing is . . . *our friends.* They're the one thing you can cling to. Your life-support system. Your family.

"So this is a show about six friends, just starting out, and how they see each other through thick and thin: bad jobs, bad dates, bad relationships. Everything we all go through, we're going to go through with them— together."

Hopefully, this little intro touched something, or reflected something, in your own life. And hopefully it would touch something in an executive. If your audience is nodding along, smiling, rapt, you're probably on the right path.

2. LOGLINE

There's not a story in the world that can't be distilled into a **logline,** a one-sentence description of the story's premise. Everything from *The Iliad* to *Casablanca* to *The Philanthropist* can be shrunk into a single sentence that encapsulates the main character, what he wants, and the obstacles in his path. A logline also gives a sense of the story's emotional **relatability.** See if you can identify these stories simply by their loglines:

- When a fatherless boy discovers a stranded alien in his backyard, he must evade parents, teachers, and government officials to help the alien return home.[1]
- A heroic soldier battles natural elements, supernatural beings, and his own townspeople as he struggles to return to the wife he loves.[2]
- When a young widower learns his father has defrauded the family business, his mother and siblings expect him to save the company—and hold their family together.[3]

It's important to know your story's logline for two reasons: first, a concise, one-sentence description helps your audience get their heads around the concept, and, second, if you can't condense your show to the bare bones of its central conflict, you probably haven't pinpointed what that conflict *is.*

When formulating a pitch, try transitioning seamlessly from the introduction to your logline. In other words, as soon as you hook your audience emotionally, hit them with a tight, digestible version of your show's concept. In the *Friends* example, I ended the introduction with "This is a show about six friends, just starting out, and how they see each other through thick and thin: bad jobs, bad dates, bad relationships." This is the logline. So, if everything works right, the audience barely knows they've heard it. They simply know they're engaged in the world of the pitch, which slides them right into the series' premise.

3 AND 4. SUMMARY AND SYNOPSIS

The summary and synopsis are slightly expanded versions of the logline. The summary is a one-paragraph description of the show that builds on the intro and logline. So a summary of *Friends* might look like this:

"The show centers around six single, twentysomething friends, three guys and three girls, all living in New York City. At the heart of it are Ross Geller, who's recently divorced, and his sister Monica, a gorgeous but anal-retentive aspiring chef. They hang out at the local coffee shop with Chandler,

---

[1]*E.T.*   [2]*The Odyssey*   [3]*Arrested Development*

Ross's wisecracking college buddy, and Joey, Chandler's womanizing roommate. Rounding out the group are the flighty, freewheeling Phoebe and Monica's self-absorbed roommate, Rachel. These six people form an ad hoc family as each struggles to find his or her place in the world. They go through horrible jobs, devastating heartbreaks, and tumultuous relationships. But through it all, no matter what happens, the one constant is their love and friendship for each other."

The synopsis is a bit longer than the summary, perhaps a page to a page and a half, and delves deeper into the characters' relationships, how the relationships affect the group dynamic, and the geographic home base of the show (a house, an office, a school, etc.).

5. CHARACTER DESCRIPTIONS

Spend a paragraph per character describing the essence of each of the show's regulars: age, appearance, background, and—of course—how they see the world. On *Nip/Tuck,* conservative Sean considers himself a moral beacon, fighting to keep a rigid grasp on his family, his marriage, and his business, even as he's constantly tempted by his own base desires. Devilishly handsome Christian, on the other hand, embraces his dark side; he believes the way to control one's darker impulses is to confront them, to scratch the itch just enough to keep it at bay. Most important, describe not only who each person is as an individual, but how he relates to the other characters and functions as part of the larger unit.

"Action is character," says *Army Wives* executive producer Jeff Melvoin. "I'm wary of 'portfolios'—'this character's Jack: he went to UCLA; his mom was this, his dad was that'—as opposed to what his function is within the pilot or the course of the series. 'He's the guy who, when in doubt, will always be found crouching in the corner. He's somebody you can't rely on.' Two or three lines of punchy description [is best]."

6. PILOT STORY

Once your pitch's audience understands the world of your series, its premise, and the characters inhabiting it, it's time to let them see a story in action. Usually, writers pitch a broad version of their pilot story, the first story viewers will see. Although your pilot story should illustrate how a typical episode works, it's also our first entrée into your world and has special needs and requirements.

"You're looking for a character at a crossroads," says executive producer Rich Hatem (*Miracles, The Lost Room, The Dead Zone*). "That character . . . has been living a particular situation, and now it's changing. 'Here's the person, and why today is different from all other days.' "

Friends begins with a distraught Rachel barging into Central Perk moments after leaving her fiancé at the altar. She's at a massive junction: Will she return to her prefabricated life and marriage . . . or will she enter the unpredictable world of the friends? (Ross, meanwhile, has just emerged from a painful divorce, so he, too, is beginning life anew.)

Your telling of the pilot shouldn't be long: one or two paragraphs will be fine. What's most important is that it engages execs in the story's world and gives them a taste of how future stories will work narratively and tonally. If every episode of your series finds your hero solving a mystery and catching a criminal, your pilot should have your hero solving a mystery and catching a criminal. If every episode involves your lovelorn romantic going on a new date, your pilot should have your lovelorn romantic going on a new date.

"It takes a lot to think about a pilot episode, but it takes a lot *more* to think about what episode five is," says Erin Gough-Wehrenberg, who—as executive vice president of Universal Media Studios—develops both comedies and dramas. "[You have to make sure] it's incredibly clear what kinds of stories are going to be told in this show and that your pilot story is indicative of the kinds of things you might see in episode eight or nine. Then it's easy to assess, 'Okay, I see the kinds of things they'll be doing on a week-to-week basis.' That's the hardest part."

7. EPISODE IDEAS

Most executives also like to hear four or five short ideas for future episodes. This gives a sense of where you envision the show going and illuminates the kinds of stories the show tells. Will stories be broad and farcical like *Three's Company*? Dark and allegorical like *Buffy* or *Dollhouse*? Intimate and character-driven like *Brothers & Sisters*?

"Future storylines," says Chambers, "should be microcosms of the overall tone and atmosphere of a show. [It helps me] know it's got an engine."

It's also important that early episodes—especially of non-procedural shows—are generated from *within* your core group of characters; stories shouldn't hinge on guest stars or outside locations. This doesn't mean you'll *never* use guest stars or locations. Procedurals, like *Medium* and *NCIS,* depend on guest stars to play each story's victims, suspects, and criminals. But with character-driven shows, execs need to know a series has legs without relying on outside elements. *Two and a Half Men*'s free-wheeling Charlie and uptight Alan, for example, are so diametrically opposed (and simultaneously inseparable) that conflict and humor arise no matter what they're doing. Even the simplest actions bring out their contrasting worldviews, from cooking dinner to deciding what to wear. So if you've developed characters correctly, their relationships should be enough to churn out hundreds of stories on their own.

8. SUBSEQUENT SEASONS (WHICH ISN'T REALLY NUMBER 8, BECAUSE YOU USUALLY DON'T NEED IT)

If you have a highly serialized show like *24* or *Prison Break,* you may want to give some general possibilities for what could happen in seasons two or three, but most of the time, laying out a show's subsequent seasons isn't necessary. If you've done your job, it should be clear how the series will work in two, three, or four years. *King of the Hill* and *Numb3rs* work the same in their fourth and fifth seasons as they did in their first. Characters and relationships grow, but the storytelling works the same. In fact, if your series idea *requires* you to explain where it will be in two or three years, you may want to rethink whether its legs are strong enough to sustain it.

WHAT TO DO WITH ALL THIS INFO ONCE YOU HAVE IT

Most writers organize this info into an organized pitch document. There's no right or wrong way to do this. Some use something similar to the order we just laid out. Many write full paragraphs; others prefer skeletal notes and highlights. What's most important is that *you* know all the information and arrange it so you can access it quickly. Also, no one should see this document but you. Don't leave it behind at the pitch.

"We never recommend **leave-behinds,**" says Chambers. "When [execs] see a piece of paper, they latch on to it and have a very hard time deviating. It's like it's in stone. If there's one thing on that piece of paper that turns them off, that's all they're going to see and that's going to be the basis for their passing."

If someone *does* ask for a leave-behind, tell them you'll e-mail it the next day. Make up an excuse: it's incomplete, full of notes, too scribbled, etc. This lets you tweak the document to address any notes they may have had before sending it. It also gives you another point of contact, one more time to get your name and project in front of the execs. Plus, it gets you their e-mail address, giving you a way to follow up and start a relationship.

SETTING THE MEETING

Once your pitch is polished, it's time to "go out with it," to set meetings and enter the marketplace. Most young writers pitch first to producers, in hopes of attaching a weighty showrunner or pod who will be excited enough to partner and take the pitch to their studio. If the studio responds, *they* partner with the writer as well and take the idea to a network.

Of course, deciding *where* to pitch is almost as important as deciding *how* to pitch. Not every idea is right for every network, and not every producer is appropriate for every show. MTV develops young, edgy, pop-culture-oriented programming; it would never buy your adult drama about divorced alcoholics. Likewise, Ron Moore, creator of *Battlestar Galactica,* has a reputation as a brilliant sci-fi writer—but he's probably not right for your slapstick sitcom about tweens trying to date. Whether pitching a network or showrunner, think about their strengths and reputation, and who's the best match for your project.

Most pitches are set through mutual connections, usually an agent or manager with whom the producer or company has a relationship. Rarely do execs take meetings with total strangers, so if you don't have an agent or manager, figure out how to find a personal connection. Perhaps your cousin works for the company's VP, or your friend babysits an assistant's daughter. If you

---

HOW DO I KNOW WHOM TO PITCH?

Partnering with a showrunner or production company isn't a matter of finding just *anyone* to help you; it's a matter of finding someone whose strengths, track record, and vision match your project. The best way to do this is to watch shows similar to your idea and your sensibility as a writer. When a show ends, stay tuned after the credits. You'll often see a handful of **cards,** the logos of companies that produce the show. One usually belongs to the studio, while others belong to showrunners or production companies.

Grey's Anatomy, for instance, displays cards for ABC Studios, as well as creator Shonda Rhimes (ShondaLand) and the Mark Gordon Company, its nonwriting producer.

You can then use the Hollywood Creative Directory (www.hcdonline.com) or the Internet to find contact info for each company.

---

don't have a connection—make one. Go to mixers and networking events where you can meet people who work with important TV companies. Ask friends and colleagues who may know someone . . . or know someone who knows someone. No connection's too weak if it gets your foot in the door. (A great place to start is part VI of this book, where we talk about finding representation and networking.)

THE MEETING

As discussed earlier, pitches usually trickle up from production company to studio to network. Although the process of pitching is often the same, each level of pitching has a slightly different tenor. Unlike a presentation for a new financial plan or a line of vacuum cleaners, pitches to production companies are informal affairs, relaxed and conversational. Some companies are decorated with a calming, Zen-like vibe. Others resemble a funky East Village artist's loft. Still others have a grungy, in-the-trenches feel. "The idea is it's a creative space," says Andy Bourne, senior vice president of development at the Littlefield Company, a production company at ABC Television Studios. "It's not a business meeting." In other words, a PowerPoint presentation would be a total faux pas.

Pitch meetings usually begin with small talk: mutual acquaintances, last night's ball game, good movies you've seen. Although this seems like innocuous chatter, it serves an important purpose. "You try to get a feel for who this person is," says Bourne. "What's his life experience? What's his view on the world? What are the kinds of things that interest this guy? Ultimately, what you're trying to get at is, 'What kind of show should this person be writing?'"

Conversation eventually moves to the topic at hand—what you want to write—when the exec says something like "So . . . tell me what you're working on." This is when the spotlight turns to you.

"Pitching is a lot like storytelling," says Bourne. "[The writer] needs to create a narrative that is engaging, usually starting with 'Here's the world I'm going to explore.' Detail that for us. Explain why [you're] interested in exploring this world."

Although you're at center stage, good pitches are fluid, inclusive, and chatty—like telling your friends a story in a bar. In fact, that's not a bad way to practice your pitch.

"Go in and have a conversation," says Hatem. Don't "worry about 'I forgot this detail, I forgot that detail.' Discuss the idea with friends; don't practice pitching it word for word, because the fact is there are going to be interruptions. They're going to ask questions, there could be a phone call. You could get thrown off in a million different ways. So you talk about the idea in a more general way, and as you're having fun doing it and engaging someone, all the little details come back."

When you finish pitching, your audience may have questions or want to talk about the concept. Perhaps they're intrigued by a certain character. Maybe they're confused by a plot point. Or excited by a fun location. Questions and conversation aren't bad signs; in fact, the only bad sign is if they *don't* want to discuss your idea.

"They know within thirty seconds whether they want it or not," Hatem says. "They know if their network needs yet another medical show or another cop show or another psychic show. Rarely will the cool act-three twist make them change their minds."

Most pitch meetings last about thirty to forty minutes. When a writer leaves, execs discuss him and his idea. Is it a universe they're interested in exploring? Will it have legs to last? Have they already developed similar ideas? Does the writer have a strong enough vision to execute it? They then call the writer's agent with feedback. Sometimes they just "didn't respond" to the writer or concept, and the writer keeps searching for a producer. Other times, producers like the idea but want to develop it further before pitching the studio. In these cases the writer works for free, developing the idea with production company execs; neither he nor the company gets paid until the project sells to a studio.

In a best-case scenario, execs love a writer's idea and want to proceed immediately. They call their studio and soft-pitch the idea. If studio execs respond, and the writer is a known commodity, the studio may make a deal without ever having an official meeting. If studio execs are unfamiliar with the writer, the production company sends them other material the writer has written and arranges another pitch.

"The production-company pitch is usually less formal [than the studio pitch]," says Joe Hipps, vice president of development for Dawn Parouse Productions (*Prison Break*). "The studio has such a high volume [of projects], you want to give them a good idea of what it is in five to ten minutes."

If the studio *dislikes* the pitch, the writer and production company part ways. A production company with an overall can't usually work on something without the consent of its studio. But if the studio *likes* the pitch, it contacts the writer's agent and negotiates a deal, hiring the writer to write the project. This happens even before the show has been pitched to a network. Remember: studios, not networks, own shows, so the studio secures the project before trying to place it with a distributor.

Once a deal is in place, the writer, studio, and production company pitch the idea to networks. Most studios pitch their sister network first, because conglomerates like to keep shows in-house.

After hearing the pitch, the network discusses the idea. Does the project fit their current needs? Do they already have other shows just like it? Do execs believe the writer can deliver a continuous stream of stories? Will the show support the network brand? Most networks take a day or two to give an answer to the studio. If the network passes, the studio can pitch to other outlets. If the network *wants* the project, they make a deal with the studio, and the development process begins.

ROUNDTABLE DISCUSSION: THE WIND-UP AND THE PITCH

Pitching's never easy, no matter how successful you are. It's easier, however, if you have some friends to coach you through it. So we've brought in some of Hollywood's best buyers and pitchers to whip you into shape:

What should I wear to a pitch?

"Writers are allowed to get away with wearing whatever they want. I've seen army pants, I've seen T-shirts. If you're a young writer starting out, look professional: jeans, sneakers. If you're going to a network pitch: khakis and a button-down."

—Jen Chambers, development executive (Maverick TV, FOX)

I'm not a great public speaker or performer. How can I navigate around this when pitching my show?

"Play to your strengths. If you're naturally effusive, rely on yourself to be a lot of the personality. If you get shy, write everything down and practice so you don't get caught up or forget key points. Come out strong . . . if it's a more character-driven show, go into the characters first; if it's a story-driven show, go into the story first. There's no one way to do it; it's about what best sets up the show."

—Jocelyn Diaz, vice president of primetime drama series, ABC

Is it okay to hold an outline or read from a "script"?

"Have an outline in front of you, but not something you go to constantly. Certainly don't read from it, but have it there in case you get lost. If you do get lost, it's not the end of the world. Just own up to whatever might go wrong. 'And . . . I forget what's next . . .' They'll [laugh]; they see these all day long, so it's not a tragedy. Stay loose, keep a sense of humor about it."

—Molly Newman, executive producer (*Brothers & Sisters, Maximum Bob, Lucky*)

What section of the pitch should I concentrate on the most?

"I always emphasize characters. Know everything you can possibly know about those characters. Every great show lives or dies based on characters. It's great if you have some high-concept idea and the network is enthusiastic, but once you get into episodes six or seven and everyone's seen your great high-concept idea, it's about the characters. Shows that go five, six, eight, ten years exist because audiences see themselves, or someone they know, in those characters."

—Yvette Lee Bowser, executive producer (*Living Single, For Your Love, Half & Half*)

I know I need to keep my pilot story short. But how short is too short?

"As an executive, you know within the first five or ten minutes if [the show idea] is going to intrigue you, so include enough to be clear about what the pilot's about

continued

thematically, who the characters are, and potential character arcs. Don't go beat by beat, scene by scene, which can go overly long and hurt you instead of helping you."

—Joan Boorstein, senior vice president of creative affairs, Showtime

When I'm "in the room," how do I know when to talk—and when not to talk?

"As soon as you get someone to agree with you, you should shut up. If you're trying to sell an idea and clearly the people in the room like it . . . keep [the other] details to yourself. They'll be amazed when you come up with them, as if by magic, later on."

—Adam Chase, executive producer (*Friends, Love, Inc., Clone*)

I know different executives will offer different notes and suggestions. But if I'm getting many different responses, does that mean my idea is flawed?

"Every network or studio is looking for their own take on something. A lot of times, in a [pitch], there are kernels of story the writer doesn't even see. Maybe something sparks for us in the room that you can't put down on paper—a character or family or setting—and we leap from there to create a whole new show. That doesn't mean we want to change everything, but studios and networks want to have input on projects."

—Lainie Gallers, director of original series, TNT

GETTING ANIMATED

From the twenty-year success of *The Simpsons* to newer successes like *The Boondocks* and *Family Guy,* animation is one of today's hottest TV genres. Of course, animation works slightly different than live-action shows. We wanted to know what it takes to pitch an animated show, so we decided to pick the brains of Al Jean, executive producer of *The Simpsons,* and Matt Weitzman, co-creator and executive producer of *American Dad*.

How is pitching an animated TV show different from pitching a scripted show?

MATT: In a lot of ways it's the same. You have to have your characters defined, your world, and the basic premise of the show. We pitched [*American Dad*] as "*All in the Family* on speed." But, in addition, you walk in with drawings. So you're not only saying, "This is Hayley," [you're] seeing her with her headband and belly-button ring. [That] helps sell the nature of who she is, in addition to "She's a loose, pot-smoking, liberal girl."

Do those pictures need to be animated, or can they just be still pictures?

MATT: Just still pictures: individual pictures and one group picture to see how they'll interact with one another. The pictures themselves sell the nature of the characters. We had a picture of Roger with his half-lidded, almost-bored expression, smoking a cigarette. That utterly sold this alien who was unlike anything anybody had ever seen before. With anything animated, you're selling a very visual show, so whatever you can do to evoke that is ideal.

The most obvious difference between live-action and animated shows is that animated shows are . . . well . . . *animated*. But are there important differences in storytelling that can help sell your animated show?

MATT: Kind of like a little movie, [animation] can go anywhere, and you want to use that to your fullest. Anyone who wants to pitch an animated show has to have that desire to get bigger. There are some shows, like *King of the Hill,* that are much smaller and might as well be live-action. I like taking advantage of the medium itself, where you can get larger than life and have more fun.

What's the most important thing execs look for in an animated pitch?

AL: Pitching a show of any kind, they're less interested in the idea than in knowing you can produce the show. Generally, in TV, it makes a big difference if you have a track record and know how to [run shows]. In film, people write a spec screenplay and it sells based on the concept or script; in TV, they want to know you can do it every week.

So, do you need a background in animation to sell an animated TV show?

MATT: It helps, but it's not absolutely necessary. As a newbie, you need as many resources as you can to get people in your corner. Everybody's ready to say no to anything, so you have to have as many resources as you can behind you, whether it's pictures or somebody with a background in animation: writers or producers who have some sort of pedigree. Our show benefits from having Seth MacFarlane in our corner. Whatever you can do to have a nationally known, desired commodity like Seth can always help.

Once you've pitched and sold your animated show, how is the development process different from that of a scripted show?

AL: In live action, you're able to write a script, shoot a pilot, test the pilot, then decide whether you want to order the series based on that one episode or not. In animation, you have a longer production time, so they generally order six, ten, or thirteen episodes based on a script, live presentation, or table read. They won't get one, test it, and order more. It takes too long.

8

The Art of the Deal

Selling your first show is a thrilling moment you'll never forget, but before you begin work, your agent or lawyer must negotiate a deal, or contract, with the buyer. Although projects rarely fall apart because two sides can't agree on a deal, it's important to know the terminology and main deal points so you can protect your own interests. Your agent or lawyer will do most of the heavy lifting, but here are the need-to-know basics.

When a studio acquires a project, it must make a **development deal** with the writer to secure its rights to the show before pitching to networks. There are two basic kinds of development deals: **if-comes** and **pay-or-play.**

An if-come deal states that the studio pays the writer only if the pitch sells to a network. If no network buys the project, the writer doesn't get paid and the studio loses no money.

With a pay-or-play deal, the writer gets paid whether he "renders services" or not. If the pitch never sells to a network, the studio still pays the writer in full. Pay-or-plays are obviously more favorable to the writer, and, because most pitches are sold by established writers, more common. (Originally designed for actors, "pay-or-play" stipulated that employers either "pay" the actor or "play" the actor. Even if the actor was fired, the actor got paid. Nowadays, pay-or-play clauses apply to actors, writers, and directors.)

A pay-or-play can be either a **script commitment** or a **blind script** agreement. A script commitment contracts a writer to a write a specific project (usually the idea pitched). A blind script binds the writer to an as-yet-undecided project. In other words, the studio likes the writer and knows it wants to work with him, but execs haven't decided what idea they want the writer to write. So they offer a blind script, committing the writer to write something once they find the right project. (Studios sometimes ask for a blind script even if they *know* what project they want; that way, if they change their mind or the project doesn't sell, they can develop something else.)

Regardless of whether a deal is if-come or pay-or-play, all the contract's deal points are negotiated before pitching to networks. The three main deal points are—fee, title, and backend. Studios negotiate through their business affairs departments; writers negotiate through an agent or lawyer (more on agents and lawyers in chapter 22). If only one studio wants to buy a project, that studio holds most of the negotiating power and the writer acquiesces to more of its demands. If *more* than one studio wants the project, the writer holds more power, and his agent creates a bidding war in which each studio tries to outdo the others' offers.

Fee negotiations begin when the studio's business affairs department calls the writer's agent to get "quotes," or what the writer was paid for his last project. The agent tries to persuade the studio to pay *more* than the writer's last quote; the studio tries to keep the price the same as, or less than, the last quote. If this is the writer's first sale, the studio may offer the lowest possible amount as specified by the Writers Guild, the labor union that regulates film and TV writers and sets minimum price tags for different kinds of work. Although "Guild minimum" changes regularly, in 2008 Guild minimum for a one-hour pilot was $47,622; a half-hour was $32,378. (Pilot minimums are calculated at 150 percent of the Guild minimum for writing an ordinary episode script, which we'll discuss more in chapter 14. Like script minimums, pilot minimums increase 3 percent each year.) The agent and studio will also negotiate what the writer gets paid in episodic fees, or fees for writing actual episodes, if his show eventually makes it to air.

Studios and agents then discuss the writer's titles for both the pilot and the actual series. Showrunners and upper-level writers are typically executive producers. Lower-level writers, or writers who won't be the actual showrunner, may take a slightly lower title, which can range from producer to co-executive producer, depending on experience and negotiating leverage. (To learn more about the hierarchy of titles, check out chapter 14.)

Writers also often get a "Created By" credit. "Created By" designates the creator of the series concept, which isn't always the original writer. If the original writer is paired with a showrunner who helps shape and develop the concept, that showrunner may insist on taking, or sharing, the "Created By" credit. "Created By" is an acknowledgment that creating a series is much more complex than simply coming up with an idea; it involves crafting intricate characters, arcs, and episodes. There's no extra fee associated with the "Created By" credit, although the writer often receives **series sequel payments,** or payments for every produced episode should the project go to series. Although different writers receive different payments depending on their level of experience, the WGA has minimums in place. In 2008, the series sequel payment for every episode of a half-hour program was $1,704 (so a writer who creates a half-hour sitcom makes *at least* $1,704 for every episode produced, whether he works on it or not); the minimum series sequel payment for a one-hour program was $3,238. These minimums increase by 3.5 percent each year.

Next, agents and studios negotiate the writer's backend. When a writer or producer sells a TV show, its backend is divided into 100 **participation points** (usually known just as "points"). As a project's financier and primary owner, the studio begins with 100 percent of a show's participation points, then carves out up to a third for other profit participants: the creator and/or showrunner, other producers, a production company, possibly even a big-name director or star. Points allotted to the show's creator and/or showrunner depend on his level of experience and involvement with developing the project. A hired showrunner who didn't create the project may get five points; a first-time creator may get ten; a successful veteran may get twenty-five. The show may never get to air, but negotiating at the outset protects both the studio and the writer.

Once fees, titles, and backend are nailed down, the studio and agent discuss other deal points as well. If the writer is working on other shows or scripts, the project may be in "second position" or "third position," meaning other commitments take priority (if it's the writer's only project, it's in "first position"). They'll discuss **separated rights,** or the writer's ownership in adaptations of the show in other mediums—if the series becomes a movie or a comic book or a novel or an opera. Agents also negotiate exclusivity, or the writer's ability to work on projects for other companies (buyers always want writers to be "exclusive" so all their time and energy are focused on one project; writers hate exclusivity). They may even negotiate a bonus if the show goes to series.

When the deal closes, business affairs sends a deal memo to legal affairs. Legal writes up a **longform contract,** which is sent to the writer via his agent. Once the writer signs the longform, the deal is done: a new TV show has officially been sold!

Of course, there's still a long road ahead. The studio must sell the project to a network. The writer must write the script. The network must pick up the pilot. The pilot must be cast, shot, edited, and delivered on time. The network must select its new series. And then, if the project is lucky enough to get picked up, it must hire writers and start production with enough time to be on the air for its premiere night. In all of this, there are plenty of things to go wrong and derail the project, but the first hurdle has been cleared.

Now the studio pitches its sister network. If the network passes, the studio shops the project to other broadcasters. If nobody buys, the studio may take the project to cable, usually pitching their own conglomerate's networks first. If there's still no sale, and the writer has a pay-or-play deal, the studio can require the writer to write the script anyway, hoping to sell it later as a **spec.** Other times, the studio rolls the writer's deal to next year, when they'll find a new idea to pitch to networks.

Of course, we hope none of this happens, because we want the network to buy the original idea.

When a network does buy a pitch, it must first figure out how much of the writer's pilot fee it will "recognize," or pay back to the studio, which has thus far put up all the money.

"Networks are incredibly cheap," says Rochelle Gerson, former executive vice president of business affairs at The Carsey-Werner Company (*The Cosby Show, Roseanne, That '70's Show*). "Maybe a writer's quote was one hundred grand for a pilot. The network would say, 'We're only going to cover fifty of that.' It's never enough, and you go into it knowing that."

The studio may also push the network for a **put pilot** or **penalty,** meaning the network guarantees, even before seeing a script, that they'll either shoot the pilot or pay the studio a substantial fine. Most networks issue put pilots and penalties only for extremely high-profile projects, or as incentives when multiple networks are fighting to buy the same show. Script penalties can range from $50,000 to $250,000, and put-pilot penalties can range from $500,000 to $1 million, depending on the importance of the project and showrunner. The CW issued *The O.C.* creator Josh Schwartz a put pilot for his 2006 development of *Gossip Girl,* which was picked up to series in 2007. The next year, CBS ordered a pilot of *The Eleventh Hour,* a sci-fi pitch from producer Jerry Bruckheimer, director Danny Cannon, and Warner Bros. TV that snagged a penalty so large it practically guaranteed a series pickup.

In rare instances, networks issue an official **series commitment** before a script is even written. FOX's *Back to You* came with such heavyweight **attachments** (*Frasier* writers Steve Levitan and Chris Lloyd, and stars Kelsey Grammer and Patricia Heaton) that it was picked up for thirteen episodes the moment it was purchased.

Once a studio and network agree on what the network recognizes, the development process begins. The network sets the pace, initiating phone calls or meetings that guide the writer and shape the script. In the next chapter we'll follow this process in depth. But first, there are a few more types of deals to discuss.

OVERALLS AND FIRST-LOOKS

Sometimes a writer has such a successful track record—creating new shows or writing great episodes—studios want to secure his talents exclusively. When this happens, a studio offers the writer an **overall,** which—as you know—is the crown jewel of TV development.

When a writer or producer signs an overall, the studio pays him a specific amount of money, over a specific amount of time, in exchange for the exclusive rights to any TV material he develops or produces during that period. So when *Battlestar Galactica* executive producer David Eick signed his overall with Universal Media Studios in 2008, UMS promised to pay him more than a million dollars to own anything he wrote over the next two years.

Overall money is, essentially, an advance. It's the studio saying, "We believe you'll produce *x* dollars worth of material over the next *x* years." Any money the writer earns counts against this "*x* dollars," or is considered part of the advance, with the exception of backend and residuals. If a writer outputs enough material that fees for that material exceed the cost of his advance, he receives "fresh cash," payment equal to the amount of additional work (but this almost never happens, since it would require a massive amount of output). Overalls are reserved for highly successful, highly prolific writers with whom the studio usually already has a relationship.

"A lot of big deals happen organically," says agent Jennifer Good of the Alpern Group. "Someone's on a show for a few years, so [the studio] locks them up."

Writing partners Eddy Kitsis and Adam Horowitz, for instance, had written on four Disney shows—*Life as We Know It, Fantasy Island, Felicity,* and *Lost*—before signing a seven-figure overall with Disney's ABC TV Studios in 2007.

When an overall expires, the producer or company must renew his deal or find another. A producer who hasn't developed quality material may not get an offer to return. As discussed in chapter 2, many writers and producers lost their overalls when studios enacted their force majeure clauses during the 2007–2008 writers strike, wiping out over sixty deals. Other writers switch on their own, perhaps for more money or a different work environment. In 2007, *Without a Trace* creator Hank Steinberg ditched Warner Bros., where he'd had an overall since 2002, for a three-year, seven-figure deal at Universal Media Studios. He remained an executive producer on the Warners Bros. series *Without a Trace* and *The Nine,* but all his new projects became property of UMS.

Studios also make **first-look deals,** which commit writers or producers to giving the studio first dibs on anything they develop, but don't give the studio total exclusivity. The studio has a brief window in which to either buy a project from the writer or producer or release it, allowing the producer to pitch to other studios. In 2008, CBS Paramount signed a first-look deal with actor-cum-producer Samuel L. Jackson, and 20th Century Fox signed one with actor/director/producer Jason Bateman, who had directed their pilot for FOX's *The Inn.*

A BIRD IN THE HAND

Although development deals and overalls are made through studios, networks sometimes make two-for-one or three-for-one deals with high-level producers and showrunners. In 2006, feature producer Armyan Bernstein (*Children of Men, The Guardian*) signed an overall deal with ABC Studios—and a three-for-one with ABC, the network. This means if Bernstein brings ABC three pilot pitches, ABC *must* pick up one to pilot.

As you excel in your career, you'll continue to get more offers and bigger types of deals. Some writers who have had great success developing new shows even begin "shopping" for overalls; their agent takes them from studio to studio, trying to get multiple offers to create a bidding war.

But before this can happen, you usually need a track record of developing successful series. So let's learn how that happens . . .

9

Development Hell

....

It's unclear whether hubris or naïveté saved Maxine Shaw's life, but either way, the credit goes to Yvette Lee Bowser.

In the fall of 1992, Bowser was in the midst of developing her first pilot, *Living Single,* a Warner Bros. comedy for FOX about four female roommates navigating life and love in the Big Apple. It was an important project for Bowser, who had cut her teeth on comedies like *A Different World* and *Hangin' with Mr. Cooper.* Not only was it based on Bowser and her friends, it was the pinnacle of a dream she'd been nurturing for the past few years.

"My main reason for wanting to create shows," Bowser says, "wasn't simply that I had something new to say. I wasn't in love with the work environment prevalent in the industry. I wasn't in love with the misogyny. I wasn't in love with the racial biases. [And] I realized that in order to set the tone in the workplace, I would have to create my own show. That was my primary motivation . . . to create a work environment where people could thrive—people who wanted to focus on the work, be creative, and not criticize other people just so they could feel better about themselves."

Yet now, as she chewed over her notes from FOX and Warner Bros., Bowser was faced with a painful decision: they wanted her to chop one of the main characters from the script.

"Some of the men involved were intimidated by [Maxine Shaw's] character," Bowser says. "They were questioning her existence because they were threatened by her."

Maxine was definitely the most headstrong and sarcastic of the show's roommates. She was sharp-tongued, brash, and stubborn. And Bowser wasn't about to lose her.

"I was young and naïve," Bowser says, "and I told the execs 'I can't do that. To take Maxine out of the show is to take part of *me* out of the show, and I don't want to do that.' [The execs] gasped, like, 'Who are you not to take our note?' So I said, 'Let me go home, think about it, and come up with a solution.' "

Bowser knew she couldn't ditch the character altogether. Sure, Maxine could be strong-willed and abrasive. But she was also hilarious. As people say in Hollywood, she "popped." But Bowser also couldn't ignore the note.

"You have to compromise," she says, "because if you don't, you may find [yourself] watching that one pilot episode in your robe, by yourself, for the next ten years. You won't see episodes two through one hundred."

So Bowser proposed a solution: move Max across the street and let her be a constant invader in the other women's apartment, the omnipresent neighbor always barging in, mooching food. The execs loved it, and Bowser soon found she could create *more* comedy by having Maxine live outside the apartment.

The following fall, *Living Single* became one of the most underrated and influential shows on television, making Bowser the first African American woman to create her own TV show. The series ran for five seasons, paved the way for *Friends,* and put Queen Latifah (who played Khadijah) on the map. It also earned Erika Alexander two Image Awards for her portrayal of Maxine Shaw.

"To this day," says Bowser, "everyone loves Khadijah, but they often claim Maxine Shaw as their favorite character."

Now, almost fifteen years later, Bowser has sold eighteen pilots, including NBC's *For Your Love.* Yet she still lives by the lessons she learned during that first time in development.

"There are always compromises along the way," she says, "but you have to make digestible compromises."

Television is a collaborative medium, and collaboration depends on communication and compromise. That doesn't mean you need to throw away your artistic vision and integrity; it just means everyone involved has their own needs and desires. Networks need to attract certain demographics. Studios need to make money in specific ways. Writers have personal stories to explore. Which is why, if you know what to expect going in—how the process plays out from story to outline to script—you can better navigate the twists and turns headed your way.

DEVELOPMENT BEGINS

"The first thing that happens [after selling a show to a network] is the story call . . . a big conference call to talk about the [pilot] story," says development executive Jen Chambers (Maverick Television, The Jim Henson Company, FOX).

The story call picks up where the pitch left off, with the writer pitching a detailed version of the pilot story to the network, studio, and production company. It's also a chance for the network to suggest any notes about the pilot or concept as a whole. Perhaps they want the main character to be younger. Perhaps they want the story to be told from a different person's perspective. Maybe they want to jettison the love interest and give the sidekick more comedy.

"It's different depending on what you sell," says Chris Parnell, VP of drama development at Sony Pictures Television, but "you try to pick the best [pilot] story to illuminate your main characters. What's the best way to challenge your characters? What are the strongest obstacles you can have them overcome? If they're cops, it's the toughest case. If it's a soap, it's a tough emotional situation. But the one thing you have to have: *it's the day something happened.* There's a reason we're picking up this story today, and not any other day. Something has happened to our main character . . . emotionally and physically. There's a reason we pick up Tommy Gavin, from *Rescue Me,* that day: it's the day he started drinking again."

If the network absolutely loves the writer's pilot story, and they trust him to start writing, they may just "send him to script," or tell him to begin writing. Usually, however, they ask the writer to return with an outline two or three weeks after the story call.

"An outline is a beat-by-beat [document] of what the story is going to be," says Joe Hipps, vice president of development for Dawn Parouse Productions (*Prison Break*). "You lay in what's going to be achieved in each and every scene. It's almost a script without dialogue, telling the story in twelve to thirteen pages for a one-hour show."

ONE-ON-ONE WITH . . . MARSH MCCALL, EXECUTIVE PRODUCER (*CARPOOLERS, TWENTY GOOD YEARS, JUST SHOOT ME!*)

Perfecting an outline is the best way to make sure your story's working before pouring time and energy into writing a script. And no one knows this better than Marsh McCall, who has executive-produced pilots and series like *My Big Fat Greek Life, Twenty Good Years,* and *Carpoolers*. Here, McCall gives a couple of his favorite tricks to make sure outlines are rock-solid.

Shape your story around commercial breaks, which provide natural act breaks and cliffhangers. "[Commercial] breaks are a ready-made litmus test. If your story has natural arcs, natural places where there's big dramatic or comedic moments, the act breaks will tell you. If you [can find] act breaks, where you succinctly leave the audience on a clear, clean twist or big character conflict, you're probably doing something right. If your story doesn't lend itself to those moments, maybe something's wrong."

Every scene of your outline must push forward the story and service the series' emotional core. "Always keep in mind: 'What is the emotional thread?' Some people write it on cards so they remember: 'This is a story about a guy who yearns for the freedom of childhood, but when he . . . becomes a kid again, he realizes he'd rather be an adult.' Always keep that in mind."

If the writer has three weeks to complete his network outline, he usually delivers a draft to the production company a week earlier. The production company reads, gives notes, and gives the writer a couple days to rewrite. The production company then sends the revised outline to the studio, where the process repeats: execs read and give notes, the writer rewrites. The goal is to give the most polished outline possible to network execs—who will undoubtedly have notes of their own.

An outline should show "the structure and the details of the pilot as clearly as possible," says Jocelyn Diaz, ABC's vice president of primetime drama series. "It should give you a scene-by-scene understanding of how each scene goes, characters' stories, characters' arcs. And if it's a good outline, the tone of the piece should also be very clear."

THE ART AND SCIENCE OF DEALING WITH NOTES

No matter what you're working on—a script, a pilot, or a series—every project receives notes along the way. You'll receive notes from your producers, your studio, your network.

These notes aren't meant to devalue or bastardize the project; they're meant to help you, the writer, realize your vision in the most compelling way possible and deliver the show the network thinks it bought. I say *"thinks* it bought" because sometimes execs and writers aren't on the same page about a show's tone or sensibility. A writer may think he did a terrific job pitching and selling a dark, acerbic satire, while the network thinks it bought a wonky, absurdist farce.

"That's probably the number-one reason why shows don't work," says Dana Shelburne, 20th Century Fox's vice president of comedy development. "You thought you were picking up something, promoting it as such, and it's a totally different show."

This is where partnering with a talented producer or production company comes in handy (and why it's important to find someone who understands your voice and vision). Part of a production company's job is to understand and strengthen a writer's vision so it can protect it down the road, where multiple layers of notes can steer that vision in the wrong direction. Successful showrunners and non-writing producers have spent years running or developing TV shows, and they're experienced in constructing series and communicating with network and studio executives. Perhaps the network wants to gear the show toward an older, more mature audience. Perhaps the studio wants it to be less serialized and more mysterious. A good production company helps the writer understand and implement these notes.

"If, at any point in time, you're confused about a note, have questions about the process, or want to have a spitball session, call me," says Jocelyn Diaz, ABC's VP of primetime drama series. "I'm at your disposal. My job is to give the writer all I can in terms of support to write the best script they can."

Many times, writers must "find the note behind the note." In other words, a network's suggestion may not be right in and of itself, but the impetus behind the note is valid. Let's say, for example, you've written a pilot for a grim prison drama series and the network says they'd like to add a funny talking monkey. While you know your prison drama would *never* work with a talking monkey, you understand the network's suggestion of injecting some "funny." So you pitch pairing the main character with a wisecracking inmate, someone who can give the show some humor without betraying its tone or vision. The network loves it. You have just dealt with "the note behind the note."

Once the network approves the outline, the writer "goes to script." He usually has about a month to get a first draft to the network, although he must first deliver drafts to the production company and studio. Most first drafts are due to production companies right around Thanksgiving.

WORDS OF WISDOM FROM . . . RICH HATEM, EXECUTIVE PRODUCER (*THE LOST ROOM, THE DEAD ZONE, SUPERNATURAL*)

"Ultimately . . . people in development are waiting to get a script, so they'll say, 'You've got two weeks to write an outline and four weeks to write the script.' Almost every writer I've talked to thinks that is a backwards system. Almost every writer I know would rather take four or five weeks on the outline and write a tremendously detailed outline. I'm talking a twenty-five-page outline for a forty-five-page script. Get all the stuff out there in the outline. If you write an outline people sign off on, writing the script takes a weekend."

Once the writer turns in his draft, the whole process repeats itself: notes and rewrites with the production company, notes and rewrites with the studio, notes and rewrites with the network.

"Every script is different," says Diaz, but many first drafts need "a lot of structure notes. Sometimes there's too little story; sometimes there's too much story and we have to trim back. Sometimes the tone that was in the pitch isn't in the script, so we have to put it back."

Traditionally, most final drafts are due to networks just before Christmas. Execs then spend the holidays reading scripts, thinking about what should be "picked up" as an actual pilot.

"It's appropriate that it's the Christmas holiday," says former NBC president Warren Littlefield, "because when you get that bundle of scripts, it is its own Christmas morning. You rip open the package and see what's inside. And like any Christmas morning, there are times when your hopes and dreams have been answered, and there are times when you think, 'I wonder if I can get my money back.' "

Writers, meanwhile, don't have quite the same excitement.

"It's a system designed to ruin your holidays," says Adam Chase, executive producer of *Friends* and *Love, Inc.* "You're hanging out with friends or family, and people who don't work in the entertainment industry are at their most jovial, drinking wine, exchanging presents, taking pictures . . .

whereas you're on pins and needles, waiting for people to make a decision that will affect the rest of your life. It's like you're on a game show, forced to wait through the commercial break to find out if you've won. But the commercial break is like three weeks long."

When network execs return in January, they discuss which projects to produce as actual pilots. They consider creative issues (which scripts they like the best), practical and strategic issues (which would best fit on the schedule), even political issues (which producers they can't afford to reject). All these factors contribute to networks' decisions, and in the end, development slates of 100 to 130 projects get whittled down to twenty or thirty.

Most projects, of course, aren't picked up. Which means that after months of passion and dedication . . . the show is dead. Sometimes, networks "roll a project over," meaning they hold the project and make a decision later. Perhaps they like the concept, but want to redevelop the script. Perhaps it's a strong project, but it doesn't fit current needs. Most projects have a window in which they can be rolled. If the network doesn't make a decision by the end of the window, usually a few months, rights revert back to the studio. Occasionally, studios can persuade a network to release a script, or give up its rights so the studio can try reselling it to other networks, but these cases are few and far between. Most of the time, when a show is pronounced dead—it's dead.

Yet for a handful of lucky scripts, January isn't the end of the road. "For a lot of people," says showrunner Bowser, getting the pilot pickup call "is terrifying. I haven't been terrified because when I go into a network or studio with a pitch, I know I've exhausted a lot of other ideas, and the one I'm pitching them, I'm pretty confident I can deliver. To me, that's the most frightening thing as a writer: getting a call to do something you're not convinced you can execute. But it happens. It happens to a lot of people."

A pilot might be picked up in one of three ways, depending on the network's level of confidence in the show.

1. A **full pilot** means the network orders a full-length, broadcast-quality episode, which—if picked up to series—could air as the series' first installment. Most one-hour pilots cost about $5 million, although they can go much higher. In 2007, ABC reportedly spent $7.4 million on an unaired pilot of 20th

Century Fox's hit movie *Mr. & Mrs. Smith,* and CBS's *Viva Laughlin* pilot cost about $6.8 million (and lasted only four days as a series). Half-hour single-cams usually cost $3–5 million, and multicams cost about $2–2.3 million. The network usually covers about 60–70 percent of this; the rest comes from the studio.

2. **Presentations** are low-budget pilots ordered when a network is uncertain about a project's viability. Perhaps execs like the idea, but they're worried about the expense. Perhaps they're conflicted creatively. Whatever a network's reasoning, presentations must cut corners or scale back production. Some shoot a truncated script or only a few key scenes. Others borrow sets from shows already in production. Because of their makeshift nature, presentations that go to series must often add or reshoot scenes. CBS's *Moonlight* and *Judging Amy* were both shot as presentations, then expanded when they received series pickups.

3. In a **cast-contingent** pilot, the network withholds a full pickup until producers find an approvable cast. The network likes the script, but the roles are so specific execs won't release the full license fee until they know they have the right actors. So they release enough money to begin casting, and if producers can't find a cast in time to start shooting, the pilot's dead. (Pilots can also be picked up with a director contingency, meaning they don't get the full pickup without an approvable director.)

Whatever kind of pilot is ordered, they all have one thing in common: they begin production immediately. And I mean *immediately.* If producers get the pickup call in the morning, the production process has begun by that afternoon. The early May deadline is often barely three months away, and if producers finish late, they've squandered their best—and probably only—chance at getting on the air.

And so begins the breakneck world of pilot season . . .

PART III

Pilot Season

From Pilot Pickup to Series

10

Preproduction

....

As soon as producers get the pickup phone call, they begin the six- to nine-week process of putting together all the disparate pieces of the show and preparing to shoot. Their first move is to hire their core production team: the **casting director,** director, and line producer.

The casting director assembles the best possible cast for the show. Casting directors not only have good eyes for spotting talent and knacks for coaching actors, they have countless relationships with agents, managers, and performers. They also keep tabs on rising stars in indie films, Broadway and off-Broadway plays, and any other venues that might yield talented performers.

A pilot director establishes a show's visual style and helps actors develop characters. But unlike in a movie, he's not doing this for just one film; he's establishing a style, tone, and characters for a film that will, hopefully, launch and define an entire series. Barry Sonnenfeld created the colorful surrealism of *Pushing Daisies*. Peter Berg established the fly-on-the-wall, cinéma vérité style of *Friday Night Lights*. Thus, experienced pilot directors are in high demand. Some projects even hire high-level film directors. The *House* pilot was helmed by *Superman Returns* director Bryan Singer; *Shark* came from *Inside Man* director Spike Lee.

Line producers manage a pilot's physical production: organizing a schedule, maintaining a budget, hiring staff and crew. But that doesn't mean line producers have no creative involvement. The best line producers blend practical skills with creative instincts, recommending the best designers, cameramen, and effects artists for the job.

Once this core creative team is in place, the hard work of preproduction officially begins. As each person gets his own specific department up and running, many different aspects of production kick into motion simultaneously. Over the next three chapters, we'll follow every move of pilot production, exploring the unique issues, steps, and key players of its three phases: preproduction, **principal photography** (often just called "production"), and postproduction.

I've organized the chapters like producers organize their production schedules, counting down to the delivery date in early May, so you can see how elements work together to culminate in a completed pilot.

13 WEEKS UNTIL DELIVERY
(6 weeks until shooting)

The casting director is often the first person to get the ball rolling. As soon as he's hired, he does two things: puts together a "wish list" of established actors, and begins searching for talented unknowns. Although pilots usually hold general auditions, most networks like casting familiar faces, people audiences recognize, rather than talented newcomers.

When "a studio [and network are] about to commit millions of dollars to a pilot or a series . . . they want to get a winner on the air," says executive producer Molly Newman (*Brothers & Sisters, Cupid, 7th Heaven*). "Any edge you can bring to that is positive, and having a familiar face or star automatically brings a certain validation. Also, stars bring fans, so there's that built-in audience."

Once producers review the wish list, discussing whom they like and whom they don't, the casting director calls agents and managers to check actors' availability and interest. Some, like A-list movie stars, aren't interested in TV at all. Others are open to television, but refuse to audition; they're considered "offer only" and must be offered the role outright. Others will audition, but only for producers and directors; they won't read for the casting director alone.

Actors not on the wish list are considered casting, meaning they have little or no recognizability, and though they may be talented, most start at the bottom and trudge through each level of auditions. The audition process begins when the casting director releases a **breakdown,** or description of the pilot's characters, through Breakdown Services, a company that informs talent agents and actors about casting opportunities in film and TV. Once the breakdown is published, agents, managers, and actors flood the casting director with headshots and **demo reels** of performers they hope are appropriate for each role. Casting directors and their staffs sort through thousands of submissions, sifting out performers they want to audition.

General auditioning is a four-step process, beginning with **pre-reads,** where actors audition strictly for the casting department. To audition, actors read lines from **sides,** script pages selected by the writer. The casting director keeps track of every person he sees for each role: who's right, who's wrong, and who deserves to make it to the next step. We'll discuss these next steps—**producers' sessions, studio tests,** and **network tests**—as we get to them.

Meanwhile, the line producer and director are gearing up their own operations: hiring staff and crew and working on a production budget and schedule.

"You can't work on the budget until you've done the schedule," says *Weeds* line producer Mark Burley. This is because much of the budget is determined by how much crew and equipment are needed, and by how long the shoot lasts.

As he figures out the schedule and budget, the line producer makes two important hires. The **unit production manager,** or **UPM,** oversees everything from details of the budget to rental of equipment and hiring of crew. One of his first duties is working with a production coordinator to find a production office, which opens in a few days. The line producer also hires a location manager, who hunts for places to shoot. Shooting on location gives a show authenticity that can't be replicated on stage, but shooting on stage is cheaper and easier because it allows more control of the production. Location managers work closely with the writer and director to help realize their vision of the pilot without exceeding the limits of the budget and schedule. Do they have time to travel to the script's exotic locales? Can they afford to rent equipment in the field? Is there enough material to make location shooting worthwhile? Will the finished product suffer if it has the artificial look of a soundstage?

Through all this, the writer/creator is bouncing like a pinball between the different processes.

"The pilot vision starts with the creator," says *Reba* creator Allison Gibson, "and that requires you to be in a lot of places."

Unlike in film, where writers are often booted from the process, TV writers are expected to be involved in every nook and cranny of their show: casting, set designs, locations, costumes, and so on.

12 WEEKS UNTIL DELIVERY
(5 weeks until shooting)

This week begins with an exciting development: the opening of the production office.

"A production office," says line producer Danielle Weinstock (*Crossing Jordan, The Agency, The Minor Accomplishments of Jackie Woodman*), "is the hub of any production or film. We provide offices for all the departments: wardrobe, art department, props, set decorating, the ADs, transportation, locations. I even set up offices for the editorial staff so they can cut in the same offices where the writers are writing and the production is operating."

The production office includes an assistant production coordinator, who supports the production coordinator with everything he needs, and two or three production assistants (PAs) or runners, entry-level employees who do everything from making copies and delivering scripts to stocking the fridge and doing coffee runs. Being a PA is one of the best ways to begin a career in Hollywood. Although you'll be doing unglamorous grunt work, you'll get to know virtually everyone involved with the show, from the showrunner and director to the lighting and sound departments. Do a good job, impress your co-workers, and they'll prove invaluable contacts when it comes time to get your next job and move up the ladder. (We'll discuss production assistants more, along with the fine arts of networking and getting a job, in chapters 23 through 25.)

The casting department, meanwhile, has used its pre-reads to amass a pool of actors for each role. They now begin **producers' sessions,** where actors re-audition for the writer, director, producers, and executives from the production company. A producers' session could have anywhere from five to forty actors, all vying for various roles. Most pilots go through ten to fifteen producers' sessions, although some have upwards of fifty. The goal is to compile a small, but strong, group of actors to take to the **studio test,** where the studio culls the herd more, sending the strongest choices to the **network test.**

Aside from narrowing the casting field, producers' sessions hold another important purpose for writers: they allow them to hear their words in actors' mouths for the first time.

"I adjust the script after hearing scenes in casting," says Gibson. "I go in and punch up jokes that aren't working or words people are having problems saying."

Producer sessions are also the first chance writers and directors have to see if they'll be successful collaborators. As a writer sees what's working in the script, the director learns more about how that writer views the characters and tone of his pilot and how he likes to communicate with the co-workers around him.

"I may realize there are certain things they care about that aren't clear in the piece," says Emmy-winning director Barnet Kellman (*Samantha Who?, Murphy Brown, Mad About You*). "I start making suggestions, helping them make their points more clearly. I'll also see things that are obstacles to actors, to me, to the audience, and we'll start to get a rewrite going."

As all this is going on, the line producer continues hiring other departments, honing the schedule and budget, and scouting locations with the location manager. Each day the production office grows busier, racing toward the pilot's first day of shooting.

11 WEEKS UNTIL DELIVERY
(4 weeks until shooting)

A new face arrives at the office this week: the **production designer,** who runs the art department and supervises the show's visuals—everything from props and sets to visual effects—and determines how to make them work within the pilot's budget and schedule.

The production designer begins by talking with the showrunner and director about their visions for the show's look. He presents them with pictures from books, magazines, catalogs, postcards, and the Internet so they can point out ideas they like and don't like. Thinking about their tastes and visions, the production designer talks to the **location manager** to figure out what will be shot on location and what must be built.

"There are a number of things that determine [where we shoot]," says Emmy-nominated production designer Tony Cowley (*Dexter, Strong Medicine*). "Are there big effects? Are we allowed to do effects on location? If you've got nineteen pages [of the script set] in a house, it's worth it to build the interior on stage because you can spend two days on stage working with your actors. Plus, you're in control of your lighting, your weather, and you don't have to go on location, which costs a lot with trucks and support and security. I always say that half of [production designers] are working just because the [schedule] dictates what we do. If not, we'd shoot most of it on locations."

While the production designer hires the rest of his art department and begins designing sets, casting continues. The production office expands. And with each new decision and addition, the line producer and UPM update the budget and schedule.

10 WEEKS UNTIL DELIVERY
(3 weeks until shooting)

By now, the casting department should be homing in on their favorite actors for each part. They schedule a studio test, where the top two to five performers in each role read for studio executives. Before actors audition for the studio, however, their agents negotiate their contracts for the entire series, hammering out details even before actors are hired (the pilot fee, episodic fee, pay bumps, etc.). This keeps an actor from having the upper hand if he does get hired. Once each deal is figured out, the studio tests commence.

"It's interesting to see how actors handle the studio process," says Gibson. "You do what you can do to guide your choice for what your vision is . . . [but] sometimes they don't do as well as you know they can. I've been to studio where your third choice jumps out and does a fantastic job, and they become your first choice going to network."

The studio then sends their favorite actors to the network test, usually scheduled for that same afternoon or the next morning. Hopefully, network execs approve the studio's choices, but this isn't always the case.

Network execs "look at all kinds of things," says Gibson, "marketing angles, promotion, cross-promotion. You put your opinion out there, but in the end . . . it's up to the network to decide."

Also this week, three new people join the production team: the director of photography (DP), the postproduction supervisor, and the **first assistant director** (**AD**).

The director of photography, or cinematographer, is responsible for how the show looks on screen. Is it bright and cheery like *Desperate Housewives*? Dark and visceral like *Battlestar Galactica*? Clean and detached like *Mad Men*? The DP talks to the writer and director, then hires the lighting department, an integral factor in how the show looks. The lighting department consists of a gaffer, who heads the team, and grips, the lighting technicians below him.

The post supervisor manages postproduction. Although the post department's main duties don't kick in until after the actual shoot, it still has important duties during and before production. During prep, for instance, post provides any audio or video elements appearing in-scene (newscasts seen on screen, music at a nightclub, etc.). During principal photography, it outputs **dailies,** daily compilations of the previous day's footage.

The **first assistant director,** one of the most important people in the whole production, schedules the shoot days and runs the set once the pilot is shooting. While the showrunner is still the captain of the ship, the AD is the boss on stage.

"The AD's job is to look at the big picture," says assistant director Steve Love, who has "AD'ed" TV shows and movies like *Pushing Daisies, The Adventures of Brisco County, Jr.,* and *Terminator 3,* as well as directing series like *Malcolm in the Middle.* "It's my responsibility to make sure everyone else knows what the director's vision is and what their part entails. [I schedule the project] in the most efficient way possible, making sure every member of the crew knows what we're shooting, when we're shooting, and what their individual responsibilities are: what props to have, what the lighting is, what camera we need, everything."

One of the AD's first jobs is to calculate a shooting schedule, a list of each day's scenes in the order they'll be shot, which he distributes to the crew as a **one-sheet,** or **one-liner.** The director uses this to arrange his **shotlist** of shots and angles needed in each scene.

As the AD, post supervisor, and DP get up to speed, other departments are racing forward. Casting continues to hold auditions. Locations continues to scout. Art illustrates props, blueprints, and visual effects. (By the way, visual effects aren't the same as special effects. Special effects are effects appearing "live" on stage, such as fire, rain, or snow. Visual effects are computer-generated images like spaceships or lasers.)

9 WEEKS UNTIL DELIVERY
(2 weeks until shooting)

With only two weeks of prep to go, the entire production feels the crush of the impending shoot. Ready or not, three main things happen this week: construction begins, the crew goes on a **tech scout,** and the entire show has a production meeting.

By this week, all final decisions must be made about the set so the construction crew can begin building. Construction is overseen by the construction coordinator, who translates the production designer's blueprints into physical sets and hires a general foreman and propmakers (who, oddly, have nothing to do with props; they're carpenters who build the set).

Near the end of the week, all the department heads (lighting, sound, camera, etc.) travel to each shooting location for a tech scout, where the director explains each scene's technical needs. How many people are needed on camera? What direction is the camera looking? Which lenses and lights are necessary? Where should the off-camera crew stand? These answers help each department figure out what equipment they need, how to set up, and how to organize their days.

A day or two after the tech scout comes the production meeting, which includes almost everyone on the crew, usually forty or fifty people. This is the first and often only time all departments come together in the same place. It's "a chance for everybody to be in the same room at the same time to discuss what part is theirs," says Love. "You go through the script [page by page] . . . then go through the schedule. There's so much going on and everyone is concerned with their little area, so you have to make sure they understand the big picture: what the important elements are, what sacrifices they have to make, whether there's enough time for a hair or lighting change."

By this time, the network should have approved the show's cast, which means another important person can shift into gear: the costume designer. Though he may have started designing earlier, it's difficult to begin building and fitting costumes until the show is cast, which rarely happens before the last minute. Once actors are hired, the costume department starts finding, buying, or making wardrobes. It also works with the production designer to ensure clothing choices work with the sets and lighting.

8 WEEKS UNTIL DELIVERY
(1 week until shooting)

For the writer, producers, director, and actors, the final week of prep is dominated by three things: the **table read,** rewrites, and **run-throughs.**

The table read, which takes place about a week before shooting, is usually the first time the entire script is read aloud by the actors. This is also often the first time the entire cast has been together in the same room. They sit at a table in the middle of a conference room, while the writer, director, producers, and network and studio execs sit around the edges, listening and taking notes. The line producer, UPM, and other people from the production office may also attend.

SSSHHH . . . DON'T TELL ANYONE

Many directors hold a **pre-table,** an unofficial reading of the pilot script with themselves, the writer, and the actors. Because pre-tables aren't supposed to happen—they're not included in actors' contracts, and networks and studio execs aren't invited—they often happen after hours at the writer's or director's house. They're informal, usually with wine and food, intended only to help the cast get comfortable with the script, and each other, before reading "for real" under the critical eyes of the network and studio.

After the table read, actors are dismissed and the network gives notes to the studio, writer, producers, and director.

"Sometimes they have cuts and trims," says Gibson. "Sometimes it's jumping on a character who really popped or a scene that's really great. You do whatever you can to heighten what's good about the script and work on what's not good."

The director then goes off to rehearse the actors, and the writer heads off to rewrite. On a drama, the writer rewrites alone and turns in pages when they're finished. On sitcoms, the writer calls in several writer friends, and often a couple of stand-up comics, to form an impromptu **writers' room.** Working together, they **punch up** the script, scrutinizing every line to make it as funny and powerful as possible. Because the writer is racing around during the day, the punch-up room usually convenes after dinner and writes long into the night. "We do a top-to-bottom, page one rewrite," says Gibson. "You do that every night [from then on out]."

That's right—sitcom writers rewrite the entire pilot script from beginning to end. *Each night.*

"I bring in anywhere from five or six to ten or eleven writers," says Gibson. "I do scene-rewriting, dealing with emotional things and restructuring, with a smaller group, maybe four to five people. Then I have another three or four off beating certain jokes."

(By the way, these writers are usually working for free. Sometimes they're hoping for a staff job if the pilot goes to series; sometimes they're just helping a friend.)

This week's other important development is the beginning of **run-throughs,** skeletal performances of the entire show, designed to give producers and executives a sense of how it looks. Single-camera pilots rarely have run-throughs, because they don't shoot the show in sequence or in one place, but **multicams** make up for this in spades. (**Single-cams,** as we'll see shortly, rehearse each scene just minutes before they shoot.)

The multicamera run-through process begins after the table read. The director and actors start by having closed rehearsals, where no one is allowed to watch or give notes, including the writer. Three days before the shoot, the director holds a producer's run-through for writers and producers—no execs. This is the first time producers see the show on its feet, with blocking and movement. Actors are usually still "**on book,**" reading lines from the script. As the writer watches, he may stop the performance after certain scenes to discuss things that aren't working. The team of rewriters also watches, marking jokes and passages that don't work. They'll address these moments in the punch-up room later that night.

After the run-through, the writer and director discuss notes for actors and improvements for the script, and the writer retreats to the writers' room for that night's rewrite session. When the new draft is finished, usually in the middle of the night, it's printed by the **writers' assistant,** or a PA, who delivers it to the homes of the actors, director, and producers so they can read it first thing in the morning.

The next day begins with a closed reading of the new script. The actors then rehearse for that afternoon's studio run-through. This time, however, actors are more **off-book** and the director has added simple production elements like set dressing and lighting cues. After the run-through, the studio gives notes, the director returns to rehearsal, the writers continue rewriting.

The next day, often the day before the shoot, comes the network run-through, which is as polished as the show can be before the actual taping.

"You want the show to look good when the network comes," says Gibson. "[You want it] to look as close to the way it's going to look when you shoot it, without stopping the flow for costume changes and things like that."

After the network run-through, writers head off for their final punch-up while other departments take care of their own finishing touches. The paint foreman paints the set. Set dressing adds electrical outlets, framed photos, and light switches. Costumers tailor clothes and costumes. Everyone's working hard toward principal photography, often only a few hours away.

PREPRODUCTION TIMELINE

Of the three stages of production—prep, principal photography, and post—preproduction is the least linear, a mind-boggling assortment of tasks and processes happening simultaneously. We've compiled the preproduction timeline on the next four pages to help you get your head around a production's various departments and how they interact to help prep a pilot for shooting:

	Week 1 (6 weeks until shooting)	Week 2 (5 weeks until shooting)	Week 3 (4 weeks until shooting)
Writer/ Creator/ Exec. Producer	The writer/creator bounces between departments, guiding, consulting, weighing in. All the while, he's continuing to rewrite and hone the script.		
Director	Begin hiring crew, helps line producer form budget and schedule.	Casting (producer sessions), work with writer to hone script, revise budget and schedule.	Work with production designer on set designs; continue casting, honing script, budget, and schedule.
Line Producer	Begin formulating budget and schedule, hiring crew.	Scout locations, revise budget and schedule, continue hiring crew.	Continue hiring crew, revising budget and schedule.
Casting/ Actors	Casting creates wish lists, contacts A- and B-list choices, releases breakdown, begins pre-reads.	Producer sessions begin, pre-reads continue.	
Locations	Location manager determines location necessities, begins scouting.	Scout locations, assistant location manager begins.	Scouting continues.
Production Office	UPM and production coordinator search for production office space, work on budget and schedule.	Production office opens/supports entire production; UPM hones shooting schedule and budget.	
Production Designer/ Art Dept.			Production designer discusses design concept, coordinates with location manager, works on design budget.

Week 4 (3 weeks until shooting)	Week 5 (2 weeks until shooting)	Week 6 (1 week until shooting)
	Tech scout, production meeting.	Table read; run-throughs and late-night punch-up sessions begin (multicams only).
Director begins compiling shotlist.	Tech scout, production meeting.	Table read; camera test; rehearsals, run-throughs, and preshoots (multicams only).
	Locations and set designs locked, tech scout, production meeting.	Table read; run-throughs and preshoots (multicams only).
Studio and network tests begin; producer sessions and pre-reads continue.	Studio and network tests finish, cast is locked.	Table read; final costume fittings; camera test; rehearsals, run-throughs, and preshoots (multicams only).
	Locations locked, tech scout, production meeting.	
	Production meeting.	
Art director, lead man, art department coordinator begin.	Studio and network approve set designs, tech scout, production meeting.	Studio and network execs walk through sets, give last-minute notes.

continued

	Week 1 (6 weeks until shooting)	Week 2 (5 weeks until shooting)	Week 3 (4 weeks until shooting)
Costume Dept.			Costume designer begins drawing costume ideas.
Camera and Lighting Dept./ Director of Photography			
Post-production			
AD Dept.			
Construction			
Other		Production accountant, PAs, and runners begin.	Transportation coordinator begins.

	Week 4 (3 weeks until shooting)	Week 5 (2 weeks until shooting)	Week 6 (1 week until shooting)
	Costume supervisor and costumers begin.	Costume dept. fits actors for costumes and begins buying/building costumes.	Studio and network execs view costumes, give notes; actors' final costume fittings.
	DP and production designer discuss how to shoot/light sets and locations, DP hires lighting department.	Tech scout, production meeting.	Camera load-in, camera prep, camera test, preshoots (multicams only).
	Post supervisor hires post dept, finds in-scene music/ video clips.	Editor begins; production meeting.	Load in edit systems.
	First AD meets with each department to discuss all the departments' needs and requirements for shooting; hones detailed budget and shooting schedule.	Tech scout, production meeting, budgeting and scheduling continues, second assistant director begins.	Organizes all departments for shoot.
		Construction begins building sets.	Construction finishes set, adding paint, set dressing, etc.
	Set dressing, gaffer, propmaster, key grip begin.	Best boy, paint foreman, sound FX, best boy grip, key hair, and makeup begin.	Script supervisor, sound dept. begin.

11

Principal Photography

This is the exciting part: actors, cameras, directors yelling "Action." Ironically, **principal photography,** or **production,** is also the "simplest" of the pilot's three phases. Sitcom pilots shoot all in one day. Drama or single-cams usually shoot over several days, but each day follows the same process. The main challenge of production, especially with single-camera shows, is staying on schedule: each day is tightly organized to accommodate a specific number of scenes and shots, and running long can cost thousands of dollars.

Two factors inform the pilot's shooting schedule. The first is the delivery deadline. If pilots deliver late, they miss their chance to be considered for the network's fall schedule. The second factor is labor laws and unions that govern the entertainment industry. TV crews and actors can only work a certain number of hours a day, a number that varies if the show is shooting on stage or on location. Also, TV crews are required to get a certain amount of **turnaround,** or hours between work days. If a shoot exceeds the maximum number of working hours, or doesn't give employees enough turnaround, the production pays expensive overtime. If the show has children in it, things get even more complicated, as there are rules regulating how many hours minors can work each day. Thus, it's important that every shoot "makes its day," or finishes on time. If a production adds shoot days, or even hours, costs skyrocket.

One way shows maximize personnel and resources is to design the shooting area, both on stage and on location, as efficiently as possible. Let's look first at the setup of a soundstage, the production's home base, then at how that setup changes when shooting on location.

SHOOTING ON STAGE

The focal point of the soundstage is the set, the artificial rooms or buildings constructed to look like the world of the show. Many soundstages are big enough to hold more than one set. The *CSI: Miami* stage holds both the CSI headquarters set and the Miami police department.

When shooting is in progress, the two most important places on stage are the set itself and **video village,** a mobile cluster of TV monitors connected to cameras, allowing observers to see what the cameras see. Video village sits a few feet from the shooting area so the director, writer, producers, DP, and script supervisor (someone who tracks which scenes and shots have been filmed and monitors visual continuity) can huddle together to watch the shoot. You can usually spot video village by the phalanx of director's chairs encircling the cart and its monitors.

Surrounding the set, usually along the inside walls of the soundstage, are several small "gold rooms" where the crew can stash their floor packages, or on-stage equipment, and prepare for the day. Each department has its own gold room: props, lighting, sound, etc. (If there's no room on the soundstage itself, the gold rooms may be in hallways just outside the stage. The goal is to keep each department's storage as close as possible to set.) You'll also find **craft services,** which keeps the set clean and provides refreshments and coffee.

Outside the soundstage are the **vanities:** hair, makeup, and wardrobe. You'll also find a green room, a small space where performers hang out before going on stage, and dressing rooms or trailers where actors can get dressed, rehearse lines, or relax.

SHOOTING ON LOCATION

Most shows spend some time shooting on location, and while the shooting process remains much the same, being away from stage presents its own unique challenges: no permanent storage areas, no dressing rooms, sometimes no local power or bathrooms. Everything the production needs must be rented and lugged along.

"You're a traveling circus," says line producer Danielle Weinstock. "Hair and makeup have their own trailer. Actors have their own trailers. Grip has a huge truck. Electric has a huge truck. You carry a generator so you can power things up. You bring in air conditioning. [And] it takes time, because when you get to a location it's not pre-rigged or pre-cabled. You have to set it up and get ready to film, and at the end of the day you make sure you leave the location as you found it."

Trailers are set up at **base camp,** a mobile facsimile of the soundstage, located as conveniently as possible to the on-location set or shooting area. Sometimes the set is walkable from base camp; other times the transportation department, or "transpo," sets up a shuttle. At base camp, every department has its own trailer, as do lead actors, the director, the writer, and any producers. There's also a catering trailer and craft services truck. If you were driving past, you could easily mistake base camp for a genuine trailer park.

Let's now look at the process of actually shooting a pilot. We'll first examine the process of shooting a single-camera show, which includes comedies like *Scrubs* and dramas like *Numb3rs,* and usually takes ten to fifteen days.

Single-Camera Pilot Shoots

7 WEEKS UNTIL DELIVERY
(week 1 of shooting)

Principal photography begins by shooting daytime exteriors, outside shots needing natural sunlight. Cameras begin rolling as early as possible, often at 6:00 or 7:00 a.m., helping to ensure that the shoot will maximize its light and make its day.

Of course, if cameras roll at six or seven, several things must happen first. Actors must get into makeup. Sound and lighting must set up equipment. Catering prepares food for hungry and grumpy workers showing up at the crack of dawn. So if the first shot is slated for 7:00 a.m., **call time**— each employee's arrival time—is even earlier. For actors who need extensive hair and makeup done, it may be 4:00 or 5:00 a.m. For makeup artists and craft services, it could be 3:45.

While actors are in hair and makeup, the director, DP, and AD review the day's shotlist. They then pull actors from makeup to **block** and rehearse the first scene. This allows lighting, sound, and camera departments to observe and know what they're doing. When the cast finishes rehearsing, they return to wardrobe and makeup, and the **second team** takes the stage. Second team is a group of stand-ins hired because they physically resemble the actual actors: similar heights, builds, coloring. Stand-ins stand on set while grips light the scene, allowing the DP and gaffer to gauge how the scene will look.

Once a scene is lit and the cast is ready, the sound department places microphones on actors and shooting begins. The first shot is usually a **master,** a wide shot covering the entire scene. Actors then redo parts of the scene while the crew shoots coverage, little shots the director specifies in his shotlist: close-ups, zooms, reactions, and reveals. With each new angle comes a different setup, or placement of the lights and camera. Depending on the complexity of each shot, a single scene can take anywhere from forty-five minutes to six hours.

"There's no rule of thumb," says first AD-cum-director Steve Love, "although we like to say, roughly, two hours per page." Most single-camera shows schedule two to four scenes a day.

Once all the shots are done, the crew moves to the next scene, which sometimes means packing up and moving to another set or location. Whether the scene is at the same place or somewhere new, the process starts over again.

Lunch, provided by an outside catering service, comes six hours after call time. Union regulations dictate that crew can never go six hours without a meal break. If they do, there's a meal penalty, which means the production pays a fine to everyone on the crew.

During lunch, the writer, producers, and director retreat to their trailers to watch **dailies,** DVDs of the previous day's footage, which have just come in from the post department. Network and studio executives also watch dailies back in their offices, scrutinizing performances, makeup, lighting, every piece of the puzzle.

"The first few days [of a pilot] are very judgmental," says post supervisor Paul Rabwin (*October Road, The X-Files*). "The studios, networks, producers, and director are looking at the film every day and making comments, judgments. Sometimes they want to change the look of an actor. Sometimes they want to change where a performance is going—or a wardrobe style."

Hopefully, execs' notes can be addressed without disrupting the **continuity,** or internal logic, of the story. After all, if an exec wants an actress's hair changed, it's tough to do if she's already been filmed with a particular hairstyle. So execs and producers must discuss what's feasible and what's not.

When lunch is over, shooting resumes where it left off. Presumably, everything is still on schedule. If not, the AD cracks the whip to make up for lost time before reaching the **Abby Singer,** the second-to-last shot of the day, named for a movie AD who used to trick his crew into thinking the second-to-last shot was actually the last. The actual last shot is the **martini,** because if all goes well, the next "shot" is in a martini glass.

Finally, the director yells, "That's a wrap," and the crew dismantles the set and returns everything to the trailers. As they head home, everyone receives a **call sheet** detailing tomorrow's schedule, location, and each person's call time.

DOWN TO THE WIRE

Many days, by the time they reach the Abby Singer, the crew is racing to finish on time and the director, showrunner, and AD must discuss options. Do they shoot the remaining material as planned, running long and starting late tomorrow? Do they cut material from the script? Or do they rethink shots and try a **"oner,"** shooting an entire scene as one long shot?

"The fun challenge," says first AD and director Steve Love, "is when you have one page left and only thirty minutes, and the director comes up with this wonderful Steadicam shot. Sometimes you can do a whole scene in one shot, moving in and out of characters to get your close-ups and your wide shots all at the same time. It's a way to take a scene that would've had three or four shots and do it as one."

But the day's not over yet. The post PA must deliver the day's film to **telecine,** where it's transferred to a high-definition (HD) video master.

"In the HD world," says Rabwin, "you can do everything [with video] you would do with film. Color-correct it, edit it. So the telecine process is taking the negative image and . . . transferring it to a digital format (like a hard drive or high-definition videotape). From that point on, you may never go back to the negative again."

This video master is **digitized,** or uploaded into a computer at lower resolution, which takes up less memory and is easier to work with. Telecine then uses the digitized version to create dailies. The next day, some sets of dailies are sent to the director and producers on set, some are sent to network and studio executives, and others are sent to the editor and assistant editor, who immediately begin putting together an **editor's cut** (more on this in chapter 12).

6 WEEKS UNTIL DELIVERY
(week 2 of shooting)

Once the production finishes shooting on location, shooting begins on the soundstage. Shooting onstage follows the same pattern as shooting on location (block and rehearse, shoot the master, shoot coverage, repeat), except it's easier and more comfortable.

"It's [also] faster," says Love, "because you can move walls and change lighting. Having said that, sometimes on location you're outside and you don't need a lot of lights, so you can shoot faster. Also, you have the sun going down, which helps . . . because you *need* to shoot faster."

Of course, as the final day of shooting approaches, producers and directors occasionally discover they don't have time to shoot everything they'd planned. When this happens, they must reexamine what they have left. Perhaps the writer cuts or rewrites certain scenes. Perhaps the director reimagines how he wanted to shoot something. Maybe they agree *nothing* should change and they add another shoot day, provided they have room in the budget or get more money from the studio.

"You need to be fiscally responsible," says line producer Mark Burley (*Weeds, Hidden Hills, Freakylinks*), "but a studio will probably pay extra if they want something good. The only rule on a pilot is that you get on the air. There's no prize for being under budget and not getting on the air."

After shooting wraps, the director and producers head to postproduction while the crew **strikes,** or disassembles, the set. There are two kinds of strike. In a "dead strike," where the producers are certain sets won't be used again, the construction team throws everything away. But if the set is hot, or potentially in use for another season or episode, they do a "fold-and-hold" and store it somewhere safe.

Multicamera Pilot Shoots

Unlike single-camera comedies and dramas, sitcoms (*Back to You, Will & Grace*) shoot on stage, before a live audience, like a play. Most shoot in one evening and take five or six hours. But the process often begins earlier in the day, or the day before, with camera **blocking,** in which the director and cameramen walk through the many camera moves for the actual taping. They also shoot **preshoots,** scenes that must be shot on location or use special effects, like explosions, that can't be done before an audience.

Sitcoms often preshoot right up to the moment the audience enters. By getting as much of the show "in the can" as possible, the director doesn't need to race through the show, and writers can spend more time playing with new jokes.

Most tapings begin around 5:00 or 6:00 p.m. The audience enters about an hour earlier and is entertained by the warm-up comic, a standup hired to boost the audience's energy before the show and between scenes. Once everyone is seated and the cast and crew are ready, the show begins.

Unlike single-camera shoots, sitcoms are performed straight through in chronological order. The director may repeat or reshoot particular scenes, but he rarely shoots out of order. Scenes not performed live, like preshoots, are shown to the audience over TV monitors.

As with single-camera shows, the director and producers huddle around video village, set up to one side of the stage. Punch-up writers huddle closer to the action, jotting alternative jokes in the margins of their scripts. Executives watch on monitors from the network and studio green room, a special tentlike room on one side of the stage, where they can discuss their reactions in private. If they have notes on specific takes or scenes, they phone them to the director. Most shoots also have an agents' green room, located on the other side of the stage from the network and studio green room, where agents, managers, and friends of the cast watch on monitors.

TALK THE TALK: LINE CUT

Because sitcoms shoot in chronological order, the director often works with a recordist, who uses a video switcher to make a **line cut,** an in-the-moment edited version of the live show, much like a sporting event being edited live. This line cut plays on monitors above audiences' heads to help them see the show and understand how it might look on television. It also serves as a template for editors, who begin splicing together the show after the taping wraps.

Once the pilot has been performed in its entirety, usually around 10:00 or 11:00 p.m., the audience is dismissed. But that doesn't mean the night is over. The cast and crew shoot **pickups,** reshoots of earlier scenes and moments. Sometimes the director wants to make sure he has certain shots. Other times writers have alternate lines or jokes. Pickups can last anywhere from a few minutes to a few hours, meaning the cast and crew wrap production in the wee hours of the morning.

Though it's a huge triumph to finish a pilot shoot, there's rarely time to celebrate. The director usually heads into post the next day, and the writer begins putting together a final package of pilot documents to deliver to the network (more on this in the next chapter).

TALK THE TALK: PRODUCTION CREW

Whether you're a writer/producer shooting your first pilot or a PA running errands, you'll prove yourself more efficient if you're aware of the many positions that make up a TV show's production crew. Here's a quick guide to some of the key departments and personnel we haven't fully discussed.

ACCOUNTING DEPARTMENT
Production Accountant
Manages the finances of the entire production. Often works with two or three assistant accountants who specialize in payroll, accounts payable, etc.

ASSISTANT DIRECTOR DEPARTMENT
Second Assistant Director (2nd AD)
Supports the first AD, often creating call sheets and organizing actors offstage. If it's a particularly hectic production, there may be a second second AD, known as the "second second," and even a third assistant director, or third AD.

ART DEPARTMENT
Art Director
Works under the production designer, often dealing with the "nuts and bolts" of executing the designer's set designs: overseeing construction, painting, etc. Usually works with an assistant art director as well.

continued

CAMERA DEPARTMENT

Camera Operator

A trained technician who runs an on-set camera; most "camera ops" are designated A-Camera Operator, B-Camera Operator, etc., depending on which camera they run. Each camera op usually has two camera assistants, known as "A-camera first assistant," "A-camera second assistant," etc.

Loader

Loads film into the camera and operates the clapboard at the beginning of each shot.

CASTING DEPARTMENT

Casting Assistant

A notch lower than the casting associate, the assistant supports both the casting director and the associate.

Casting Associate

Supports the casting director in organizing casting submissions, scheduling auditions, videotaping readers, etc.

Extras Casting

Hires extras, or background, nonspeaking performers who fill the background of shots.

CONSTRUCTION DEPARTMENT

Construction Lead

Works under the construction coordinator, purchasing materials, scheduling crew, keeping tools in order, etc.

Greensman

Member of the construction crew responsible for on-set greenery: plants, flowers, grass, shrubs, etc.

Toolman

Ensures that the department has all necessary tools on hand, keeps tools in working order, repairs broken parts, maintains stock of expendable parts (nails, screws, blades, etc.).

COSTUME/WARDROBE DEPARTMENT

Buyer

Shops and buys clothes, costumes, wardrobe pieces, or accessories for the department. (This person is truly a professional shopper—a great job if you like to shop.)

Costumer

Works under the costume designer, making actual costumes and handling them in the wardrobe department.

Costume/Wardrobe Supervisor

Reports to the costume designer and oversees the wardrobe department, including costumers, assistants, etc.

GRIP DEPARTMENT

Best Boy

Both grip and lighting departments have best boys, who act as assistants to the key grip (grip department) or gaffer (lighting).

Key Grip

Heads the grip department, which works with the DP and operates camera equipment like dollies and cranes. These grips are slightly different from grips in the lighting department, who work under the gaffer to light the set.

PROPS DEPARTMENT

Prop Master

Finds or makes onstage props. The prop master often works with an assistant prop master and, occasionally, a props buyer, who shops for actual props. Props departments often acquire props from prop houses, stores specializing in collecting random paraphernalia to sell or rent to film and TV productions.

SCRIPT SUPERVISOR DEPARTMENT

Script Supervisor

Monitors which scenes have been filmed and tracks the production's continuity, making sure visual details and story points are consistent from one shot to the next.

SET DECORATING DEPARTMENT

Lead Man

Reports to the set decorator and supervises the set dressers.

Set Decorator

Heads the set department, which embellishes a set with details like outlets, curtains, framed photos, knickknacks on shelves, etc.

Set Dresser

Physically "dresses" the set, placing elements designated by the set decorator.

continued

SOUND DEPARTMENT

Boom Operator

Operates the on-set boom, a microphone held at the end of a pole so the sound department can record dialogue without placing body mics on actors.

Sound Mixer

Heads the sound department, records and mixes all sounds during shooting: dialogue, onstage noises and effects, etc.

STUNTS DEPARTMENT

Stunt Coordinator

Choreographs, supervises, and sometimes performs on-camera stunts (jumping off buildings and rolling cars, leaping from trains, etc.).

12

Postproduction

Postproduction "is, essentially, the last rewrite," says executive producer Adam Chase (*Friends, Love, Inc., Clone*). "You eliminate parts of the story, you speed up the story, you rearrange scenes. If there are things that don't work, you can fix them in editing."

In other words, "post" is the process of compiling all the pilot's video and audio elements into the final product, and this happens in four basic phases:

Phase 1, creating and delivering **dailies,** begins during shooting and entails digitizing each day's footage and making DVDs so producers and execs can analyze the look of the show (as discussed in chapter 11).

Phase 2, the **producer's cut,** involves the editor, director, and showrunner working together to compile a cut they're happy with. This takes three steps: the **editor's cut,** the **director's cut,** and the **producer's cut.** Although most of this happens after the completion of principal photography, editors on single-camera pilots often begin their cuts at the commencement of principal photography, as soon as dailies begin coming in.

Phase 3, studio and network notes, entails delivering cuts to executives and incorporating feedback into the pilot.

Phase 4, finalizing the pilot, readies the pilot technically for delivery. Picture is locked, sound is mixed, visual effects are inserted. Final dubs are made and final cuts sent to the network.

There may be only four phases, but with five weeks to go, this is a massive amount of work.

5 WEEKS UNTIL DELIVERY

The process of compiling the pilot begins with the editor splicing together the first complete cut. On a single-camera show, this often begins as soon as dailies come in on the second day of production.

"The whole process during dailies is trying to 'stay up to camera,' " says editor Scott Wallace (*Traveler, The X-Files, The Inside*), "meaning you cut as quickly as you can so you're finished by the end of the day. You don't have much time in the television world, especially on pilots."

This portion of the process, known as **offline editing,** is the most creative period of post because shots and scenes can be rearranged, tweaked, and swapped in or out. The **editor's cut,** the first fully assembled version of the pilot, is often rough, but its intention is merely to give the director a complete version from which to work.

Once the editor's cut is finished, the director begins his cut. He and the editor work together, cutting, rearranging, and trying different takes as they mold a tighter, more cohesive product. A director usually gets four days for his cut on an hour-long show, and one or two days on a half-hour (or less if time is short).

The writer, meanwhile, is juggling other duties. He may visit the **title house,** the company hired to design the pilot's main titles and credits. He may check in with the **effects house,** the company creating the show's visual effects. He's also working on a packet of additional material to be turned in with the pilot.

"You have to put together story ideas," says showrunner Allison Gibson (*Reba, Living with Fran, Home Improvement*). "These will be tested by marketing people and they'll be a part of the sales presentation of the show."

The writer usually submits about ten short paragraph-length episode ideas. As in every other aspect of television, these pages wind their way from production company to studio to network, evolving along the way until the writer finally delivers his five or six strongest storylines. The writer may also turn in character descriptions, write-ups on the show's history or mythology, interesting articles, and other pertinent pieces of information. These help the network decide whether or not to pick up the series.

4 WEEKS UNTIL DELIVERY

Once the director's cut is finished, the writer and producers begin to edit the producer's cut. Depending on how tight the schedule is, they may have only a couple of days.

"You look through everything you have, find the gold, and put that together," says Chase. "You can actually change an actor's pace by cutting to their reaction more quickly than they gave that reaction on stage. You pick your best takes, cut parts that didn't work, go to close-ups to underscore emotional moments."

Producers also "cut for time." Although a typical sitcom lasts twenty-two minutes, editors' cuts intentionally come in at twenty-seven or twenty-eight minutes. The director then siphons off two or three more minutes, leaving producers with many choices to continue shaping.

At about this time, two important people join the post department: the music editor and the music supervisor. The music editor puts together the score, instrumental music that plays behind scenes. Most pilots can't afford actual composers, so "you put in temporary music from other shows, soundtracks, and CDs," says Wallace. "If the show is picked up, a composer will score new music that will emotionally do what those tracks are trying to do."

The music supervisor has a similar job, but he finds actual songs to incorporate into the show. On an airing episode, songs can't be used without paying the artist a royalty. But in a pilot, which may never air, rules are looser.

"You can put in a song by the Rolling Stones if it's going to sell a scene," says *October Road* post supervisor Paul Rabwin. "A pilot is about making something that will excite the network. It's a sales pitch. You want to present the flashiest, best-looking show you possibly can."

Finally, the producer's cut is delivered to the studio as the **"studio cut."** Yet even this is often incomplete, missing specific shots, music, and effects, and producers frequently insert the word "TEMP" where elements have yet to be added.

3 WEEKS UNTIL DELIVERY

The studio usually watches the studio cut and turns around notes overnight. Producers then begin work on their **network cut,** the first cut to be seen by the execs who decide the show's fate. Stakes are high to make this cut shine, so producers often do a temp **sound mix** and **color correction** before delivering the cut to the network.

Sound mixing involves working with an engineer to balance the sound tracks, or strips of recorded sound, running through the show. Each sound lives on a different track of the videotape; sound effects take up fifteen or twenty tracks, dialogue uses about eight, music could have up to sixteen. Several other tracks are used to add new bits of sound and dialogue. Most often, fifty or sixty tracks must be blended together to make the biggest emotional impact.

Color correction involves adjusting the pilot's lighting and color from one shot to the next. If shots in the same scene were filmed at different times, their lighting and coloring may be different. Color correction fixes these problems and smooths out the picture.

Even though producers are likely to repeat these processes later, "it's critical to sell the show," says Wallace, and "if you don't get a good response [from the network], you don't have a show. So there's big pressure to make it look good. Producers don't care if they spend the money and later have to do it all over again."

When the network receives their cut, they give notes like everyone else. But they often "test" the pilot as well, screening it for a small audience to get feedback. Sometimes they test a finished pilot to determine whether or not it will go to series; other times they use test results to gauge what's working and what's not, and how to fix it.

Testing takes place at a testing facility, where audiences watch the pilot in a specially designed testing room. Everyone in the audience has a remote control with a knob, which they turn one direction if they like something and the other direction if they don't. These bits of data are aggregated by a computer, which generates a real-time evaluation of how the audience feels. The writer, director, producers, and editor sit behind one-way glass and watch as the audience watches the show. They can see the pilot on their own monitor, which has onscreen graphs monitoring the audience's responses: one for males, one for females. When the pilot ends, moderators ask the audience a series of questions. What did they like about the pilot? What didn't they like? Were characters likable? Some audience members are pulled aside and asked individual questions. This information is compiled, analyzed by the testing facility, and presented to the network, studio, and producers in a comprehensive report.

2 WEEKS UNTIL DELIVERY

Based on test results and network notes, producers use this week to make final creative changes: adding moments, deleting scenes, changing actors' performances. Hopefully, these are minimal changes that take only a few days, but sometimes they can be more extensive.

"On *Freakylinks,*" says Mark Burley, who line-produced FOX's short-lived supernatural series in 2000, "we tested the pilot and it didn't test well. So we went back and shot new scenes that made it test better. But hopefully one doesn't have to do that."

Once notes have been addressed, producers **lock picture,** agreeing not to change any more of the edit. They may swap out visual effects, or sound and music cues, but they won't alter anything that changes the length of the cut. The delivery date is just around the corner, and it's time for the fourth phase of post: readying the pilot technically.

1 WEEK AND THEN . . . DELIVERY!

As the pilot heads into the final week, something interesting happens. The assistant editor splits the pilot into two components, sound and picture, which won't come back together until the end of the process. He does this by creating an **output** of the show, a tape of the edited pilot thus far (sound, picture, everything), and two **edit decision lists** (**EDLs**), electronic lists of the pilot's cues and edits. One EDL is of the pilot's hundreds of visual cues and edits; the other is of audio cues and edits, which often number in the thousands.

The picture EDL is taken to a special facility to be fed into an editing system with the pilot's masters. This begins the day-long process of **online**

editing, where a replica of the edited pilot is reconstructed from the original high-quality footage. Following the instructions in the electronic EDL, the computer re-creates a high-resolution version of the show. (Remember, the dailies were digitized, reducing their resolution in order to upload onto the editing system. Online editing is where low-res cuts become high-res pilots.)

Meanwhile, sound effects editors and dialogue editors create a high-resolution version of the pilot's sound cues. Using the sound EDL, they return to each sound's original source and retrieve its highest-quality version. Sounds may come from a music CD, an effect on a hard drive, or the unmixed production track itself.

When the online facility finishes its picture output, the assistant editor checks it against the offline, making sure everything is in place. He then sends it to color correction, usually in the same building. Once color correction has been completed, which takes a day or two, the final visual effects, graphics, and titles are inserted.

The producers and director, meanwhile, are **spotting** the pilot, watching it with music, dialogue and sound effects editors. They discuss how sound effects are working, which lines can't be heard, what scenes need new dialogue. Sound effects editors add effects and clean up noise while producers head to **automatic dialogue replacement (ADR)**, or **looping,** where actors rerecord or add new lines of dialogue. Maybe lines weren't audible the first time, or producers need additional lines to help the story. Either way, the actor sits in a booth while a section of the pilot plays over and over on a loop, repeating lines of dialogue until he finally nails it.

By this time, the pilot's delivery date is often twenty-four hours away and there's still much to be done. One of the biggest tasks is the official sound mix, where sound mixers adjust the level of each track so they blend together naturally. This usually takes place on a mixing stage, where the pilot is projected on a theatrical-size screen and sound mixers go through, bit by bit, tweaking each individual piece of sound.

The mix often finishes late at night, hours before the pilot must be delivered. Yet one more important thing needs to happen: the sound and picture, which have been separate elements ever since the assistant editor split them up, must be reunited through a video-audio synchronization process called **layback.**

After layback is completed, the final pilot is outputted, usually to a **D5** videotape, and raced to a **dub house,** which makes DVD copies to be delivered to executives, writers, and producers. The DVDs are picked up a few hours later by the post PA (who probably hasn't slept in over twenty-four hours) and delivered to the homes and offices of everyone who needs them. Most producers like their pilots delivered first thing in the morning, so network executives arrive to a shiny new show sitting on their desk.

Delivering a pilot is a relief, a rush, and completely terrifying—all at the same time. It may feel great to be done, but after months of painstakingly nurturing, shaping, and molding the pilot, your project's fate is now completely out of your hands.

"At the same time you're turning it in, all across town and probably in New York, other producers in your same shoes are doing exactly the same thing," says *Brothers & Sisters* executive producer Molly Newman, who has developed pilots for Sony, Warner Bros., and 20th Century Fox. "You can almost feel the hopes of these dozens upon dozens of producers sending over their babies, the thing they've worked so hard on for so many weeks and months. The competition is fierce, and it's like winning the lottery—the odds are so stacked against you. You have to remember that. And you almost never do, because hope springs eternal and you worked so hard and you think it's so good and you want it so badly and often the answer will come quickly . . . you could find out literally in a day or two if it's a go."

THE PICKUP

For networks at the end of a traditional pilot season, the beginning of May is a flurry of incoming pilots. As each comes in, execs watch and discuss what they like and what they don't.

"We go through a screening process that includes all the executives," says Michael Benson, ABC's executive VP of marketing, "[as well as] assistants and other people working around the division so [the president] can get the vibe of how things are being perceived before they're picked up."

The best shows often become apparent during screenings. But that doesn't make networks' decisions any easier. Sometimes there are only four time slots and five great contenders; other times there are five slots and three contenders, forcing the network to pick up shows it knows aren't great quality.

"That's where scheduling comes in and lays out different scenarios, [plus] competitive scenarios," says Dan Harrison, senior VP of emerging networks at NBC Cable. They look "at it from a holistic point of view. Sales may weigh in and say, 'Show A is more salable than Show B; let's put that on a bigger night.' Even if they believe a show might get a smaller rating, it might have a higher **CPM** [see below], in which case they say, 'Show A, which might be a smaller show, might be a more *profitable* show.' "

TALK THE TALK: CPM

Ad prices are calculated in **CPM,** or **cost per mille** (*mille* is Latin for "thousand"). So let's say the CPM of advertising in a particular show is $25, or $25 for every unit of one thousand viewers. If that show pulls in 7 million viewers (which is 7,000 units of 1,000 viewers), the cost for one ad spot would be $175,000 ($25 × 7,000 = $175,000).

This entire time, showrunners are reading stacks of scripts and meeting with writers to decide whom to hire if their show goes to series. They have no idea if that will happen—or if, in a month, they'll even have a job—but they need to be prepared. Staffing season begins immediately after the networks' May upfront presentations, and producers want to grab their first choice of writers.

"It's different for every creator," says Gibson. "Sometimes you know your show is a hot show and has a really good chance. Sometimes you know you're 'on the bubble' and competing with one other show. It comes down to the last minute, and you're either on or you're not."

Then, one day, usually within a few days or a week of delivering, the phone rings.

For most writers, that phone call is the heartbreaking news that their blood, sweat, and tears have been for naught: their series wasn't picked up. Although producers know odds are slim, it's impossible for writers not to get attached to projects they care about, and after a year of passion and hard work, it all comes crashing down in a few seconds.

I've seen people practically have to take to their beds after being turned down on a pilot," says Newman. "You put so much of yourself into it, and then to be disappointed like that is difficult emotionally. You *have* to put your heart and soul into it, and then your heart can be broken."

Yet for a small handful of producers, the phone call is life-altering good news. Their hard work and late nights have paid off—the network is picking up their show!

Different shows receive different orders. Some, like FOX's *Back to You* and ABC's *Private Practice,* receive thirteen-episode orders, or a half-season, right off the bat. (Also, most orders include the pilot. So a thirteen-episode order is actually for twelve new episodes.) Others receive smaller orders: CBS's *Welcome to the Captain* began with six episodes (and was canceled in five); FOX's *The Return of Jezebel James* began with seven (and was canceled in three); ABC's *Masters of Science Fiction* was ordered for four (and never continued). Yet however many episodes the network wants, the show has now started down the path of an on-the-air, people-will-see-it, we-might-actually-make-it-to-syndication TV series.

Not that there's time to celebrate.

Showrunners get the call only days or hours before networks make their new-season announcements, which means there's no time for champagne. Writers and producers must pack their bags, race to the airport, and hop a plane to New York for the biggest event of the TV year: the network **upfront presentations.**

13

Upfronts

....

Writer Rich Hatem slid into the front seat of his car and smiled. He had just left his therapist's office, and he felt good.

It was a beautiful Wednesday in May 2003. The past five months had been a whirlwind of pilot production on *Miracles,* Hatem's pilot for ABC, Touchstone Television (now ABC TV Studios), and Spyglass Entertainment, a Touchstone-based pod. It had been barely a week since Hatem turned in the pilot, and for the first time in months he had actual downtime to think about how his life could change if *Miracles* went forward: what it would mean for his family, his career, his lifestyle. After all, Hatem had had a successful feature career (*The Mothman Prophecies, Under Siege 2: Dark Territory*), but he hadn't had the same luck in television. He'd developed scripts, but none had gone to pilot.

Until this one.

The story of a Catholic priest investigating paranormal phenomena, *Miracles* had been a passion project for Hatem, and the pilot had turned out beautifully. Director Matt Reeves had delivered one of the best pieces of film in his career. Actor Skeet Ulrich was as talented as he was handsome. And the network, which would announce their series pickups next week, had already declared it one of their favorite projects. So after nearly a year of pouring himself into writing, rewriting, and producing, Rich Hatem had finally said to his therapist the words every superstitious TV writer hates to say out loud:

"I want this. I know it's a long shot, but I love this show and I want to be working on it."

So when Hatem saw the message light blinking on his cell phone, he knew his show was getting picked up.

Until he heard his agent's voice. "Michael Eisner [then the CEO of Disney] walked out of the screening. The show's not going. It's over."

The last year of his life hurtled through Hatem's mind. The late-night rewrites, the endless casting sessions, the countless location scouts. Then, just like that . . . because one guy didn't like it—*one guy*—it was all for nothing.

"It was the most devastating phone call I've ever received," Hatem says. "I went into a tailspin, a full-scale freakout. I was screaming into the phone."

Hatem called everyone he knew. His lawyer. His girlfriend. Nothing helped.

It was Megan Wolpert, Spyglass's VP of production, who finally stepped in.

"Listen to me," she said, pushing Hatem against a wall. "I have heard too many stories about pilots that were dead, then they were alive, then they were dead, then they were alive again. We're not going to hear anything official from the network for a matter of days. This can go a million different ways and change direction twenty-five times. So, until we hear something official—*shape up.*"

The next three days were a taut, stifling blur. On Friday, Hatem received the pilot's test results. They were good, but the network still had no decision. On Saturday morning Hatem received another call. The network would have an answer that afternoon.

A few hours later Hatem's phone rang. It was Thom Sherman, president of ABC Television. Hatem listened carefully, his heart racing, as Sherman spoke.

"We're picking up the show," Sherman said. "It's midseason. But we're picking up the show."

And that, says Hatem, "began the best week I've ever had in this business. Upfronts. International upfronts. You won the prize."

Less than a week later, Hatem was in New York, stumbling in and out of limos, partying with the cast of his show and the ABC development execs at Radio City Music Hall.

"I'd always had this vague fantasy that when something really good happened in my career it would feel like the industry was throwing a party in my honor," Hatem says, "and this was pretty close. Everyone there has just had big success, so everyone is congratulating everyone they see. It's like New Year's Eve and Mardi Gras. Wherever you go, you're running into people you usually only see when you're pitching, but now they're drunk and dancing with their shirts off."

Yet behind all the glitz and glamour, something far more important is happening at the networks' upfront presentations: the prologue to the **upfront buying season.**

The upfront buying season, which usually lasts from June through July or August, is the most critical time of year for broadcasters, when they often sell 80 percent of their next year's ad space. During this time, advertisers are offered special incentives, like lower prices or guaranteed audience levels, to buy more ad time, or **inventory,** in upcoming shows. In other words, the upfront buying season is like a giant bargain presale before the new TV season begins. Unsold ad space can still be bought after the upfront season ends, but it's available only on the **scatter market,** meaning prices rise, audience levels aren't guaranteed, and buyers can't back out of purchased ads.

So although upfronts feel like massive parties in honor of TV's writers, actors, directors, and producers, they're actually carefully choreographed events designed to woo advertisers, the lifeblood of broadcast television. (In 2007 alone, advertisers spent a total of $22.4 billion on broadcast television. Compare that to $17.8 billion on cable, $11.3 billion on the Internet, and $4 billion on outdoor billboards.)

PREPARING FOR UPFRONTS

Although broadcasters schedule announcements for mid-May, buyers and sellers start preparing much earlier. Beginning in January, network marketing departments read pilot scripts and brainstorm how they can sell them to advertisers. As actual pilot cuts roll in a few weeks later, they cut trailers, develop key art, and organize presentations for each pilot in contention. Most of these never see the light of day, but marketing must stay ahead of the curve to be ready for May upfronts.

Advertisers, meanwhile, are learning what pilots are in development. In actuality, advertisers themselves rarely talk with networks; they instead use **media buyers,** like Starcom and Carat USA, who act as middlemen. Media buyers represent multiple clients and do everything from gathering information to making buys and negotiating contracts. (Starcom's clients, for instance, have included Kellogg's, Allstate, and Miller Brewing Company; Carat USA has repped RadioShack, Papa John's, and Hyundai/Kia.)

As media buyers and advertisers learn what's on networks' development slates, they ponder what brands and products they can advertise in each program. Although they don't know which will make the networks' fall schedules, they—like networks' marketing departments—begin formulating advertising strategies for each show. They also give feedback to networks on which shows they find appealing and which turn them off. Advertisers rarely get the final say in which series are picked up, but this info helps networks make their decisions in May.

THE UPFRONT PRESENTATIONS

"As a broadcaster, you throw a lot of parties," says former NBC Entertainment president Warren Littlefield, "but the biggest party you throw is the May upfront presentation. If you've got the goods, and you present them well, within a number of weeks you're going to take in several billion dollars. So it's a multibillion-dollar party you're throwing. And who are you talking to? Advertisers. Advertisers whose job in life is selling. So you're dealing with a sophisticated, intelligent, very savvy audience."

Aside from advertisers, upfront invitees include representatives from affiliate stations and members of the press. The network is trying to drum up enthusiasm on every level for its new and returning shows.

Most networks' upfront announcements begin with massive presentations, often held at Radio City Music Hall, Lincoln Center, Madison Square Garden, or Carnegie Hall. Hosted by the network's entertainment president, each presentation often last an hour and a half to two hours, incorporating music, video clips, even live appearances by casts and producers. ABC once had *Desperate Housewives* creator Marc Cherry perform a song-and-dance routine with the women of Wisteria Lane. The CW, promoting 2007's *Life Is Wild,* had its president, Dawn Ostroff, cuddle with a baby black leopard. FOX produced a mini-episode of *24* in which Jack

Bauer defused a bomb while begging network president Peter Ligouri to shorten his upfront speech. Amid all this, the network president discusses last year's goals, next year's objectives, and exciting shows and projects the company has on tap. The audience then adjourns to a tent or party room where they can eat, drink, and rub elbows with TV stars and creators. The whole evening usually costs between two and five million dollars.

"We want to make it fun, we want to make it enjoyable," says Michael Benson, who—as ABC's executive vice president of marketing, advertising, and promotion—helps plan the entire presentation. "We want the audience to walk away saying, 'It looks like they've got some good shows coming out this season.' "

ALL SHAPES AND SIZES

Broadcasters aren't the only ones with upfront announcements and upfront buying seasons. Kids' networks, like Nickelodeon and Cartoon Network, often hold announcements in February, and cable upfronts take place in March and April. Because these outlets don't reach as many viewers as broadcasters do, their presentations are rarely as extravagant; many times execs simply visit ad buyers' offices and present shows themselves. Some networks, like Discovery, even have overseas channels and host international upfronts for foreign advertisers. (Discovery has networks in more than twenty countries, on every continent but Antarctica.) In fact, the success of cable networks has led many people—on both the television side and the advertising side—to wonder if broadcasters' multimillion-dollar presentations are archaic.

"There was a point in time," says Erin Gough-Wehrenberg, executive VP at NBC Universal's Universal Media Studios, "where [upfronts] were an intimate experience, where advertisers were getting close, in-depth looks at what was going on at a network and what their plans were. They were able to base their buys on knowledge of the product. [But upfronts have] become much bigger than that . . . a press event, a celebration of the year of work. From advertisers' perspective, it became less about them."

Thus, some broadcast networks are overhauling their upfront-presentation process. Instead of announcing its schedule at a gala bash in mid-May, NBC revealed 2008–2009's entire sixty-five-week schedule at a press conference in April. Its sales team then held one-on-one meetings with ad buyers and clients, hoping to help them find new, more tailored, even nontraditional ways of using NBC's schedule to reach consumers. They then invited advertisers to "The NBC Universal Experience"—an interactive upfront party/presentation featuring *American*

Gladiator battles, culinary samplings from *Top Chef,* and a live *Hardball* segment with Chris Matthews—in New York in mid-May. Similarly, the CW revamped its 2008 upfront announcements by swapping its traditional high-profile presentation in favor of a casual cocktail party. ABC and CBS canceled their parties altogether, instead hosting shorter, streamlined business presentations. Some networks have even toyed with holding upfront presentations online, digitally.

Meanwhile, online production companies are beginning to hold their own "digital upfronts." On April 3, 2008, the day after NBC revealed its 2008–2009 schedule (and just over a month before regular upfronts), Microsoft hosted its first-ever Digital Showcase, where it announced its own slate of original shows, all intended for the Internet (*In Need of Repair, The Men's Room, 50 Greatest, Seven Secrets About . . . ,* and *What on Earth Is Going On?*). Less than three weeks later, Broadband Enterprises (producers of the hit online series *Cube Fabulous*) held an upfront to introduce ten new Internet series, including *Threads, Dorm Storm, Sports Court,* and *Sock Puppet Television.* These weren't the online world's first stabs at upfronts, but they were two of the most prominent.

Although it's too soon to tell if any of these changes will become permanent, they highlight companies' attempts to adapt to an evolving media and society.

After the upfront presentations, advertisers and media buyers have about two weeks to revise their advertising strategies based on networks' official schedules. First they look at each show's target demographics. A Maybelline ad, for instance, is better placed in the female-skewing *Grey's Anatomy* than the male-skewing *The Unit.* A preview for a teen movie is more appropriate in *Aliens in America* than *Law & Order: SVU.*

Next they look at leverage points, shows or dayparts where networks have special needs. In 2007, for example, when NBC replaced its soap opera *Passions* with an extra hour of *The Today Show,* they were anxious to rally advertising support. So advertisers who were willing to fill that need were able to negotiate better prices and incentives.

Advertisers also designate **flightings,** or weeks in which their ads should air. Perhaps Doritos has a new ad campaign coming out this winter, so they want a six-week flighting in *The Big Bang Theory* beginning in January. Colgate may want a three-week November flighting in *Pushing Daisies.*

Once advertisers decide how to spend their money, they dispatch media buyers to purchase the actual time. Because media buyers represent multiple companies, they bundle clients' strategies together into one big plan, giving themselves more bargaining power when approaching networks.

TALK THE TALK: CLUTTER

Advertisers also study each show's amount of **clutter,** or nonprogram time per hour. Although it seems like advertisers would champion *more* ad time, they actually favor *less,* as longer commercial breaks keep viewers away from the TV and dilute each spot's effectiveness. Networks used to have twelve or thirteen minutes of commercial time, or clutter, each hour (about twenty-four or twenty-six thirty-second spots), but many now have almost fifteen or sixteen (thirty to thirty-two spots).

THE BUYING SEASON BEGINS

The buying season, which usually begins around Memorial Day, is a strange dance of feints and negotiations. Because ad sales work according to supply and demand—levels of demand drive prices up for some spots and down for others—advertisers never want to buy until they know they're getting the best deal possible. Thus, each upfront season begins with networks and buyers jockeying for position. Buyers try to learn what rival companies are intending to pay, and networks try to play buyers off each other, propelling prices as high as they can. Finally, one of the media buyers makes an official "buy," setting a price precedent for the rest of the season.

When media buyers make a buy, they present a network with their overall strategy. The network's ad sales department then studies the strategy and maps out pricing plans and programming mixes (schedules of which shows will air the ads). The media buyer can then negotiate for better pricing or a different mix of shows.

There are several points networks and media buyers negotiate. First, certain shows and dayparts are more expensive than others. Primetime ads are usually the most expensive; ads in broadcast daytime shows, like *The View* and *General Hospital,* are the least expensive. (Because these daytime shows are programmed by the network itself, they're different from first-run syndicated shows, like *The Oprah Winfrey Show,* which also often air during daytime but are programmed by individual stations or station groups. We'll discuss first-run syndication in chapter 26.)

Media buyers also negotiate ratings guarantees. CBS may ensure that commercials in *NCIS* receive at least a rating of 8.8 (about 9.93 million viewers). ABC may promise that *Ugly Betty* ads receive at least a 4.5 among women aged eighteen to thirty-four. If a show doesn't meet expectations, the network must offer **make-goods,** usually free ad space in a comparable time slot. If the network is unable to offer acceptable make-goods, it resorts to **give-backs,** refunding advertisers' money. This is obviously not a position in which a network ever wants to be.

TALK THE TALK: C3, OR "LIVE-PLUS-THREE"

When using Nielsen TV ratings to evaluate the value of an ad spot within a particular show, the ad world doesn't use quite the same ratings as everyone else. After all, advertisers don't care how many people watch a particular show. They care how many people watch *commercials* within that show. So advertisers use C3, or live-plus-three ratings, which—though calculated the same as regular ratings—measure how many people watch commercials live, as well as how many people watch DVR-recorded commercials up to three days afterward. Interestingly, even on recorded shows, viewers tend to watch 30 to 45 percent of commercials.

Buyers buying upfront ads also get **option** dates, allowing them to back out of ads by a certain day without losing all their money. So if Coke buys several flightings to launch a new soda next spring, then decides to delay the launch before their options expire, they can back out and get a refund.

All these factors get discussed as the network and media buyer negotiate a fair price. Not only do ad prices vary from show to show, but different advertisers often pay different prices for ads within the same show. As the 2007–2008 season began, a thirty-second ad in *Smallville* averaged $77,000; *Family Guy* averaged $198,000; *Survivor* and *Private Practice* each pulled in $208,000. (Some quick math: At the beginning of the 2007–2008 season, the average thirty-second spot in a primetime broadcast drama cost $145,400. So if the average drama had thirty thirty-second spots, it grossed $4.4 million per night—which means that if its license fee was $1.8 million, the average drama netted its network about $2.6 million each airing. The net is obviously much higher for in-demand dramas like *House,* which charged $294,000 per spot, and lower for shows like *Life Is Wild,* which managed only $40,00 per spot. *Grey's Anatomy,* with the most expensive ads of any scripted show on television, nets an average of over $10 million per episode.)

WHAT ADVERTISERS *DON'T* CHOOSE

Although advertisers pick which shows to advertise in, most *don't* select the **pod,** or commercial break, in which their ad will air. It's the networks' job to rotate ads evenly throughout their programs. Having said this, as Nielsen ratings get more accurate, many advertisers want to use minute-by-minute ratings, allowing them to see not only which pods—but which positions *in* those pods—are the most valuable commercial slots. Even now, certain powerful advertisers (i.e., movie studios, who spend millions of dollars on TV advertising) have enough clout to demand certain pods, but networks play these deals close to the vest.

As fall premieres draw closer, ad prices rise and drop based on supply and demand. Most broadcast networks haul in about $2 billion during their up-front buying season. (In 2008, the five main broadcasters, collectively, made a total of $9.23 billion in upfront sales.) Once networks and media buyers have closed all their deals (which is usually by early July, but sometimes as late as August), unsold inventory becomes available on the **scatter market,** where buyers can buy individual ads without upfront incentives and usually at higher prices, often up to 40 percent higher than upfront prices. Thus, networks intentionally hold back about 20 percent of their inventory in hopes of selling it at higher prices on the scatter market. Eventually, May and the new upfronts roll back around, and the entire cycle begins anew.

HOW TELEVISION ADVERTISING IS CHANGING

Although TV's current system of **participation advertising** has been in place since the 1950s, it's suddenly going through seismic shifts. DVRs allow viewers to zip through commercials or watch them at their convenience, sometimes days after a particular ad has lost its timeliness. (According to a 2008 TiVo report, the most "ad-zapped" show on television is *Grey's Anatomy,* with 75 percent of TiVo users skipping through commercial breaks.) This, combined with the rising amount of clutter, has motivated advertisers to find nontraditional forms of promotion, such as **product integration.** Unlike product placement, in which advertisers pay to insert products into shows' shots or scenes, product integration weaves products into a show's actual story. *Desperate Housewives* wrote a storyline about Gabrielle Solis posing as a model for a Buick LaCrosse promotion. *The Apprentice* partnered with Crest and Mars, leading to contestants competing to sell toothpaste and candy on air. *The Office* concocted a story about Dwight creating his own version of Second Life.

Because there are few business templates for product integration, various deals work differently. Each year, advertisers pay almost $125 million in integration fees, which are split among a show's network, studio, and—sometimes—producers. In 2007, for instance, brands like Kodak, Quiznos, and Crocs were paying up to $2 million per episode to integrate their products into NBC's *The Apprentice*. (Interestingly enough, only ABC, CBS, and NBC charge integration fees. The CW, FOX, and MyNetworkTV do not.) Other advertisers commit to buying more ad space or doing cross-promotional swaps, as when NBC's *American Dreams* wrote an episode about a soup-sponsored essay contest in exchange for promotion on Campbell's Soup labels and ads. And in 2007, Telemundo announced it would air *Idolos de Juventud (Youth Idols),* a forty-episode, commercial-free **telenovela** buoyed only by product integration.

Advertisers have also found new opportunities in cyberspace. As networks stream more shows online, advertisers jump to support them. As discussed in chapter 3, media buyer Starcom USA estimated that streaming TV shows earned networks $120 million of ad revenue in 2007, and technology and market research firm Forrester Research predicts that number could increase to $1.7 billion by 2010. In fact, NBC Universal and News Corp. joined forces in 2007 to create Hulu, an ad-supported online distributor that allows viewers to stream TV shows and movies from over fifty providers—including FOX, NBC, Sony, and Warner Bros.—then keeps 20 to 30 percent of each show's ad revenue. And when CBS broadcasts the 2008 NCAA March Madness basketball tournament via both TV and the Internet, it drew 132 million television viewers and 4.8 million Internet viewers. But because online ads were more scarce and tended to connect better with audiences, CBS's ads earned $4.83 per online viewer and only $4.12 per traditional TV viewer, helping the network bag $23 million in online ad sales.

Advertisers have also begun partnering with TV and Internet companies to produce **branded entertainment,** original shows and projects based around specific brands or products. Much branded entertainment is appearing on the Internet, providing new opportunities for advertisers, studios, and producers alike. As part of its online campaign to promote Sunsilk shampoo, Unilever joined forces with TBS for *Love Bites,* a **webisodic** series about a twentysomething couple. Volvo sponsored *Driving School,* an Internet comedy about a driving teacher, produced by Reveille Productions, the production company behind *Ugly Betty* and *The Office.* We'll discuss branded entertainment more in chapter 20.

For now, of course, television is still the reigning champ of advertising and media, and networks have no intention of losing that crown—which makes the summer upfront season one of broadcasters' most crucial periods.

Yet ad departments aren't the only ones who spend their summers working overtime. TV series are racing toward fall premiere dates: hiring writers, assembling crews, pumping out scripts, and producing enough episodes to make their air dates in September and October. They no longer have five cushy weeks of prep, two weeks of shooting, and several weeks of post as they did for the pilot. TV shows must churn out a mini-movie every week.

And it ain't easy.

PART IV

Staffing Season . . .
and Beyond

Getting the Series Up and Running

14

Staffing Season: How Showrunners Staff New Shows

The frenzy of staffing season, the traditional May–June period when new TV shows hire writing staffs, shifts into high gear as soon as showrunners and executives return from New York upfronts knowing which shows are headed for air. (Hit shows that already know they're returning often begin staffing *before* upfronts, usually in late April or early May.) Most writing staffs must begin work by mid-June in order to start shooting by mid-July or early August and make fall premiere dates, leaving showrunners little time to form staffs.

(Even series receiving pickups outside normal pilot/staffing seasons usually begin hiring writers as soon as they're greenlighted. So as networks move away from a traditional development calendar, shows getting picked up in February, October, or July still go through the same staffing process.)

HOW A STAFF IS STRUCTURED

"Unlike a movie," says showrunner Adam Chase (*Friends*), TV shows "aren't telling just one story. In a half-hour sitcom, there's typically an **A-story** (the main plot) and a **B-story** (the subplot). If you do twenty-two episodes, that's forty-four stories. In *Friends,* we did three stories an episode and threw out [more] stories that didn't work. In one season, we might go through a hundred stories. It's impossible for one person to come up with a hundred stories."

This is why showrunners need writing staffs, or a **writers' room** (also known as just "the room"), a team of writers who brainstorm, outline, write, and rewrite all the stories of a show. Most writers' rooms consist of eight to twelve people arranged in a three-level hierarchy, each level representing the experience of its writers: upper level, mid-level, and low level. Each level is then subdivided into smaller levels.

THE HIERARCHY OF A WRITING STAFF

As TV writers gain more experience, they move up the ladder of the writing staff. Each rung is a different level, and as writers ascend they take on more duties, earning titles as producers as well as writers. Here's how the ladder works:

UPPER LEVEL

Executive producer (although the series' creator/showrunner is often an EP, many shows have more than one exec producer)

Co-executive producer

MID-LEVEL

Supervising producer

Producer

Co-producer

LOW LEVEL

Executive story editor

Story editor

Staff writer

Many shows also hire **consulting producers,** upper-level writers who don't fit into the regular hierarchy. Some work only three or four days a week. Some come in to polish stories. Others are technical experts who advise the writers.

In fact, when you see names of producers at the beginning of an episode, most of these are writers. Low-level writers, however, rarely get credit at the beginning of a show. Story editors' and exec story editors' credits flash by during ending credits, but staff writers don't get credit *anywhere*—unless they actually write the episode and get a "Written By" credit at the top. "It's a recognition of the greater participation of those higher up the writing staff's hierarchy," says Charles Slocum, assistant executive director of the Writers Guild of America, West. "It's a reason to move up the ladder."

Upper-level writers, executive producers and co-executive producers, are the most experienced. One is always the showrunner, who, as we know, is the head writer responsible for organizing the staff, "running the room," and dealing with everything from casting and wardrobe to postproduction and publicity.

"The showrunner is managing a $25-million company that goes from zero to $25 million dollars in eight weeks, which is basically your pre-production time," says Kevin Plunkett, ABC's VP of current comedy programming. "It's a monster job. What makes a good showrunner is the ability to wear different hats and—not unlike what we do on the corporate side of things—hire good people to work for you. It's impossible for one person to do all those things alone."

To help keep the show afloat, showrunners often hire a "number two," a second-in-command EP or co-EP who runs the room when the showrunner is approving set designs or picking out music or helping choreograph a stunt.

"As you get into production, the showrunner starts being less and less in the room," says Melissa Rosenberg, the number two on Showtime's *Dexter*, "so the number two is giving notes on scripts, rewriting, making sure outlines are moving forward. [You're] constantly moving ahead, pumping out stories, keeping the train running."

Next come mid-level writers: supervising producers, producers, and co-producers. Mid-levels aren't as seasoned as EPs or co-EPs, but they help with many of the producing duties: editing cuts, supervising preshoots, scouting locations, approving wardrobe choices, or sitting in casting sessions.

Low-level writers are executive story editors, story editors, and staff writers. Although these writers participate in the room, they have less experience than writer-producers, and aren't expected to carry the same load of duties. They're also often paid and contracted differently, which we'll discuss in a moment.

Many rooms are a mix of levels. Some showrunners surround themselves with younger, fresher voices. Others prefer top-heavy staffs of mostly upper-levels. Each showrunner architects the staff most appropriate for his particular show and management style.

HOW STAFFS ARE HIRED

In January, TV literary agents look at their client rosters to review who's working, who's not, and who will need a new job in a few months. Some clients are unemployed. Many work on shows about to be canceled. Others are **baby writers,** aspirants hoping for their first writing jobs.

Agents then assess what writing materials each client has given them to work with. Writers usually need two types of writing samples. **Spec scripts** are sample episodes of shows already on the air, used to showcase a writer's talent. Original material could be any original pilot, screenplay, short story, stage play, column, or essay not based on preexisting properties. We'll talk more about specs and originals in chapter 21.

In March, several weeks before hiring season officially begins, agents call executives at networks, studios, and production companies. They pitch comedy writers to comedy execs, drama writers to drama execs, and both to current execs (who cover both genres of returning shows). The agent's goal is to persuade executives to read a writer's material and take a general meeting, a meet-and-greet, with the author. Execs start taking generals in March, meeting first with mid- and upper-level writers, then moving to lower levels and babies.

NETWORK AND STUDIO WRITING AND DIVERSITY PROGRAMS

Some writers come through special writing programs established by networks and studios to help find and foster fresh voices. These programs not only help struggling writers gain entrée into the industry, they give sponsoring companies the first look at young talent. Networks and studios even have diversity programs designed to seek out talented minority writers. Danielle Sanchez-Witzel was accepted into NBC's diversity program in 2002 and landed her first staff writing job on *In-Laws*. Six years later, after working her way up the ladder at *My Name Is Earl*, she signed a two-year, seven-figure overall with Universal Media Studios.

Each writing program works a bit differently, but some of the most popular are these:

- **CBS Diversity Institute Writers Mentoring Program:**
  www.cbscorporation.com/diversity/cbs_network/index.php
- **The Disney-ABC Writing Fellowship:**
  abctalentdevelopment.com/programs.htm
- **Fox Diversity Writers Initiative Program:**
  www.fox.com/diversity/creative/writer_initiative.htm
- **NBC: Writers on the Verge:** www.diversecitynbc.com
- **The Warner Bros. Television Writers Workshop:**
  www2.warnerbros.com/writersworkshop

In a general meeting, "I look for personality," says development executive Jen Chambers (Maverick TV, FOX). "If you get along with me, I'll feel comfortable putting you in a room with my executive producers and other writers." She also looks for "knowledge about the pilot, [and] your thoughts about what you've read or seen in regard to projects I'm staffing."

As a writer preparing for a general, brief yourself on what pilots and series that particular executive covers. Peruse any appropriate pilot scripts, most of which aren't available publicly, so don't be afraid to be resourceful and use connections. (Ask friends who are assistants at agencies, networks, studios, or production companies. If the exec has shows on the air, watch recent episodes and know what's happening with plots and characters. (You can sometimes find scripts of produced shows online. See chapter 21 for some great online script-hunting resources.) Also, know what projects rival companies are developing. Read the morning's trades so you're informed about industry news.

Most important, says Barry Kotler, a literary agent at The Gersh Agency, "know what [shows] you think you'd be right for, and sell yourself in the room."

This means you shouldn't be afraid to talk about your favorite shows and pilots, or what you think you'd bring to a writing staff. As a writer, your main skill sets are your talent and life experiences. So you need to know how to articulate both.

Each exec keeps a list of writers he meets for each level of a staff. Then, in late April, as showrunners finish pilots and begin thinking about staffing, execs send them their lists. This helps showrunners weed through their own stacks of submissions. When they read material they like, they call the writer in for a showrunner meeting. Showrunners look at several factors when hiring writers. They obviously look at talent, but different writers have different strengths. One may be great at dialogue, while another's a genius at structure. Some are brilliant joke writers while others choreograph action scenes. Just as football teams need strong linemen, fast runners, great receivers, and powerful quarterbacks, showrunners select writers to service each aspect of the series.

"I'm looking for talent," says Rosenberg, but "I'm also looking for life experience. What have they done with their lives? What are their families like? Where have they been? Someone who's lived in L.A., straight out of film school, worked as a PA, and their family is really normal—what are they going to give me? What are their stories? Someone who's lived in Afghanistan, whose parents were missionaries, whose brother was a drug addict—they bring stories to the table."

Writers, therefore, must be able to articulate their own unique perspectives on the world. If you're a white, middle-class woman from Nebraska, it may be difficult to make a case for hiring you on a gritty urban cop show. This doesn't mean it can't happen, it just means you need to understand how you connect to the show's characters and themes. How does the dangerous, dirty world of the series reflect your life experience? How does your worldview provide a vital element no other writer can provide?

Showrunners also hire people they know they *like.* After all, if you're going to be trapped together in a room for twelve hours a day, showrunners need to know they like you.

"After good experiences and bad experiences," says *Carpoolers* executive producer Marsh McCall, "you learn life is too short to work with people you don't like."

Thus, many showrunners simply call or rehire writers they've already worked with, which is why it's often difficult for even the best agents to **break a baby,** or get a baby writer his first break.

WRITER Q&A: PREPARING FOR A SHOWRUNNER MEETING

Congratulations! The showrunner of a hot series read your material, likes it, and wants to meet. If it goes well, you could be only days away from being a professional television writer.

To help answer your last-minute questions, we've brought in four of our favorite writers to whip you into fighting shape. Say hello to executive producer Jeff Melvoin (*Army Wives, Alias*), co-EP Jane Espenson (*Battlestar Galactica, Gilmore Girls*), supervising producer Craig Turk (*Boston Legal, Cold Case, Private Practice*), and staff writer Tracy Grant (*Lincoln Heights*).

I have an upcoming staffing meeting on a particular show. How should I prepare?

CRAIG: [If it's a returning show,] watch as many episodes as you possibly can. Know the characters, know the arcs, have a thorough familiarity with what the show's about and how it works. You have to watch TV fairly closely sometimes to really get down the structure of what shows do. All shows have their conceits. Some delve into the personalities of characters deeply, some not at all. Be aware of things like that. Get a sense of how writers write the show and how the showrunner likes the show to be presented. You want to give the showrunner a sense that you understand and appreciate what they do, and you'll be able to execute it. They're not looking for you to re-create their show; they're looking for you to be an effective implementer of their vision.

Should I pitch story ideas?

JEFF: Have ideas, but you shouldn't come in to pitch those ideas necessarily. Be prepared with what you like about the show, what intrigues you, and why you would like to write for that show. Have questions: "This was great, but I was curious about where you were planning to go with it." What you *don't* want to do is tell the showrunner what he's doing wrong: "Gee, I didn't like when this happened," or "That character was a wrong turn." It's fine to have questions: "I wonder what's going to happen after the pilot, since you killed two of the main characters." But it's funny how many first-time writers make the mistake of being overly critical. It takes so many bumps and bruises to get your show on the air, the idea that somebody's going to come in and tell you what you're doing wrong usually isn't appreciated.

My dream has always been to write for television, and this is the kind of show I love. I've read the script and seen the pilot, and I *really* want this job. How enthusiastic should I be in the meeting?

JANE: Bring enthusiasm, ideas, and energy. If you've gotten a meeting at all, the showrunner likes your writing, so this is the "show-up-wearing-pants meeting." Mostly, they're checking to make sure you're not crazy, that you're a presence they're going to be able to stand having in the room. Make sure your enthusiasm doesn't cross the line to "this person is unbearable to be around," but nobody's offended by you loving their show. You get no points for being too cool for the room.

Sometimes writers meet on shows they're not crazy about. When that happens, do you lie about liking the show? How do you feign enthusiasm for a show you don't really like?

JANE: Find enthusiasm in yourself. It doesn't have to be a lie. Find something about the show you can totally embrace. "The third male lead is hilarious!" Go into the meeting raving about them. Think of stories and all the things you would do for them. Find enthusiasm.

What should I wear to the meeting?

TRACY: One of the mistakes I made early on was not dressing properly. I came from a corporate environment, so [at] one of my first meetings, I had a [three-piece] suit on, a shirt and tie. It made me appear out of place and out of touch with the

continued

environment I was in, and I was. Here was a guy who didn't know enough not to wear a suit in this casual arts-and-entertainment environment. And a tie, for men, is an absolute no-no. I should've worn a more business-casual outfit. If you wear a suit, you look like an agent or an attorney.

Finally, the show's budget always plays an important role in hiring writers. Most broadcast shows budget between $75,000 and $125,000 per episode for their writing staffs (about 10–15 percent of a half-hour show's total budget and about 5 percent, or less, of a one-hour show's budget). Cable shows allot less; a half-hour single-cam on the Disney Channel, for instance, may budget only $60,000 for each episode's writing budget. Higher-level writers cost more than lower-levels, so showrunners balance their wants with what they can afford (upper-level writers' salaries, on a first-year broadcast show, often begin at $40,000 to $45,000 per week; lower-level writers can cost anywhere from $3,817 to $12,000). Unfortunately, this means staff writers are often the first positions eliminated from a show with a tight budget. Babies may be cheap, but they offer little in terms of experience, so showrunners hire them only if there's leftover money.

TWO'S COMPANY: WHY WRITING TEAMS ARE MORE STAFFABLE

Like it or not, economics often play into showrunners' staffing decision. Some writers may be very talented, but their price is too high. Others may be more affordable, but they don't have much experience. One of the ways showrunners maximize the bang for their buck is by hiring writing teams, two writers who write their scripts and projects together.

When people work as a team, they don't get paid as two people, but as a single writer.

"You're getting two people for the price of one," says producer Lesley Wake-Webster (*Notes from the Underbelly, What I Like About You*). "If you only have in your budget money for eight entities . . . if you get a writing team you're getting an extra person. The writing team splits the money."

As you watch TV shows and movies, you can spot writing teams in the credits because they join their names with an ampersand (*American Dad*'s Kenny Schwartz & Rick Weiner); if two names are connected simply by the word "and" (Todd Smith and Joan Ponzio), it means the second writer was hired to rewrite the first.

All these stars must align for a writer to get hired; he must have great writing samples, click with the EP, fill a need on the staff, and get approval from the network, studio, and production company. There also needs to be money in the budget, and the writer (usually) needs to have a preexisting relationship with the showrunner—which is why "breaking a baby" is a Sisyphean task. In truth, most babies are hired simply out of the goodness of the EP's heart.

THE BEST WAY TO BREAK IN

There's one important staff member we haven't yet discussed, someone who's not an official writer, but is indispensable nonetheless: the **writers' assistant.** Writers' assistants support the writing staff in everything they do: taking notes, researching stories, archiving scripts and paperwork. Thus, good writers' assistants form strong bonds with staffs, which means—in an industry where showrunners hire people they know and trust—starting as a writers' assistant is often the best way to get your first staff job.

"Being in the room gives you an opportunity to experience how the process works for that particular show," says *Boston Legal* co-producer Karen Wyscarver. "It allows you to see how the showrunner works the room in regard to ideas and stories. You're also able to form relationships with other writers and let others know what your goals are: to figure out who will and won't help you."

Unlike executive assistants, who spend days answering phones and organizing calendars, writers' assistants sit in the writers' room and type notes on everything the writers talk about: every joke pitched, every story suggested, every idea mentioned. They're like the staff's personal court stenographer. At the end of each day, they organize this info into a readable document, print it, and leave copies for the writers to use the next morning.

"Being a television writer is a specific skill that can't be learned in any training program or college major," says *Scrubs* co-executive producer Janae Bakken, who worked as a writers' assistant on *Oh Grow Up* and *Malcolm in the Middle* before staffing on *Scrubs* in 2001. "I learned the proper way to pitch a joke by observing others. My joke-writing skills also got better. Most important, I learned outline and story skills that made me a much better writer. My spec scripts improved exponentially once I got in the room as an assistant."

Although it has many perks, being a writers' assistant is hard work. Writers' assistants arrive earlier and stay later than the rest of the staff, which means—since many staffs work long hours—they often have little downtime. Still, an

continued

industrious writers' assistant with a good attitude is frequently the best candidate when a show has an open staff writer position.

"[Getting staffed] these days is more about relationships than anything else," says Barry Kotler, a literary agent at The Gersh Agency. "It's about working for the right people, having the right relationships, so they essentially *do you the favor* of inviting you to be on their staff. Sure, you're probably a good writer. You're probably a wonderful person to hang out with. But the bulk of the work is done by senior-level people. You're there to learn the process, write a couple scripts, and chime in when appropriate."

Writers' assistants are also sometimes assigned **freelance episodes**, episodes not written by a show's official staff. The WGA requires any show with at least a thirteen-episode order to give at least two episodes to writers not on staff. "The idea is to help struggling writers and bring in new voices," says writers' assistant David Wright (*Notes from the Underbelly, Malcolm in the Middle, Suddenly Susan*). So if the staff likes their writers' assistant, they usually assign him the freelance. (Wright has written two freelances for *Malcolm* and received a "Story By" credit on *Susan*.) We'll talk more about writers' assistants in chapter 24.

When a showrunner wants to hire someone, he first tells the studio and network, who have hopefully already approved the writer through lists and general meetings. Next, the showrunner informs the writer's agent he'll be getting a job offer. The offer usually comes from the studio's business affairs department, after they call the agent to get the writer's quotes, or his salary on his last writing job. This gives the studio a starting place from which to form an actual offer. The job offer, and the writer's contract, consist of several main points negotiated between the studio and the agent.

The first thing the agent and studio determine is the writer's title, or level. Agents usually try to get the writer a title bump from his last job; so a staff writer last year becomes a story editor this year, a co-producer becomes a producer, etc. (provided they've had their last credit for at least twenty-two episodes). Agents also negotiate *future* bumps, so if a writer stays on a particular show, he's guaranteed to move up the ladder each year.

Next, the agent negotiates the length, or term, of the deal. Most writers sign three-year deals, binding them to the show for three years—as long as the series stays alive and the showrunner wants them back. Although the showrunner and studio can always fire writers earlier, most writers are guaranteed a certain number of weeks: usually six, fourteen, or twenty. If, at the end of those weeks, the showrunner is happy with the writer's work, the writer gets to keep his job. If the writer's not carrying his weight, or isn't the right fit for the showrunner, the showrunner doesn't **pick up his option,** and the writer is let go.

Once the agent and the studio have agreed on the writer's title and length of term, they figure out the writer's salary, or rate. Staff writers are usually paid week-to-week. Writers above staff level are paid per episode. Some are paid for "all episodes produced," meaning they get paid for every episode of the series that actually gets made, whether they write those episodes or not. But if the show gets canceled after four episodes, the writers only get paid for four episodes. Other writers are guaranteed payment for a certain number of episodes. This is obviously preferable to writers, because it ensures they get a set amount of money, even if the show gets canceled or they don't work on all the episodes. So a staff writer and a supervising producer may both be hired for fourteen weeks, but while the staff writer is guaranteed a $3,548 minimum weekly salary (regardless of how many episodes he writes), the supervising producer is guaranteed payment for thirteen episodes (regardless of how many he actually writes).

Although mid- and upper-level writers' per-episode fees are negotiated for each show, no writer can ever make less than the Writers Guild's weekly minimum, which increases each year. There are different minimums for staff writers and all writers above staff level, and the minimums vary depending on how many weeks writers are contracted for. In 2008, for instance, a staff writer contracted for six weeks on a broadcast network show made a minimum of $3,817 a week, with the studio having the option to extend the contract for more weeks at the same rate. A staff writer contracted for fourteen weeks made $3,548 a week; a staff writer contracted for twenty weeks made $3,272 a week.

Although the WGA only decrees studios pay writers its minimum weekly payment, writers often move up the payscale as they rise from level to level. Mid-level writers' salaries, on a first-year show, typically range from $12,000 to $22,000 per episode. Of course, upper-level writers with overalls aren't paid directly for the show at all. Rather, their work on a show counts against their overall. (Remember: overalls are advances, so writers are simply working off money they've already been given.)

WGA WEEKLY MINIMUMS

According to the WGA's 2008 Minimum Basic Agreement (the collective bargaining agreement negotiated with the Alliance of Motion Picture and Television Producers), the weekly minimum salary for writers on primetime broadcast TV shows increases 3.5 percent each year. Here are week-to-week minimums, based on the length of term, for both staff writers and other writers working on broadcast series until 2011, when the MBA will be renegotiated:

	Effective 2/13/08– 5/1/09	Effective 5/2/09– 5/1/10	Effective 5/2/10– 5/1/11
Week-to-week	$3,817	$3,951	$4,089
6 out of 6 weeks	3,817	3,951	4,089
14 out of 14 weeks	3,548	3,672	3,801
20 out of 20 weeks	3,272	3,387	3,506
40 out of 52 weeks	2,991	3,096	3,204
All writers above staff level			
Week-to-week & term employment up to & including 9 weeks	$7,120	$7,369	$7,627
10 to 19 weeks	5,934	6,142	6,357
20 weeks or more	5,336	5,523	5,716

Most writers above staff level operate under a different set of WGA minimums because their per-episode salaries are actually considered payment for producing and management services *other* than scriptwriting: helping with casting, editing, line producing, etc. Which also means whenever a mid- or upper-level writer writes an actual script, he gets paid a script fee *in addition to* his weekly salary. (In 2008 the minimum payment for an hour-long episode of broadcast television was $31,748; a half-hour was $21,585. An hour of cable was $20,816; a half-hour was $12,002. Each year, these minimums increase 3 percent, and you can look up the current schedule at the WGA's website: www.wga.org.)

Staff-level writers, unfortunately, are considered pure writers, not writer-producers, so they do *not* receive script fees on top of their weekly salaries.

In other words, let's say a staff writer on *Lipstick Jungle* gets paid Guild minimum of $3,817 per week. During the first season, he's assigned one episode to write, with a script fee of $31,748. His weekly paychecks of $3,817 are considered installments of that $31,748, so he doesn't get paid the additional script fees. Of course, if he ends up writing enough scripts that his accumulated script fees total *more* than his weekly paychecks, he gets the extra cash. But this almost never happens, since staff writers rarely (and by rarely, I mean never) get assigned enough scripts to outweigh their weekly paychecks.

There are several other deal points agents also negotiate. Most studios want exclusivity, meaning the writer isn't allowed to write, or "render services," for other shows or companies. Some deals ask for exclusivity in all media (film, TV, radio, print, etc.), while others simply cover television. Writers hate giving up exclusivity, as it prevents them from doing other writing elsewhere. It's the agent's job to find a happy medium.

When a writer is hired as an actual showrunner, his agent may also try to obtain **participation points** in the show's backend. Other agents try to guarantee clients a certain number of scripts to write. Or yearly raises. Or a special office and an assistant.

"The more senior the person," says Kotler, "the more bells and whistles there are, the more leverage and elbow room. At lower levels, there's not a lot of negotiation."

Eventually, all issues are agreed upon and the writer begins work. In the next chapter, we journey into the depths of the writers' room to look at how staffs work—and how you can survive.

15

The Writers' Room

As he hung up the phone, Drew Goddard had never been more terrified in his life.

A few weeks earlier he had begun his first job as an official TV writer: the staff writer on the seventh season of UPN's hit series, *Buffy the Vampire Slayer*. But as Goddard quickly discovered, walking into a writers' room for the first time is no easy task—especially when that room's been up and running for six years.

"It's like going to a new high school in a small town where everyone knows each other and you're the new kid," says Goddard. "It's like a fear of public speaking, times a thousand. It was particularly terrifying with *Buffy* because there was no job I wanted more. It was that dream job."

Goddard hadn't spoken much since he'd started at *Buffy*; he'd spent most of his time in the writers' room listening quietly, observing, watching the process. But now, as he hung up the phone, he knew that was all over.

Five minutes ago Goddard had been sitting alone in the writers' room, brainstorming ideas for his episode, which he knew he'd eventually have to write. No other writers were around. Some were on script. Others were helping on *Buffy*'s spinoff series, *Angel*. Three were on maternity leave. And that's when the phone rang.

"Who's in the writers' room?" asked Joss Whedon, *Buffy*'s creator and showrunner, calling from set.

"Just me, sir," said Goddard.

"Just you?"

"Yes."

"All right," said Whedon. "Come to the set and we'll work from here."

Goddard was suddenly aware of two things. One: he was heading to the stage to meet with his showrunner, completely alone. And two: *this was his shot.*

"It was clear to me," he says, "that if this didn't go well, *maybe* I would get a second chance, but you never *really* get a second chance. It's hard to counter someone's first impression of that first script you do on a show. You want to make it count, and I was painfully aware of that."

Goddard and Whedon spent the week on set, watching production and brainstorming stories for Goddard's upcoming episode.

"I came every day from 6:00 a.m. to 8:00 p.m.," says Goddard, "and in Joss's ten minutes of free time every couple hours, I'd say, 'Here's what I'm thinking for act one,' or 'Here's an idea for this scene.' Some he'd like it, some he'd say no, and sometimes he'd say, 'I can't talk right now, I'm busy with all this other stuff.' I learned when to approach and when not to approach, and that worked well."

It worked so well, in fact, that Goddard wound up writing the fifth, seventh, and ninth episodes, becoming one of the most renowned writers of the season. He eventually graduated to *Angel, Alias,* and *Lost,* and in 2006 signed a seven-figure overall with Touchstone Television (now ABC Studios). And while he has come a long way from that day alone in the writers' room, Goddard looks back at those early "terrifying" days as education.

"The mistake a lot of staff writers make is they don't listen," Goddard says. "They're so desperate to make their mark and do a good job, but you can actually end up doing more damage at first. No one's expecting you to dazzle right away. [The staff] knows you're green and they want you to absorb, figure out how to pitch and be helpful. No one coached me, I was just terrified, so I shut up."

Indeed, being a first-time staff writer isn't about proving you can hang with showrunners and EPs. It's about following the flow and learning the ropes in a bizarre, brutal, often intimidating environment. So if you know what to expect going in, life can be a lot easier—especially since many baby writers *don't* know what to expect going in.

STARTING THE ROOM

Because writing staffs need to generate several scripts before the first week of shooting (in a traditional development calendar, dramas usually begin shooting in mid- to late July; comedies start in early to mid-August), showrunners like to begin working as soon as possible after upfronts. Many studios budget six weeks of writing before shooting commences. Of course, because episodes have immovable air dates, they must be shot and edited by specific times, which means each script has a specific deadline. If writers fall behind, the entire ship sinks.

The first few days of revving up a staff are often lazy and uneventful. Writers meander in around ten, sometimes a bit later, get their coffee, check e-mail. Eventually the showrunner corrals everyone into the writers' room.

As we know, the term *writers' room* is another name for a show's writing staff, but it's something else as well: *an actual room.* This sounds obvious, but it's important to recognize the writers' room as a part of the production office for two reasons:

One: all writers' rooms look fairly similar. Drab and nondescript, they're just large enough to hold a table so that writers can face each other as they discuss the show. Dry-erase or bulletin boards hang on each wall. One is used for story ideas; others are used to **beat out,** or outline, actual episodes.

Two: the room is a sacred space; typically, only writers and writers' assistants are allowed inside. This is because writers often generate ideas from personal experiences, sharing painful, private, and embarrassing moments that could lead to interesting stories.

"People reveal things they would *never* reveal if they weren't in the room," says writers' assistant David Wright, who has worked on *Malcolm in the Middle, Notes from the Underbelly,* and countless other series and pilots. "The writers' room can turn into these group-therapy sessions. A lot of showrunners have this mantra, or rule, that nothing will leave the room. And ultimately it does serve some story you're writing."

Privacy also provides writers with a safe space to brainstorm without having to censor themselves.

"To find what's funny, you have to push past what's socially accept-able," says comedy writer Lesley Wake-Webster (*Notes from the Under-belly, That '80s Show*). "A lot of times, the things we laugh at are things that are embarrassing or things we'd like to say out loud, but don't. And in a comedy room, we get to say those things. But if you're trying to be polite or nice or protect some person in the room, you can't find those things."

GETTING THE ROOM ON ITS FEET

Getting a series up and running is no easy task. You're not only thinking up individual episodes, you're crafting characters and stories that can sustain the show for months and years to come. Plus, each room has its own differ-ent political dynamic, and it often takes a few weeks to settle into a pro-ductive, creative groove.

"There's a chemistry to the room," says *24* story editor Matt Mich-novetz. "You don't want to be out of sync with the group; you want to be harmonized. You write when it's time to write, listen when it's time to lis-ten, speak when it's time to speak. Like an orchestra. Everyone has the in-strument they play, and you have to wait for your moment."

The staff's hierarchy dictates much of the room's politics. In other words, says *Life* staff writer Melissa Scrivner, "there's an order in which peo-ple speak. The most important people usually speak first, and once every-one's had their say, the staff writer gets to chime in."

Many staff writers don't open up at all during their first few weeks in the room.

"You fight the urge to speak just for the sake of speaking," says *Private Practice* staff writer Sal Calleros. "Whenever I've done that, it's always a bad idea that comes out. It's tough because you're sitting there thinking, 'Oh my God, I'm not saying anything.' You feel like they're all thinking about you, but they couldn't care less . . . they don't expect you to be tossing out ideas every ten minutes. And honestly, you probably shouldn't be."

Of course, eventually even staff writers must speak up, or the studio won't renew their option.

"Wait until you know you can pitch a really strong joke or a really strong idea as your first suggestion in the writers' room," suggests showrunner Adam Chase (*Love Inc., Friends, Clone*) "because no matter what people say, that's going to be their first impression of you as a writer."

The first few weeks of a new staff are especially chaotic as writers figure out what stories the show wants to tell this season. Showrunners focus first on big-picture, long-term arcs, then funnel down to individual episodes and beats. They do this in five basic steps: figuring out macro-level stories, themes, and arcs; identifying episodes within those arcs; assigning and outlining individual episodes; going to script; and rewriting.

FIGURING OUT SEASON ARCS, THEMES, AND STORIES

Many showrunners first concentrate not on the series' actual stories, but on characters and themes. They make sure all writers are on the same page with who characters are and what ideas the show is exploring. This is especially important on new shows that have no past seasons to use as guides.

On *24,* says story editor Matt Michnovetz, "we spend the first couple of weeks tossing out every idea we can think of. They can be as big-picture as 'here's the threat for the season' to tiny things. We come up with some idea of where Jack is, what his mindset is, and what the terrorist threat is, then work those together, so stories are always rooted in [Jack's] 'emotional adventure.' [In season six] we came up with the idea of suicide bombers and suitcase nukes, but the story was, 'How do we get Jack back in the game? Where are his emotions, apart from just being a do-gooder?' [We decided] to tell the story of his father, his brother, and the few things that tied him to the world and gave him relevance."

The showrunner writes all ideas on one of the whiteboards. The writers then take those ideas and discuss how they might play out as season arcs. As writers home in on areas they like, they send a list of their favorite big-picture story ideas to the studio and network's current departments. Current execs may agree with the staff's season arcs, or they may have suggestions and other ideas.

"Networks are usually looking to protect their characters and the world," says *Lincoln Heights* staff writer Tracy Grant. "They may not want to see a certain storyline used [or a] character to be a certain way. Maybe a story is not specific enough to your lead character. It could be a great, interesting story, but the main character of the show has to be involved. There are times when you can, and should, pick your battles and defend what you've done, but it still may not fly."

Once the studio and network sign off on story ideas, the staff moves to the next step.

BRAINSTORMING AND CHOOSING EPISODES

With the season approved, the room begins to talk about how it actually plays out: where characters start, where they end up, and the logical steps, or **beats,** required to get them there.

In the final season of *Sex & the City,* says EP Cindy Chupack, "showrunner Michael Patrick King knew he wanted Carrie to end up with Big, partially since that's where the show started, and partially since that relationship was what attracted Michael to the show in the first place. And even then, believe me, we debated *a lot* in the writers' room, just as we knew viewers would. Ultimately, once we made the decision, we knew we had to build episodes into that last season to satisfy our objections—like Big's heart surgery, where we got a glimpse of his heart opening up and wondered if he might be changing. Or his talk with the other women—where he told Carrie's friends they would always come first, and he was just hoping for second."

All potential beats get written on the storyboard. Writers then lay these beats out over the course of the season, which usually consists of twenty-two episodes. Slowly, loglines for each episode to take shape. Of course, not every episode contains plot points of the season arc, so the staff must decide what stories these "empty" episodes might tell.

After writers determine their stories for these first episodes, they send descriptions to network and studio current executives. Once execs sign off, writers get to work on the next phase.

TALK THE TALK: BEATS AND BEAT SHEETS

A **beat** is a single piece of information that pushes a story forward. It may be a scene, sequence, or moment, but it propels the story from one step to the next. Here's a possible beat sheet for "Goldilocks and the Three Bears."

- The three bears want to eat their porridge, but it's too hot. They decide to go for a walk while it cools.
- While the bears are out, Goldilocks, tired and hungry, enters the house.
- Goldilocks spots three chairs. The first is too big, the second too small, the third just right.
- Goldilocks spots the porridge and decides to eat. The first bowl is too hot, the second too cold, the third just right.
- Goldilocks decides to nap. The first bed is too hard, the second too soft, the third just right.
- The bears return to find their chairs used, porridge eaten, and beds slept in. Goldilocks wakes, terrified, and flees the house.

BREAKING INDIVIDUAL EPISODES

Just as they "beat out" season arcs, the staff now beats out, or "breaks," individual episodes. First, however, the showrunner assigns episodes to specific writers. He usually assigns only the first four or five, doling them out in a hierarchical fashion: first to EPs, then to co-EPs, then to supervising producers, and so on. Once he's cycled through the top of the staff, the showrunner assigns episodes based on other factors, like who connects most to the material.

"We often assigned episodes at *Sex & the City* based on who had the original impulse," says Chupack, "or the most 'heat' around a story idea. Who was going through something similar? Who was uncomfortable with the discussion? That usually led to good writing."

Remember, in the preceding chapter, when we talked about producers and executives looking for writers with unique perspectives, personalities, and life experiences? This is when that starts to be important. Brilliant writing often comes from experience, and showrunners want to hire writers whose experiences match the stories being told on the show. That doesn't mean *Heroes* writers need to have superpowers or know what it's like to save the world. But it does mean they need to understand, share in, and articulate what those characters are going through emotionally. So it's crucial to be open and vocal about yourself, your life, and your experiences; showrunners want writers who are willing to bring these things to the table as the room brainstorms characters and stories.

"If you're not a person who likes to interact with others," says Goddard, "television is not for you. Most writers . . . like to be alone with their pad and pen, which is the exact opposite of writing for television. Half the job is writing, the other half is interacting with human beings."

As the room begins beating out stories, great attention is paid to a new show's first episodes, as they're critical in amassing an audience. In fact, "some people say the first thirteen episodes are the pilot [and] should, in different ways, retell the premise," says Chase.

This helps "someone finding the show on episode three or four enjoy the show, as opposed to being confused," adds Kevin Plunkett, ABC's VP of current comedy programming. "You may have missed the premiere, but a friend tells you, 'I saw this great show, *Carpoolers*. You should check it out.' [So] we reset the show [each episode]: what's the show about? What are the key relationships? Give some insight on the backstory of our main characters."

Once the showrunner has assigned the first episodes, the staff goes in order, breaking each story in detail. To **break a story,** the showrunner divides one of the whiteboards into acts. Half-hour shows usually have a teaser with two or three acts; hours have a teaser with four or five. Much like beating out a season, the staff looks at where each character begins, where he ends up, and steps required to get there.

"We often go character by character," says *24* writer Matt Michnovetz. "Jack does this, CTU does this, the President does this. 'What do we need to happen? What kind of drama do we want to take the characters into? Where are we taking Jack [both emotionally and physically], and how does that relate to other characters?' Then we break those beats into acts and come up with an act outline."

It often takes close to a week to fully break a story. While this may seem like a long time, the room is juggling countless other duties and distractions: punching up scripts, rewriting outlines, dealing with network notes on previous episodes. Finally the staff completes a beat sheet, or cursory outline. They then expand these beats into detailed scenes. Sometimes the assigned writer does this alone; other times the staff helps. A complete out-line's level of detail may vary from one showrunner to another. Some showrunners like short, terse outlines of four or five pages. Others like more in-depth outlines—say, twenty or twenty-five pages. Once the showrunner okays the outline, it's sent up the ladder for studio and network approval.

TALK THE TALK: SITCOM JARGON

Succeeding in the writers' room means being able to communicate with your fellow writers. Like all jobs, writers often have their own vernacular. Here's some of the specialized sitcom lingo that comedy writers use in the writers' room.

A-side or B-side: Before or after a particular moment in a story. Imagine Blair has a big revelation in a scene of *Gossip Girl* and writers are debating whether to put it before or after Chuck's snide come-on. The writers will discuss whether to put the revelation on the *A-side* or *B-side* or Chuck's wisecrack.

Callback: A joke or line referring to a previous joke or line. In "Nice in White Satin," a sixth-season episode of *Will & Grace,* Will takes Karen to the doctor. As her exam begins, Dr. Hershberg (played by Jack Black) asks Will to leave the room. Will insists on staying, saying, "I'm her attorney, which makes me a lawyer, which is just as good, no matter what my parents say." Later, Dr. Hershberg tells Will he attended Harvard. "I went to Columbia," says Will, "which is just as good, no matter what my parents say." This line—"which is just as good, no matter what my parents say"—calls back to the earlier joke.

Clam: A joke that's been pitched or used so many times it's old and clichéd. Most writers would probably agree that "Talk to the hand" or "You had me at hello" have become "clammy."

House number: A bad example, used solely to explain a joke or story beat. Perhaps Barney has a new girlfriend on *How I Met Your Mother,* and the story ends with a revelation that will prevent him from being able to date her again. You're not sure what that right revelation is, but the "house number" might be suggesting he discover she's his long-lost half sister. It's not quite the best beat or the right answer, but it explains how the moment should work.

Nakamura: A joke that gets called back over and over . . . and is never funny. No one's sure exactly *where* the term comes from (I've heard *Taxi, Happy Days,* and *The Bob Newhart Show*), but it supposedly originates from a guest character named "Mr. Nakamura." Apparently, this name was supposed to be hilarious. It wasn't, but other characters kept "calling back" to the name, repeating "Mr. Nakamura," "Mr. Nakamura," as if it were the funniest thing in the world, and each time it only got *less* funny.

Schmuck bait: False jeopardy, a piece of information used to raise stakes that clearly can't come to pass. In season one's "Cleveland" episode of *30 Rock,* Liz tells Jack she's thinking of moving to Cleveland. Obviously, the series' main character can't move away from the show, so this is "schmuck bait," a threat that can never actually happen (and the show acknowledged this by having Liz standing before a ramshackle bait shop called Schmuck's Bait).

GOING TO SCRIPT

When a writer "goes to script," he leaves the room and writes the **writer's draft.** Sometimes he writes in his office. Sometimes he writes from home. He can write anywhere he wants, as long as he meets his deadline. He may have a week or ten days to finish his script, or if the show's running behind, only two or three days.

"WRITTEN BY" VS. "STORY BY"

Whenever a writer writes a script, or **teleplay,** for a particular episode, he gets a "Written By" credit in addition to his official title. If a writer creates *only* the story idea for an episode, not the actual script, he gets only a "Story By" credit. The actual writer then gets a "Teleplay By" credit. You can always spot "Story By," "Teleplay By," or "Written By" credits at the beginning of a TV show.

Writing your first script can be a daunting experience. The stakes are high. You want to do a great job. It's easy to go wrong.

"On my first script," says Michnovetz, "[all the other writers] were off writing, so I worked with whoever was available. A couple of guys sat me down and we broke it out. It was an episode where Jack rescued his girlfriend and the Secretary of Defense from terrorists. I pitched my ideas and they were terrible. [The writers] gave me an idea to run with . . . and I took a week and a half and poured my guts into it. When I came back, it was awful. Maybe one or two people read it, and everyone else . . . they didn't even need to read it. There was no point. Plus, by the time we got around to rebreaking it—and I had already rebroken it twice—the previous episodes had changed entirely. So my entire previous writer's draft became the first act, and the rest of the episode became a new threat. I was lucky to get in *any* of my own writing. But it was my first assignment, and it's incredibly difficult."

(Fortunately for Michnovetz, his script, "Day 4: 12:00 p.m.–1:00 p.m.," *did* turn out okay—and he ended up spending the next two years writing on *24*.)

Once the writer's first draft is done, the showrunner reads and gives notes. The writer makes changes, then distributes it to the rest of the staff for other notes and suggestions.

"No one ever hands in a perfect script," says Wright, which is why "[early] drafts are distributed just to the writing staff, not the production office. Everyone reads, then gathers to discuss what needs to be fixed. Those changes are [often] made that same day."

THE WRITER'S GUIDE TO WRITING YOUR FIRST SCRIPT

A staff writer's first episode assignment can be an intimidating moment, and nobody knows this better than former *Sex & the City* writers Cindy Chupack and Aury Wallington, who are here to offer a few helpful tips on acing that first script—and making it to your second.

AS SOON AS YOU GET THE ASSIGNMENT . . .

CINDY: Have your laptop in the room for all discussions of your episode. Don't expect a writers' assistant to take your notes for you. They might miss something great! And, if a higher-level writer is pitching a riff that could go into your episode, get it down *word for word*, because you can bet somebody will be expecting to see that, if not in the outline, in the script.

STRAYING FROM THE OUTLINE THAT WAS BEATEN OUT IN THE ROOM . . .

CINDY: Some baby writers feel it's cheating to turn in jokes and scenes that have been spoon-fed to them, but even if the whole episode is given to you beat for beat, it still takes skill to put it together and make a great script. So don't stray from what was pitched in the room. Instead, try to capture all the fun and spirit, then make it sparkle.

AURY: You can't change actual story beats when you're writing a script. If there's a hole or a gap, [don't] try to figure it out yourself. Knock on the door of one of the executive producers or let the other writers know and they will help you solve it. You shouldn't try to figure it out on your own, because what you do may not be what the showrunner wants.

REWRITES

Every script—and I mean *every* script—gets rewritten.

"It's not a slap in the face," says story editor Aury Wallington, "it's just the way TV works. Scripts go through a zillion permutations."

Yet *how* a script gets rewritten depends on the type of show. Dramas are usually rewritten by the episode's writer, who gathers notes from the showrunner or staff, then goes off to make changes. Comedies are rewritten by the entire room, which rewrites scene-by-scene as a group, tweaking lines and punching up jokes.

This revamped version, the **studio draft,** is sent to the studio for notes. Based on those notes, the writers do a **network draft,** which gets network notes and another revision. The showrunner then takes one last pass to polish the script's voice and tone. This **shooting draft,** or **production draft,** is handed to the line producer about a week before shooting so the director can begin prepping.

(On an interesting side note: as with pilots, multicamera shows shoot only one night a week, so they're often rewritten every evening until the taping. "Because [multicamera] is such a joke-driven format," says Wright, "rewriting is more last-minute. A joke that was funny at Monday's table read is no longer funny by Friday's shoot. Rewriting usually happens after dinner, so you can end up working till midnight." So even though the director preps all week, there may not be a final shooting draft until the actual day of the shoot.)

STAYING AFLOAT

As the season progresses, the staff continues generating stories, outlines, and scripts to keep production from falling behind. This would be easy if all writers had to do was tell the stories they wanted. But writers balance hundreds of intrusions and diversions affecting the course of the series, from budgetary issues and casting to scheduling and product integration. And it's their job to adapt accordingly. For instance, writers may create a brilliant character, only to discover the actor can't pull it off and their only recourse is to reconceive the character and his scenes. Or they may set a critical scene at a specific location, like a nighttime scene in an abandoned warehouse, only to learn it's not financially feasible to shoot there and they must reset the scene somewhere else—like a swimming pool where they've already scheduled an expensive daytime shoot. Now the staff must figure out how to transplant their creepy warehouse scene to the brightly lit swimming pool.

As the year goes on, staffs often find themselves racing to keep up.

"Usually, you're lucky if the script is done before you're in prep," says co-executive producer Melissa Rosenberg (*Dexter, The O.C., Love Monkey*). "Half the time you're prepping some kind of outline or rough draft."

As the end of the writing season approaches (usually in March for half-hours and April for hours, on a traditional development/production schedule), staffs begin winding down and preparing for hiatus, the period between the end of one writing season and the beginning of the next. Showrunners may meet with network and studio execs to discuss arcs and storylines for next season, especially if they need to plant seeds for new stories in the season finale. If the show's not guaranteed to return, writers may lobby the network and discuss what can be done to ensure survival.

Once the season is over, the entire staff goes on hiatus. Most hiatuses last four to twelve weeks, depending on when the show must be back in production. Many writers use this time to write new specs or original material. Some produce a pilot or do **punch-up,** helping fellow writers tweak and rewrite their pilots, as discussed in chapter 10. Others take vacations. But most writers make sure they're back by mid-April to take meetings for staffing season, hoping they have a job when June rolls around, either on their old show or another one, and the whole cycle begins again.

Fortunately, getting your second job is rarely as difficult as getting your first.

"The first job is the hardest," says Lesley Wake-Webster, "because one of the main things people rely on is calling other writers who have worked with you. You can only figure out so much in an interview. Everyone's got their game face on, everyone's on their best behavior. You can read someone's spec script, but you don't know how many people helped them. So one of the few things you can rely on is calling another writer who was in the room with that person and asking, 'How is this person *really*?' If you haven't worked on a staff, it's harder for people to make that call. I've actually heard people say you need to get the *second* job before you can breathe a sigh of relief."

THE WRITERS' ROOM SURVIVAL GUIDE

Your first time in a writers' room can be an intimidating experience. The good news is, every writer in television has gone through it. So we've rounded up a few veteran writers (and one exec) to answer some baby writers' questions about staying afloat in the writers' room.

It's my first day on staff. Should I go in with stories and ideas to pitch?

"I've had showrunners say 'Come in with four storylines' and I've had showrunners not say anything. I always go in with at least three storylines, whether or not [I actually] pitch them."

—Aury Wallington, story editor (*Veronica Mars, Courting Alex*)

I know writers' rooms can be extremely political. What's the best way to navigate writers'-room politics?

"Keep your head down. Don't come into a show thinking you're going to save the show or fix the show. Push in whatever direction you're asked to push. [And] don't hang out with other writers complaining about other writers."

—Jane Espenson, co-executive producer (*Battlestar Galactica, Gilmore Girls*)

If I have notes or suggestions on someone else's script or idea, should I offer those up?

"If you're going to point out problems in a script or a pitch, be ready with a solution or alternative. If I don't like where a story is headed, rather than spending time explaining what I don't like, which can sound negative and not supportive, I find it useful to say, 'Maybe it would be interesting if so-and-so did x instead.' Just cut to an idea you like better."

—Cindy Chupack, executive producer (*Sex & the City, Men in Trees, Everybody Loves Raymond*)

Will I get fired if the showrunner never uses any of my jokes or ideas? How many pitches should I expect to get in the script?

"One of the hardest things about being a comedy writer, period, is learning that nine out of ten jokes you pitch are not going to go over. Even the best comedy writers, if you

continued

look at what they pitch in a room versus what they get in a script—maybe people who are really amazing get four or five out of ten things in a script. But for most of us competent working professionals, it's one or two things out of ten."

—Lesley Wake-Webster, producer (*Notes from the Underbelly, Kitchen Confidential*)

How can I best position myself to get good writing assignments?

"[When I first started,] I said, 'If my bosses are here working, I'm going to be here, even if there's nothing to do—just in case they need me.' Several times they'd come out at 9:00 p.m. and say, 'What are you still doing here?' And I'd say, 'I'm just here in case you need me.' They'd look at me like I was crazy, then they'd say, 'But come to think of it, I could use some help with this. Will you do this scene?' And they start giving you more just because you're there and willing to do it."

—Drew Goddard, co-executive producer (*Lost, Alias, Buffy the Vampire Slayer*)

What's the best way to deal with network or studio notes I disagree with?

"If I'm [reading a script] for the first time, why am I any different from a viewer who's watching it for the first time? If I have a reaction, and my colleague has the same reaction, and someone at the network has the same reaction, we can't all be wrong; it's just opinion and instinct. We're more than happy to have a writer say, 'You're not right and here's why,' or 'Here's how I'm going to address it,' but to just shoot down a note is a narrow way of looking at it. [Learn] the phrase, 'We'll take a look at that.' "

—Dana Shelburne, VP of comedy development, 20th Century Fox Television

---

THIS SUDS FOR YOU: WRITING FOR DAYTIME SOAP OPERAS

Ever since Procter & Gamble first transplanted the soap genre from radio to television with 1950's *The First Hundred Years,* daily serials like *Guiding Light* and *As the World Turns* have been a staple of daytime programming—until recently. As cable networks and daytime talk shows have grown in popularity, soap operas have watched in a cold sweat as audiences trickled away (viewership dropped 41 percent between 1999 and 2006). This, coupled with the influx of more women in the workforce, has eroded soaps' Nielsen ratings and ad revenue.

Still, millions of people continue tuning in to classics like *Days of Our Lives* and *The Bold and the Beautiful,* which means these programs continue needing talented writers. Of course, because daytime soaps are **stripped,** or air every day, their writers' rooms have their own unique rules and processes, quite different from those in the primetime world.

How do writers' rooms on daytime soap operas differ from writers' rooms on primetime scripted shows?

"The difference with writing [on daytime soaps] is it's both continual and very first-draft-oriented," says head writer Christopher Whitesell (*One Life to Live, Sunset Beach*). "Unlike in nighttime, where almost every show has hiatus, daytime doesn't, [so] you have to get it right the first time. That's not to say there aren't rewrites and corrections, [but] you can't fall too far behind."

Most soaps have staffs of ten to fifteen people: the **head writer** or co-head writers organize the room and supervise the storytelling process, three or four **breakdown writers** specialize in detailed episode outlines, and about five **scriptwriters** use those **breakdowns** to write actual scripts.

At the beginning of the writing cycle (which could happen any day of the week, but for the sake of simplicity we'll say it's Monday), head writers and breakdown writers spend a day or two "laying out" the story **thrust,** the series' direction for the next couple of weeks. They then dissect the thrust into individual episodes, which breakdown writers write as **breakdowns,** thirteen-to-twenty-page outlines describing each scene of an episode. At the end of the week, the breakdowns are sent to the head writers and network execs to be read over the weekend.

On Monday, execs give breakdown notes and the writers rewrite. Once each breakdown is approved, it's sent to a scriptwriter, who has one week to transform it into an actual script. Scriptwriters can work from anywhere: home, a different city, a hotel room, or a Swiss chalet (some rarely even come to the writers' room). When their script is finished, they e-mail it to an editor, who checks for **continuity,** making sure dialogue and events are consistent with other episodes. If the script is approved, it goes into preproduction, to be shot about two weeks later. The entire process, from idea to script to shooting, takes about four weeks, far less time than that of most primetime dramas.

How should an aspiring soap writer start a career?

As with primetime shows, many soap writers are hired by people they know. So unless you have an uncle who's an exec or a sister who's a head writer, the best path is to land a gig as a writers' assistant or PA, where you can learn from writers above you. "Many head writers, breakdown writers, and scriptwriters have started that way," says Whitesell. "If you're the writers' assistant or production assistant . . . and you've been writing, have ideas, and know the characters and voices, you're more likely to make a good impact."

Do baby soap writers need writing samples and spec scripts?

Absolutely. Whitesell suggests using plays, screenplays, or even novels—"things that show you have a command of dialogue, characters, structure, plot." Unlike

continued

primetime, however, soap writers rarely write **spec scripts,** sample episodes of current series (we'll talk more about specs in chapter 21). "You don't have to have written what would be a great *All My Children* episode," Whitesell says. "Daytime is so fluid and quick, those things don't usually work."

What about writers who have ideas for new soap operas? Where are the best places to pitch and sell new soap ideas?

Because soap viewership has been declining, it's tough—if not impossible—to sell a daytime soap in today's TV marketplace. But that doesn't mean networks and studios aren't experimenting in other arenas. "Think in terms of alternative media," suggests Whitesell. In 2007, NBC debuted its Internet soap *Coastal Dreams* at NBC.com. SoapNet, which strips daytime soap reruns during its primetime daypart, introduced *General Hospital: Night Shift,* a spinoff of ABC's long-running serial. And Procter & Gamble, soaps' founding father, launched *Crescent Heights* online to help sell Tide laundry detergent. "The medium is changing," Whitesell says. "The form is evolving."

16

Production

....

Forty-five seconds doesn't seem like a long time.

Unless you're Anya Adams, first assistant director of *CSI: Miami,* and you're attempting to get a forty-five-second shot of an AVP volleyball tournament. (Not a real tournament, of course; the entire thing has been re-created for the show—except for Misty May, who's actually there.) Your duty is to make sure everyone on the crew does his or her job, two hundred extras perform as they're told, and there's not a single outside interruption, from an airplane overhead to a passerby in the background. One misstep costs valuable time and thousands of dollars—*and is completely your fault.*

"To choreograph all that can be a huge, huge challenge," says Adams. "You only get one or two chances, and if you don't get it, you have to move on."

These are the kinds of challenges a production staff and crew tackle on a daily basis. So as writers begin writing, the rest of the show is preparing for the chaos and excitement of producing a full TV series. And though basic production processes don't change much from pilot to series, there are two new important challenges affecting every aspect of the show: less time and less money.

"We usually ask shows to deliver at least ten episodes in a row," says Eric Kim, former vice president of current at the CW (which folded its current department into its drama deparment in 2008). "So if you premiere in

September, we want enough episodes to air from the launch through the end of November sweeps."

Thus, series have relatively little time to film each episode. Multicams still shoot in one night (just like their pilots), but half-hour single-cams shoot over five or six days (as opposed to seven to ten for pilots), and hours shoot over seven or eight (as opposed to ten or fifteen for pilots). Shows also work on multiple episodes simultaneously. At any given time, one episode's in prep, one episode's shooting, and several are in different stages of post (not to mention the various episodes being broken, outlined, and written in the writers' room).

Episodes also have much less money than pilots. Because pilots are ultimately selling tools designed to woo executives, studios invest many more millions of dollars into pilot production (like the $7.5 million NBC pumped into 2007's *Bionic Woman*, which lasted less than a single season). "The line you hear all the time is 'We want this to look like a feature,' " says TV director Steve Love. "And when you spend eight million dollars for a pilot, you're spending feature money. The trick is [re-creating] it on a much smaller scale once the series goes."

A smaller scale means smaller budgets for every deparament, but producers have ways of making the most of the cash they have. For one thing, shorter shoots cost less money. Hiring a crew can cost nearly $100,000 per day, so shrinking principal photography saves thousands of dollars. Second, pilots tend to hire expensive directors—either experienced pilot directors or high-profile film directors. In series, however, directors are simply hired to keep a rolling stone rolling, and are often less expensive than pilot directors. Some direct a handful of episodes; others direct one episode and leave. Many never even stay to see their final cut.

Finally, series amortize costs in ways pilots can't. "When you do a pilot, all costs are going toward that pilot," says line producer Mark Ovitz (*October Road, Karen Sisco*). "When you do a series, you get ordered, say, twelve more. So all of a sudden you have costs you can divide by twelve: set construction, set decoration, props, wardrobe, hair and makeup supplies, grip and electric supplies, lighting, stage space, office rent. It all gets amortized. Also, your cast gets more money for a pilot—double what they get for an episode. They get double because there has to be a holding fee to carry them long enough to get the show ordered and keep them off the market."

GETTING STARTED

Production on a series begins with the line producer hiring the production staff and crew: director of photography, production designer, costumer designer, etc. Often, workers from the pilot return for the series, but sometimes the same people are no longer available and new people must be found.

The showrunner and line producer then reevaluate the pilot, discussing what worked, what didn't, what needs to be changed creatively and practically. Based on these decisions, they begin making other choices. Will the series be shot on film or HD? How many days will each episode shoot? Is the visual look of the series the same as the pilot?

At this point, they also take the crucial step of locking in a production schedule. This helps both writers and production staff stay on track. For a single-camera camera show slated to premiere in September, writers usually need to finish their first script by the end of June. If everything's on schedule, the first episode begins prepping in late June or early July, and shooting begins three to five weeks later (sitcoms prep in mid-July for an early-August shoot). If production or writers fall behind, the show's already in danger of not meeting its air date.

"Once cameras start rolling," says showrunner Jeff Melvoin (*Alias, Army Wives*), "every seven or eight working days you need a new working script. So before the first episode is filmed, you want to have at least four or five shows in some form of being written. If you don't, you'll get behind so fast that you're just reacting to the clock and calendar—and that's not where the best creativity is done. If there's a mantra about making a television show, it's: 'Quality scripts on time,' and both those things have to be satisfied in order to have a long-running, successful series."

As shooting begins on a series, the day-to-day processes are mostly the same as on a pilot. There are, however, some important production differences between multicams and single-cams.

MULTICAMERA PRODUCTION

Sitcom episodes, like pilots, shoot on a stage, all in one evening. Most shoot every Friday and use the preceding week to prep (pilots, remember, get several weeks). Unlike single-cams, however, many sitcoms take a shooting hiatus every fourth week.

"[We're] giving writers time to take a breath and catch up," says Ovitz. "They're rewriting, every day, what they're shooting that week, so they don't have much time to get ready for the next couple weeks. So they get behind after their initial prep of eight weeks, whereas with dramas, you're not rewriting every day."

The week of multicamera prep begins with a Monday morning production meeting, where department heads gather to discuss practical issues of that week's show. Do they need to build new sets? Are there night scenes? Location shoots? Special props or costumes?

An hour after the production meeting comes the table read. This is the first time the script's been read aloud, so network, studio, and production company executives often have notes for the writers and director. Writers then head off to rewrite, actors block and rehearse on stage, and the production staff implements decisions made during the production meeting. (On rare, unfortunate occasions, the table read goes so horribly that the network demands the script get entirely rewritten. In such cases, actors are sent home—what's the point of rehearsing?—and writers scramble to rewrite the entire story.)

On Tuesday morning, actors rehearse new pages put out by the writers office. (As on a pilot, the script gets rewritten on a daily basis.) If the show's schedule is tight, writers continue rewriting even as actors memorize revisions; if the show's running on schedule, writers use the morning to break future episodes. In the afternoon, current execs from the studio and production company arrive for a studio run-through, which generates more notes and rewrites.

This process repeats on Wednesday, culminating in the network run-through. While the studio run-through is fairly low-key, Wednesday's run-through has much higher stakes.

"The network is the boss," says Lesley Wake-Webster, who's written on both multicamera (*What I Like About You*) and single-camera (*Notes from the Underbelly*) shows. "They're the ones who can throw a story out or say, 'We're not airing this unless you change it.' So actors wear makeup and nicer clothes, and they have important props. It's in everyone's interest that Wednesday's run-through goes well. If it doesn't, writers are there late, rewriting."

Thursday and Friday are packed with intense rehearsals, preshoots, and locking camera movements. Writers continue to grind out new pages. Actors hone performances and incorporate new lines and jokes.

Friday's taping itself usually begins at 6:00 p.m. and lasts until 10:00 or 11:00 p.m. As on a pilot, the writing staff watches from the stage, scribbling jokes throughout the show. After the audience leaves, actors shoot pickup, retakes, and new lines.

On Monday the episode enters postproduction and a new episode begins prepping. Post on a multicamera episode usually lasts about three weeks, with three episodes going through post at a time. Thus, the cycle continues: one episode prepping and shooting while others progress through post.

Because multicams prep and shoot in the same week, some—unlike single-cams—are able to use the same director week after week. James Burrows directed entire seasons of *Will & Grace*. Gil Junger directed much of the first season of *According to Jim*. Single-camera shows, however, work a bit differently. . . .

SINGLE-CAMERA PRODUCTION

Unlike multicams, single-camera comedies and dramas can't use only one director. That's because they shoot every day, with no downtime between episodes. One episode shoots as the next preps. When one wraps, the next begins, sometimes even the same day.

As a result, single-camera shows must alternate directors. Some use many each season; others have a rotating staff of two or three. They also have more than one assistant director, so while one AD/director team shoots, another preps its episode.

Single-camera prep begins about a week before the shoot with a production meeting and table read. Because actors are shooting all day, the table read takes place during lunch, so actors can read as they eat.

Single-camera prep also may begin with a **tone meeting,** where the showrunner and director discuss the tone and nuances of the script.

"The first tone meeting I ever had was with John Wells for *ER,*" says director Barnet Kellman (*Murhpy Brown, Alias, Samantha Who?*): "We sat in the same room and started turning pages of the script. He'd mention the issues on each page—'This is what I see happening,' 'Make sure this woman isn't too shrill.' It gives the writer, the executive producer, a chance to communicate to the guest director '[Here's] what our company is like, what my concerns are with a given actor, what I love about that actor and what I don't love.' "

Preproduction unfolds much as it did during the pilot, the main difference being that the showrunner, who was involved and available during the pilot, is now bouncing back and forth between the writers' room, the production office, the stage, and post.

As in the pilot, the first day an episode begins shooting starts as early as possible, usually with on-location exteriors. As the week progresses, days slide later and the shoot moves inside for night scenes and interiors. The on-set process is also the same as pilots: actors rehearse a scene, the crew sets up lights and cameras while actors finish their makeup, the scene is filmed in a series of shots and setups.

Unlike on a sitcom, the writing staff doesn't stay on stage during the shoot. The showrunner, or the episode's writer, may be there to answer questions from the director or actors, but that's it. The rest of the staff remains in the writers' room, beating out stories and working on future episodes.

The main obstacle on a single-camera series is the time crunch. Because there's so much less time, production is a constant race to stay on schedule. Shows must shoot five or six pages a day to stay on target. Yet it's not the page count itself that makes things difficult.

"It's the number of camera setups," says Lesley Wake-Webster. "You could write a scene where people are just talking to each other, and that might be only a couple camera setups if you're in a park, shooting from a couple of camera angles. But if you have characters walk through a house and into the street, you're looking at a bunch of camera setups. You have to think about who's in the background, how much coverage you need. And if you do a shot where you widen to reveal, or reverse, you're adding camera setups. Camera setups equal time, so that's one of the things your showrunner and director talk about in the production meeting. 'Is this joke worth it? Do we want to take the hour it takes to shoot this reveal?' Sometimes the answer's yes. Sometimes it's no."

When an episode wraps principal photography, it goes immediately into postproduction. Another episode takes its place in production and another begins prep. So there's not only a constant flow of episodes, but most departments are working on multiple episodes at the same time. Wardrobe deals with this week's clothes while preparing next week's. Set dressing readies everything for today's shoot while putting together tomorrow's. Post, the longest of the three processes, juggles three or four episodes at one time.

As days go on, shows get into a groove. Although this eases the production process, it's still a struggle to stay on schedule and turn in quality work week after week. By the end of the season, many shows are delivering episodes only a day or two before airing.

Once an episode's final network version has been completed, a PA delivers two digital D5 videotapes, a master and a backup, to the network. First, Standards and Practices makes sure the episode contains no objectionable content that could incur a fine from the FCC. Next, quality control checks to make sure the tapes meet the network's technical specs. Is the sound at the right levels? Does the color look right? Finally, the network adds closed captioning and **bumpers,** the promotional intros and outros leading into and out of commercial breaks. The show is now ready to be aired. Except for one problem: shows aren't aired from Los Angeles, where most series are actually made. So the network's L.A. headquarters uplinks the episode via satellite to broadcast headquarters in New York. (They also FedEx a D5 videotape as backup, just in case something goes wrong.) The episode is then uploaded into a computer, which satellites use to send the program to the network's local stations at the scheduled airtime. Affiliates then downlink the show and broadcast it live over local radio waves to TV sets in viewers' homes. Local stations also transmit their content to cable headends, which deliver it via wires into subscribers' homes. At commercial breaks, broadcast headquarters inserts national ads (which have been sold and arranged by the network's ad sales department, as we discussed in chapter 13), while local stations insert local ads.

(Eventually, once bandwidth becomes faster and cheaper, this will be all done via the Internet. But for now, satellites are the most economical way.)

"The interesting thing," says post supervisor Paul Rabwin, is "there are often glitches and quirks that happen at the local level. There might be a sync problem. Or a color that's washed out. And not only does [the show] get broadcast a little differently in different cities, but everyone's television is calibrated a little differently. So the big irony and paradox is that we spend many dollars and a great amount of time fine-tuning shows, getting the exact color, exact sound, everything perfect—and there are a thousand different interpretations. The common denominator isn't as high-quality as the product we deliver."

ONE-ON-ONE WITH MARSH MCCALL, EXECUTIVE PRODUCER (*CARPOOLERS, TWENTY GOOD YEARS, JUST SHOOT ME!*)

Single-cam and multicam shows obviously work differently—but how do these differences affect writers and storytelling? We spent a few minutes with show-runner Marsh McCall, who has worked on multicamera shows, like *Just Shoot Me!,* and single-camera shows, like *Carpoolers,* to find some answers.

On a single-camera comedy, you have the freedom to leave the stage, shoot on location, do special effects. How does this affect how writers approach comedy and storytelling?

"In single-camera, budget and time allowing, many more things are possible. You're shooting a little movie every week . . . [so] it's important to think visually and not just verbally, maybe even more so. You also have to learn to trust your instincts, because there's no audience telling you what's funny."

On multicamera sitcoms, you're basically confined to a stage. Is this restrictive? Does it make writers' jobs harder?

"The thing about multicamera . . . writers grumble about restrictions, but it's also reassuring. You don't bother wondering what you could've done if you could've gone outside and shown the crazy car accident, because you can't. So you skip the part where you wring your hands over how to shoot that, and instead think of the funniest way to have a guy walk in with his coat all dirty saying, 'I just got into a car accident.' "

How does the live audience affect the jokes and comedy of a multicamera show?

"The danger in multicamera is to be a whore to the audience. You hear those laughs, actors do things more physically on stage, and perhaps it gets a little over the top because the audience in the bleachers loves it. But you're not shooting the show for those two hundred people; they're the prop. You're shooting for the audience at home, and what plays to people [in the bleachers] might seem over-the-top and character-betraying to viewers at home."

17

Staying on the Air

....

Joe Hipps did not like StairMasters. But on this breezy afternoon in late summer 2005, there was nowhere Hipps wanted to be more than right there, at his West L.A. gym . . . *on a StairMaster.* Because Hipps was staring out the window at the coolest thing he'd ever seen: a massive *Prison Break* billboard looming over Bundy Drive.

"There were people next to me," Hipps says, "and in that cheesy Hollywood way, you want to say, 'Hey, I was involved with coming up with the concept of that.' "

Hipps was director of development at Original Television, a small television production company at 20th Century Fox. Original had had two programs on the air so far: *Tru Calling,* FOX's short-lived time-travel drama, and *Point Pleasant,* a teen/horror series that barely lasted six weeks.

But this time everything was different, because Fox president Peter Liguori, who came from a marketing background, loved *Prison Break.*

"Billboards, marketing, radio ads, commercials," says Hipps. FOX made "sure everyone in major markets knew the show was premiering. It was the first time I actually saw that."

FOX's efforts paid off. When *Prison Break* debuted on August 29, 2005, it garnered a 6.8/11 (Nielsen rating/share) and became the third-most-watched scripted show that week, behind *CSI: Miami* and *Two and a Half Men.*

"Every time you have a show on," says Hipps, "you e-mail all your friends and family: 'Hey, we have a show on—check it out!' With *Prison Break* . . . people were already calling to tell me they watched. It was the first time I realized that if you promote a show, and promote it well, people will tune in."

Of course, launching a new show involves more than pasting up billboards. It's a coordinated effort between networks and studios' marketing, promotions, and scheduling departments. And though most shows premiere in the fall, networks often begin planning weeks earlier, even before they know what shows are picked up.

"As pilots come in [each May]," says Michael Benson, ABC's executive vice president of marketing, "we watch them and immediately think about how we're going to package them and sell them in the upfronts. You start to define the sellable elements, bring those things out, and put them into a trailer. We also develop key art for a lot of the shows that come in. Then the ones that aren't picked up, we stop working on."

Once new series have been picked up, usually in early May, just before upfronts, the network begins strategizing their launches. Blueprinting a premiere begins when the scheduling department determines when the show should begin. As we discussed in chapter 4, they look at holes in the schedule, returning programs, and competition from other networks. Though most series begin in the fall, some have better shots at success by debuting at other times. Many networks have started to air shows at midseason, in winter or early spring. This is a popular time for "smaller," offbeat shows, like ABC's *Miss Guided,* or serialized shows like *24* and *Lost,* which often air entire seasons without interruption. Broadcast networks have even started using summer, a time previously reserved for scripted reruns, to kick off high-concept reality series like *Kid Nation* or *High School Musical: Get in the Picture;* cablers use it to launch high-profile scripted fare like USA's *In Plain Sight* and TNT's *Saving Grace.*

As soon as scheduling cements the schedule, it forwards this info to the network and studios' current departments, which coordinate all the producers and departments working to keep shows on the air.

"Current needs to know when we're expecting delivery of shows for premieres," says Preston Beckman, FOX's executive vice president of strategic program planning and research. Meanwhile, "press and publicity [tell] current when they need to get shows to critics [which is usually about four weeks before the premiere]. Generally, especially with a new show, press will want two episodes, not just one. Most critics are skeptical of pilots because of the money spent, so the second episode reflects what the show's going to be."

Publicity also works to get shows' stars in fall preview sections of pop-culture publications like *TV Guide* and *Rolling Stone,* as well as on magazine shows like *Entertainment Tonight* or talk shows like *Jimmy Kimmel Live!*

Meanwhile, the marketing department pays for print, radio, billboards, and online campaigns. It also works with advertisers who could have tie-ins or promotions on certain shows. Some marketing campaigns take place on the national level; others are coordinated locally through the network's O&Os and affiliates.

The network's promo department is also in high gear, creating on-air spots to steer viewers to new shows. "The most valuable resource we have is on-air promotion," says Benson. "It's the number-one thing that drives people to watch our shows."

Because every thirty minutes of television contain about eight minutes of commercial time, networks usually sell six to advertisers and keep two for themselves. The network often retains the **bookends,** one-minute positions on either side of the commercial break. These are the most valuable spots in the break because audience drop-off is at its lowest (leaving the show and heading back into the show). The network then uses the bookends to promote itself and its programs. (Research has shown that even when watching shows recorded on a DVR, more than 60 percent of viewers watch the first bookend, then fast-forward through the rest of the pod, reinforcing the value of bookends.)

There are three main types of on-air promos: branding, **tune-ins,** and **episodics.**

Branding spots promote the network itself. Unrelated to any show, they simply reinforce the network's brand. MTV's famous "moonman" spot, for instance, has nothing to with its shows; it simply pounds home the uniqueness of MTV. Tune-ins promote one-time **tentpole** events like series premieres, finales, the Oscars, or the Super Bowl. And episodics tease storylines from upcoming episodes. For example, "in the premiere of a show," says Gaurav Misra, VP of Programming at MTV, "we'll take the first bookend and tease next week's episode. We'll do it two or three times during that half hour. [So] everything is driving to the episode next week," bringing audiences back over and over.

As various promo campaigns gather steam over the summer, shows themselves are chest-deep in production. Writers break stories. Line producers manage physical production. Post supervisors refine editing processes. And supervising everything and everyone, from promos to production, is the network's president of entertainment, who's also in the middle of overseeing the summer's freshly started development season.

Finally, at long last, comes the moment everyone's been racing toward: the premiere. The night when, all across America, viewers have their first chance to see the new show.

Of course, while this may be a big night for the series itself, it's barely a blip on the radar for writers, crew members, actors, and executives who have been living with the show for several months.

"Usually, the writers . . . all get together at someone's house," says writer-producer Lesley Wake-Webster (*Notes from the Underbelly, What I Like About You, That '80s Show*). "You watch the episode as it airs, even though you've already seen it. You watch the commercials and discuss: 'We have a car commercial—that's good! It means men eighteen to forty-nine are watching!' It's a fun, nervous energy. At the moment it's airing, there's nothing you can do except watch. The hand-wringing is the next morning as you wait to find out the Nielsen ratings."

The morning after the premiere, execs and showrunners wake early to check ratings. They look not just at their own show's numbers, but at how their numbers compare with other programs'. Did the premiere hold its lead-in's viewers? Did it find its desired demographic? Did it improve its time slot's ratings from the last show there? And how did the premiere hold up against other networks' shows at the same time?

Occasionally a pilot will debut as an instant hit, like 2004's *Desperate Housewives*. But these cases are few and far between. It's more likely that a show will be an instant flop—as when ABC's highly promoted *Emily's Reasons Why Not* premiered in 2006 to a 2.8 Nielsen rating among adults 18–49. Or when FOX's *Anchorwoman* debuted the next year with a miserable 1.0. Both shows were canceled after a single airing.

Most programs take a few weeks to find their audiences, and many shows, even successful ones, drop off a bit in their second week, so programmers watch to see how they perform during their third, fourth, and fifth airings. If a show holds its ratings or grows, producers and execs are ecstatic, but it's not always easy to determine what constitutes success.

"When I started in the business [in 1980]," says Beckman, "you were canceled if you went under a 30 share of households. Now the biggest shows on TV, like *CSI* and *American Idol,* get around a 25 share. At some point, maybe a 15 share of 18–49 viewers will be considered a hit."

Networks are also learning to evaluate shows' success based on measurements other than traditional TV ratings. Executives at the CW, for example, were disappointed when *Gossip Girl* premiered on September 19, 2007, to only 3.5 million viewers. But when it quickly became the number-one downloaded show on iTunes and viewers streamed it at the CW's website 1,250,000 times over the next month, execs changed their tune, giving it broadcast television's first full-season order of the year.

GETTING LUCKY

Remember when we talked about how studios lose money by deficit-financing every show they produce? (If you don't, reread chapter 2.) Well, a show's license fee *does* grow a bit each year—just enough to cover the rising costs of the annual production budget. But when a show is massively successful, like *24,* a studio may persuade the network to put up a full-cost license fee, covering the entire cost of the show. It often takes five or more seasons for a series to get this lucky, and many never make it that far. But like syndication, getting a full-cost license fee is another landmark moment in the life cycle of a series.

If a show picks up steam from week to week, networks feel good. Most new series begin with thirteen-episode orders. If ratings rise, a network will order the show's **back nine,** making a full season of twenty-two episodes. If a show's ratings continue to sink, people worry.

"There are a lot of things that affect ratings," says Eric Cardinal, senior VP of research at the CW. "If you're in a tough competitive time period, if you've got a lousy lead-in, if you don't have a budget to promote a show . . . there's a bunch of reasons why a show can flag in the ratings, besides being rejected by the audience."

Researchers may discover that audiences don't know when the show is on. If this is the case, marketing and promos create more ads to inform people about the show. Sometimes, a show's overall number may have dropped, but it's growing in certain demographics. Perhaps the show's general audience is shrinking, yet it's attracting women eighteen to thirty-four. Promos and marketing then pump up campaigns geared toward that demographic.

If those tactics don't work, producers and execs look at the content of the show itself, possibly even testing an episode. Are audiences not under-standing specific relationships or storylines? Do they dislike certain charac-ters? (When *Lost* found itself in a ratings tailspin during its 2006–2007 season, writers and execs discovered people were aggravated by its countless characters and unanswered mysteries.) Executives and writers then discuss where storylines are going and whether they can address what's repelling audiences. Unfortunately, when a problem is systemic, it's nearly impossible to make quick fixes.

"By the time you air an episode," say Eric Kim, the CW's former vice president of current, "you've already shot . . . the next four to five episodes, so you can't go back and change things. It costs too much money, and it's physically impossible. You have to air what you have."

Thus, there's little a staff can do to save a dying series. Sometimes they try stunts like killing a regular, giving someone a baby, or having a special guest star. But because there's so much time between concocting an episode and airing it, such tricks rarely work.

"Stunt casting is a big thing networks always think will work," says Lesley Wake-Webster. " 'If you get Tom Hanks, the ratings will go up!' And that never happens. On *That '80s Show,* when our ratings started to decline very early on, [FOX] felt we needed to bring on a character similar to Ash-ton Kutcher on *That '70's Show*—a sexy, dumb guy. So we did. And it did not save the show."

When a series is **"on the bubble,"** perched between survival and cancel-lation, the network weighs the pros and cons of keeping the program alive. Does the show have critical acclaim? Is it growing with a small but faithful demographic? Will it cost more money to cancel than leave on the air?

In fall 2006, for instance, ABC canceled *Six Degrees* after thirteen episodes when it lost 54 percent of its *Grey's Anatomy* lead-in and averaged a 4.2 Nielsen rating among adults 18–49. But when NBC's expensive *Studio 60 on the Sunset Strip,* which the network had acquired only by promising massive penalties, lost 44 percent of its *Heroes* lead-in and mustered a mere 3.4 rating (adults 18–49), it limped along for a full twenty-two episodes. It was more expensive, NBC calculated, to cancel the show and pay penalties than simply air the show and offer make-goods to advertisers. (In fact, NBC killed *Studio 60*'s regular season after its sixteenth episode, then opted to "burn off" the final six episodes, airing them during a slow period the following summer.)

Normally, however, a show's ultimate kiss of death is plummeting ad revenue.

"If we're losing money on the show," says Kim, "if the license fee we're paying is more than the ad money we're bringing in, or we're losing ad revenue because we're giving money back, [the decision] is much more clear-cut."

The decision to deep-six a show comes from only one place: the top. Only a network president can cancel a show, and even he usually needs the approval of the CEO.

Canceling a series is a delicate political process. Once the decision has been made, the network president calls the studio president. One of them breaks the news to the showrunner. Sometimes the show shuts down that very day, or it could be that the show must finish a certain number of episodes, even though everyone knows they'll probably never air.

"Most [writers] don't even decorate their offices because they want to be able to sweep everything off their desk and leave at a moment's notice," says Wake-Webster. "It's a tough business, and chances are really good you're going to be canceled. It definitely is depressing, and generally the day you find out you're canceled, everyone goes out and gets drunk together. The longer you work in TV, the more you realize this is just part of the cycle."

A YEAR IN THE LIFE OF A BROADCAST TV NETWORK

Like a living organism, a television network is a collection of separate sections, each conducting their own functions while synergizing to keep the greater whole alive. We've so far explored each section individually, but the magic of TV happens when they work together. The following chart gives you a bird's-eye view of a typical year in the life of a broadcast network, from development and current to marketing and advertising.

	July	August	September
Development	Development season begins: network/studio retreats; agency begins hearing pitches and acquiring projects.	Networks, studios, production companies, and writers develop concepts, take pitches, sell and buy projects.	Networks build development slates of 100–130 projects.
Scheduling/Research	Schedulers and researchers present development departments with holes and needs for upcoming season.		Fall premieres begin.
Current	Oversee series' story and script development; coordinate fall launch campaigns with marketing and promos.	Oversee series production: guest casting, scripts, etc.	Fall premieres begin; monitor ratings to determine which shows survive and which are canceled.
On-Air Series Production/Writing Staffs	Series' writing staffs working, production offices open; single-camera series production begins.	Multicamera series production begins.	Series in production:
Marketing/Promos	Television Critics Association (TCA) fall press tour in L.A. (networks promote new and returning series to press and media).	Deliver episodes of new series to critics.	Fall premieres begin.
Advertising Sales/Advertisers	Broadcast network upfront buying season.		Fall premieres begin; ad spots are sold on scatter market.

October	November	December
Networks close (stop buying); networks, studios, and production companies work with writers to develop outlines.	Writers "go to script," or begin writing pilot scripts.	Writers deliver first drafts of pilots, get notes, execute rewrites, deliver final drafts to networks just before Christmas.
Research monitors ratings to determine successful and failed shows.	Fall sweeps.	Research monitors ratings.
Oversee series production: guest casting, scripts, etc.		
writing, prepping, producing, posting episodes.		
Monitor shows' ratings to finesse marketing campaigns, target specific demographics, promote special episodes or guest stars, etc.		
Advertisers and media buyers monitor shows' ratings to maintain buys, back out of options, get make-goods, etc. More ad spots are sold on scatter market.		

continued

	January	February	March
Development	Pilot season begins: networks select 20–30 scripts to shoot as pilots.	Pilot production; execs take general meetings with writers for staffing season.	
Scheduling/ Research	Midseason premieres begin.	February sweeps.	Research monitors ratings.
Current	Midseason premieres begin; coordinate midseason launch campaigns with marketing and promos.	Oversee series production: guest casting, scripts, etc.	
On-Air Series Production/ Writing Staffs	Series in production: writing, prepping, producing, posting episodes.		
Marketing/ Promos	Television Critics Association (TCA) winter press tour in L.A. (networks promote new and returning series to press and media).	Midseason premieres continue; marketing and promo departments begin brainstorming upfront and marketing campaigns for potential pilots and series.	
Advertising Sales/ Advertisers	Media buyers confer with networks about shows in development; advertisers and media buyers formulate strategies for upcoming broadcast TV season.	Kids upfronts (Nickelodeon, Disney Channel, etc.); advertisers and media buyers continue strategizing upcoming broadcast TV season.	Cable upfronts; advertisers and media buys continue strategizing upcoming broadcast TV season.

	April	May	June
		Networks receive final pilot cuts, greenlight 4–8 series, broadcast network upfront announcements. Staffing season begins.	Staffing season.
		Schedulers receive new shows from development, strategize new season schedules; May sweeps.	Researchers and schedulers analyze last season, determine new needs and holes.
	Meet with showrunners of returning series to discuss possible story directions for next season.	Broadcast network upfront announcements: new and returning series receive episode orders; staffing season begins.	Staffing season wraps up, writing staffs begin writing, new shows transition from development to current execs.
	Hiatus; staffing general meetings kick into high gear.	New and returning series receive episode orders, begin staffing.	Staffing season wraps up; writing staffs begin writing.
		Finalize campaigns for new and returning fall series.	Marketing promo campaigns begin for fall shows: on-air promos, print, radio, out-of-home, online, talk shows, etc.
		Broadcast upfront announcements; upcoming fall and midseason shows revealed.	Broadcast network upfront buying season begins.

Most of the time, canceled series are dead, never to be seen again. On rare occasions, however, a studio can sell a canceled show to another network. In 2001, when the WB canceled 20th Century Fox's *Roswell,* UPN stepped forward and picked it up. And in 2008, ABC grabbed ahold of NBC's canceled *Scrubs.* On even rarer occasions, canceled shows have been resurrected thanks to rabid audiences and fan buzz. After canceling *Family Guy* in 2003, stellar DVD sales persuaded FOX to bring the series back in 2005. And when CBS nuked *Jericho* in 2007, fans bombarded the network with twenty tons of packaged peanuts (a reference to a line in the season finale), persuading execs to revive the series for seven more episodes.

Still, such cases are anomalies, and most canceled shows never get a second chance.

Canceling a show isn't fun for anyone. Like fans and audiences, producers and executives get attached to favorite stories and characters, and even the best shows run out of steam. The hope, of course, is that the show survives long enough to make it into other windows of its lifespan: broadcast syndication, cable repurposing, or—as TV evolves—broadband and mobile distribution.

PART V

New Frontiers
Where TV Is Headed

Cable

....

John Walson had a problem. It was the spring of 1948, and as owner of the Service Electric Company, Mahoney City, Pennsylvania's local GE appliance store, Walson needed to sell more televisions, the newest appliance craze sweeping America. But nestled amid the hills and mountains of eastern Pennsylvania, Mahoney City was unable to receive TV signals from Philadelphia, the nearest city with broadcast stations. So Walson did the only thing he could think of: he erected an antenna atop New Boston Mountain, smack in the middle of the Alleghenies, thirty miles away. He then ran heavy-duty, twin-lead cable across the thirty miles to TV sets on display in his shop. The antenna, he hoped, would nab signals from Philly's three broadcast stations and transmit them over the wires to sets in Walson's store. It was an unconventional plan, but it was Walson's only hope.

It worked.

It worked so well, in fact, that Walson's customers not only wanted to buy his televisions, they wanted to tap in to his innovative system for delivering pictures. Walson agreed—for a hundred-dollar installation charge and two dollars per month. Little did he know it, but John Walson had just sparked a revolution that would change the world of television—and the way the planet received and consumed information far into the future.

John Walson had invented cable.

Now, over six decades later, cable is still, at its most basic level, a TV distribution system, with more than 65 million households receiving cable (as of 2007). America boasts over 7,000 cable systems, localized networks of viewers receiving content from a **cable operator** (Time-Warner, Cable-vision, Buckeye), and over 500 hundred TV networks producing content solely for cable distribution (Bravo, Sleuth, CMT, etc.). A 2007 Nielsen report calculated that, thanks to cable, the average TV watcher now has 104 traditional TV channels at his immediate disposal.

In fact, the very term "cable network" has become a catchall used to refer to any non-broadcast TV distributor, including satellite providers like DirecTV and Dish. Even phone companies, like AT&T, and online companies, like Google, are beginning to distribute television. Meanwhile, cable operators, or providers, like Cox Communications and Comcast, have started using the cables intended for television to deliver Internet and phone service. Walson's cable system of 1948 has evolved from a three-channel delivery system into a digital data web encompassing the entire globe.

As new cable technologies become more powerful and pervasive, cable networks themselves become more and more indistinguishable from broad-casters. Randomly surfing channels, it's nearly impossible to tell ABC from USA from VH1 from MyNetworkTV. But there *are* differences, both in how cable networks function and the kinds of shows they develop and distribute. MTV and Food Network, with their glut of low-budget reality programming, work differently from NBC and CBS, with their costly dramas and comedies. And though many writers, producers, and studios participate in both broadcast and cable, understanding differences between the two is essential to having a career in either.

As we learned in chapter 2, cable "networks" don't have their own system of local stations to distribute programming, so they're not genuine networks. This is important for two reasons:

One: cable outlets only reach paying viewers, so they have smaller audiences than broadcasters that provide free programming. This also means they have dual revenue streams. First, they receive **license fees,** or **affiliate revenue,** from service providers who pay to distribute their content (e.g., Mediacom, Comcast, Suddenlink). This is different from most broadcast networks, which pay affiliates network comp to distribute their programming. (Cable networks function a lot more like the CW, which—if you remember chapter 2—charges affiliates reverse comp.) Two: cable networks, like broadcasters, sell advertising within their shows.

The amount of affiliate revenue a cable outlet earns from service providers is negotiated between each network and the providers carrying it. Larger networks usually generate between one and three dollars per customer per month (in 2007, ESPN received $2.96 per customer per month; TNT received eighty-nine cents). Midsize networks bring in twenty to forty cents per customer per month (The Golf Channel's 2007 license fee was twenty-three cents; CNN got forty-four). Small startups may get absolutely nothing. A startup network's best chance is to give its content to operators for free while it gathers viewers and sells advertising, hoping that after two or three years it will have a solid enough audience to negotiate some small license fees, often no more than a few cents per customer per month.

Though this seems like little money, a cable network making eight cents per customer per month makes ninety-six cents per customer per year. If that network is being carried by Comcast, the nation's number-one cable provider, it's reaching approximately 25 million customers, bringing in $24 million annually. Also, most networks are carried by multiple providers, so they're getting money from every service provider that carries them. Combined with ad revenue, this gives cable networks a healthy income. Most enjoy an ad revenue to affilliate revenue ratio of 50-50 or 60-40. Bravo, for example, hauled in just over $200 million in ad revenue in 2007, and over $150 million in cash flow.

Despite dual revenue streams, cable outlets still don't generate the level of income enjoyed by broadcasters (in 2005, CBS raked in $4.7 billion; its closest traditional cable competitor was Nickelodeon, with $1.7 billion). Not only must cable networks charge advertisers lower rates than broadcasters, but they're not entitled to all the money from subscribers' fees because a good portion goes to cable operators. Thus, cable networks have much less money to buy and develop projects.

The second effect of cable networks not having a web of local stations to program much of their own air is that cable networks are responsible for scheduling every second of their airtime. Broadcasters, remember, only program a few hours a day, leaving the rest in the hands of their local stations. As a result, cable networks require much *more* content than broadcasters. This affects both the *kinds* of shows cablers develop and how shows are programmed.

TALK THE TALK: PREMIUM CABLE NETWORKS

There are two kinds of cable networks: **traditional** networks, which receive both affiliate revenue and ad money (Bravo, SoapNET, The Military Channel), and **premium** networks, which don't sell advertising and receive only affiliate revenue (HBO, Showtime, Starz). Because the latter are subscription only, they usually receive a license fee of a few dollars per subscriber per month, much more than ad-supported networks. Of course, this can be an incredibly lucrative income. In 2005, HBO's 28 million subscribers helped it collect more in license fees than FOX, the year's most watched broadcast network, made in advertising, giving HBO a total revenue of $2.9 billion dollars compared with FOX's $2.6 billion.

HOW THIS AFFECTS CABLE NETWORK PROGRAMMING

With less money and more airtime, cable networks must stretch dollars as far as possible. This affects kinds of content they program, how original content is developed, and how content is scheduled and promoted.

When new cable networks launch, their purses are often too small for splashy original shows, so they instead invest in **acquisitions,** second-run movies or reruns of other networks' shows. AMC began by acquiring classic movies, but as its fan base and pockets deepened, it developed series and films like *Remember WENN, Sunday Morning Shootout, Mad Men,* and *Broken Trail.* Nascent cable channels also program their air with noisy **stunts,** easily promotional, sensational "events" like VH1's Rock and Roll Hall of Fame Induction or Discovery's "Shark Week." Even though stunts are rarely long-running programs, they help gather eyeballs and brand the budding network.

As cable startups grow both their audience and their bank balance, most eventually try their hand at original programming. But because they have less money and more airtime, they can't jump right into the world of expensive scripted shows like *Burn Notice* and *The Tudors.* So they begin by developing inexpensive reality series.

"When Food Network first launched, it was producing programming for $3,000 per half-hour," says Cathy Rasenberger, president of Rasenberger Media, a consulting company that helps launch new cable networks and digital media platforms. "It was [all shot in a production studio]: you could put up a set, bring in the talent, do six shows a day, and do a whole series in one week."

Even bigger shows are relatively inexpensive. MTV's *The Hills* costs about $500,000 per half-hour episode. Episodes of *Next* cost between $100,000 and $150,000. Thus, for the cost of *one hour* of broadcast television (about $2.5 million), cablers can produce up to *twelve* hours of low-budget reality programming. (In the next chapter we'll talk more about reality TV: why it's cheaper, how it's developed, and how you can get your foot in the door.) Even scripted cable shows are less expensive; Starz's *Crash*, for instance, cost about $2 million per episode, $500,000 less than a typical broadcast hour, and it was considered a pricey venture.

Although most unscripted shows have little backend potential, scripted cable fare often *does* have syndication value. HBO resold *The Sopranos* to A&E for $2.5 million per episode. Likewise, distribution company Debmar-Mercury sold the first run of *House of Payne* to TBS, then turned around and sold its second run to FOX's O&Os. So the business model for scripted cable shows is similar to that of broadcast, but on a smaller, less expensive scale. Still, it usually takes many years of airing acquisitions or unscripted content before cable channels are ready to take the leap into traditional scripted programming.

Finally, unlike broadcasters, cable outlets **wallpaper** their air with repeats of their own shows. In other words, broadcast networks rarely rely on reruns for primetime programming. Sure, they may show an occasional repeat of a hit like *CSI* or *Heroes,* but that's usually just to fill an incidental gap in programming. Cable, however, depends on reruns not only to fill surplus air, but as a calculated effort to snag viewers. (I just checked my TiVo, and over the next twelve days, Style Network is showing thirty-seven episodes of *Kimora: Life in the Fab Lane,* and most are repeats of the same episodes. Guess how many episodes of ABC's *Ugly Betty* are airing in the same time period? Two. Not a single repeat.)

"When cable shows repeat," says Brandon Riegg, ABC's director of alternative series and specials (who worked as VH1's director of development and original programming prior to joining Disney), "it's a scattershot approach to hooking viewers into the show. When *Laguna Beach* came out, it didn't do well out of the gate. But MTV had the luxury, like all cable networks, of repeating it ad nauseam. You could barely watch MTV without coming across the show, and as [viewers] became more and more exposed to it, they were interested enough to keep coming back."

This leads to one of the fundamental differences between broadcast and cable networks: how they program and develop their air. Broadcasters use **horizontal programming,** scheduling "destination programming" that draws people back to the same time slot, or destination, every week. *Heroes'* audience is not the same as *ER's* audience, but NBC knows *Heroes* fans will show up every Monday and *ER* fans will show up every Thursday. Each audience has its own destination on NBC's schedule.

Cable outlets use **vertical programming,** which operates on the philosophy that a network's target audience can tune in at any time, but once they're there, it's the network's job to keep them.

Cable networks have two main ways of doing this. First, they often air encores of a show's exact same episode back-to-back, or half an hour later. They then pepper these encores with **episodic promos** driving viewers to the series' next new episode (remember chapter 17?). This gives them multiple chances not only to hook viewers on the current episode, but to point them to the next episode's premiere. They also "stack" episodes of the same program, or air large blocks, like when Discovery celebrated Earth Day in 2007 with a *Planet Earth* marathon. Stacks work because once a viewer is watching a particular show or storyline, they tend to stick with it rather than change the channel.

THE FAST AND FURIOUS WORLD OF CABLE DEVELOPMENT . . . AND HOW IT AFFECTS YOU

Because cable networks need cheap, highly repeatable programming, they employ a slightly different development process than broadcast networks. Unlike broadcasters, which follow a gigantic year-long process, developing over a hundred projects per season, cable outlets divide their year into multiple development cycles. Each cycle (usually three or four months), they develop only a handful of shows and pick up a higher percentage than their broadcast friends. Comedy Central may develop fifteen to twenty projects a year, shoot eight as pilots, and pick up two to four as series. TNT usually develops around ten, shoots three to five, and airs two or three.

This not only allows executives to give more time and energy to each project, it "gives us the option to pick up another season, if we want to, as quickly as possible," says Gaurav Misra, MTV's VP of programming. Also, "if something's not firing we can get it off the grid really quickly."

When a cable network greenlights a series, it also usually greenlights an entire season at one time. Of course, one season of a half-hour unscripted cable show is astronomically cheaper than one season of a half-hour scripted broadcast show. (Cable seasons, both scripted and unscripted, are also shorter—often only six to thirteen episodes.) A broadcast scripted show costs about $2.5 million dollars per hour. An entire season of a cable reality show can cost less than five or six million.

This system allows cable networks to be in constant motion, continually looking for, buying, and trying new programs. If something sticks, they quickly order a second season. If something fails, they yank it without losing much money.

As discussed earlier, broadcast networks are experimenting with similar models, ordering scripts straight to series and trying shorter seasons. They still tend to program more expensive, often less efficient shows, but the success of cable models—as well as the 2007–2008 writers strike—has spurred broadcasters to try new paradigms (like we talked about in chapter 5).

So, given the clockworks behind cable's programming and development models, how does this affect writers and producers like yourself hoping to sell shows to Animal Planet or Discovery Kids?

Because cable networks need less expensive programming, they're often more willing to work with younger, greener, less proven talent. In 2005, former casting executive Cara Coslow, who had never before produced a television series, helped sell the supernatural soap *Dante's Cove* to Here!

"What's going on in cable . . . is opening up the whole world," says Coslow, now a co-producer on the series. "[Cable networks] have to take chances with newcomers because they can't afford big stars. [So] it's less pressure. It's less formal. It's a good place to cut your teeth."

Because cable networks target niche audiences, they also take chances on narrow shows that wouldn't find a home on broadcast TV. A racy show about a pot-dealing mom would probably never attract viewers or advertisers on ABC or CBS. But on Showtime, *Weeds* reaches audiences who accept and appreciate it. NBC Universal learned this the hard way when, on April 6, 2008, it tried transferring quirky cable hits *Monk* and *Psych* from USA to NBC and found they pulled in about the same number of viewers that they did on cable (5.7 million for *Monk,* 4 million for *Psych*). Yet while audiences this size may be successes in the cable world, they're far from acceptable on broadcast, and the shows' NBC premieres landed the network in fourth place for the night. Also, since cable networks aren't using public airwaves, they're not regulated by the FCC, allowing them to push boundaries of language, violence, sex, and subject matter (although many cable networks self-regulate for fear of repelling advertisers).

Finally, most cable networks don't follow broadcasters' yearly production cycle, so they develop and premiere shows year-round, allotting more time and attention to writers, directors, and actors' creative processes. Showtime's *Dexter* took nine months between its first season, which ended in December 2006, and its second season, which debuted in September 2007.

"We started shooting in May [2007], but we started meeting to break story in February," says Melissa Rosenberg, the show's co-executive producer. "We [are given] time to break the entire season, smartly, and really think through character. [We] have time to break story in the room. If it's not working, [we] rebreak it and rebreak it and rebreak it till it's right. Then I have time to write the outline in tremendous detail, get feedback, and hone it. I have time to write the actual script. It makes all the difference in the world. If you have more time to do something, it's going to be better."

For all of these reasons—the need for inexpensive content, the ability to try riskier programming, the willingness to work with less experienced writers and producers—cable has become a great entry point and training ground for young up-and-comers. Writer Silvio Horta created *The Chronicle* for SciFi Channel before exec producing *Jake 2.0* for UPN and *Ugly Betty* for ABC. Blake Masters had written only a few little-known independent films when he sold *Brotherhood* to Showtime. And reality producer Kirk Durham worked on Animal Planet's *Ultimate Zoo* and TLC's *Resolutionaries* before graduating to ABC's *The Big Give* and FOX's *Hell's Kitchen.*

"Cable is an easier place to cut your teeth for a number of reasons," explains Durham. "For one, there are many more cable shows than there are broadcast. Plus, many production companies have more than one cable show happening at once, so once you get in, there's good possibilities for promotion on later shows. Finally, when you produce a cable [reality] show, you wear lots of hats. You develop the story, find characters, set up the shoot, get permits and releases, produce the story in the field, and follow it through post. While exhausting, you become equipped to handle most anything."

In fact, as countless cable shows and networks continue to emerge, they grow more and more powerful and pervasive, eating away at audiences once dominated solely by broadcasters. In 2007, USA (cable's top ad-supported network) averaged 2.67 million primetime viewers per night, only about 104,000 viewers behind the CW, the fifth-ranked broadcast network. And on Wednesday, March 5, 2008, Bravo's *Project Runway* season finale pulled in 5.2 million total viewers and 3.8 million adults 18–49, making it that night's second-most-watched show on all of television among adults 18–49, just behind NBC's *Law & Order*. This would have seemed impossible only a few years ago, when cable channels claimed only a fraction of American audiences. Eroding broadcast networks' rule even further, broadcasters' business-to-business ad revenue increased a mere 0.1 percent from 2005 to 2006. Cable networks' ad revenue, however, increased a full 6 percent.

"[My] prediction is that cable will keep exploding and more channels will continue popping up," says reality show producer Tracy Wilcoxen (*Last Model Standing, Identity, The Bachelor*). "The more channels we have, the more specialized they'll be. More channels means more content . . . and that translates into more jobs."

19

Reality TV

From *Ghost Hunters* to *Wipeout*, reality TV—also known as **unscripted** or alternative—comes in all shapes and sizes, genres and formats. Which leaves many people wondering: what exactly *is* reality TV? I mean, *American Idol* is clearly reality. But so is *Rob and Big*. And *Good Eats*. And *The Steve Wilkos Show*. Yet these shows have almost nothing to do with each other. So what's the common denominator?

"Alternative," says Brandon Riegg, ABC's director of alternative series and specials, "is the term that signifies something that, in a broad sense, falls outside the realm of scripted comedy or scripted drama."

At ABC, this includes everything from *The Bachelorette* to *Dancing with the Stars* to *Jimmy Kimmel Live*. At NBC, it could be *The Apprentice* or *Deal or No Deal*. In fact, "reality" isn't one genre at all. It's a dizzying array of subgenres.

Some alternative series are splashy competition/elimination shows like *Top Chef* and *Rock of Love*. Others are docu-series: unscripted "sitcoms" like *Gene Simmons Family Jewels*, or "dramas" like *The Real Housewives of Orange County*. There are also game shows (*The Price Is Right, 1 vs. 100*), makeover shows (*Pimp My Ride, How Do I Look?*), and talk shows (*The Ellen Degeneres Show, Talk Show with Spike Ferestein*). And don't forget how-to shows (*30 Minute Meals*), clip shows (*The Soup*), court shows (*Judge Judy*), magazine shows (*Entertainment Tonight*), and dating shows (*Change of Heart*). (And, if you think about it for half a second, or flip through your TV guide, I'm sure you'll find several genres not listed here.)

People often marvel at or complain about today's "sudden" proliferation of reality shows, but the truth is: reality has been around since the dawn of television, when shows like *Cash and Carry* and *Arthur Godrey's Talent Scouts* pioneered the medium and captivated audiences. During the late 1950s, game shows like *The $64,000 Dollar Challenge, Twenty One,* and *Dotto* were the highest-rated shows on TV. (You may recognize *Twenty One* and *Dotto* as two of the shows at the center of the 1950s notorious quiz-show scandal, which was the subject of Robert Redford's 1994 film *Quiz Show.*) The 1970s and 1980s were filled with reality shows like *Real People, That's Incredible,* and *Star Search.* But like all cultural trends, television genres are cyclical, and primetime nonfiction programming faded in the 1990s . . . until *Who Wants to Be a Millionaire* reopened the door in 1999, allowing *Survivor* to come along the following year and introduce America to a whole new kind of game. Since then, reality has rivaled (and often surpassed) traditional scripted shows for ratings and helped grow countless cable networks. But why? What makes alternative so popular among both audiences and executives?

Well . . . audiences watch reality because, like it or not, much of it is compelling television. Reality has given us amazing characters, like *The Real World: San Francisco*'s antisocial Puck and *Survivor: Borneo*'s Machiavellian Richard Hatch. It has given us terrific moments of drama (and comedy), like Justin Timberlake phoning his mom on *Punk'd* and the Osbournes hurling ham over their neighbors' fence. You couldn't write that stuff—literally.

But executives like unscripted shows for other reasons as well.

First of all, they're less costly than scripted shows. One-hour dramas often allocate a third of their budgets to above-the-line expenses: costly writers, actors, directors, and producers. Unscripted shows usually allocate 15–20 percent to above-the-line costs. Reality shows also save money because they rarely need to build expensive sets, costumes, or props. Plus, they take less time to shoot. One episode of a half-hour, single-camera scripted show like *Everybody Hates Chris* or *30 Rock* often takes five or six days to shoot. An episode of a half-hour reality show like Food Network's *Everyday Italian* or MTV's *A Shot at Love with Tila Tequila* can be shot in a few hours or a couple of days.

Second, most unscripted shows aren't governed by unions like the

Writers Guild of America (WGA) or the Directors Guild (DGA), so there are no rules mandating what anyone gets paid from one show to the next. People still establish quotes, so they continue to ascend the pay scale, but rates are determined only by what the market will bear, not by a regulatory organization. Most reality shows allocate 10 percent of their budgets to executive producers' fees, but that 10 percent is often split among *all* executive producers. Showrunners may make between $25,000 and $35,000 per episode on broadcast shows, but on cable series, where budgets vary wildly, showrunners' fees can drop as low as $3,000 per episode. Compare those numbers with scripted TV, where EPs' salaries often *begin* at $40,000–$45,000 per episode and can sometimes go higher than $60,000.

STRIKE ZONE: GETTING REAL

Reality television was one of the hot issues of the 2007–2008 writers strike, when the Writers Guild of America fought to bring reality producers and writers (yes, reality TV is written—more on that in a moment) under its jurisdiction. Ultimately, as negotiations drew on, the WGA sacrificed reality to make headway on fair compensation for Internet content, but it hasn't given up the fight.

The WGA began its campaign to unionize reality in 2004 when reality workers began reporting that without a union or governing body, networks and production companies were running roughshod over workers' rights. Reality employees not only had no standardized pay scale, they were working illegally long hours with little or no overtime. According to a 2007 study by Goodwin Simon Victoria Research, 88 percent of reality workers worked more than forty hours a week, but only 9 percent received overtime. Fewer than 12 percent received health-care benefits, and only 5 percent were offered 401K benefits.

In 2005, the Writers Guild helped reality writers and producers file lawsuits against ABC, CBS, NBC, FOX, the WB, TBS, and several reality production companies, claiming workers on shows like *The Bachelor, Trading Spouses,* and *Joe Millionaire* regularly worked over eighty hours a week, were denied meal breaks, and had been told to falsify time cards so they wouldn't receive overtime. In July 2006, twelve writers from the CW's *America's Next Top Model*—organized by the WGA—walked out on their jobs, striking for salary minimums, residuals, and pension and health benefits. Three months later, with virtually no movement from *Top Model*'s network or production company, their jobs were replaced, the picket lines dissolved, and the striking workers were forced to find work elsewhere. The strike had failed.

According to networks, reality shows *can't* compensate reality workers the same as scripted because reality shows operate on smaller budgets. This may be true, but broadcast reality shows command the same ad dollars as scripted shows (and often, in cases like *Survivor* and *American Idol,* they get *higher* ad prices), meaning networks' profits are much larger on successful reality shows.

To this day, most of reality TV remains nonunion. But reality writers and producers, backed by the Writers Guild, continue their fight for equitable treatment. You can learn more at the Writers Guild's website: www.wga.org.

Thus, most high-concept, hour-long broadcast reality shows, like *Survivor* or *The Amazing Race,* cost between $700,000 and $1.3 million, far below the average cost of a broadcast scripted hour. Cable reality shows are even cheaper; per-episode budgets at startup networks often range from less than $50,000 to $200,000. And because reality shows are inexpensive, networks can cut out studios and own shows themselves (or co-own them with creators and production companies), meaning they pocket not only shows' advertising revenue, but most of their product integration money as well.

When networks own reality shows, they also keep most of the license fees generated from foreign sales of a show's **format,** or premise. Because unscripted programming has no writers, producers must create formats designed to continually generate conflict and story. *Survivor*'s format strands strangers in a remote location and forces them to compete in a series of challenges to win a million dollars. *The Amazing Race*'s format sends a gaggle of duos on a global scavenger hunt to win a cash prize. No matter who these shows cast, or what country they're produced in, their competition and challenge-based formats force contestants into dramatic, confrontational situations. This is why great formats often have massive salability overseas. *Temptation Island, The Bachelor,* and *Extreme Makeover: Home Edition* have all sold in Sweden, Norway, Denmark, Belgium, and multiple other foreign territories. *Survivor* is based on a format developed in the UK; *Expedition: Robinson, Survivor*'s original name, aired first in Sweden before being sold to more than forty other countries. No matter where you live, watching a group of sequestered people fight for their life's dream provides dramatic conflict—and a hefty paycheck for a format's owners.

Networks also like owning reality shows because if they fail, they don't lose much money. And if they succeed, their profit margin is much larger than that of a scripted show. In 2007, thirty-second commercial spots in both *The Amazing Race* and *Cold Case* (both CBS Sunday-night shows) cost about $140,000. But scripted hours like *Cold Case* cost their networks license fees of about $1.8 million per episode, while large-scale reality shows like *The Amazing Race* cost their networks between $700,000 and $1.3 million. So a sleek, well-produced reality program can generate over twice the profits of a comparable scripted show. (A massive hit like *American Idol* can bring in even more. In 2007, it brought FOX $810 million in ad revenue, a 39 percent increase from the previous year.)

Alternative series can also be developed and rushed to air more quickly than scripted programs. So when a failing scripted program must be abruptly canceled (and broadcasters always expect to cancel some of their new scripted programs), it's easy to have a reality show waiting in the wings.

The downside of reality is that because many big broadcast shows are serialized competitions, like *Last Comic Standing* or *So You Think You Can Dance,* episodes have limited repeatability.

"If you've seen game seven of the NBA finals, do you need to watch it again?" asks Riegg. "Reality is the same way. There's usually a big endgame, and once you know how it turns out, you're not as inclined to watch. You see similarities with serialized dramas, like *Lost* and *24,* where they don't repeat as well as traditional dramas. Once you are aware how it turns out, watching the journey isn't as compelling."

Having said this, cable networks *do* occasionally buy repeats of successful broadcast shows, but only the biggest hits. And even then, price tags are low. In 2005, VH1 bought second-run rights to UPN's *America's Next Top Model* for $75,000 an episode. Comcast's Outdoor Life Network (now Versus) acquired CBS's *Survivor.* And TV Land picked up *Extreme Makeover: Home Edition.*

Cable networks, of course, program unscripted shows a bit differently from the way broadcasters do. Cablers use acquisitions, like other networks' reruns, to attract new viewers and their own reruns to promote shows. Yet even on cable, certain series have limited rerun value.

"MTV offered up the first six seasons of *The Real World* [on demand]," says Riegg. "Almost nobody watched. The only thing they wanted was the current season. You're going through such an emotional journey, and it's an arc over the course of the season. [Thus, networks] only repeat the season in play right now, and that's purely a device to garner as many eyeballs as they can."

DEVELOPING YOUR OWN REALITY SHOW

So what does all this mean for you, a young writer or producer hoping to sell the next *Don't Forget the Lyrics* or *The Surreal Life*? First and foremost, it means you need strong conflict, compelling characters, and relatability, just as with any other kind of storytelling.

ARE REALITY SHOWS WRITTEN?

"While a [show like] Survivor doesn't have 'writers' per se, it has producers who are producing stories, called 'story producers.' And what do writers normally do? They write stories. So [reality writers are] not writing lines for actual contestants, but they're certainly crafting stories and storylines . . . and that's as much writing as anything. Go to a show like Letterman—of course he has writers. Then there's a show like American Idol, and . . . Ryan Seacrest's host copy needs to be written. The host of The Amazing Race—whenever he's like, 'You've reached the next leg of our trip,' someone's written that. So there's a lot of crafting of story and dialogue being written that is just as legitimate as anything else being written on TV."

—Brad Wollack, writer/producer (*Chelsea Lately, Parental Control, Celebrity Duets, The Wayne Brady Show*)

Conflict

Reality shows can be divided into two main categories: **format-driven** or **talent-** and **personality-driven** shows, and each finds or creates conflict differently.

Format-driven shows, like *Nashville Star* and *The Biggest Loser,* find conflict and story by engineering situations that force people to butt heads.

"[A strong format] creates conflict that reveals characters," says senior producer Matt Short (*Farmer Wants a Wife, Manswers*). "Take people out of their element and put them into strange elements. It's artificial to have ten women living in a house, competing for one guy . . . but it puts them in a foreign environment that's a pressure cooker. That's the basis for any thriller: people in a pressure-cooker situation."

Like *Project Runway* or *High School Musical: Get in the Picture,* a salable format is simple to understand, generates endless conflict, and can be easily replicated, season after season, with entirely new people.

"[If] there's no format . . . it's just a social experiment that falls flat," says *Beauty & the Geek* showrunner Biagio Messina. "*Beauty & the Geek* has tentpoles . . . every week they're going to get a challenge. The geeks are going to do something out of their comfort zone. And the beauties are going to do something out of *their* comfort zone. And if they don't win . . . they could be screwed, because the winners get to send people to elimination. It all culminates in a head-to-head battle, which is basically the stuff of every story you've ever watched."

That isn't to say casting is unimportant; casting is *always* important because—especially without a script with compelling prewritten characters— you need to find participants who are colorful enough to attract audiences. But even before you've cast *Hell's Kitchen,* the mere idea of forcing aspiring restaurateurs to compete for their dream job creates conflict. Some people may be more fun to watch than others, but the format automatically generates drama.

If you're pitching a format-driven show, think of it the same way you'd think of a scripted story. What's at stake for each "character" or participant? What kinds of dramatic decisions do they face along the way? Will each episode resolve with an elimination (*I Love New York*)? A reward (*Fear Factor*)? The reveal of a transformed home or person (*Flip That House, What Not to Wear*)?

Talent-driven shows, like *The Girls Next Door* and even *The Oprah Winfrey Show,* are based around a specific person or group of people who propel each episode's action. Without Phil McGraw, *Dr. Phil* wouldn't exist. *Living Lohan* couldn't find stories without Dina and Ali Lohan. Audiences come to these shows to do one thing: spend time with the central "characters." It doesn't matter what Oprah's doing on any given day, we just like being with her.

This means that if you're pitching a personality-driven reality show, the talent must be attached. You can't pitch TLC a show about Kobe Bryant if you don't have Kobe Bryant on board. It's your job to present the network with a complete package, because without the central cast or talent, your idea is nothing but that: an idea.

Like scripted series, unscripted shows can also be categorized as **stand-alone** or **serialized.** In stand-alone shows, each episode's story has a complete beginning, middle, and end. Stand-alones, like *Bridezillas* or *Moment of Truth* are attractive to networks because audiences can watch any episode without being confused. Serialized shows, like *Dancing with the Stars,* stretch stories across many weeks or episodes. Though a single episode may be enjoyable, viewers need to watch the entire series for the full experience.

Characters

Although your series needs to be "casting-proof"—riding on the strength of its premise, not the hope of finding good participants—it's still important to think about kinds of "characters" your show will use. Many use familiar stereotypes. *Beauty & the Geek,* for instance, pairs socially awkward nerds with airheaded bombshells. Because we understand those stereotypes, we know exactly what that show's cast will look like, even before casting has begun. *Extreme Makeover: Home Edition* finds decimated families and mends their lives by rebuilding their houses. *Shear Genius* and *I Know My Kid's a Star* put people with specific dreams through physical, mental, and emotional obstacle courses.

"You need characters who have big personalities," says supervising producer Kirk Durham (*Student Body, The Big Give*), "but underneath, you need vulnerability. No matter what situation [a] person is in, they [need to] reveal an emotional vulnerability such as falling in love, fear of rejection, fear of failure, cracking under pressure, et cetera. Scripted shows have characters revealing these emotions . . . but it's not always certain with reality shows. Unfortunately, you won't know what reality characters are going to give you, if anything, until you're in the middle of filming . . . and that can sometimes be frustrating for the producer."

THE REALITY CASTING COUCH

Even though most shows need to be "casting-proof," casting is an integral part of any nonscripted show. But how do you cast something with no script and no actors? How can you tell who will make a great character when they're "playing themselves?"

continued

> *"Have one person you love to hate, who will cause conflict. Have a few people you're rooting for. A lot of times, we take characters from different movies and put them together, then use that as a guide when we're casting. So we'll say, 'We need a Paris Hilton type.' So when your casting goes out, that's who they're looking for."*
>
> —Sara Auspitz, director of programming, Endemol (*Deal or No Deal, 1 vs. 100*)
>
> *"The best characters are people who don't self-censor and speak without overanalyzing or thinking about what they're going to say. Usually, people who think they'd be great on a reality show wouldn't be. It has nothing to do with gender, age, walk of life. It has to do with . . . having their own opinion and their own outlook on things that are important to what the show's about."*
>
> —Joke Fincioen, executive producer (*Beauty & the Geek, Scream Queens*)

Relatability

Like any piece of art or entertainment—a scripted series, an Oscar-winning movie, a classic novel, a beautiful sonata—great reality shows connect with audiences and reflect viewers' lives. In some programs, like HGTV's *Design on a Dime,* this reflection can be literal; we all share the problem of decorating on a limited budget. In others, the reflection may be allegorical.

"*Beauty & the Geek* is relatable to anyone who went to high school," says Messina. "You start there [with that universal concept, and] you've got something people can relate to on an emotional level."

Just like scripted series, reality shows become relatable by having strong, specific voices, or points of view. Alternative programs may not be written in the conventional sense, but they still tell stories and explore worlds through particular lenses, and understanding yours is often critical to selling a successful show.

Survivor, for instance, seems to say, "At first glance, the world is a beautiful place, full of gorgeous locations, wonderful friendships, and romantic opportunities. But the truth is, we're all here for one thing: ourselves. To protect our own interests, accomplish our own dreams. And when those interests or dreams are threatened, we do whatever it takes to get what we want. We lie, cheat, backstab, and steal to protect ourselves and our goals. So *Survivor* takes sixteen strangers, each with a different goal or dream, and strands them in the world's most breathtaking location, with one shot at winning a million dollars . . . the money they each need to make their own dream a reality. We then put these people through a series of mental, emotional, and physical challenges . . . and watch as they manipulate, use, and destroy one another to make their own dream a reality."

Similarly, *The Osbournes* (in its first season) seemed to say, "No matter how much money you have, parenthood is hard. We all want to do right by our children, help them make smart decisions, and avoid the mistakes we made. But that's not easy . . . especially when you look in the mirror and see nothing but a *lifetime* of bad decisions. How do you tell your teenage daughter not to have sex . . . or your teenage son not to smoke and drink . . . when your past is a well-chronicled history of sex, drugs, and rock and roll? How do you teach your children to be mature adults when you sometimes get so angry with your neighbors you throw ham over their fence? It doesn't matter whether you're a Midwestern farmer or the world's greatest rock star . . . for parents struggling to navigate parenthood and help their kids become better people than they are, the dilemmas and emotions are the same."

Think about the perspectives and voices of some of your favorite reality shows. How do they reflect your life experience? Are they earnest, dark reflections like *Breaking Bonaduce*? Romantic comedies like *Newlyweds: Nick and Jessica*? Are they "train-wreck" shows that illuminate your nightmares? Or fanciful escapes that highlight your fantasies? Explore these questions in the context of your own projects. Knowing how to articulate the answers will give your shows the extra edge they need to be TV's next big reality hit.

WHAT TO DO WITH ALL THIS INFO ONCE YOU HAVE IT

When organizing a reality pitch, I usually create a document consisting of the same seven areas as a scripted pitch: the introduction; the logline; summary/synopsis; character descriptions; a sample episode; episode ideas; and subsequent seasons (see chapter 7). But with unscripted pitches, some sections work a bit differently.

When it comes to character descriptions, for instance, your characters—unlike in a scripted pitch—aren't fully imagined and fleshed out. Rather, you're pitching character types, as we discussed earlier. Does your show cast down-and-out families like *Extreme Makeover: Home Edition*? Adulterous lovers like *Cheaters*? Lovelorn romantics like *The Bachelorette*? Washed-up celebrities like *Celebrity Fit Club*?

Similarly, your "sample episode" needs to be a walk-through of the format. Explain the structure of an episode, possible segments or challenges, how characters respond and progress through the "story," and the ultimate resolution.

Finally, give examples of possible episodes. If you were pitching *Wife Swap,* you might explain how one week you'd swap a conservative redneck with a liberal vegan, and the next you'd swap a deadbeat with a disciplinarian. With serialized shows, like *Big Brother,* you might describe how challenges become more difficult and tension becomes thicker as contestants drop out and the finale approaches.

Many reality producers also pitch with **sizzle reels,** two- to five-minute videos introducing the shows' personalities or formats. Because talent-driven programs are dependent on specific "characters," buyers need a sense of what those people are like on camera. Just as scripts illuminate these things in comedies or dramas, sizzle reels do it in alternative. Are characters likable? Relatable? Are personalities big enough to leap off the screen? Sizzle reels also help execs get a sense of the show's tone. Is this broad, hijinks-filled comedy like *Gene Simmons Family Jewels*? An earnest soap like *Laguna Beach*? A gritty adventure like *Ice Road Truckers*? Think of sizzle reels as movie trailers for un-scripted shows.

(Of course, shooting a sizzle reel takes a bit of money, time, and energy . . . which is why reality production companies often have their own equipment. If you're not already stocked, you can buy—or rent—your own tools for minimal investment. Check out the sidebar below for great suggestions on how to get up and running.)

GIVE YOURSELF SOME SIZZLE

Beauty & the Geek showrunner Biagio Messina has produced countless hours of television for both broadcast and cable networks. But no matter how massive his series budget, one thing remains the same. "If you have talent and determination," Messina says, "you don't need money to be successful, beyond getting yourself a computer and a camera." Here Messina gives you everything you need to be a "one-man band" capable of producing top-of-the-line sizzle reels, promo tapes, online content, or your very own show.

THE BASICS

- A **reliable 3-chip camera,** such as the Panasonic DVX100B or the Canon GL2, both available for less than $3,000.
- A **clip-on electret microphone,** available at Radio Shack for about $25 (you may want an extension cord for mobility).
- User-friendly **editing software** like Apple's Final Cut Pro (about $1,300), Final Cut Express (about $300), Adobe Premiere (about $800), or Avid Express Pro (about $1,700).

GRAPHICS: ICING ON THE CAKE

"If you're going to go out and pitch a show to the CW, or NBC, or CBS," says Messina, "look at what their promos look like. That's where their head is at graphically, where their branding is at. If you bring in a video pitch or presentation tape inspired by what they're using, they're going to feel like you're bringing something that's already part of their brand."

Messina recommends two graphics programs: Adobe After Effects (about $1,000) or Zaxwerks ProAnimator (about $700).

"That's where a young producer's work can really shine," Messina says. "When you've got great story, great camera work, great sound, and—on top of that—terrific graphics? . . . You rise above the crowd."

NOW WHAT? SELLING YOUR REALITY SHOW

As in the scripted world, showrunners are one of the most important factors in buying and selling unscripted shows. Networks need to know that the captain of the ship has the knowledge, experience, and vision to deliver episodes on a regular schedule. So if you're not a seasoned producer, you increase your odds of a sale by teaming with someone who is. But in order to find the right person, you have an important decision to make: whether your series is for broadcast or for cable.

"If [a show] is for a broadcast network, it has to feel 'big,' " says Red Varden Studios president Zig Gauthier, who used to head development at SciFi Channel, Fox Sports Net, and GSN. "If it's for cable networks, it has to feel especially unique or distinctive."

Broadcasters favor sensational competitions, like *America's Got Talent* and *American Gladiators,* or high-concept stand-alone shows like *Trading Spouses* and *Supernanny.* They rarely program docu-series like *The Two Coreys* or *Blow Out,* which have little rerun value and struggle to find large audiences. In fact, most broadcast forays into docu-series, like FOX's *Nashville* and *The Princes of Malibu,* have been dismal failures.

Also, if your show appeals to only one segment of the population, even a seemingly large segment, it's probably not a broadcast show. Millions of people love Broadway musicals, but that wasn't enough to sustain *You're the One That I Want,* NBC's search for new actors to star in Broadway's *Grease* revival. The show premiered in January 2007 with 11.6 million viewers and a 12 share among females 12–34, then dwindled to a disappointing average of only 8 million people per episode and was canceled after one season. Would it have found a better life on a younger, more female-centric network like the N or Oxygen? Maybe (which helps explain why TV's next Broadway-related reality show, 2008's *Legally Blonde The Musical: The Search for Elle Woods,* played only on MTV rather than a broadcaster).

Because cable and broadcast are such different worlds, most producers and production companies specialize in one or the other. As in scripted, there's only a handful of showrunners and production companies that broadcasters trust, such as Mark Burnett Productions (*Survivor, Rock Star*) and Rocket Science Laboratories (*Temptation Island, My Big Fat Obnoxious Fiancé*). In fact, the division between broadcast and cable showrunners is often more pronounced in alternative, where running *The Amazing Race* is a whole different ball game from running *Miami Ink.* (This isn't to sneeze at cable shows; it's simply to highlight that different showrunners specialize in different kinds of shows.)

Your job, then, is to partner with a producer who has enough muscle to sell your project to the appropriate buyer. Some producers have overall deals, like documentarian Morgan Spurlock (*30 Days, Supersize Me*), who signed a two-year deal in 2008 with Fox Television Studios. Other successful companies, like Authentic Entertainment (*Cities of the Underworld, Ace of Cakes*), remain independent.

And remember: because most reality shows are inexpensive enough not to need deficit financing and there's little syndication value in unscripted programming, there's rarely a need for studios. So once you find the right producing partner, you can pitch directly to networks.

Networks usually buy unscripted shows as either a **work-for-hire** deal or a **license fee** deal. With a work-for-hire arrangement, the network owns the show in its entirety and simply hires you (and whoever you're partnered with) to make the series. With a license fee deal, you or the other producers maintain ownership of the format and simply license it to the network (just like a studio does with scripted shows). License fee deals allow producers and creators to sell formats overseas and participate in product integration revenue. Of course, networks don't like making license fee deals, since they often exclude the network from huge shares of money, and only allow them with hugely successful production companies that wield a lot of leverage.

On most reality shows, executive producers are paid 10 percent of the budget, but how that 10 percent breaks down varies from show to show, depending on the clout of the EPs, showrunners, and production companies. Sometimes the 10 percent is split evenly; sometimes the production company takes 5 or 6 percent and forces the other EPs to split the remainder; other times a powerful production company persuades the network to pay 10 percent to the company and additional fees to other producers or showrunners.

Once deal points are worked out, the development process proceeds similarly to that of a scripted project. Some networks order a pilot or presentation; others thrust you right into series production. One thing, however, is for certain: once you've sold that first show, it becomes much easier to sell another . . . and another . . . and another.

HOW TO GET YOUR FOOT IN THE DOOR AND BEGIN WORKING IN REALITY TELEVISION

Of course, maybe you're not yet looking to create and sell your own show. Maybe you'd first like to begin working in alternative television to see how it's done and learn a bit about nonfiction storytelling.

The heart of an unscripted show's storytelling operation is its **story**

producers, reality's version of writers. They design each show's story and characters, from defining episodes and season arcs on *Tori and Dean: Inn Love* to inventing challenges and dramatic situations on *Parental Control.* Unlike in scripted TV, the bulk of most story producers' work is often done in postproduction, when they pore over hours of footage to find moments they can use to build a story.

"With scripted stuff," says Riegg, "you write the story before you actually shoot it. [In reality shows] we put everything in place, but nobody knows what's going to happen between the start and the finish line. Once you get to the finish, you take a look back, put the pieces together, and come up with something that's coherent and interesting."

Being a story producer can be extremely creative and fulfilling. Story producers need strong writing chops, a good sense of narrative structure and character, and great people skills. And just as in scripted shows, the best way to get a story producer gig is to start at the bottom. Most people begin as production assistants, fetching coffee, making copies, running errands. Check out the sidebar below to learn more about the hierarchy of a reality show's story department (and in chapters 24 and 25 we offer practical tips for landing that first PA job).

THE HIERARCHY OF A REALITY STORYTELLING DEPARTMENT

Although different shows and companies use different titles, most reality employees still start at the bottom and climb their way up. Here's how the ladder often works, from top to bottom:

Executive producers and **co-executive producers** are usually the showrunners, overseeing all practical and creative aspects of the show. They also interact with executives at networks and production companies, taking notes, working with network promotions departments, etc.

Supervising producers work with story, but they're also in management positions, serving as liaisons between story producers, in-the-field production teams, and showrunners.

Senior story producers supervise story producers responsible for individual episodes. While a story producer often focuses specifically on two or three episodes, the senior story producer makes sure all episodes come together as a whole.

Story producers, reality's version of mid-level scripted writers, oversee t
storytelling of specific episodes, craft challenges and events in preproductio
conduct "OTFs" (on-the-flys, direct-to-camera interviews with reality "characters")
and come up with "story bombs" (sudden, produced events that force characters
to interact).

Story editors track stories on storyboards, find footage in postproduction, log
in the field, and write questions for OTFs. They also work with editors to create a
"string-out," the earliest, rawest cut of a reality episode.

Story assistants log in the field, then work in postproduction by helping story
editors and producers find specific moments they need to reconstruct the story.

Loggers transcribe raw footage shot in the field, watching every moment of the
tapes and typing up action and dialogue. In other words, they reverse-engineer
the script. "Live" loggers sit in the field and type everything that happens as it's
happening.

Production assistants are entry-level workers who do everything from buying
office supplies to delivering tape stock to making copies.

THE FUTURE IS HERE

Regardless of the kinds of shows you choose to work on, alternative is no
longer TV's red-headed stepchild; it's a thriving part of the television landscape. *American Idol* is the number-one show of the new century, and one
of the most powerful programs in the history of television. *The Amazing
Race* weaves complex, multidimensional characters into sophisticated storytelling structures. *The Hills* ushers us into a sexy, soapy world as enticing as
anything on *The O.C.* or *Gossip Girl*.

Thus, reality producers can not only have long, successful careers, they
can springboard to other genres and mediums. Reality producers Steve
Sobel and Alan Wieder worked together on *Joe Millionaire* and *Meet My
Folks* before teaming up to write *Stallions*, a feature comedy about young fathers, which they sold to Warner Bros. in 2007. Wendy Calhoun was a co-
producer on *Hell's Kitchen* before becoming a scripted writer on NBC's
Raines and *Life*.

As television continues to evolve, so will alternative, offering many

᠍ writers, producers, and artists eager to tell new sto-
television.

television has been around for decades," says Gauthier.
95 percent of cable networks are driven by nonscripted
Even at broadcast networks—while primetime program-
ᵣn dominated by scripted—nonscripted programming drives
niddays, early fringe, and late night, whether it's *Blind Date,*
ortune, or *Oprah Winfrey.* Nonscripted drives most of broadcast
s and local affiliates—and it'll be around for a long time to come."

20

Digital Media and the Internet

Okay, folks, here's the truth: writing one chapter on **digital media—** what it encompasses, how it works, where it's headed, how to break in—is like trying to write a chapter on the history of the world, how it's changing, and how to be successful in life . . . in twenty pages.

Because it's still so new, digital media, aka **new media,** is a lawless frontier that's constantly changing. A successful business model one month could be obsolete the next. A wildly popular YouTube video today can be completely forgotten tomorrow. Digital media is an out-of-control teeter-totter, with few rules or paradigms.

Of course, when people talk about "new" media, there's obviously nothing new about it; the Internet has been an integral part of our lives for almost twenty years. Yet even after two decades, cyberspace is such a wild, constantly evolving beast that no one has come close to conquering it.

Only one thing is certain: digital media is here to stay, and when it comes to how people distribute and consume television and video, it's changing everything . . . not just how people *watch* TV and video entertainment, but how it's produced and distributed. A 2007 survey from Deloitte and Touche found that 45 percent of Americans make their own audio and video entertainment to post online, with 32 percent considering themselves "broadcasters." And while these armchair entertainers may not have the money or marketing power of actual broadcasters, they can certainly generate audiences that make advertisers and distributors take notice. In the fall of 2006, Internet marketing company The Viral Factory reported that *Star Wars Kid,* the video of fourteen-year-old Ghyslain Raza practicing his light-saber skills in his school's AV room, had been viewed 900 million times since its release three years earlier. (To put that in perspective, that's more views—in three years—than all the Super Bowls put together received between 2000 and 2008.) And while *Star Wars Kid* wasn't a written or produced Internet show like Disney's *Squeegees,* it speaks to the reach and power of Internet video.

Yet even as the Internet nips at TV's heels, no one has figured out exactly how to use it. Although more and more people are watching TV online, Internet technology isn't yet strong enough to deliver high-def content to large-screen TVs. Likewise, most TVs can't yet process large video streams. While this technology may be just around the corner, no one's sure how far away that corner is. Likewise, no one's cracked the formula for a successful online series that rivals the entertainment value (and revenue stream) of a traditional TV show. Sure, there have been breakout hits, like *Lonelygirl15,* but these are few and far between. So when it comes to discussing the future of Internet television, the **convergence** of TV and the Internet, the conversation consists mainly of questions. How long until content on our TV screen is delivered not by radio waves, cable wires, or satellite signals, but by an Internet connection? How much money can be made online in the meantime? Will Internet distributors like YouTube, Crackle, or Joost wipe out traditional TV networks? Will we ever reach a day when TV and the Internet are virtually indistinguishable from each other?

No one knows, but these are questions facing and worrying the industry.

Thus, the best way to approach the world of digital media is to look at what has happened so far, how it has changed, and how it will likely continue to change. And, of course, how you can use this information to break in.

So the first thing to understand is . . . what *is* digital media?

Digital media is, quite simply, anything that's not "traditional media"; i.e., television, radio, or conventional recording/playback devices like VCRs and Blu-Ray discs. The three main components of new media are **digital video recorders** (**DVRs**) like TiVo and Moxi, online streaming like ABC's broadband player, and electronic sell-throughs (ESTs) such as video-on-demand services (VOD) and downloads, which allow consumers to keep copies of the content they acquire electronically.

These inventions are affecting entertainment by both introducing new distribution and viewing methods (and, therefore, new revenue streams) and by creating, in the Internet, a whole new artistic medium, with unique rules, restrictions, and creative freedoms.

DIGITAL MEDIA AS A DISTRIBUTION METHOD

It's no news flash that many people no longer watch TV on actual televisions. We stream *Swingtown,* download *Robot Chicken,* catch *Entourage* on-demand. And when we *do* watch those ancient boxes known as TV sets, DVRs help us pick and choose what we watch and when we watch it. These new technologies have three main effects:

First, they decentralize TV content. In other words, each show used to be available exclusively in one place. To watch this week's *Law & Order,* you had to go to NBC. To see *King of the Hill,* you went to FOX. That's no longer true. You can now watch *Law & Order* on NBC . . . or stream it at NBC.com, Veoh, or Hulu . . . or record it on your DVR . . . or download it through an online retailer like Amazon Unbox. Networks are no longer the sole destination for their own content.

Second, thanks to DVRs, portable multimedia players (PMPs) like the Archos 405 or the iPod Touch, and 24/7 on-demand services and streaming, audiences have the ability to **time-shift** programming, or watch it on their own schedules, as opposed to network schedules. VCRs gave us some ability to do this, but nowhere near the combined flexibility and power of DVRs, VOD, and electronic sell-throughs. In fact, a 2008 study by Information Resources Inc. found that 42 percent of CBS's shows were time-shifted, as opposed to 18 percent of Lifetime's and 10 percent of Food Network's. It also discovered 34 percent of Friday shows were time-shifted, in contrast with 15 percent of Sunday shows.

Third, traditional television has always given us **lean-back entertainment,** where audiences remain passive and just watch, but the Internet has brought us **lean-forward entertainment,** allowing audiences to interact with content. Some Internet shows, like *KateModern,* allow viewers to communicate directly with characters and affect a story's outcome. Others, like *Sanctuary* (which was picked up as a full TV series by SciFi Channel), allow

viewers to interact with other viewers, chatting, sharing show-inspired art-
work, even re-editing scenes into their own shorts and videos.

Though audiences love the power and freedom offered by digital media,
certain people aren't so crazy about the changes. Namely, TV networks. Networks like to control content by being its sole distributor. But digital media
has loosened that control. Also, networks are dependent on ad revenue, and
if time-shifting viewers download ad-free episodes, fast-forward through
breaks, or watch programs days after commercials lose relevance, ads don't
do much good. And if ads stop being effective, advertisers stop paying TV
networks.

So, on one hand, networks are terrified of digital media and the power
it affords customers. On the other, they realize progress is inevitable and
that, in order to survive, they must adapt. Thus, studios and networks are
scrambling to figure out how to monetize new platforms so they can remain
the big dogs of the entertainment industry. Some use digital media as a distribution device to repurpose TV shows and movies. Others use it to produce original content. *Lost, The Office, Deadliest Catch,* and *Battlestar
Galactica* have all produced original **webisodes** and **mobisodes** expanding
the worlds of their series. CBS produced *BBQ Bill,* a mockumentary series
available only at CBS.com. And NBC launched its first online soap, *Coastal
Dreams,* on NBC.com.

But before we discuss new kinds of shows being developed, let's look at
online business models and how—much like in TV—these models affect
shows companies create.

THE DIGITAL MEDIA BUSINESS MODEL
FOR ORIGINAL CONTENT

Unfortunately, the first problem with explaining the online business model
is: There's not just one. There aren't just two. There aren't just three. There
are many, and none has proven particularly successful at monetizing digital
media, whether producing original online content like *Afterworld* or *Sam
Has 7 Friends,* streaming *30 Rock,* or **storing and forwarding** *CSI* to set-
top boxes. Sure, a few million bucks are being made via electronic sell-
throughs and video-on-demand, but "those millions are a mere rounding
error for the amount of money made in theaters and on television," says

Rich Hull, film producer (*Daddy Day Camp, She's All That*) and chief content officer of Blowtorch, a youth-oriented entertainment company. "Some people are making millions, but that's with delivery mechanisms like iTunes. Steve Jobs is making millions; the guys that own content are not."

As a result, many networks and studios currently view new media simply as a marketing tool to promote programs already on TV. In fact, a 2006 CBS study determined that more than half the people watching shows online didn't actually begin as regular viewers of those shows—but they got hooked online, then sought the shows out on traditional television. In other words, online episodes of, say, *Numb3rs,* act like giant trailers, captivating audiences and sending them back to broadcast television, which is why NBC's *The Office* spiked 13 percent among adults 18–49 after making episodes available on iTunes. Thus, networks and studios focus less on how to produce and distribute original shows online, like ABC's *Voicemail,* and more on how to use the Web to promote existing shows like *Pushing Daisies* and *Samantha Who?*

That doesn't mean Hollywood's not dabbling in making online originals. Many studios *are* producing original content, but it's often in the context of promoting either the networks' larger products (à la the *Lost* mobisodes, which drive viewers back to the actual series), the network brand itself (NBC's *Coastal Dreams*), or advertisers' products, like TBS's *Love Bites,* a shortform romantic comedy sponsored by Unilever shampoo that airs both online and on the actual network.

Naturally, these different views of new media have led to almost as many business arrangements, although four models seem to be emerging as the most prevalent.

Business model 1. The "television model." A financier funds a show, then licenses it to an outside **portal,** or distributor, who sells advertising against it. So rather than licensing to NBC or FOX, the financier licenses the show to AOL, Yahoo!, etc. This is how Electric Farm Entertainment and Sony Pictures TV International sold their sci-fi series, *Gemini Division,* starring Rosario Dawson, and *Woke Up Dead,* to NBC Universal. Sometimes, a portal even contracts a production company to produce exclusive online content, much like a network laying off a show on a studio or a pod. MSN, for instance, partnered with Reveille, the production company behind *Ugly*

Betty and *The Office,* to co-produce online shows like *The Big Debate* and *Chef to the Rescue.*

Business model 2. Branded entertainment. As with product integration, where brands are "discreetly" woven into TV shows' storylines, advertisers often pay production companies like For Your Imagination (*Break a Leg, Dad Labs*) to design online shows promoting specific goods. Some, like Tide's *Crescent Heights,* are simply advertiser-sponsored; others, like *Sprays in the City,* from I Can't Believe It's Not Butter!, are constructed to organically showcase specific products.

Business model 3. Revenue-generating services and sites like Google's Ad-Words and Revver. These services match ads with user-generated content, then split the ad revenue with content creators. They usually charge advertisers for both **CPMs** (based on how many people merely *see* the ad) and **cost per clicks,** or **CPCs** (based on how many people *click* on the ad). While this arrangement works, in theory, revenue generated by online ads is so incremental it's nearly impossible to make any "real" money. Most prices per click are between one and fifty cents, and that's split between the ad-matching service and the content creator. Thus, producers use these services simply in hopes of breaking even on the cost of maintaining their website.

Business model 4. "If we make it, they will come." Or, quite simply, creating something on spec, posting it online, and hoping it can find financial support later. "If it's good enough quality," says Hull, you "can . . . sell advertising against it [or] find a market overseas and in a handful of other places." This, of course, is the riskiest model, and most successful shows that have tried this—such as *Lonelygirl15*—have been independent productions that happened to become "viral" enough to garner attention. In fact, the "if-we-make-it-they-will-come" model paid off in a big way for LG15/Telegraph Avenue Productions, the production company behind *Lonelygirl15,* when—in 2008—it received $5 million in funding from a group of investors from Netscape, Google, and Mark Burnett Productions. (A year earlier, *Lonelygirl15* had also struck a product placement deal with Hershey's, in which the producers had the show's main character, Bree, offer other characters a piece of Icebreakers Sours Gum.)

2. Keep it short. Most online shows last about two to four minutes. According to a 2007 report from research firm comScore, 75 percent of American Internet users watch an average of six minutes of online video a day, usually "snacking" on two or three short videos averaging 2.8 minutes each. "You could say it's short attention spans, but that short attention span is fostered by the Internet," says writer/producer Ari Eisner, who landed an MTV development deal after two parody trailers he made with partner Mike Dow, *Must Love Jaws* and *Ten Things I Hate About Commandments,* racked up over a million views on YouTube and Spike. "You could be watching a *Lonelygirl15* video at the same time someone sends you an e-mail for something else, and a lot of people will just click over halfway through. [So Internet content] needs to hold your attention, then fly away."

3. Have a strong marketing hook. This doesn't mean you need to be able to sell your show to Procter & Gamble; it simply means you need a splashy premise to grab viewers' attention. "There are hundreds of thousands of people banging around new media creating something," says Nemcoff, "so you need a reason why your show stands above the fray . . . a hook you can sell quickly, whether it's the most outrageous comedy show you'll ever see, the best tech news on the Internet, or the most frank political discussion you can find."

4. Make it Internet-specific. Audiences come to the Internet expecting a different media experience than what they get on television, so "there should be a reason you have to find this show online," says TV and new media producer David Armour (*Ricki Lake, Sunset Hotel*). "If you're going to make a television show and just put it online, it's not going to work. *Lonelygirl15* was . . . nothing you could see on television, nothing people had seen online, and it hit an emotional chord," so take advantage of the connectivity and interactivity that make the Internet unique.

As we've already mentioned, the most unique trait of the Internet is its ability to be interactive and create community. This is the brilliance of YouTube, MySpace, and FunnyorDie. Whether posting comments on a favorite short, e-mailing its creator, or live-chatting with fictional characters, users get a connective experience they can't get in any other medium.

Your job as an online creator is to "build content that draws people into interacting with your content," says Dann Webster, a software and scalability architect at Jacked.com who has also worked for CBS.com and MySpace. Fortunately, the Internet is full of free tools and applications you can use to give your work full interactivity.

VIRTUALLY SPEAKING: TOOLS FOR CREATING INTERACTIVE CONTENT

Whether you're creating a daily podcast or scripted webisodes, here are suggestions for making your material interactive. If you need help implementing any of these ideas, a quick Internet search should provide a wealth of information.

Blogs & vlogs (video blogs)
Online journals where you can share thoughts and opinions with your audience. Like the director's commentary on a DVD.

Chat rooms
Text-based conferencing where users can post comments and respond in real-time.

Easter eggs
Hidden messages planted within content. A great way to get users chatting and speculating about secrets and conspiracies within your content.

Message boards
Online forums where users can post thoughts and opinions about your content or related topics.

Polls
People love expressing opinions in polls. A quick Internet search will give you countless free sites to help place polls on your website, blog, or podcast page.

Ratings systems
People enjoy rating things. TV.com lets people rate shows. Spike lets people rate shorts. HotOrNot lets people rate people.

Social networking sites
Create pages for your project and yourself on social networking sites like MySpace and Facebook. If you're making a fictional show, give your characters pages as well.

Wikis
Software allowing users to quickly create and link webpages to form evolving, user-generated websites. A great tool if you want people to theorize on your show's mysteries and mythologies.

ONE-ON-ONE WITH . . . OLIVER LUCKETT,
CO-FOUNDER/CEO, DIGISYND, INC.

Web shows don't work the same way as TV shows, and if you're going to learn to do something, learn from the best. I sat down with Oliver Luckett, pioneering co-founder of production and distribution sites like DigiSynd, Revver, and iBlast, to learn how he's helped grow countless Internet phenomena, from *Lonelygirl15* to the explosive Diet Coke/Mentos clips to the conspiracy-based game/wiki *Nowheremen*.

You've worked with shows, sites, and shorts in almost every genre under the sun. Creepy soaps, mysterious thrillers, outrageous reality stunts. What kinds of topics work best on the Internet? Is there a unifying factor?

"You need content that makes somebody say, 'Have you *seen* this?' No one forwards a nine-minute video of someone droning on. 'Viral' is fifteen seconds of pure comedy. Parody works. Compelling music works. Timeliness and relevance work. Conspiracy theories—people eat them up."

People talk about how important interactivity is to the Internet, but what if I just want to use my Internet show as a calling card for television? Do I really need to make it interactive?

"Audience interaction, most of the time, is more entertaining than the show itself. You know you have a viral hit when audiences are interacting at a high rate of people-who-view-it to people-who-interact-with-it. Putting up a page with your episode and nothing else is stupid. You can't treat it as television."

But I don't know anything about building a website or posting videos. How can I build a home for my show?

"You don't have to build anything . . . it's all there for free. Construct a storytelling architecture from things that are freely available. You know what MySpace is, you know what Facebook is, you know what YouTube is. They're all open systems that are self-publishing . . . and they're only as good as the content that goes through them."

So many online successes are successful simply because they're viral. Is there a way to help my content be viral-friendly?

"Edit it down to the essence. Think about television shows . . . then think what the audience does when they put them on YouTube. They cut them down to thirty seconds of essence. Name ten viral hits, and they're either the length of a song or the thirty-seconds essence. [Also,] use music. It allows a lot of

continued

engagement at an auditory level that allows a lot of mistakes at the visual level. A large majority of traffic online has been lip-syncing [or] remakes and parodies of music videos. There's a formula; it's not rocket science, and it's easy to replicate."

I don't want to post my show until I know it's perfect. How do I know when the show is ready to be seen?

"Just throw it up. If it gets popular, it gets popular. If it doesn't, move on. Don't be afraid to try things. Put up ten cuts of the same video. We work on campaigns where the first ten videos don't hit, then we make the eleventh, the audience remixes it, and it pops! The audience version of the video we created, done in slow-mo or spoofed over, ends up popping the most. If the message is in the video to begin with, your message is out there."

Once you've nailed your show's concept, shoot and edit it as cheaply as possible. Aspiring filmmaker Joshua Trank produced his popular Internet short, *Stabbing at Leia's 22nd Birthday Party*, for only $200, shooting with an old DV camera and editing with Final Cut Pro. The film was so successful it garnered almost 4 million views its first week, landing Trank a development deal with Spike TV. (Check out the "Give Yourself Some Sizzle" sidebar in chapter 19 for a guide to affordable equipment to help shoot your online projects.)

Finally, you're ready to post your work. Some people begin by posting to a small handful of sites, gathering feedback so they can revise, improve, and repost. Others like to "go wide," posting to as many portals as possible. Successful shows tend to be those that get passed "virally" from person to person, so your job is to get your content to people who want to pass it on. This is the true challenge of being an Internet producer: it's not enough to make great content; in the clutter of cyberspace, you need to be half artist, half marketing genius.

"Know where your audience is, how to find it, and who may be interested in promoting your product as a benefit to their own project," says Nemcoff. "It's a barter system: you have to find a reason why somebody will want to talk about your show . . . because it's the kind of content they need for their specific blog or podcast."

SEEING YOUR NAME IN LIGHTS (REALLY, REALLY TINY LIGHTS)

Every day, new online distribution sites rise up and fall away, so the best places to post new work are constantly changing. Over the past few years, however, a handful of heavily trafficked, go-to sites have emerged. Here's a short list of popular portals, great places to both see new work and post your own.

Bebo (www.bebo.com)
A social networking site that not only has sections for filmmakers to post work, but also for musicians and authors to post music, stories, and book chapters.

Blip.tv (blip.tv)
Provides free hosting, as well as multiple formats like Quicktime, Flash 8, and 3gp to make content compatible on multiple platforms. They also have an optional ad revenue sharing plan.

Crackle (crackle.com)
Sony's online network and studio for emerging Internet writers and creators.

Digg (www.digg.com)
Doesn't actually host content, but aggregates and organizes the Internet's most popular videos, blogs, and podcasts.

FunnyorDie (www.funnyordie.com)
Created by Will Ferrell, Chris Henchy, and Adam McKay, FunnyorDie specializes in comedy shorts on which users vote to keep on or remove from the site.

iFilm and Spike (www.spike.com)
Originally founded as a portal for independent short films and music videos, iFilm was bought in 2005 by MTV Networks and combined with Spike.

Metacafe (www.metacafe.com)
Focusing on entertainment shorts, Metacafe lets users preview, select, and rate videos appearing on the site.

MyDamnChannel (www.mydamnchannel.com)
Started by MTV exec Rob Barnett, MyDamnChannel splits ad revenue with artists and has commissioned content from talents like Harry Shearer, Andy Milonakis, David Wain, and Don Was.

MySpace (vids.myspace.com)
Aside from being a powerful networking tool, MySpace has become a go-to outlet for viewing and posting user-generated shorts, shows, and videos.

Podshow (www.podshow.com)
An online network of user-generated videos, blogs, and music.

Revver (www.revver.com)
A hosting site that matches online ads to user-generated content.

Second Life (www.secondlife.com)
A virtual world where users can upload and screen videos, promote work, or network with other artists.

continued

Veoh (www.veoh.com)
Online distributor hosting user-generated content as well as product from NBC, FOX, CBS, and Comedy Central.

Videosift (www.videosift.com)
Like Digg, Videosift aggregates content from other sites, then lets users vote and rank different videos, shows, and podcasts.

Vimeo (www.vimeo.com)
A hosting site for user-posted content. Unlike YouTube, which allows non-user-generated clips of movies, TV programs, and videos, Vimeo allows *only* user-generated material.

YouTube (www.youtube.com)
The heavyweight site of user-generated content, YouTube also features a Directors Program for aspiring filmmakers and content producers.

As in the real world, success online depends on networking. But the virtual world has its own set of rules and etiquette. In the sidebar below, we go over some tips and advice for marketing your way through cyberspace.

As more young producers distribute content on the Web, the Internet is quickly becoming the "independent film" of television, not only a vibrant playground where young artists showcase their work, but a hunting ground where Hollywood searches for fresh talent. Sketch groups Human Giant and The Whitest Kids You Know snared TV deals with MTV and Fuse, respectively, after putting shorts on YouTube. Tennessee vlogger Chris Crocker scored a reality development deal with 44 Blue Productions (*Split Ends, Mega Movers*) after posting a hysterical vlog begging people to "leave Britney [Spears] alone." And comedian Tom Green launched *Tom Green Live,* a talk show shot from his living room, on his personal website before partnering with Debmar-Mercury to sell the show into first-run syndication.

"The best way to get noticed . . . is to go out and shoot something yourself," says Hull. But be warned: if you're planning on using the Internet as an entrée into television, you need to be ready when Hollywood calls. Don't expect to "catch lightning in a bottle twice" by simply taking your Internet show and doing it on TV. You need to have more to show for yourself, something Hollywood can use.

"[Write] ten spec scripts so you understand how to tell a story in televi-

WITH A LITTLE HELP FROM YOUR FRIENDS: HOW TO BECOME A CYBERMARKETING GURU

The key to online success is producing content that goes viral and creates community. Though viral hits often seem to be arbitrary phenomena, here are some easy ways to make friends, influence people, and help content get passed along in the interconnected world of cyberspace:

Post your work on more than one site. Make sure your work is on the top ten or twenty distribution sites. Although these are constantly changing and require keeping your finger on the pulse of the Internet, certain sites have established themselves as online distribution giants: MySpace, YouTube, Revver, Spike, Facebook, etc.

Link to other peoples' shows and blogs. Connect your sites and shows to those with similar content. Become a link in the Internet chain.

Chat and comment on other people's message boards. Be active in chat rooms where people talk about content similar to yours. Make yourself a presence, don't be rude, and you can subtly push your work.

Ask people with similar sites to link to your content. Find people doing similar work and ask them to link to your projects. Offer to link to theirs as well.

Find favors you can do for other people. Seek out people with related content and think of ways to help them. This could be promo-ing their work, linking to their sites, or passing along their content. You'll quickly gain a network of grateful friends.

Don't be afraid to cold-call or e-mail. The Internet's based on communication. Don't be afraid to call or e-mail strangers to see if they'll promote your work— though you may have better luck if you offer them cross-promotion in return.

Get on other people's blogs and podcasts. Make friends with people who have blogs and podcasts; see if they'll interview you or talk about your work on one of their shows.

Have consistent metadata. Always describe your show the same way. Use the same title, key words, and spelling. This makes your work more findable online.

Use "search engine optimization" techniques. Every search engine, like Yahoo! and Google, uses its own technology. SEO techniques help search engines find your site. You can learn more about SEO through a quick online search.

sion," Hull says. "You can't say, 'I've done one thing on the Internet; now that I've got my big break, I'm going to learn how to do it.' "

WHERE ARE WE GOING?

No matter how much the television industry tries to resist or deny it, the cold hard truth is: traditional television, as we've always known it, is slowly disappearing.

"The idea of watching shows in your living room on your plasma screen is not going away," says Rosenthal. But what *is* going away is the notion that your plasma screen and your computer get content from separate places. TV and the Internet are rapidly converging into a single medium . . . and while no one's entirely sure how Internet TV will work or what it'll look like, we're racing toward a world where TVs and computers are attached to the same massive distribution web. Soon we'll be able to watch Hulu and TidalTV on our TVs, NBC and Food Network on our computers, and it'll be nearly impossible to tell the difference.

In many ways, the revolution is already in full swing. Websites like Joost and Hulu stream TV shows straight to computers. **Set-top boxes** like Apple TV transfer content from computers (and, in Apple's case, the iTunes store itself) to televisions. And select high-end TVs, like Sony's Bravia, now come with pre-installed Web connections, allowing consumers to stream YouTube videos and watch on-demand TV shows. In 2006, in fact, Switzerland's Swisscom AG Bluewin service used Microsoft software to give TV consumers genuine Internet TV, with over 100 TV channels and more than 500 on-demand movies—all delivered via the Internet.

Cell phones and handheld devices are also greasing the wheels of Internet/ TV convergence, enabling viewers to watch shows on Web-enabled screens like BlackBerries and iPhones. According to a 2007 study from Deloitte and Touche, 24 percent of all Americans watch entertainment on their cell phones, as do 62 percent of thirteen- to twenty-four-year olds.

These numbers aren't good for the nerves of people working in television. Networks are jittery because advertisers are flocking to digital media faster than they're coming to television. According to Accustream Media Research, online video streaming—not just TV shows, but *all* streaming video—generated close to $1.3 billion in ad revenue in 2007. And Forrester Research predicts that number could reach $7 billion by 2012. (To put that in perspective, the five broadcast networks typically bring in about $9 billion dollars, collectively, during each year's upfront buying season.) TV ad revenue, on the other hand, was predicted to increase a scant 2.7 percent in 2008, according to a study by TNS Media Intelligence. Thus, TV execs are frantically trying to figure out how to protect or adapt business models without sacrificing the elements that make them powerful. (If your entire business plan is built on being the sole owner and distributor of a product, how do you suddenly embrace a medium that hinges on decentralizing that very product?) Writers and artists are nervous because they want to be paid fairly for online work. And in a world where Joshua Trank's $200 short can find 4 million viewers in a week, studios and networks are loath to pay talent the same big-budget dollars they've been paying in TV.

These were the issues at the heart of the 2007–2008 WGA writers strike. For writers, the strike was a battle for the future; if they didn't stake their claim for equitable payment then, they argued, they would be left in the cold, still making pennies a year, long after the Internet had become America's dominant distribution system. For conglomerates, the strike was about protecting themselves in an untamed, unshaped, and unpredictable digital world—a world that was starting to make money, but still had an uncertain future.

Ironically, the strike itself helped hasten digital media's expansion. As original scripted content evaporated from airwaves, millions of people migrated to the Internet. Broadcast audiences plummeted 21 percent, making December 2007—one month after the strike began—the Web's busiest month ever for online video-watching. According to ComScore Media Metrix, in December 2007, the average user went from watching 7 minutes per month of online videos to a whopping *111* minutes (and 20 percent of users watched 14 hours).

The strike also acted as an incubator for online talent and programming. With no TV to write and produce, writers, directors, producers, and actors began churning out their own online content. *Heroes* star Milo Ventimiglia and producer Russ Cundiff (*It's a Mall World*) shot a series of Internet shorts in which they battled each other with light sabers. *Carpoolers* stars Jerry O'Connell and Jerry Minor hooked up with editor Ryan Case to produce O'Connell's now-famous Tom Cruise spoof, which garnered more than 1.7 million views in two weeks. Executive producers Tom Fontana (*Oz, Homicide: Life on the Streets*) and Warren Leight (*Law & Order: Criminal Intent*) invested in Virtual Artists, a financing company for online movies and series. And writer/producer Tom Smuts (*Close to Home, The Guardian*) got on board with Founders Media Group, an Internet company designed to create shows for specific demographics.

Although the strike officially ended and TV production resumed on February 13, 2008, the "damage" was already done. Twenty years earlier, during the 1988 writers strike, broadcast viewership declined 9 percent and never fully recovered, thanks in large part to burgeoning cable networks. This time around, there were hundreds of cable channels and a nearly infinite number of online portals, all of which were gobbling up traditional TV's audience share. With almost no scripted programming on broadcast networks, the top-ten cable outlets saw audiences increase close to 25 percent. Online video viewing grew to approximately fifteen times its pre-strike levels, and in December alone, Internet users watched more than 10 billion videos.

So like it or not, convergence is on its way. The only questions now are: What will it look like when it gets here, and when will that be? TV is still a powerhouse, but its chokehold is slipping. And although answers aren't yet clear, writers, producers, studios, and networks are scrambling to be ready. After all, our definition of "TV" may change, but the world's need for entertainment won't.

At that point, "whether there's a good reason to have NBC rather than NBC.com, that's up for discussion," says Rosenthal, but "right now . . . the money is still in television. Ad dollars are still there. No one's getting rich making content for the Web, regardless of how you're distributing it."

STRIKE ZONE: HOW THE STRIKE CHANGED NEW MEDIA

Of all the issues swirling about the 2007–2008 writers strike, none was more important—or more contentious—than compensation in digital media. Before the WGA and AMPTP came to terms on the Writers Guild's new Minimum Basic Agreement, there were virtually no rules regulating payment for writers of either original or repurposed Internet shows. But thanks to the tenacity of the WGA, groundbreaking advances were made. Here's a brief rundown of the deal's main terms for original online content.

COVERAGE

The WGA obtained jurisdiction over most original content produced for the Internet. This means that like TV shows, most scripted Internet shows would be covered by the Writers Guild, allowing the union to establish salary minimums, residuals, credits, pension and health benefits, etc. It also meant that writers of online content must be members of the WGA or join upon being hired. Online shows must meet one of three requirements to be covered by the Guild:

- Be written by a "professional writer" (someone with at least one TV or film credit; at least thirteen weeks of paid writing work in film, TV, or radio; a professionally produced play; or a published novel)
- Be based on a TV show or movie already covered by the Writers Guild
- Have a budget over $15,000 per minute, $300,000 per show, or $500,000 per series order

SALARY MINIMUMS

Prior to the 2008 Minimum Basic Agreement, many scripted online shows, especially those based on existing properties, such as *The Office: The Accountants,* paid writers nothing to write their scripts. Studios claimed webisodes were "promotional" and not actual writing work. Here are the new online salary minimums, according to the WGA's 2008 Minimum Basic Agreement:

- Shows based on traditionally scripted TV series of movies: $618 for the first two minutes, $309 for each additional minute
- Shows based on comedy/variety shows or daytime soaps: $360 for the first two minutes, $180 for each additional minute
- Shows based on all other types of programs: $309 for the first two minutes, $155 for each additional minute
- Totally original online shows, Internet programs based on no preexisting series or movie, have no minimums

To help put the above in perspective, remember this: the writer of a traditional hour-long drama (forty-four minutes of actual script) receives a minimum of just over $700 per minute.

RESIDUALS FOR REUSING ORIGINAL ONLINE CONTENT

For the first time, the WGA also established online residuals, reuse fees similar to those for television (see chapter 3). Here's how Internet residuals work:

continued

Residuals for original online programs kick in after thirteen weeks for ad-supported streams and twenty-six weeks for downloads. At that point, writers receive at least 1.2 percent of the distributor's gross on paid downloads, and there's no minimum for streams (it must be negotiated with each show). Also, if a program's production budget is at least $25,000 per minute (which almost never happens with online shows), the writer receives the TV reuse rate described in chapter 3.

Also, an interesting note: if an original online show is repurposed on television (like *Quarterlife*), usual TV residual formulas apply (see the residual chart on page 47).

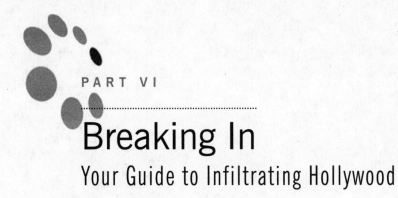

PART VI

Breaking In
Your Guide to Infiltrating Hollywood

21

Write Your Ass Off

···

Spring 2006. This wasn't the conversation writers' assistant Aaron Korsh was supposed to be having. He was supposed to be shouting with joy, celebrating over getting his first staff writer job. But instead he was struggling to process the words coming over the phone.

"Limited budget . . . unable to come up with the money . . . so sorry . . ."

Korsh was talking to comedy writer Stacy Traub, who'd just had her first pilot—*Notes from the Underbelly*—greenlit to series at ABC. Korsh had been certain that if Traub's show was picked up, she'd hire him on staff. He was wrong. Traub wasn't sure she had the money for a staff writer, and if she did, there was a more experienced writer up for the same job. Now Korsh found himself finishing another staffing season without a job.

"I remember thinking, 'If I can't get Stacy to hire me, who *can* I get to hire me?'" he says. "It wasn't the first time I'd had a personal relationship with a showrunner who had been impressed with my writing and wanted to hire me and wasn't able to."

Korsh had known being a TV writer would be difficult. He had known barriers to entry would be high. He'd known he'd start at the bottom, work long hours, and claw his way up. But none of that stopped him. Years as a real estate investment banker had taught him all about hard work. But to come this close—after years of waiting, hoping, working, praying—and then to have it ripped away . . .

As Korsh hung up the phone, he forced himself to face the one question he didn't want to ask.

Was it still worth it?

"My initial goal was to get staffed on a show *one* time, and then I wouldn't feel like I had failed. I could leave the pursuit with my head held high," Korsh says. "[But now] I was ready to be a writer. I was ready to be at the table. I had proven myself in the room, and I couldn't help wondering when my shot would come."

It had been a long road for Korsh, who—ten years earlier—had been working as a New York suit at Dean Witter and Victor Capital Group. But when a college roommate was killed in a drowning accident, Korsh had a wake-up call.

"I realized, 'Life is precious,' " he says. " 'I'm doing something I really don't like—and I shouldn't be wasting what few years I have doing that.' So I quit."

After spending two years traveling the country, Korsh found himself in Los Angeles, thirty-one years old and wondering what to do with his life. A college buddy was working as a TV writer, and "I thought if he could do it, I could do it. I had always loved television . . . and thought I was funny."

Korsh's buddy told him he needed to do two things. One: learn to write. Two: get a writers' assistant job, which—his friend assured him—would be "grad school for comedy writing." So Korsh stocked up on every TV writing book he could. Then, following a friend's lead, he landed a $400-a-week gig as a production assistant on *Everybody Loves Raymond*.

"My first day on the job, I show up, and I'm looking at Peter Boyle and Doris Roberts, people I'd been fans of my whole life, and I thought, 'This is fantastic!' " Korsh says. "I wasn't looking at it like, 'I'm getting coffee . . . this sucks.' I was looking at it like, 'Wow—I get to be around *this*!' "

For the next year, Korsh—an Ivy league graduate used to flying first class, hanging out at the Plaza Hotel, and designing cash-flow models for $50-million commercial properties—ran errands, made copies, and stocked his bosses' fridge. And, of course, he began to write, trying his hand at spec scripts for shows like *Friends* and *Raymond*.

"I worked on my spec *Raymond* for about a year," says Korsh. "I had no fundamental understanding of how to structure a story, so . . . I didn't outline it, I just wrote things. It was terrible . . . [and] I realized I had to go back to the drawing board and learn how to structure an episode of TV and understand how story worked."

Korsh's aim was to snag a writer's-assistant position on *Raymond* at the end of the year. Unfortunately, his hopes vanished when the current assistants stayed in the job. Undaunted, Korsh approached showrunner Phil Rosenthal with an offer: he'd work for free as a third writers' assistant in exchange for being able to sit in the room and listen. Rosenthal agreed (and even found the money to pay Korsh part-time). "He was very good to me," Korsh says. "The guy was all about helping people move up." Rosenthal was so good, in fact, that he agreed to let Korsh pitch and write a freelance episode. "Fairies" was the fourteenth script produced the next season, and Korsh was on his way to being a staff writer.

Or so he thought.

Once again the following year, there was no room to move up, and Korsh didn't get staffed.

He didn't get staffed the next year, either.

Or the year after that, when he took a writers' assistant job on *Just Shoot Me* and wrote his second freelance episode.

Or the year after that, when he was the writers' assistant on ABC's short-lived *The Big House*.

Or the year after that, on FOX's *Kitchen Confidential*.

"It was difficult," Korsh says. "[That] first job, I was so excited . . . [but] when you've been doing it three or four years, and you feel like you've put in the time and you're still not getting the opportunity, that's difficult to persevere through."

Through it all, Korsh kept writing—a spec *Scrubs,* a short story, two spec pilots, a freelance episode of *Love, Inc.* He would show his work to showrunners, co-workers, friends, anyone he thought might help.

"The more you write, the more you learn how it works, how to think about it, and different options you [have when writing] a scene," says Korsh. "It helps you be a better writer, but also be better in the room, [if you can] say, 'Oh, we have a situation like this, [so] we're able to approach it from this angle or this angle.' It gives you more experience and makes you better."

It was on *Kitchen Confidential* that Korsh and Traub hit it off—he even helped her punch up her *Notes from the Underbelly* pilot—and a few weeks later ABC announced *Notes* as part of its 2007 schedule. Korsh was over-joyed; this was his shot. Until he got Traub's gut-wrenching phone call. She wanted to hire him, but didn't think she could.

"I was devastated," says Korsh. "I basically wrote off the job as a possibility."

So Korsh did the only thing he could do: he started looking for another gig. He called friends, pursued job leads, met with showrunners. Nothing materialized. Then, weeks after staffing season had officially ended, the phone rang. It was Traub. Korsh's competitor had staffed on another show, and she was trying to find money to hire him. "Stay tuned," she said. "I think it's going to happen." Korsh was dubious. He'd been close before, and he knew what it felt like to fall from the heights of hope.

Two weeks later the phone rang again. The voice on the other end said just one word—"Korsh"—and he knew exactly what it meant.

"I remember screaming, 'STACYYYY!' and feeling like it was one of the greatest days of my life," he says, beaming. "Then . . . almost immedi-ately . . . the panic hit. It's one thing when you're sitting at the writers' as-sistant desk saying, 'I can do this.' It's another when someone says, 'We're giving you the opportunity to do this.' You get afraid: 'Can I really do this job?' "

But Korsh *could* do the job. Years as an assistant had not only taught him how to write, they had taught him how to handle himself in the room.

"It's unlikely the first thing you ever write is going to be good enough to get you a job," Korsh says, "so it's important that you do it as long as it takes, do a quality job, and learn the lessons from it. Keep getting better no matter what that entails. If you fail, do what you need to do to get back on the horse."

As Korsh learned, and as discussed in chapter 14, writers usually get hired when two elements come together: connections and actual writing ability. We'll talk about connections and job-hunting techniques in the next few chapters, but let's first talk about the kinds of writing samples writers need to prove they have talent. What if you've never written television be-fore? Or if you've had a successful career in a different medium? Can a tal-ented novelist or a seasoned journalist convince showrunners they're the perfect person for a staff?

Before storming the walls of television, you need to arm yourself with two tools: writing samples, which showcase your talent, and **credits,** or a résumé, which showcase your actual experience. This holds true for every writer in Hollywood, from the lowliest assistant to the mightiest showrunner.

WRITING SAMPLES

Most writers need two types of writing samples: **spec scripts** and original material. The term "spec script" (short for "speculative script") refers to both **sample specs,** or sample episodes of shows already on the air, and **spec pilots,** uncommissioned pilots for original series. Most of the time, however, "spec scripts" refer only to sample specs.

Sample Specs

The most common use of the term "spec script" refers to scripts written as mock episodes of existing shows. In other words, if you want to be a procedural writer, you write your own episode of *The Closer* or *House;* if you write multicamera comedies, you spec *Two and a Half Men* or *Rules of Engagement.*

Sample specs can't be sold; they're written simply to highlight your talent. In fact, most producers won't even read specs of their own show for fear of stepping into legal tangles.

"At *Sex & the City,*" says executive producer Cindy Chupack, "we rarely read spec *Sex & the City*s, because invariably there would be something in a spec that we had discussed or had in the works. Maybe we had talked about something similar, and then we would worry we couldn't do it because the writer would think we stole it." Instead, most showrunners read specs *similar* to their own show. Producers at *Eli Stone* may read *Boston Legal* or *Damages.* Execs covering *Samantha Who?* may read *30 Rock* or *How I Met Your Mother.*

Each staffing season, writers usually need two sample specs that showcase their versatility and present them as a specific "brand." In other words, you need to prove you have range, but you also need to know that agents, execs, and producers like to pigeonhole you as an "edgy drama writer" or a "wisecracking multicam guy." This isn't because they're lazy; it's because it's easier to sell (or hire) a writer who knows his own voice, as well as the conventions of his chosen genre. Most writers have specific strengths and proclivities, and you want yours to be obvious. Ray Bradbury doesn't write

SCREENWRITING AND STORYTELLING SOFTWARE

In today's high-tech world, help with any writing questions you may have is only a keystroke away, whether it's a technical issue or second-act writer's block. Here are pieces of software that do everything from format your screenplay to break your stories . . .

FORMATTING SOFTWARE

- **Final Draft.** The most widely used screenwriting program in Hollywood, Final Draft allows you to format teleplays, screenplays, or stage plays. **Final Draft AV** formats two-column scripts used for commercials, reality TV, and live broadcasts.
- **Movie Magic Screenwriter.** The industry's second-most widely used formatting program.

CREATIVE SOFTWARE

- **Storyview.** Outlining software that allows you to brainstorm, construct, and organize ideas and outlines.
- **Writer's Dreamkit.** Storytelling software that helps you cast characters, beat out plots, and uncover the themes of your stories.
- **Dramatica Pro.** Sold with Writer's Dreamkit, Dramatica Pro is storytelling software to help you explore the worlds of your stories, asking questions about plot and character.
- **StoryCraft Pro.** Helps overcome writer's block by perfecting story premises and organizing ideas according to classic story paradigms.
- **Power Structure.** Helps build story by concentrating on conflict and identifying conflict-weak scenes.
- **John Truby's Blockbuster.** Identifies the strongest moments of your stories and uses a "drag and drop" feature to facilitate easy reoutlining.

metaphorical science fiction *and* broad romantic comedy, just as Jimmy Page and Robert Plant don't write bluesy rock and roll *and* poppy ska.

"Figure out what area you're most comfortable writing in and you're best at writing, and exploit that to the fullest," says APA agent Lindsay Howard. "Be specific about what you're going after. It makes it easier for everyone to be able to target specific things for you."

So don't pair a *CSI: Miami* with *Worst Week Ever;* pair it with another hour, like *Without a Trace* or *Rescue Me.*

Your first goal in writing a spec is to prove you can mimic another writer's tone and sensibility, so your spec script must read *exactly* like a reg-

> **WORDS OF WISDOM FROM DREW GODDARD,**
> **CO-EXECUTIVE PRODUCER, *LOST***
>
> "If you're not inspired to write TV, be it a spec script or a pilot, then why are you trying to get into TV? If your answer is, 'That's where the jobs are,' you're never going to make it. This is not a waystation for anyone. For people you're competing against, this is their final destination. This is what they want more than anything in their life. And if you can't get it together to write a spec script, how in God's name are you going to make it through a twenty-two-episode season where you're required to write multiple episodes? That's not to degrade people; that's just a sign that television is not for you. You need to write what excites you."

ular episode of the show. A spec of *The Office* must have all of Michael's manchildish quirks, the romantic playfulness of Jim and Pam, and Dwight's and Andy's Machiavellian subversions. A *Grey's Anatomy* should incorporate Meredith's romance with Derek, the tumultuous relationships of the other characters, and a quirky, allegorical patient-of-the-week.

"The job of any TV writer, other than the creator of the show, is to channel the creator of the show's vision, to mimic their voice, to inhabit the world they've [created]," says producer Lesley Wake-Webster (*Notes from the Underbelly, What I Like About You*). When you write a spec, "you're doing that as if you're on a show. It's like if you said, 'I want to write a Petrarchan sonnet.' Is that still creative? Yes. You're following someone else's rules . . . because most of us don't speak in iambic pentameter, but it's still a creative exercise. Writing a spec is really good practice for what being a TV writer actually is."

Your second goal with a spec is to show off your own unique voice and vision.

"Create a plot or premise that's fresh, original, and puts the major characters into really rich situations," says executive producer Jeff Melvoin (*Army Wives, Alias*). "You *don't* do it by creating outside characters that you play most of the action to. That's the biggest mistake you can make in a spec script: showing your originality by saying, 'Here's this outside character,' or creating characters in addition to what's already there. You may have to invent some characters, of course, but the key is, can you write those lead characters well? Put them into situations that force them into interesting and

> ## GOOD BOOKS ON HOW TO WRITE A SPEC
>
> *Small Screen, Big Picture* is obviously not a book that teaches you how to write a spec. It's a book that teaches you *why* you need a spec—and what happens once you've finished. But there are resources out there that *can* help you write it. Here's a list of books and guides to help you learn, and perfect, the craft of writing for television:
>
> - *Successful Television Writing,* by Lee Goldberg and William Rabkin
> - *Writing the TV Drama Series,* by Pamela Douglas
> - *Crafty TV Writing: Thinking Inside the Box,* by Alex Epstein
> - *Writing Television Sitcoms,* by Evan S. Smith
> - *The TV Writers Workbook: A Creative Approach to Television Scripts,* by Ellen Sandler
> - *Gardner's Guide to Television Scriptwriting: The Writer's Road Map,* by Marilyn Webber
> - *The Hollywood Standard: The Complete and Authoritative Guide to Script Format and Style,* by Christopher Riley
>
> Also, check out TV writer Jane Espenson's (*Buffy the Vampire Slayer, Gilmore Girls, Battlestar Galactica*) blog, JaneEspenson.com, which has terrific practical advice on writing for television. In the appendix of this book, you'll find other great blogs, books, and TV-writing resources.

dramatic situations. If TV episodes were sonatas, you've got the form . . . but your melody, harmonization, and rhythm are [what make it] interesting. It's clearly recognizable as a sonata, but [your uniqueness makes it] a good one. It's taking the elements of that show and using them to good advantage."

Not surprisingly, those two goals—mimicking someone else's voice while inserting your own—are often at odds, making spec-writing a strange and delicate process. But there are a few things you can do to make it easier.

Pick a series you enjoy and relate to, but is also watched and buzzed about by the entertainment industry. That doesn't necessarily mean the show is a huge hit; *NCIS* and *Bones* are both successful shows, but few industry insiders watch them. *30 Rock,* on the other hand, isn't a blockbuster, but it has the attention of producers and agents, making it a much more spec-able series.

The best way to identify "hot specs" is to ask friends in the business. Agents and executives always know what specs are being read. If you don't have industry contacts, try these hints to help find a spec-able program:

- Don't choose mainstays that have been around for many years, like *Law & Order* and *ER*. You want to spec a show that's familiar to a wide audience, but still feels fresh and sexy. Also, if a show has been around for many years, readers are probably sick of reading its specs.
- Don't choose a new show in its first weeks of airing. New shows have uncertain futures (if they're canceled, your spec is useless), and they haven't been around long enough for readers to fully know their tone, characters, and storylines. Plus, new shows are often in the process of figuring out themselves what stories work and who their characters are, making them difficult to spec. Pick a show that's been on for a season or two (or, if it's a monster hit that clearly isn't going anywhere, at least thirteen episodes), but still feels young, vibrant, and creative.
- Get a sense of shows the industry appreciates by reading reviews in *Variety, The Hollywood Reporter,* and the *New York Times.* Check the most downloaded shows on iTunes. Watch the Emmys. There's no better way to see what the industry likes than to watch it congratulate itself on its favorite shows.
- Don't spec a show that's highly serialized. A spec should fit nicely into place with the current state of the series, and while shows like *Heroes* and *24* are popular within the industry, stories and characters change at breakneck speed.

Once you've selected your series, watch as many current episodes as possible. "Way back when, when I specced a *Law & Order,* I watched four or five seasons nonstop," says co-executive producer Melissa Rosenberg (*Dexter, Love Monkey, The O.C.*). "I just got into the middle of it, got into the voice of it, and analyzed it. How many scenes per act? How long does a scene run? How do they get into scenes? How do they get out of scenes? Do they pop in in the middle of conversations, or do they start walking in the door?"

It also helps to read shooting drafts of the actual show. "There's a different narrative style for every script," says Rosenberg. "Look at it on screen to get a sense of the voices and structure. Then look at it on the page. What's the scene description like? How does it lay out on the page? Do speeches rarely go over one sentence? Do they have huge blocks of monologues? How long are scenes, how many pages?"

Although shooting scripts aren't usually publicly available, most agents

and execs can track them down. You can also snail-mail a letter to shows'
writers or line producers; some are generous about letting people read
scripts of already-aired episodes. They may say no, but it doesn't hurt to
ask. (Also, pay a visit to the Writers Guild Foundation's library in Los Angeles, where they have a mind-boggling collection of produced TV and
movie scripts. Scripts can't leave the library, but it's free to read there. Learn
more at www.wgfoundation.org.)

DOWNLOADABLE TV AND MOVIE SCRIPTS

If you're looking for a particular script from a specific episode of a TV show, you
may need to do a bit of legwork. But if you're simply hoping to get a sense of how
TV scripts look and read, here are some websites featuring a wide variety of
(mostly) free produced scripts and screenplays.

Daily Script
www.dailyscript.com

Drew's Script-O-Rama
www.script-o-rama.com

Internet Movie Script Database
www.imsdb.com

Script City (this is a pay site)
www.scriptcity.com

Simply Scripts
www.simplyscripts.com

Q&A: SPECS APPEAL

Writing a TV spec script is an art form unto itself. In the sidebar on page 296, we
listed some great books to help you get started. But here are some things those
books *don't* offer—a real-life Q&A with industry insiders who are reading and
writing specs every day.

What are some of the details that turn a good spec into a great spec?

*"Stage directions. So many people skip over normal stage directions, but there have
been scripts where I've actually laughed at the description of somebody, or been
intrigued by how they set up a scene. So you have to pay attention to every little bit of
that spec script."*

—Jen Chambers, development executive (Maverick Television, FOX)

What's the biggest mistake you read in young writers' spec scripts?

"The single biggest mistake I see is the scripts aren't about anything. When I get to the end of it, I always ask: 'Why? You told this story, but why did you tell this story?' Ninety-five percent of them have no answer other than 'I thought it would be a cool story.' That's not good enough. You can have the coolest, most elaborately constructed plot and expert dialogue, and all the things people look for . . . but if you're not saying anything at the end of the day, that script is not going to stand out."

—Drew Goddard, co-executive producer (*Lost, Alias, Angel*)

What's the most important thing to study when writing a spec script?

"The structure of the show: whether it's five acts, six acts, or a teaser and four acts. Analyze each scene. Study the show, scene-by-scene, and get a copy of the scripts. Analyze what's happening in the last scene before the commercial break, the act out. Know where those 'impactful' moments have to be."

—Tracy Grant, staff writer (*Lincoln Heights*)

So lemme get this straight: I have to mimic the voice of the show *and* let my own unique self shine through? How is that possible?

"Choose an emotional story that reflects who you are and will be remembered. I just finished a House spec, and I didn't start with a disease. I started with emotional arcs of the characters. Then I picked a disease based on that, [on what] fit my theme and character arcs the best."

—Melissa Scrivner, staff writer (*Life*)

How many drafts do you recommend doing of a spec script? Two? Three?

"Rewrite that thing to death. After you have that first draft, do a second, third, fourth. Don't be afraid to make big changes. The best specs I've written have always come out after I've done huge overhauls on certain stories or character arcs. Don't get precious. Rewrite that sucker until it's gold . . . and you'll never know when it's gold, but the number-two draft compared to the number-ten draft: the number-ten draft is always going to be better."

—Sal Calleros, staff writer (*Private Practice*)

Once I get staffed on a show, I'm done writing specs, right? Surely I don't need to keep writing spec scripts after I'm a professional TV writer?

"You're almost never out of the spec-writing game until you're really high-level, and even then, sometimes you still have to write a spec. I'm by no means immune from having to write a spec, [and] the other producer-level writers I know—they're still writing specs. When someone's going to staff a show, and they don't know you, they want to read a spec, and they don't want to read a six-year-old spec."

—Aaron Korsh, staff writer (*Notes from the Underbelly*)

Original Material

Aside from specs, writers hoping to get staffed usually need two pieces of original material. These could be anything from screenplays to sketches to short stories. Although original material can be in whatever medium best captures your voice, producers and execs often like reading things in script form. "Write in the medium you want to sell yourself in," says manager Michael Valeo of Valeo Entertainment. "I won't read a magazine article and say, 'This person should write a script for me.' If you want to be a playwright, show me a great play. If you want to be a TV writer, show me two great TV samples. If you want to be a feature writer, show me two great feature scripts. Certainly, feature and TV scripts are close enough that there's crossover . . . but a lot of great feature writers don't understand the jump to television."

In recent years, thanks to the success of shows like *Desperate Housewives* and *The Shield,* which both began as spec pilots, showrunners and execs have been hot on reading spec pilots. A spec pilot, like any other pilot, is a script designed to sell a TV series—but it's written without being sold to a network first. A writer may write a spec pilot on his own, independent of a studio or production company, or he may write under the tutelage of a particular producer (often for free, since most production companies don't have their own money).

As we know, studios and networks rarely acquire already-written scripts, but lately the tides have been shifting. Like *Desperate Housewives* and *The Shield, The Oaks* and *The Class* were both sold as specs, igniting a spate of spec sales. CBS's *The Class* was a spec from *Friends'* David Crane and *Half & Half*'s Jeffrey Klarik. Writers' assistant Ari Eisner sold his action-thriller pilot *Target* to McG's Warner Bros.–based Wonderland Sound and Vision. And newcomers Ben and Dan Newmark sold *The Wilton* to the CW.

While this seems like great news for newbies with series ideas, "if you look at [most of] the spec pilots that have sold . . . the people who wrote them had been writing for twenty-five years," says Kevin Plunkett, ABC's VP of current comedy programming. Indeed, *Studio 60 on the Sunset Strip, Desperate Housewives, The Oaks,* and *Californication* all came from seasoned TV writers (Aaron Sorkin, Marc Cherry, David Schulner, and Tom Kapinos). "They wrote partly out of frustration that they couldn't sell this pitch, or had such a clear vision in their head of the show they wanted to do, that they found it more effective to write than to pitch it. So . . . if you're a baby writer trying to get a job on a writing staff, a spec pilot is about the hardest thing you can do. Whereas if you spec an episode of *Grey's Anatomy* or *How I Met Your Mother,* so much of that work is already done for you, and you get to showcase your skills as a writer [by] taking existing characters and an existing situation and telling the story you want to tell."

Although selling a spec pilot remains a long shot, writing one as a piece of original material, as a calling card for your talent, can be an effective way to capture the attention of showrunners and executives.

"If the voice is different or the plot outlandish, that's when you write [the pilot on spec]," says Allison Gibson, whose spec pilot *Reba* became a hit show on the WB, "especially if you can bring [a unique voice] to it and put it down exactly the way you see it. Then you have a terrific sample of your work, and hopefully you'll sell the idea in a way no one can see till you put it on paper."

PROTECTING YOUR WORK

One question on many writers' minds is "How can I protect my work before sending it to agents, producers, and execs? What if it gets stolen?"

Well, the truth is: *Ideas, especially in television, rarely get stolen.* I know you may think they do. I know you may have heard horror stories about writers having pitches stolen. I know you may see something on a show that's frighteningly similar to a concept you pitched last year. But that doesn't mean it was stolen. And here's why:

There is no idea you, or anyone else, could possibly think of that hasn't been pitched. Think you've got a brilliant premise for a pilot? I promise: it's been thought of. Have a hilarious idea for a *'Til Death* episode? Trust me: the staff was there first.

"Most good ideas are sort of in the 'collective unconscious,' " says *Sex & the City* executive producer Cindy Chupack, "and it's good if you're tapping in to that . . . it means you're on the right track. The real trick is execution, because an idea can be great or terrible depending on how it's executed, and the idea itself—unless it's crazy original and high-concept and specific, like . . . I don't know . . . *Defending Your Life*—isn't worth much."

In other words, it's not an idea itself that's valuable; it's the unique vision *behind*

continued

the idea. Look at *The Cosby Show* and *Everybody Loves Raymond*. On paper, those shows are nearly identical: befuddled fathers trying to navigate families and maintain control of their households. But the visions of those shows, the way they see the world, are completely different (as we discussed in chapter 6). And no one would accuse Ray Romano of stealing his idea from Bill Cosby.

So what am I saying? Don't protect your ideas? Well . . . yeah, kinda. Or, put differently, if your idea is capable of being stolen, you haven't done your job as a writer or producer. You haven't stamped it with the one thing that makes it unstealable: a strong enough sense of you and how you see the world. So when studios and networks pick up a show, they're not investing in the strength of the concept; they're investing in the strength and unique vision of the artist executing it.

Which is why, Chupack says, you shouldn't "be afraid to talk about your ideas, let people read your work, or go into a show and pitch freelance ideas. Your biggest fear should be that people *won't* want your ideas, not that they will! Your ideas, if they're good enough, will forge your career, so don't spend your creative energy worrying about protecting your work. Worry about making it so good people will want you (or your script), because you're worth it."

Having said all this, the Writers Guild *does* offer a script/idea registry service. You don't have to be a member to use it, and it costs about twenty dollars per idea. You can register your script online at www.wga.org.

(One last word of advice, however. Don't write "WGA Registered," or a WGA registration number, anywhere on your script. It's the sure sign of an amateur and immediately downgrades your credibility.)

CREDITS

In addition to writing samples, you also need a writer's résumé, or **credits,** which is different from a résumé you'd use to get a regular job. Credits list a writer's produced or sold writing projects, his title on those projects, and the companies that produced them. Credits also list notable writing experiences such as published novels, short stories, and awards.

Beginning writers often think credits should only include high-profile publications and productions. *Not true.* Any published or produced work is valuable, whether it's writing for your hometown newspaper or a regional theater production of your original play. These experiences still prove you possess a certain level of professionalism and someone liked your writing enough to acquire it. You may also include interesting nonwriting jobs that could raise your value in a writers' room. Perhaps you worked as a NASA scientist or an undercover cop. Maybe you spent time as a cult deprogrammer or a deep-sea fisherman.

"You're never *just* a writer," says Terri Lubaroff, senior vice president of actor-writer-director Eriq LaSalle's Humble Journey Productions. "You're hopefully a writer who's had some life experience to bring to the table. [So] whether you're a former FBI agent, or a lawyer who worked in the inner city, use it."

You can check out some sample credits below.

Another way to showcase your work is with a demo reel: a DVD or video containing clips of shows, movies, or other material you've written or produced. Although reels are mostly used by actors and directors, writers occasionally use them as well, especially in alternative and unscripted mediums

---

Hot Shot Talent Agency **HSA**

JOE SCRIPTER
Writer/Producer

TELEVISION

Take It or Leave It	Producer	BIG Network/Karma Prods.
Cold Lunch	Co-Producer/Exec. SE	BIG Network/Rich Studios
Sweet Tooth	Story Editor	FUN Network/Rich Studios
All Dried Up	Story Editor	WIN Network/Great TV
Three and Counting	Staff Writer	FUN Network/Rival Prods.

FILM

Untitled Joe Scripter Project	Writer	Smoke & Mirrors Pictures

THEATER

The Big Tantrum	Playwright	Podunk Playhouse/Dallas
Eat 'Em and Smile	Playwright/Director	Carnival Theater/Chicago

like reality TV and digital content. Hollywood is full of professional services that can help edit your reel. Or you can create your own with a computer, a DVD burner, and a little tinkering on Final Cut Pro.

GETTING YOUR MATERIAL TO THE RIGHT PEOPLE

Once your specs are polished, your original material is ready to go, and your credits have been whipped into shape, it's time to get your work into hands of people who can hire you. Like it or not, networking is everything in Hollywood, and from the greenest PA to the most experienced showrunner, most writers get jobs by knowing someone, which brings us to our next two chapters: representation and networking.

"[Going through an agent or manager] is the best way," says *Life* story editor Wendy Calhoun. "The system is in place and it's pretty difficult to buck the system, but some other alternatives are to befriend writers and executives. Get to know them, get them to read your work. Ultimately, they'll refer you to an agent. But if you don't come with some kind of recommendation . . . [from] someone they're in business with—you don't get any serious attention."

Of course, if you don't live near the industry or have connections, you need to attract industry eyeballs through other means, such as contests, festivals, and writing programs. Although these aren't the most direct routes to a career in television, they can open doors and garner attention. In chapter 26, we'll review alternative paths to breaking into Hollywood.

THE WRITER'S COMMANDMENT: THOU SHALT NOT STOP WRITING

So you've got your specs. You've got your original material. You even have some respectable credits. Now you can put down the pencil, close the laptop, and concentrate on getting a writing job—right?

Hardly.

One thing you must never do, no matter how much brilliant material you've written, is stop writing. A writer's job, whether you're getting paid or not, is to create, to constantly stay imaginative and churn out new material.

"I'm a big believer in putting your voice out there in whatever form you like," says showrunner Cindy Chupack (*Men in Trees, Sex & the City*). "Each time you do, it's like sending up a flare, and you never know who will spot you."

This is essential to a writer's career—not only because creativity is a muscle that must be exercised, but because showrunners and execs like hiring writers who are continually busy. Here's how some of TV's top writers recommend staying fresh—even when you're off the clock:

"Form a writers' group. I've had a writers' group for sixteen years, and I wouldn't have a career if it weren't for them. It's the equivalent of having your own writers' room. You're constantly getting feedback and experience in a room because you've created your own. That's half the battle of learning to be in a room. How do you pitch ideas? How do you feel confident pitching? When do you talk? When do you not talk? It's essential. And it shouldn't become a therapy group; it should only have people for whom this is a professional endeavor. No hobbyists."

—Melissa Rosenberg, co-executive producer (*Dexter, The O.C.*)

"Take an acting or improv class. Writers tend to get in their heads and construct sentences that aren't always easy for a person to say. When you're [performing], you quickly discover that how it looks on the page and how it sounds out of your mouth are two different things. Your jokes are going to be better if you actually hear how they sound."

—Lesley Wake-Webster, producer (*Notes from the Underbelly, What I Like About You*)

"Write plays you can put up. Once you put a play together, you can see your strengths and weaknesses. That's really helpful for developing your writing."

—Wendy Calhoun, story editor (*Life, Raines*)

"A writer writes from experience. Because of that, once you become a professional writer, your well of experiences dries up a bit because you spend most of your time writing instead of doing things. Make it a point to go out and experience new things. Travel. Start a conversation with somebody you wouldn't normally talk to. Put yourself outside your comfort zone. Say 'yes' versus saying 'no' to opportunities that come up."

—Daniel Hsia, staff writer (*Psych, Four Kings*)

"However you write when you work . . . if you do a lot of your basic work on a computer, which most people do, then when you want to be creative, do the opposite—handwrite—because your brain will start to think you're not working; it'll think you're just having fun. If you do a lot of your writing in handwriting, then do it on

continued

a computer, or some other way. I still handwrite all my scripts because it doesn't feel like I'm working."

—Drew Goddard, co-executive producer (Lost, Alias, Angel)

"Read a lot. In the early days of TV, people came to it as playwrights or novelists. [But today] young TV writers, and executives as well, are drawing [ideas] from years and years of television. My theory is: you get better stuff if you're 'dumbing down' high art than if you're coming at it from 'all I know is other TV shows.' Not to say television is dumb, but funnel down from more sources."

—Maggie Bandur, consulting producer (Life Is Wild, Malcolm in the Middle)

22

Representation

Agent Lindsay Howard knew she was trying the impossible.

Selling a spec pilot—a pilot written independently without being sold on pitch to a studio—has always been a Herculean task, and most specs that *do* sell come from experienced writers like Aaron Sorkin (*Studio 60 on the Sunset Strip*) and David Crane (*The Class*). But Howard, a literary agent at APA (Agency for the Performing Arts), was trying to do the unthinkable: sell a spec by a complete nobody.

Ari Eisner had been recommended to Howard by some executive friends shortly after she had been promoted from assistant the previous year. As soon as she read his work—a *Without a Trace* spec and two pieces of original material—Howard knew he was something special. But Eisner wasn't the world's easiest sell. He'd spent eight years as a writers' assistant, bouncing from sitcom to sitcom before transitioning into dramas like *Dr. Vegas* and *The 4400*. But still no staff job. His only real credit: cowriting a freelance episode of *Still Standing*.

That is, until he'd handed Howard a pilot about a guy who walks into a bar, sees a newscast about a man wanted for murder—and it's his own face. Howard loved it. The next day she sent *Target*—the story of an amnesiac assassin—to nearly every exec in town. Within days she found herself at the center of a heated bidding war between CBS Paramount and Warner Bros.

"I was frantically pacing the halls of my office," Howard says. "The whole process went on for two weeks, with studios trying to see how they matched up against each other. My adrenaline would skyrocket, then I'd be sitting and waiting to see who'd make the next move. It was [like] playing chess and riding a wave [at the same time]."

Howard knew how high the stakes were. Not only would selling this script be a huge coup for her—who, at twenty-six, was one of Hollywood's youngest agents—but Eisner needed this. Desperately. After eight years of not staffing, he was at a professional low, he'd just broken up with his girlfriend, and he was seriously considering leaving the business.

"You work really hard for people and sometimes, no matter what you do, you just can't break them," says Howard. "There are incredibly talented writers who just don't get their shot, and I didn't want him to be one of those people."

And then the phone rang. It was Warner Bros.' business affairs exec calling to say whether the studio was accepting Howard's latest counteroffer.

Howard listened carefully . . . hung up the phone . . . and called Eisner.

"It was one of those things you wait so long for it feels surreal," Eisner says. "You think there's a catch, it's a dream, there's a candid camera on you."

But there wasn't a catch. *Ari Eisner had just sold a spec pilot.*

"It's never easy to get somebody a job," says Howard, "but to expose the town to someone new and feel like you've made a great discovery, it's the equivalent of finding gold. That was the moment when I said, 'This is why I do this. This is why I'm an agent.' "

As an agent, Howard is part of an integral section of the Hollywood machine. She's a representative, or "handler," whose job it is to protect and further the professional interests of clients, usually creative types like writers, actors, and directors. This can entail anything from finding them work to cleaning up PR disasters, depending on the type of representative involved, whether an agent, manager, lawyer, or publicist.

Agents handle everyone from writers and actors to directors, designers, and composers. Their job is to procure work for clients by staying informed about current needs of networks, studios, and production companies, then filling those needs with clients from their rosters. They also negotiate clients' deals with employers, ensuring clients get the best possible contracts and are financially, creatively, and legally protected.

Managers focus less on obtaining immediate work and more on constructing clients' big-picture, long-term careers. Most represent writers, actors, and directors, and they're very hands-on in helping clients develop material and grow as artists. Unlike agents, managers are not allowed to negotiate contracts.

Lawyers rarely help clients find work or plan careers. Instead, they come in when a client gets hired or makes a sale to peruse contracts, execute deals, and make sure the client is protected legally.

Publicists help clients find opportunities to publicize themselves or their work (photo shoots, talk-show appearances, etc.), and protect them in the midst of PR disasters (like Isaiah Washington's gay-bashing incident or Denise Richards and Charlie Sheen's divorce battles). Thus publicists deal mostly with actors and celebrities who lead extremely public lives. A handful of A-list producers like Jerry Bruckheimer or J. J. Abrams may have a PR person, but most only hire publicists on a case-by-case basis to promote a project in need of special media attention.

In this chapter we discuss how agents, managers, and lawyers function differently—and how to know which type of representation is best for you. (Because publicists don't procure work for clients and rarely work with writers, producers, or directors, they won't get much ink here, but they're still an important piece of the Hollywood puzzle.)

Agents

Agencies are essentially employment agencies, like AppleOne or Manpower or any other traditional job-placement firm. But instead of finding jobs for analysts or secretaries or bankers, they place actors, designers, writers, and artists.

Because agencies procure work for clients, many states require them to be licensed or bonded (California agents are regulated according to the 1978 Talent Agencies Act, which differentiates them from managers). Employees within the agency are then considered sub-agents working under the license or bond of that particular company. Costs and terms of the bonds and licenses vary from state to state. You can check state-by-state specifics through the Association of Talent Agents (www.agentassociation.com), but most agents commission clients 10 percent of their gross income. Some only commission jobs they procure or negotiate; others take 10 percent of *any* income, but 10 percent is industry standard.

There are two types of agencies: **above-the-line** and **below-the-line.** Above-the-line agencies represent "creative" clients like writers, directors, actors, and producers. Below-the-line agencies rep "technical" clients like editors, DPs, and visual effects artists. (The distinction comes from the old days of film, when budgets contained actual lines separating creative employees, whose fees were calculated before preproduction, and technical employees, who were factored in during prep.) In this book we focus mostly on above-the-line agents, which are of either the talent or literary varieties. Talent agents represent actors and performers, while literary agents represent writers, directors, and producers. Some agencies handle strictly one or the other; others have departments for both. Because we're talking about writers, producers, and directors, our focus is on literary agencies.

Hollywood has three levels of literary agencies, based on the size of the company: the Big Five, midlevel, and boutiques.

The Big Five are Hollywood's largest, most powerful agencies: CAA (Creative Artists Agency), WMA (William Morris Agency), ICM (International Creative Management), UTA (United Talent Agency), and Endeavor. These companies often have more than 200 agents (William Morris and CAA have almost 500) in many different departments, ranging from talent and "lit" to sports, commercials, music, books, voice-over, online, below-the-line, and endorsements, with offices in multiple cities around the globe (most have 75 to 150 in their L.A. office, where TV is headquartered). A single agent may have thirty to fifty clients on his roster. The most successful agents have even more, as well as two to three junior agents dedicated to helping with the workload. Representing the majority of A-list writers, directors, producers, and stars, the Big Five agencies propel much of the industry's commerce, especially in television, which is a writer-driven industry and depends on big-name lit clients. These agencies not only represent most of the high-powered showrunners, but, thanks to their sheer manpower, can surveil more of the industry, fill needs more quickly, and package together various clients to create stronger, more salable projects.

The midlevel agencies—Innovative Artists, Paradigm, Gersh, and APA (Agency for the Performing Arts)—are slightly smaller than the Big Five. Most have about twenty to forty agents, each with fifteen to thirty clients, although many still have departments for talent, lit, music, or books. Midlevel agencies must work a bit harder to cover the vastness of Hollywood, but smaller client rosters allow them to give clients more personal attention.

Boutiques, like Kaplan-Stahler-Gumer-Braun and The Rothman Agency, often consist of fewer than ten agents, with under twenty clients per agent.

Boutiques believe bigger isn't always better. Although they lack the recon or packaging abilities of the Big Five or midlevels, they provide clients with much greater levels of personal attention.

THE JOYS OF PACKAGING

Aside from commissioning clients, agencies generate income by **packaging,** bundling together various clients to make projects more attractive to buyers. In August 2007, for instance, showrunner Tim Minear and director Todd Holland sold a one-hour pitch for *Miracle Man,* about a failed televangelist, to 20th Century Fox and ABC. Both Minear and Holland were repped at Endeavor, making the show an Endeavor **package.**

When an agency sells a package, it "becomes a minority owner of the show, meaning it participates in the license fee and backend profits," says Barry Kotler of The Gersh Agency. Although different deals work differently, an agency with a package usually gets 3 percent of the show's license fee, 3 percent of half of the show's net profits, and 10 percent of the show's backend. The agency then has "an obligation to service that show its entire life," Kotler says. "If I package a show [that gets on] the air, it's my responsibility to keep that show on and make sure it's being treated properly by the network. Let's say it's lucky enough to [have] a second window of reruns or syndication . . . it's my obligation to make those deals happen. I'm a profit participant, [and] there's a lot of money at stake, so I'm going to work my ass off to make sure that piece of business matures."

Because packages make agencies part-owners in shows, packaging revenue can be much more lucrative than sheer commissions. And an agency with a package is incentivized to staff clients of all levels on that show, so packageable showrunners make attractive clients.

Sometimes, rival agencies partner to create a package. If a director from ICM and a writer from Innovative want to sell a show together, ICM and Innovative can create a package and split the 3-percent fee. Also, when an agency receives a packaging fee, it doesn't commission the clients involved. So packages are often in the best interests of both agents and clients.

Managers

Unlike agents, managers aren't legally required to be licensed, so their job is more difficult to define and is, in fact, so nebulous that virtually anyone can call himself a manager. "The management landscape is much more like the Wild West," says Matt Schuler of Levity Entertainment, one of the industry's leading comedy management companies.

So what are managers expected to do? In short, managers counsel clients, plan their long-term careers, advise on projects, and act as intermediaries among their other handlers. Some writers, for instance, have separate agents for TV, film, new media, etc., but they usually only have one manager. "Your manager is your communication line to all those different entities," says Schuler. "You and your manager will have one conversation, and your manager will call the other people in your life and manage the whole situation."

A manager also helps clients develop projects, find or fire agents, and set general meetings with executives or producers. Clients often have closer, more personal bonds with managers, and managers—conversely—try to keep smaller, more intimate client lists. (Many successful managers have as few as fifteen clients.)

"Because of that closeness . . . you know your clients' hopes, dreams, goals, strengths, weaknesses," says talent and literary manager Chris Henze, a partner at Thruline Entertainment, and "presumably you understand better how to help them navigate their career on a day-to-day basis."

What most managers *can't* legally do, because they're not licensed, is procure work for clients. But that doesn't mean it doesn't happen, and managers can be as aggressive and productive as actual bonded agents (although managers aren't technically allowed to negotiate contracts). Also, because managers aren't licensed, they're allowed to commission clients however they want. Most charge between 5 and 15 percent, but they also make money by attaching themselves as producers to clients' projects. When a manager produces a client's TV show or movie, he often doesn't charge commission, instead collecting a "producer's fee" from the project's budget. Managers, unlike agents, are allowed to produce clients' projects because they're not (technically) procuring work. This regulation dates back to the 1930s, when MCA, Hollywood's largest talent agency at the time, would produce films, then hire its own clients to star in them. Citing a conflict of interest, the Screen Actors Guild outlawed the practice of talent agencies both procuring work and engaging in film or TV production.

Not surprisingly, the best managers are well connected, possess sharp eyes for talent, and have enough legitimate experience to know how to build a long-running career from beginning to end.

Lawyers

Most people don't need a lawyer until they actually *need* a lawyer. Lawyers step in after agents or managers have found and negotiated their client's job to peruse the minutiae of contracts and ensure that everything's properly executed. Some charge on an hourly basis; others charge 5 percent of each client's gross earnings.

HOW TO KNOW WHAT KIND OF REPRESENTATION IS BEST FOR YOU

Deciding whether you need an agent or manager (and what *kind* of agent or manager) depends largely on where you are in your career.

As a fledgling writer or producer, you need someone who can invest the large amounts of time and energy required to build a career, step by step. Perhaps, if you're just starting out, you want a small management company that has fewer clients and can give you more attention. Or perhaps your career is already moving and you need an agent to help take it to the next level. Different agencies have different strengths; your job is to find the right one for you.

"Some agencies are good at breaking writers; others are good at helping them break through the ranks to become a showrunner," says ICM co-president Chris Silbermann. "Good representation comes down to having a group of people who are passionate about *you*. Passion leads to the ability to knock down doors."

Would you rather be at one of the Big Five, where agents have massive clout with networks and studios, but less time for low-level clients? Or would you rather be at a boutique, where they may nurture babies, but wield less influence with buyers? Many times, the best fit for an ambitious young writer is an equally ambitious young agent, someone who has recently been promoted and is eager to make a name for himself, regardless of the size of his agency.

"[Staff writer] is the most competitive slot there is," says Howard, and "because lower-level writers take up so much time . . . you want someone who's young and hungry and aggressive about getting you out. It's not common for older agents to be able to devote that time. If they do, it's a massive rarity."

Whether you sign with a young agent or an established manager, the most important thing is finding someone who understands you, your work, and how to sell you to producers and executives. They don't have to be your best friend; you just need to feel comfortable that they "get" you. Young writers often get enamored with the idea of "having an agent," but the truth is: getting an agent is rarely what writers need to be focusing on.

"Don't spend time worrying about getting an agent," says staff writer Sal Calleros (*Private Practice, Three Moons Over Milford*). "Spend your time worrying about your next spec and how good it's going to get. Eventually, you're going to come across somebody who can forward your material or refer you, and when that time comes, you want a really good piece of material. If you're sitting there writing query letters instead of writing samples, you're not doing your job."

WORDS OF WISDOM FROM DREW GODDARD, CO-EXECUTIVE PRODUCER, *LOST*

"The dream scenario with an agent doesn't really exist, where an agent discovers a young talented writer, says, 'This script is great, I'm going to back this person and stake my career on them.' Agents are wonderful and very useful, but one thing they don't do, that people think they do, is discover talent out of the blue and get them jobs. What's more likely is talent's going to get themselves a job, and agents come after that. When you look at it with that framework, you say, 'What things are going to get me a job?' First off, it's the writing, so focus on writing. If you don't have a good script, you're never getting anywhere, [and] you want not *one* good script, but several, so you're ready when the time is right. The energy spent trying to get an agent is, by and large, useless. Because at the end of the day, you're going to get yourself a job through your own writing."

HOW DO I KNOW IF I WANT AN AGENT OR A MANAGER?

While agents and managers often function in similar ways, they also have different strengths and weaknesses and work differently with various kinds of writers. Some young writers argue managers are more valuable; others prefer agents. Ultimately, it comes down to who makes the best "teammate" for you, your writing, and your career. Here are some criteria to help you decide which representation is best for you.

You might need an *agent* if you . . .

- already have an official TV writing job, or an official job offer
- have had a certain level of success writing in another medium (feature films, novels, journalism)
- have a solid "library" or portfolio of usable writing material
- have strong contacts and relationships with showrunners, executives, and producers who would champion you and your work
- are hireable and need someone to find you work *today* (sure, we'd all love to get hired immediately, but being hireable "today" means you have two or more of the essential elements above already in place, making it easy for an agent to find you a job quickly)

You might need a *manager* if you . . .

- have a solid "library" or portfolio of usable writing material (yup, this applies to both; the more great material you have, the better)
- don't have many strong relationships and need to meet showrunners, execs, and producers
- would like a creative "partner," i.e., someone off whom to bounce ideas, someone to give you detailed notes and suggestions, etc.
- have many seemingly unrelated career areas that need coordinating (TV writing, stand-up comedy, short-film directing)
- aren't immediately hireable and need someone to help plan your long-term career (what kinds of things to be writing, what kinds of jobs to be seeking, etc.)

HOW TO ATTRACT AN AGENT OR MANAGER

For better or worse, there's one way—better than all others—to make yourself attractive to agents and managers.

"Get yourself a job [writing on a TV show]," says TV agent Jennifer Good of the Alpern Group, a boutique literary agency that also handles film writers and novelists. Then, "call up an agency and say, 'Wanna broker it for me? I'll start paying you tomorrow.' All of a sudden, we all pay attention. It's funny how that works."

Sure enough, baby writers are so difficult to "break" that agents rarely take them on until they already have a writing job. Or, at the very least, a writers' assistant gig that could lead to a staff position. But assuming you don't have that job, the best way to get representation is—like everything else in this industry—through connections and relationships.

"Because there are so many people trying to get into the business," says Henze, "[we] don't have time to just pick up [a writing sample] that shows up in the mail, read it, assess it, and talk to people desiring to get in. So we look to referrals—people who have been right in the past, people who have discovered talents, friends who we respect—and say, 'Hey, there's something I read,' or 'There's someone I know and you have to meet them.' If we just did it in an unsolicited fashion, we wouldn't have time to devote to our current clients and jobs." Thus, referrals not only validate you in the eyes of an agent or manager, they let the agent know you have your own relationships to help pave your way.

As Henze suggests, one of the least effective ways of attracting representation is sending cold queries. Not only do most reputable companies not accept unsolicited submissions, but cold calls or letters are sure signs of an amateur. "I get the occasional well-written query e-mail," says Good, "and I think . . . 'They're not in L.A., they don't know anybody, they're not diversity writers . . . I don't have the time.' I've broken a lot of people, but often jobs are given to writers' assistants, the PA, script coordinators. So you're competing with someone like that on every show."

The moral of the story: You want representation? You gotta know somebody. If not agents and managers themselves, people who can refer you to them—which means it's your job to get out there and meet people. (Not sure where to start? Check out chapter 23, on networking your way across Hollywood.)

Even working with a representative, you'll need to utilize every connection you have to get that first job (and second . . . and third . . .). "[Your agent] gets you the meeting; they don't get you the job," says Calleros. "It's your job in the meeting to make that person your contact. Follow up, meet for drinks, develop a rapport. That's where jobs come from—not [from] an agent. Once you're [hired], you get to know other writers, and when they go on to other shows and you're looking for a job, you hit them up. Suddenly, you have all these contacts and it snowballs. Then your agent steps in and negotiates a deal. So most jobs come from contacts, not [from] your agent."

Of course, once you're in the door, meeting potential agents, then what? What do agents and managers look for in future clients? How do you convince them you're the next big thing? "I wouldn't be meeting with you if

I didn't already like your writing," says Silbermann, "but there has to be something behind the words—a person, not just a robot. In film, you can be just on the page; you don't have to be a leader or a personality. In television, showrunners have to have social skills, leadership skills, and a personality. So I'm looking to see if you have those qualities."

Agents also want laser-focused clients who know what they want and what assets they bring to the table. Just as it's difficult to market someone who says, "I write everything: multicamera comedies *and* edgy cop dramas *and* sexy soap operas," don't try to impress agents with an overabundance of projects you're writing or developing. "When someone comes in with too much material, you feel bogged down," says Howard. "You want to know the thing you're taking in is the one thing you're really jazzed about. I'd rather see someone who's passionate about a specific thing and gets me really excited . . . [so] I'm putting all my energy into one or two things instead of five."

Sometimes, if an agent likes a writer but isn't ready to take him on as a full client, the writer may be **hip-pocketed.** "When you sign a contract client, you're under a fiduciary obligation to try and find them work," says Good. But sometimes "you say, 'I'm not going to get my entire agency behind you, but I like you, so I'm going to keep you in my hip pocket. If an opportunity comes up, I'll submit you. If you get the job, great, you're a client.'"

HOW TO KEEP AN AGENT OR MANAGER

Contrary to many newcomers' beliefs, working with a representative is a partnership; it does not mean you can simply sit back while your agent pounds the pavement, selling your scripts, sliding you into jobs. It's a two-way street, and though your agent's job is to be aware of as many opportunities as possible, your job is to be talking to contacts, searching for openings, and keeping your reps informed. It takes months, and more often years, of hard work and cooperation to "break a baby," and young writers need patience and perseverance, even when working with representation.

"Occasionally, [clients] put managers and agents on a problem-solving pedestal," says Generate talent and literary manager Kara Welker. "[They think,] 'If I could only get an agent or a manager, then I'll be active in this business and realized in Hollywood.' The reality is, agents and managers *do not* do the work for you. They guide, advise, educate, and help you through the processes, but the cold, hard reality is that the product starts with you, the talent. The idea starts with the talent. The *hard work* starts with the talent. So I'm inspired to work for people who want to work as hard as I do, if not harder. People who want to have the pitch ready to go, the script samples in shape, the live show really well produced. When a client provides me with material I can sink my teeth into, be it live or on the page or on the Internet, I have a sales tool and can do my job of getting you out there."

AGENTING YOUR AGENT

Agents and managers aren't known as Hollywood's wheelers and dealers for nothing. Their job is to "agent," to pitch, sell, and get execs excited about buying clients' shows. But as a client, sometimes you need to "agent your agent," or keep them excited about you and your projects. Here's some advice from some of Hollywood's top agents and managers on how to keep your representation passionate—and how to turn them off.

"A good client is on time to meetings and prepared. They know where it's at, why they're taking the meeting, who they're taking the meeting with. If they don't have the information, they call their manager or agent and get prepared by asking questions."
—Kara Welker, talent and literary manager, Generate

"My biggest pet peeve is someone calling to find out if I know anything yet. If someone calls once a week, totally cool. Even if someone calls once every couple days, totally fine. But people who call every day for updates get annoying. [If your agent's] a good agent and you trust them and they know something, they're going to call you. Back off."
—Anonymous agent

"Someone loses my interest if they're not scoring where they need to score . . . if I've given them a ton of opportunities and they're just not booking or starting to make me money. Or if they are booking, but they're difficult. If someone is always unavailable for [meetings] or wanting to reschedule or push deadlines . . . I'm not interested. I don't want to work harder on your career than you do."
—Michael Valeo, talent and literary manager, Valeo Entertainment

"Saying 'thank you' to your agent is often forgotten but always appreciated. Don't harp on every rejection. There will be many more noes than yeses. That's part of being a writer. [Also,] don't complain about your financial woes. You made the decision to be a writer and embraced the high level of financial risk that comes along with that."
—Anonymous agent

Communicating with your handlers is essential. If you meet a new showrunner at a restaurant or party, tell your agent. There may not be anything to do at the moment, but this can be valuable info down the road. Likewise, if you have an idea for a script or series, bounce it off your reps. "Never write anything without checking with me first," says Good. "I can't tell you how often someone writes this amazing idea and says, 'Here it is!' And if they would've told me three months ago, I could've said, 'There are three of these set up.'"

An agent's job is to know the marketplace: what's buying, what's selling, what's a MOP (Most Often Pitched). They use this knowledge not only to gauge what's commercial and what's not, but to give notes and help make clients' projects as salable as possible.

"There's a weird misconception that agents give notes to annoy people, like notes are something to make ourselves feel better," says Good. But "an agent is the conduit to what buyers say they want. When we give a note, it's because we're told that's what the market wants. We're trying to do our best to help you sell something."

HOW TO FIRE YOUR REPRESENTATION

Like everything in life, having an agent or manager is a relationship. And sometimes relationships run their course. People meet other people, have fallings-out, outgrow one another. And while no one ever wants it to happen, we occasionally have to break up.

"When it's working, things are getting done, your career is progressing forward, you feel like you're getting the right guidance through good times and bad," says Welker. "When it's not working, the client can sense their representation isn't that into them, or vice versa. The client runs out of gas on the relationship, or [the manager] runs out of gas. I've had to pick up the phone on more than one occasion and admit to a client I just don't know what to do with them, or I feel we have a failed connection."

As with any relationship, talk openly with your representation before closing the door. An agent might have no idea you're upset and try to rectify the situation. Or he may agree things aren't working, and you can part ways amicably. You may even discover the problem's on your end.

"Artists' expectations can sometimes be completely off," says Henze.

"They can expect way too much, way too fast, and sometimes they don't expect enough. The only way to know where you are on that spectrum is to communicate with the people representing you. They could be honest when they say, 'Here are twenty-seven places we've sent your material. We've had twenty-seven passes, and here's what they felt were weaknesses in your scripts.' You realize, 'These people are working as hard as they can, but there's something I need to do better.' "

If things can't be fixed and you need to pull the plug, talk to your agent in person. "Have a conversation in advance, a 'warning shot,' " says Welker. "Let's discuss and take a shot at fixing the problem. If, after an agreed-upon amount of time, we're not firing on all cylinders, let's mutually move on." Don't burn bridges; reps frequently switch companies, often hopping to other agencies, management firms, and even production companies or studios, so you never know when your paths might cross again.

Also, be aware: just because you part ways doesn't mean your representation stops making money off you. If your agent landed you your current job, he's entitled to her commission for that job, under the terms he negotiated, for as long as you work there.

Ultimately, it's important to remember that while having representation can be a huge boon, it neither makes nor breaks writers' careers. Your job is to keep writing and networking on your own, whether you're repped or not repped, paid or unpaid. Keep churning out quality material and meeting new people, and the rest—from paid gigs to representation—will fall into place.

MAKING CONTACT

Looking for contact info for Hollywood's agencies? We list many of the biggest agencies in our list of job-hunting resources at the end of chapter 25, or you can check out the Writers Guild's list of licensed agencies at www.wga.org/agency/agencylist.asp.

23

Networking

....

I've said it before and I'll say it again: networking is essential to surviving Hollywood. Execs buy projects from writers they've worked with. Agents sign clients they already know. Showrunners hire friends. Yet for many people, networking is one of the most difficult parts of managing a career. Shouldn't the skills of a writer, director, or producer speak for themselves? How can there be justice, let alone logic, in hiring someone on anything other than talent?

Well, the truth is, there *is* logic behind it, even if it's not readily visible logic. Think of it this way: Whether you're a writer, director, or even a network suit, you are—at the end of the day—some form of artist (or someone who works with artists). You create a product designed to move people emotionally—to make them laugh, cry, sit on the edge of their seats.

But emotion and art are subjective; what moves one person may not move another. You love comedies; your neighbor loves horror flicks. You like Beethoven; your sister likes Bowie. You watch *Breaking Bad* on AMC; your mother watches *Color Splash* on HGTV.

Each of those preferences is perfectly valid. But in an industry where you're peddling emotional stimuli, you need to work with people who respond emotionally to the same things you do. You wouldn't hire your horror-fan neighbor to write a romantic comedy, and you wouldn't enlist your rock-loving sister to produce an album of classical music.

So networking is a way for people of like minds and interests to find each other and work together.

It's also a way to find people you *like*. And this is important. Not just because you should enjoy time you spend at work, but because in an industry where getting a TV show on the air is a nearly impossible task, it's even more difficult if your partners don't share your passions or sensibilities.

Thus, it's essential to know people on a personal as well as a business level. In Hollywood, personality and emotional preferences—and the ability to articulate them—are both your skill set and the criteria by which others judge whether or not you're a good match to work with.

In this chapter, we'll look at practical networking skills and tips. We'll talk about whom to meet, where to meet them, and how to nurture relationships.

WHOM YOU NEED TO MEET

It's obviously important to meet whomever you can. If your dog-walker's uncle is the president of FOX or you run into the head of CAA at a barbecue, by all means get to know them. But these aren't necessarily the people you should be targeting.

Newbies often make the mistake of thinking they should form relationships with bigwigs at the top of the food chain. The truth is, however, you actually build your network faster if you aim for people lower on the ladder, only one or two steps above you: assistants, coordinators, low-level execs. These are the people best poised to help. Here's why:

Low-level employees are more accessible. Higher-ups rarely have time to answer their own phones or make their own coffee—which is why they hire assistants and low-level execs to help them. Lower-levels have (slightly) more time to deal with you.

Lower-levels are hungrier to prove themselves. "A lower-level executive has plenty to prove and less to lose than a senior executive," says Gabriel Marano, director of scripted programming at Fox TV Studios. "[Upper-level execs] have reached a level where they have a certain pedigree and an association of people bringing them [projects], so they don't need to go after something that would require more attention [such as a talented young upstart like yourself]."

Assistants have access to their bosses. One of an assistant's main duties is to decide what information trickles up to superiors: which calls get returned, which meetings get scheduled, which scripts get read. "[Assistants] are gatekeepers," says Beth Schwartz, a writers' assistant on *Brothers & Sisters*. "They work so closely with [their bosses], and they're in charge of so many aspects of their lives. If I didn't like something [I read], my boss wouldn't even bother reading it. If someone's rude to an assistant, they're going to tell their boss, and their boss isn't going to like someone who's doing that."

Information is power. Befriend those who have it. In an industry where knowledge is currency, some of the most powerful people are those controlling the flow of information: who's pitching what, which projects have sold, who's getting hired or looking for a replacement.

"Assistants trade information you couldn't find in *Variety* or Perez Hilton or a gossip blog," says C. J. Yu, manager of development, digital media at Endemol USA (*Big Brother, Deal or No Deal*). "A lot of times, assistants trade information off the record to facilitate their own company. For example, every year when upfronts happen . . . a lot of speculation goes on: what shows should be picked up, what talent is attached. And you can bet most assistants already have a good idea of the final schedule before it's published anywhere."

Assistants ascend the ranks together. "There's a camaraderie among people in the trenches," says producers' assistant Karen Jacobs, who has worked for former FOX president Gail Berman, Carsey-Werner principals Marcy Carsey and Tom Werner (*The Cosby Show, Roseanne*), and *Carpoolers* showrunner Marsh McCall. "With some of the upper-level executives I've worked with, a lot of their closest colleagues are people they were assistants with." Which means that by networking at lower levels, you're not forging friendships with today's underlings, you're seeding relationships with tomorrow's network presidents and producers.

WHERE TO MEET PEOPLE

Like it or not, there's one way, better than all others, to build your database of contacts.

"Get a job," says Rick Muirragui, a script coordinator on NBC's *Life*. "At the entry level, there are always jobs. Intern, PA, whatever you can. That first job opens all the doors, [because] all of a sudden you know dozens of people who know dozens of other people."

That's right: disabuse yourself of the romantic notion of spending nights waiting tables and days writing in coffee shops until you sell your magnum opus. There are thousands of disillusioned wannabes all across L.A. and New York doing the exact same thing, 99.9 percent of whom will never sell anything but a blue plate special. TV writing is a business, and while you need to hone your craft, you can't succeed in a business without immersing yourself in it. You must learn how the industry works—and, more important, meet players who can help you move forward. And the best way to do that is to get a job.

Of course, you often need to network in order to find that first job, and this requires more legwork and savvy.

"A lot of places have industry mixers you can go to," says story editor Wendy Calhoun (*Life, Raines*) "Any kind of industry party is good." Industry mixers are often hosted by official organizations like mediabistro .com or the Junior Hollywood Radio & Television Society, groups that specialize in helping people network and connect. See the sidebar on page 325 for some great networking organizations and resources. We'll discuss more of these in chapter 24.

You can also meet TV professionals by hanging out at industry hot spots. Whether in New York or L.A., the industry is full of bars, clubs, and restaurants where up-and-comers like to congregate. "Usually, hot spots [are] places you see in the tabloids," says Yu. "If they're places celebrities are going, you can bet assistants are going, too, and so are agents and executives. It's the notion of 'where are the top places to go?' Remember, assistants are the ones setting dinners and drinks between [their bosses], so—in a way—assistants determine what those places are."

You can find those places by reading blogs and websites frequented by the industry, such as Defamer, Gawker, Perez Hilton, and TMZ (and new ones pop up every day). Perusing these sites regularly not only gives you juicy industry gossip, but clues you in to where Hollywood hangs out. (You can find a list of helpful sites in the appendix of this book.)

NETWORKING ORGANIZATIONS AND RESOURCES

Association of Celebrity Personal Assistants (www.acpa-la.com): Networking and support for L.A.-based celebrity assistants, the ACPA hosts mixers, classes, and speakers introducing products and services of interest to celebrities. It also has a job bank, as well as an e-mail system to help assistants communicate and gather information.

The Biz (thebiz.variety.com): *Variety*'s social networking site specifically for people in the entertainment industry.

Connecting Reality (connectingreality.com): Set up specifically for and by professionals in reality TV, Connecting Reality hosts an online job board, a chat forum, and periodic mixers.

Hollywood Radio & Television Society (www.hrts.org): One of the oldest, largest nonprofit organizations in Hollywood; the premiere networking group for high-level TV producers, agents, and execs. Their periodic luncheons have become the biggest forum of Hollywood luminaries in the industry.

Junior Hollywood Radio & Television Society (www.jhrts.com): This Hollywood Radio & Television Society offshoot is open to assistants, coordinators, and junior execs working in TV or new media. Aside from hosting several yearly mixers, it holds regular speaker panels.

mediabistro.com (www.mediabistro.com): We host parties in New York, L.A., San Francisco, and more than twenty-two cities around the world. Many are tailored specifically for people working in television. There's no better place to meet working professionals and up-and-comers.

New York Celebrity Assistants (www.nycelebrityassistants.org): New York's premier organization for personal assistants, with a membership including assistants to luminaries in TV, film, music, sports, fashion, and business. They offer monthly meetings, discounts on special products and services, and a job referral service.

NextGenFemmes (www.nextgenfemmes.com): Open to women working in entertainment, including tangential fields like PR and marketing, NextGenFemmes's ranks include assistants, trainees, executives, and producers. They host monthly brunches and semiannual speaker panels, as well as a tracking board open to members with full-time entertainment jobs.

Women In Film (www.wif.org): One of the oldest and most prominent networking organizations for women working in film and television, WIF has renowned internship and mentoring programs.

Also, most colleges have alumni associations in every major city. Some even have branches dedicated solely to the entertainment industry: Vanderbilt has Vandy-in-Hollywood, Stanford has Stanford in Entertainment, Yale has Yale-in-Hollywood. Learn more by contacting your school's alumni department, career center, or film program.

Churches, synagogues, and religious groups also have mixers for young professionals, and some even have groups dedicated to various industries. The Jewish Federation of Greater Los Angeles has its own Entertainment Division, and Catholics In Media Associates or Hollywood Connect bring together Catholics and Christians. A few minutes on Google will uncover a wealth of resources.

Finally, join TV groups on social networking sites like MySpace and Facebook, or filmmaker-specific sites like JumpCut, the Biz, Flixster, YouTube, and Vimeo. Cyberspace isn't just the next great distribution outlet—it's the networking mixer of the future.

HOW TO MEET PEOPLE

Although everyone in Hollywood networks, and everyone *knows* everyone networks, the key to being a successful networker is to not look like you're networking. "As important as it is to make relationships," says Lisa Lenner, production coordinator at Lifetime Television, "you don't want to come across as the kind of person who's only talking about getting ahead in the business. I wouldn't want to hire someone whose only concern is their next job. It comes across as not having a well-rounded personality. There should be more to your life than that."

While this book can't give you a "well-rounded personality," it *can* give you tangible pointers on meeting people and nurturing relationships. I'd like to identify four steps to forming strong relationships: the introduction, the follow-up, asking for help, and staying in touch.

The Introduction
Whether it's a blind date or a potential business colleague who could get you a job, meeting new people can be an uncomfortable situation. That's why much Hollywood networking takes place in social situations like bars and parties.

"It has to be organic," says Mike Dunham, NBC Universal's coordinator of digital entertainment strategy and operations. "To go out and meet someone with the express purpose of landing a job—that's almost fruitless. If people perceive you have an agenda, that can be a turn-off."

It's often easier, therefore, to go to networking events with a friend or group of buddies, especially if one knows other people there. Once you meet someone, it's your job to spark scintillating conversation. I can't teach you the art of small talk, but I will say this: stay on top of pop culture. Know the weekend box office, the top TV shows, the number-one books. Watch iTunes's most popular music videos. Keep up with Internet fads. Though these sound like useless bits of trivia, topics that would be idle chatter anywhere else are the bread and butter of the entertainment industry, so arm yourself appropriately. Then, as conversation evolves, ask more specific questions about where your new acquaintance works and what they do.

"It's a lot like dating," says Lenner. "It's more important to be good on a social level than to come right out and ask for a job."

Indeed, it's rarely effective to ask for a job on that first meeting. Rather, get your new contact's phone number or e-mail, then follow up a few days later.

The Follow-up

Once you've met that "special someone," your job is to keep the ball rolling and get that all-important second date.

"Within a week," suggests Lenner, "e-mail and say, 'It was nice meeting you. Just wanted to let you know I think your job's really interesting. I want to talk about it more; I want to talk about how I'd get started.' If the person responds and says, 'I'm glad I met you, too,' ask them out for drinks. [Don't] include your résumé or be too pushy. It's easing into it, very slowly, not pushing too hard. You just want to form a relationship."

This is where I like to offer a little pearl of irrefutable wisdom: never underestimate the value of taking someone to lunch.

Everyone likes being taken to lunch. Especially assistants at the bottom who spend days getting yelled at by muckamucks above them. Lunch doesn't need to be pricey; it just needs to be someplace you can chat and get to know each other. If you can't go to lunch, go to drinks or coffee after work.

Try taking out one or two new people a week. While this can get expensive, remember: you're not just buying a sandwich, you're investing in your career. A lunch today lays the groundwork for a job tomorrow.

Asking for Help

Assuming lunch goes well, you can usually make your move. Wait a few days after the meeting, then e-mail to ask your favor (helping you job-hunt, reading your script, looking at your reel, etc.). There's no hard-and-fast rule, and knowing when to ask a favor involves feeling out the relationship and being sensitive to the appropriate timing. Some contacts may be receptive immediately, others may take more nurturing. The key isn't rushing but developing the relationship so it serves you (and the other person) for years to come.

When the time is finally right, be as specific as possible. "Don't 'ask' for a job," says *Life* staff writer Melissa Scrivner. "Let everyone know you're looking for work, and . . . *exactly* what you want to do. Say, 'I'm looking for a writers' assistant gig,' or 'I want to work for a talent manager,' so people know *exactly* what you're looking for. You have to know what you want."

It helps to be specific if you already know what jobs might be available or to whom your contact may have connections. Does his company have a show in production? Did a co-worker recently get promoted or fired? Does he work with someone who just sold a big project?

Sometimes, of course, you may not be looking for a specific favor, you just want to meet more people. In that case, tell your contact you'd like to treat them to another lunch—if they bring someone else. If you've just had lunch with an assistant from UTA's motion-picture talent department, but you'd like to meet someone from TV lit, tell your motion-picture contact you'd like to take him out again, if he brings a friend from the TV department. Slowly, you begin building your network of contacts.

Staying in Touch

Regardless of what happens—whether you get a job or someone likes your script—networking is never about immediate results. It's a game of long-term investing that may take years to return dividends. A PA you met last night may not help you now, but in ten years he could be running NBC. And the writers' assistant you met at the movies may not be much use today, but next month he could be looking for his replacement. Your job, therefore, is to stay in touch—with everyone.

"Keep a line of communication open," says Monika Zielinska, Comedy Central's manager of development. "A face-to-face every six months is good, even every year. But being in touch over e-mail and phone is just as useful."

Try to do no-pressure favors for people. If someone you know sells a pilot, send a congratulatory e-mail. If a contact is casting a series and you see a great actor in a play, send him the actor's name. Small favors are a great way to keep in touch because they're selfless; you're asking nothing of your contact, just making their day easier.

Remember, networking gets easier the more you do it. So jump out there and start meeting people. And if we ever run into each other at a party, I'm *always* up for going to lunch (I'm partial to In-N-Out).

THE DO'S & DON'TS OF NETWORKING: HOW SOME OF HOLLYWOOD'S BEST NETWORKERS DO—AND DON'T— RUB ELBOWS AROUND TOWN

DON'T ask people for favors right away. "Establish the relationship first. A lot of times at networking events, you see people and right away they say, 'Who do you work for?' And because you work for a certain person, they want something out of you. Just because you work somewhere doesn't mean you want to recommend some random project [to your boss]. Establish the relationship before asking a favor.'"

—Rachel Abarbanell, assistant, Lynda Obst Productions

DO "get business cards. Actual business cards with an actual corporate logo are obviously sexier than ones you make on your laser printer, but if it has your e-mail address on it, it serves the purpose."

—Jennifer Godwin, associate editor, E! Online

DON'T "get drunk. Everybody's drinking at networking events. There's free booze flowing; it's part of the culture. But just have one cocktail. It's not necessary to have more than that."

—Elise Friemuth, PR assistant, mPRm Public Relations

DO "ask real questions: anything about production or post or network or studio relations. Whoever you run into, whoever you think is smart, whoever is in the top

continued

jobs . . . ask. Keep asking. You can't get enough knowledge. It's not about schmoozing to be my friend. That's not going to help. What's going to help is knowledge."

—Mark Ovitz, line producer, *October Road*

DON'T cold-call or query execs and agents you don't know. "It's uncomfortable, because the sad reality is, most people who are sending query letters and calling probably don't have the chops to cut it."

—Mike Dunham, coordinator of
digital entertainment strategy and operations, NBC Universal

DO go to industry panels, mixers, and seminars. "[I used to use them] to practice introducing myself to people who were important, even if I knew they weren't going to remember me. If there was a TV exec on a panel . . . when the panel concluded, I'd [shake their hand and] say, 'My name is Tracy Grant, I really enjoyed what you had to say. I appreciate you coming out.' I knew they weren't going to remember, [but] it was practice. I just committed myself to doing it."

—Tracy Grant, staff writer, *Lincoln Heights*

"DON'T sleep around with too many other assistants. Whether you're a man or a woman, it will come back to haunt you. Dating a few people is normal. Leaving a trail of dozens of co-workers in your wake is the kiss of death."

—Joel Begleiter, literary agent, UTA

DO "follow up. [The day after meeting someone], I drop a quick e-mail to them saying, 'Thanks for meeting with me . . . it was a pleasure.' If you talked business, include a sentence about that piece of work, showing that you're interested in your career and how you can help each other."

—Janelle Young, development assistant, The Littlefield Company

DON'T "make negative comments about the industry or another person you've met. No matter what you're talking about, make sure it's upbeat so whoever you're talking to will remember you had a great attitude and would be a pleasure to work with."

—Alexandra Gaines, production assistant, *24*

24

Assistants

....

Ninety percent of all careers begin at the assistant level. *Friends* showrunner Adam Chase began as a production assistant for James Brooks. The Endeavor agency's Patrick Whitesell began in the CAA mail room before representing superstars like Matt Damon and Christian Bale. Universal Media Studios president Katherine Pope worked her way up the ladder at NBC. And though there are exceptions, almost everyone in Hollywood— no matter who they are or where they come from—begins their career as an assistant.

"You could be the most experienced CEO or business owner in another field," says C. J. Yu, who worked as an assistant at Mark Burnett Productions before becoming an executive at Endemol USA (*Big Brother, Fear Factor*), "but when you come to entertainment you have to start at the bottom."

This can be a sobering wake-up call for people transferring from other industries, especially since most assistants make about $30,000 a year.

"No one's going to give you that high-level job right away," says Loren Elkins, a former development assistant at HBO who now works as a personal assistant to stars like Nathan Lane and Bradley Whitford. "There were people at HBO who'd been lawyers and came in as assistants. I've seen lawyers, people with major careers, intern for free. They're fast-tracked, so maybe they're only 'on a desk' [working as an assistant] for six months or a year. But even just to get an assistant job, you're fighting everyone."

But what makes this business so unique that other professional experience doesn't transfer over? Why can't someone with an MFA in screenwriting or an MBA in entertainment jump right in as an executive, agent, or writer?

Though assistants perform many standard secretarial duties, like keeping bosses' calendars and organizing phone sheets, they also gain three key elements necessary to forming a career in Hollywood: relationships, information, and an understanding of industry culture.

"As with any business, part of it's about knowing the game and knowing the players in the game," says manager Michael Valeo of Valeo Entertainment. Few bosses will even hire or promote someone who doesn't already have relationships in place. Assistants are expected to take lunches and attend industry mixers to meet and schmooze with other assistants. A boss may not expect his assistant to know the VP of drama at CBS, but he'll certainly expect him to know the VP's assistant.

Another important assistant's duty is the gathering of vital industry information: which projects have been picked up, which actors have holding deals, who's writing on what shows. Much information is collected from trades, but news is also swapped over **tracking boards,** online information lists maintained by groups of peers. Although most boards are by invitation only, there are several membership-based tracking services. TVTracker and FilmTracker are popular, yet cost several hundred dollars a year. TrackingB.com is newer, but costs much less.

Assistants also glean information by "rolling calls" with their bosses. They listen on mute to all their bosses' phone calls, so—when the boss's conversation is over—they can place another call without their boss hanging up. This allows the boss to "roll" through calls while in the office, the car, or at home. It also allows assistants to take notes, stay abreast of information, and learn how business is done.

Finally, assistantships teach people the bizarre culture of the entertainment industry. Although Hollywood is run by corporate behemoths, it still eschews much of corporate culture. The workday often begins at ten and ends between six and eight. Lunch is at one. Major power players wear everything from Armani suits to shorts and flip-flops.

"You can read every book in the world and take every class," says Mike Dunham, who began as a literary assistant at APA before becoming NBC Universal's coordinator of digital entertainment strategy and operations, "but you don't understand the attitude of Hollywood until you're in it.

There are all sorts of situations where—if you haven't been an assistant and started at the bottom—you'll come off seeming incredibly naïve."

Of course, not all assistant jobs are identical. There are six main kinds of assistants—agency assistants, executive assistants, writers' assistants, producers' assistants, production assistants (which are different from producers' assistants), and personal assistants—and each has its own unique responsibilities and privileges.

Agency Assistants

Agency assistantships are generally thought of as the best learning ground for anyone hoping to break into Hollywood, whether they want to be an agent, showrunner, or executive.

"Agencies are the center of all commerce in the entertainment business," says Matt Schuler, a manager at Levity Entertainment Group, who began his career at United Talent Agency (UTA), one of Hollywood's powerful Big Five agencies. "An agent deals with everyone in town. And as an assistant, you listen to all the phone calls and learn how business is done. You hear [everything from] how a deal is done to how an agent sells a client to how projects are set up."

Many companies—including most studios, networks, and production companies—won't even hire assistants who don't have agency experience.

"[Companies] know if an individual has agency experience, he or she learned the basic skill set of being a good assistant: rolling calls, managing a phone log, setting meetings, etcetera," says Red Varden Studios president Zig Gauthier. "By working at an agency, you [also] immediately find out about the next best opportunities, whether that's going to a network or studio, or an individual writer or producer. Even for budding writers, producers, and directors . . . who don't want to be agents, they can go to an agency and establish relationships with other assistants. A year or two or three later, when those assistants become agents, they have to sign clients, and they're more apt to sign clients they know and have developed relationships with."

Most agents' assistants begin in the agency's mail room: sorting mail, binding scripts, delivering packages. Although this is tedious, grueling work, mail-room employees have access to thousands of scripts to read. They form relationships with agents in every department of the company. They often work as "floaters," filling in for assistants who are out of the office. When a job opens up, someone from the mail room steps right in. Thus, a mail-room employee gets to see every nook and cranny of the business. If he decides he wants to work in reality TV, he tries to "get on the desk" of an alternative agent. If he wants to be a writer, he angles for a desk in the lit department.

To learn more about life inside an agency, pick up David Rensin's book *The Mailroom: Hollywood History from the Bottom Up.* It's not only a great glimpse into the intense world of agencies, it's a terrific chronicle of Hollywood history.

LIFE IN THE TRENCHES: ADVICE ON BEING AN AGENT OR MANAGER'S ASSISTANT

Know when to "keep your mouth shut and play dumb." Working at an agency gives you access to privileged information, but "there have been a number of times where someone would call and ask what's going on with a situation, and your first instinct is to be helpful. But you have to be aware of what situations are explosive. If you're too loose . . . you can get fired."

—Mike Dunham, former APA agent's assistant (now coordinator of digital entertainment strategy and operations at NBC Universal)

"Bring good information to the table, don't be afraid to work late, communicate with your bosses, and be out in the community so you know what's going on in the trenches. Share information with other assistants."

—Kara Welker, talent and literary manager, Generate

"I wasn't a good agent's assistant. I was fired after three months and probably shouldn't have lasted half as long. It was my first job out of college and I took it for granted. I only did what I was told . . . I didn't go the extra mile because I didn't have the foresight to look at the big picture. I could have made so many more contacts and learned so much about the industry. I only knew I didn't want to be an agent, so I didn't see the value in learning anything. That was a major mistake. I had so much at my fingertips . . . if I had only made use of it."

—Tracy Wilcoxen, former agent's assistant, The Paul Kohner Agency (now a successful reality producer on shows like E!'s *Last Model Standing* and ABC's *The Bachelor*)

Executive Assistants

Executive, or administrative, assistants work at networks, studios, and production companies, where they have windows directly into TV's development and production process.

"An executive assistant," says Yu, "is there to do anything and everything to keep their boss running. That's everything from making sure their calendars, appointments, and travel plans are set to getting coffee and the paper on their boss's desk before they walk in. You need to be the eyes, ears, and arms of your boss when he's not available, and his presence when he's not in the office."

Because most executive assistants are suits-in-training, they often read scripts and give notes on shows in development or production. Many sit in on pitches or development meetings. Some even find and shepherd their own projects.

Administrative assistants frequently begin as agency assistants, where they form relationships with assistants at networks and studios. Some begin as unpaid interns. Others come through corporate training programs, like NBC's Associate and Page programs, which teach the ropes to aspiring execs.

LIFE IN THE TRENCHES: ADVICE ON BEING AN EXECUTIVE ASSISTANT

"If you're going to be at a production company, studio, or network, read everything. Go home every night with three or four things to read. There are a lot of times you don't want to read but you have to. You never know where a good script or a good writer is going to come from. A good assistant is willing to look everywhere for good material."
—Joe Hipps, VP of development, Dawn Parouse Productions

"Going above and beyond shows a lot of initiative. Some scripts came in while I was on vacation, and when I came back, [my assistant] had stacked the scripts on my desk. There was a buckslip on each one, and I figured it was from the agent. When I went to read the scripts, which was a big pile, [I realized my assistant] had read all the scripts, and on the buckslips she'd written coverage. It was so helpful, and she never said, 'I read all these scripts . . . here's what I think!' "
—Amanda Tracey, director of development, 20th Century Fox Studios

---

Writers' Assistants (and Script Coordinators)

Writers' assistants work for the writing staff of a particular show, where their main duty is to sit in the writers' room, taking notes on everything that's discussed. They also do story research, execute administrative paperwork (like writers' contracts), and print or distribute scripts. Writers' assistants often work closely with **script coordinators,** who track script changes, distribute new pages, archive drafts, and back up the writers' assistant when he's not in the writers' room.

Getting hired as a writers' assistant or script coordinator requires speedy fingers, quick ears, and great organizational skills. Most important, showrunners have to like you enough to be in a room with you for twelve hours a day—which is why showrunners usually hire people they already know. The best way to get the job, then, is to begin as a production assistant, doing menial tasks like getting lunch and making copies, so you can form relationships that can get you promoted. Many shows even have PAs who work solely for the writers' room. It's not glamorous, but it provides direct contact with writers and producers.

Because most showrunners hire writers they know, working as a writers' assistant is also the number-one way to get an official writing job. Writers' assistants are occasionally allowed to pitch jokes or write freelances scripts, and if they do a good job, they'll likely get promoted the following year.

LIFE IN THE TRENCHES: ADVICE ON BEING A WRITERS' ASSISTANT

Scrubs co-executive producer Janae Bakken worked as a writers' assistant on *Oh Grow Up* and *Malcolm in the Middle* (as well as a producers' assistant on *Caroline in the City, Union Square,* and *Mad About You*) before getting her first writing job on NBC's *Scrubs*. Having been on both sides of the writers' table, here are Bakken's six rules for surviving as a writers' assistant:

Be a stellar typist. "I hate when I'm a better typist than the assistant. Take a typing class or program on a computer if you have to; there's no excuse for being bad at your job."

Know Final Draft inside and out. "Practice typing dialogue into Final Draft from a show on television. The warp speed of people talking will be much like it is when writers are rewriting a script in the room."

Take good notes in a usable format. "[This] goes along with being a good typist: organize the notes well. Use bold type, or italics, and new paragraphs to separate ideas and emphasize important stuff. It helps when writers read the notes later."

Don't talk too much. "Know your audience, when they want to hear your pitch, and when it's better to stay quiet."

Have thick skin. "A lot of offensive stuff can be said in the room . . .[and] you have to learn to laugh at it, which can be hard, especially as a woman or a minority, and realize it's in jest and most likely not meant in truth. It probably means [the writers] like you. Also, you can never tell what you've heard in the room. As the saying goes, 'What's said in the room, stays in the room.' "

Go the extra mile. "[Always] be willing to help out, stay late, answer a phone, whatever it takes. Don't think something's 'beneath you' . . . it just makes you look bitter and entitled. If you are always helpful and good at your job, people remember it, love it, want to hire you, and are willing to help when you're trying to move up."

Producers' Assistants (and Directors' Assistants)

For aspirants who want to remain close to the creative process, being the assistant to an EP or a director may be a better path than joining a network or studio. Just ask Karen Jacobs, who has assisted former FOX president Gail Berman; Marcy Carsey and Tom Werner of Carsey-Werner Productions (*The Cosby Show, Roseanne, That '70s Show*), and *Carpoolers* showrunner Marsh McCall. She's seen how television works from almost every possible angle.

"The network was the business side of the business: scheduling, marketing, publicity, comedy, drama, reality," Jacobs says. "At Carsey-Werner, it was more creative. They were selling as opposed to buying, so they spent time perfecting the pitch, working with writers, getting things network-ready. Where I work now, for an actual writer, I see the *other* side of perfecting the pitch: the treatment, the story, the bare bones of creativity from the birth of an idea through the script."

While there are still general assistant duties to be done, EPs' assistants experience the creative process up close, one on one.

"My duties include everything from answering phones and keeping [my boss's] calendar," says Correne Kristiansen, assistant to *Samantha Who?* showrunner Donald Todd, "to proofreading scripts to coordinating with the studio and network to doing research to assisting him on set. I am basically responsible for staying on top of the hundreds of things he has to do on a given day and making sure they get done."

Like being a writers' assistant, working for an EP or director is a great way to form relationships with other writers and artists, and it frequently leads to staff jobs or freelance scripts. But like all jobs in Hollywood, it requires connections.

"I got to where I am today by working for [Tom Werner,] the (non-writing) EP of the last pilot Marsh wrote," Jacobs says. "I met Marsh [at Carsey-Werner] . . . he trusted me . . . and he brought me over to be his assistant. The old adage about this industry is 'relationships are everything,' and relationships *are* everything."

LIFE IN THE TRENCHES: ADVICE ON BEING A PRODUCERS' ASSISTANT

"Be sensitive about wasting the showrunner's time. Save nonessential questions for the end of the day [and] try to reroute issues that can be handled by someone else. Generally, act as a 'bouncer' so they can focus on the important things: writing and producing a great show."

—Correne Kristiansen, showrunners' assistant, *Samantha Who?*

"Don't ever tell callers what your boss is really doing. They don't need to know he's at the dentist, at a basketball game, or taking his dog to the vet. Your boss is either out of the office or on a call. [Also,] don't let your boss get to the office before you. By the time he comes in, have the messages checked, his computer turned on, and his coffee ready."

—Tracy Wilcoxen, former showrunners' assistant (now producing reality shows for MTV, Lifetime, FOX, and NBC)

Production Assistants

Production assistants, or PAs, work for specific shows, where they're the lowest rung on the assistant ladder. They're "all-purpose assistants . . . picking up whatever other people won't do," says Kate Burns, who worked as the writers' PA on CBS's *Shark* before becoming the writers' assistant on the CW's *90210*.

Being a PA often involves tedious and dirty grunt work. Office PAs work in the production office: making copies, ordering supplies, answering phones. Set PAs lend a hand on stage: helping the crew, delivering messages, fetching things for actors or directors. Writers' PAs stock the writers' kitchen, pick up lunch, and deliver scripts in the middle of the night.

Although it's a thankless job, PAs meet everyone on the production, from writers and producers to grips and gaffers, which means a smart PA makes relationships that can lead to his next job or promotion.

Because PAs are entry-level positions, employers often post them in public forums like Showbizjobs.com or The Grapevine, which we'll discuss in chapter 25. Still, the best way to find a PA gig is to know someone.

"Use your alumni association, call family friends, people you went to high school with, anybody you know in the industry," says Burns. "They'll be able to refer you to jobs, which is the [biggest] way to get employed."

(For a fun glimpse at the day-to-day life of a production assistant, check out The Anonymous Production Assistant's Blog at anonymousassistant .wordpress.com.)

LIFE IN THE TRENCHES: ADVICE ON BEING A PRODUCTION ASSISTANT

"Always follow through on whatever task it is you were given. The production office gets blamed for everything that goes wrong, both in the office and on set, so . . . if someone asks you to do a task, see it through and tie up all loose ends."

—Alexandra Gaines, office PA, *24*

"When I was a PA [on The Keenan Ivory Wayans Show*], we had food for guests in the green room . . . and I got promoted because I would make sure the food was organized. It sounds ridiculous, but I was neurotic about it, and they saw that. I took pride in every little thing I did. If there was a dish that was empty, I'd take it to the kitchen. I used to bring a bagel to this one writer every single morning. Just do your job and stick with it."*

—Sara Auspitz, director of programming, Endemol

"Anticipate and have things ready. If you're the one who's supposed to get there in the morning and make the coffee, get there ten minutes before everybody else. Make it look as seamless as possible."

—Kate Burns, writers' assistant, *90210*

"[Don't] personalize the shit you get thrust upon you every day. Most of the stuff you're on the receiving end of has nothing to do with you. Even more important, [if you're an aspiring writer], keep writing. Dealing with a jerky boss is easier when you incorporate his antics into your pilot."

—Rafael Garcia, staff writer, *Samantha Who?*

Personal Assistants

Personal assistants run the personal and professional life of an individual— usually a celebrity.

"[Celebrities] are a corporation in and of themselves," says personal assistant Loren Elkins. "They're a business, and the business has to be run. So I deal with all the business aspects of their lives: agents, managers, business managers, publicists. Everything gets filtered through me. [I cover the] schedule, answer phone calls, filter everything."

Some personal assistants perform strictly business tasks: answering phones, keeping calendars, reading scripts. Others do personal things: gift shopping, car washing, grocery shopping. Your job, after all, isn't just managing the life and business of a celebrity—it's helping that person *be* a celebrity.

"You have to be discreet," says Elkins. "They don't want you being the center of attention, even if you're out with them and they're talking to other people. You're in the background. You're listening and a participant, but let them do what they do. If you're out in public and people start hounding them, you have to be able to push them away. Sometimes you have to be the bad guy because the celebrity doesn't want to be the one to say no."

Some people become personal assistants by applying through specialized employment agencies like The Help Company or the Elizabeth Rose Agency. But most get jobs through their own relationships with celebrities or people who know them.

"Agents, publicists, business managers will often look for personal assistants for their celebrity clients," says Elkins. You can also start by getting "a job on a movie set or a TV set. Like anything in this business, it's about saying what you want when you meet people."

Personal assistant positions can be great steppingstones to other jobs because you work closely with high-powered people. Prove yourself capable, articulate, and trustworthy, and you may find yourself positioned to hop into a staff job or a writers' assistant gig. Even if your boss isn't a writer, working as a personal assistant gives you access to your boss's co-workers, associates, and friends—many of whom are probably writers, agents, execs, and directors themselves—giving you more relationships to nurture and use when the time is right.

OTHER ENTRY-LEVEL JOBS

While being an assistant is square one for almost any TV career, assistant jobs are highly competitive. So many positions go to friends and contacts of employers that even human resources departments have a tough time placing people. Thus, here are several other ground-floor paths into Hollywood:

Internships are one of the best ways to start a career in television. Everyone loves free labor, and most interns are unpaid college students or recent graduates. Interns do everything from buying office supplies and fetching coffee to reading scripts and filling in for assistants.

"You'd be surprised how much access you have as an intern," says Ryan Quigley, whose internship at ABC Studios led to his development-assistant job at Brancato/Salke Productions (*North Shore*), an ABC-based pod. "I got to be on notes calls with writers, attend development meetings, even get ahead on future episodes of *Lost*. And, of course, it involved many hours at the copy machine."

Check with your university's career center or alumni association about how you can find a TV internship. Unfortunately, many employers won't hire interns who aren't currently enrolled students, so if you're not a current student—become one! Part-time enrollment at a local community college often costs only a few hundred dollars and allows you to get credit (even if you don't actually need it) for an unpaid internship.

You can also begin as a runner, which is similar to being a PA, except runners do little but run errands. They run to the set, edit bays, grocery stores, studios—wherever their bosses send them. If you're applying for a job as a runner, be sure you have your own transportation and a working knowledge of your city. Most employers won't even consider runners who don't have a car and don't know their way around (which usually means you've lived in that city for several months).

Companies also hire **script readers,** freelance employees who read scripts and write **coverage,** "book reports" synopsizing the story and detailing the reader's opinion. If a script reader doesn't like a script, his boss will probably never read it. If he raves about a script, his boss may read it that very night. Most companies keep databases of coverage, allowing them to look up readers' opinions on writers years later. Though script-reading gigs aren't high-paying or prestigious jobs, it's still best to know someone or be an intern in order to get them.

If you're trying to break into reality TV, being a **logger** is a great starting place. Loggers create transcriptions, or logs, of taped footage, which producers use to find scenes and moments needed to edit an episode. It's a low-paying, tedious job, but logging is a good way to meet people and learn the process.

HELPFUL RESOURCES FOR ASSISTANTS

As an assistant, you'll be expected to have answers at the drop of a hat—everything from which agents represent which writers to where to find the hottest new Chinese restaurant. Though we can't give you every answer you might need, here are several resources that will turn you into an encyclopedia of up-to-the-minute Hollywood news and information.

Hollywood Creative Directory (www.hcdonline.com). A regularly published directory of names and contact info for nearly every company in the entertainment business, whether it's film, TV, music, or new media. Online subscriptions are also available.

IMDb and IMDbPro (www.imdb.com). A massive database of film and TV titles, casts, and crews, including release dates and box office information. For a monthly fee, IMDbPro also offers contact info, production charts, and industry news. **IMDbResume** allows actors to post headshots and résumés.

Thomas Guide (www.randmcnally.com). A must-have for any assistant living and driving in L.A., Thomas Guides are detailed street maps of all of L.A., Orange County, and the San Fernando Valley.

Studio System (www.studiosystem.com). Most Hollywood companies subscribe to Studio System, an up-to-date tracking system that monitors everything from where individual agents and executives work to different companies' development slates.

TrackingB.com (www.trackingb.com): A subscription-based tracking board following script sales, hires and fires, job opportunities, and other industry news.

TV.com (www.tv.com): Like IMDB, a massive database of current and past TV shows, including information on writers, directors, and casts, as well as air dates and episode guides.

TV Tracker (www.tvtracker.com). Like Studio System, this subscription-based service traces everything from current cable series to broadcast development. You can find a film version at www.filmtracker.com.

Who Represents (www.WhoRepresents.com). A subscription-based database that tracks talent and representation. Who Represents can tell you George Clooney's agent, Jerry Seinfeld's manager, or Glenn Close's publicist.

25

Getting a Job

Getting a job in Hollywood may be all about relationships, but relationships can only get you so far. You still need to have a résumé. And ace the interview. And prove you're right for the gig. In this chapter we'll explore how to go from pavement-pounder to professional, whether you're aiming to be a writer, producer, agent, or executive.

FINDING A JOB

"More than 75 percent of jobs people get are through some kind of connection or word of mouth," says *Life* script coordinator Rick Muirragui. But that doesn't mean Hollywood's not filled with countless other great job-hunting resources, from industry websites to employment agencies. We list many of these resources in our Job Hunting Guide at the end of this chapter, but there are other ways to find jobs as well.

One of Hollywood's most popular job-hunting resources is the UTA joblist (maintained by United Talent Agency), an e-mailable document containing openings for execs, producers, assistants, and interns in every area of TV, film, music, and PR. Unfortunately, the joblist isn't available to the public; the only way to get it is to know someone at UTA (or know someone who knows someone). Still, it's widely considered one of the industry's most current resources, and if you're scrappy, it shouldn't take long to find someone to get you a copy.

You can also contact companies directly. Most networks and studios

POUNDING THE PAVEMENT: HELPFUL TIPS
ON HOW TO FIND A JOB

"Learn where your interests are, whether it's in development, marketing, [etc.]. These areas are so specific in terms of ways to go. I started here twenty-six years ago and became a producer by going into edit bays and watching how people actually formulated a campaign. Put yourself in a place and . . . educate yourself as to what your interests are."

—Marla Provencio, executive vice president, marketing, ABC Entertainment

"Go for jobs in an area . . . you're passionate about. It doesn't make sense to approach interviewing as, 'I need a job and will do anything to be in the business.' Know what you love going in. Be focused."

—Kara Welker, talent and literary manager, Generate

"Think about entry-level jobs that let you learn needed skills on the side. My first job in New York was as a receptionist at a postproduction company that let me learn the Avid at night. Gradually they let me do digitizing work that I could put on my résumé."

—Rebecca Short, editor (The Bachelor, Rob and Big, Flavor of Love)

"There are ways to get internships even if you're in school. Look into programs such as AFI (www.afi.com) or UCLA Extension (story.uclaextension.edu) where you can take an 'internship class.' "

—Correne Kristiansen, executive producers' assistant, Samantha Who?

"[If you don't live in L.A. or New York], check out craigslist. When we travel for our [reality] shows, we advertise in cities we travel to, looking for local PAs. Impress a traveling company coming in, be the local PA who knows their shit, and any producer will tell you, 'Move to L.A. and I'll get you a job.' "

—Joke Fincioen, executive producer, (Scream Queens, Beauty & the Geek)

"Know what you already like and what you like to do. You probably aren't going to be the anointed one who gets a job assisting Joss Whedon, but if you have a list of writers you admire, finding out where they work and reaching out to them couldn't hurt."

—Jennifer Godwin, associate editor, E! Online

have contact info online, and many have their own employment websites (some of which we'll include at the end of the chapter). Another valuable resource is the *Hollywood Creative Directory,* a collection of regularly published books (*The Hollywood Creative Directory, The Hollywood Representation Directory, The Hollywood Distribution Directory*) that contain contact info, executive rosters, and credits for nearly every network, studio, production company, and agency in the business. If you don't want to buy the books, they also offer Internet subscriptions and an online job database (www.hcdonline.com).

APPLYING FOR JOBS IN ENTERTAINMENT

Like it or not, there's one important rule when it comes to looking for entertainment jobs: you have to be living in L.A., New York, or whatever city you wish to work in. I hate to say it, but it's true. Most places won't even consider you if you're not already local.

"In the 'real world,' " says Levity Entertainment manager Matt Schuler, "you get a job and they set up a start date so you have time to give notice to your [current] job. Here [in Hollywood] they hire people based on people leaving. They interview people on a year-round basis, so . . . if three people quit, they just call and have [three more] start the next day. They want people who are available right then and there."

Bosses also want assistants and execs who are familiar with the landscape. This not only means knowing your way around geographically, it means having strong networks of contacts already in place, which usually takes living somewhere for several months.

Most entertainment jobs require two pieces of application material: a résumé and a cover letter. These often look different from résumés and letters in other fields, so be sure yours are Hollywood-friendly.

RÉSUMÉS

A résumé should be easy to read. Contrary to many beginners' beliefs, organizing a résumé is not about cramming in as much info as possible; it's about creating an easy-to-read, one-page document that imparts important bullet points in a ten-second glance. You can do this by dividing your résumé into four sections: entertainment experience, other employment, education, and additional information (you can see an example on the next page).

Begin with any entertainment-related experience—even if it was unpaid.

"Any skills you can show on your résumé that might translate into this

KELLY PENMAN

5150 Rewrite Drive
Los Angeles, CA 90069
555-316-1984
kpenman@hireme.com

ENTERTAINMENT INDUSTRY EXPERIENCE

• Production Assistant, "Outta Love Again"   **2009**
Scatterbrain Productions
Delivered dailies, stocked supplies, loaded sets, orgianized script rewrites, filed location permits on low-budget indie film.

• Intern, "Paradise City"   **2009**
Double Dip Films
Answered phones, wrote press releases, obtained releases from doc subjects, archived footage.

• Intern, Smoke & Mirrors Pictures   **2007–2008**
Served as backup administrative assistant, answering phones, maintaining executives' calendars, filing paperwork; read and covered over 400 scripts; ran errands and deliveries from office to set.

• Assistant Director, "House of Pain"   **2007**
Student Film, Ivory Tower University
Assisted director on $15,000 short film; scheduled five-day shoot, managed budget, organized entire crew before and during shooting.

• Box Office Manager, ITU Theater   **2006–2005**
Oversaw sales of tickets for twelve student theater productions, supervised staff of four people, helped balance annual theater budget and write proposals for additional funding.

OTHER EMPLOYMENT EXPERIENCE

• Concessions Attendant, Dawe Cinemas   **2007**
Served customers at local movie theater, calculated receipts, maintained concessions area.

• Teacher's Assistant   **2006**
English Dept., Ivory Tower University
Assisted professors in "Eighteenth Century English Literature" class: organized lectures, graded papers, filed administrative paperwork.

EDUCATION

• B.A., Ivory Tower University, 2009
• Wisconsin Theater Institute, Midwest Summer College Conservatory, Summer 2008

SPECIAL SKILLS

Adept at Final Draft and Final Cut Pro; fluent in French, Spanish, German; karate brown belt.

industry should be used," says Muirragui. "Maybe you worked in an administrative office for a summer. Maybe you wrote a newspaper column for your college newspaper or [worked at] a radio station. Anything related to the industry is important."

Internships, part-time jobs, and local productions all provide valuable experience and knowledge. They also prove you're proactive in pursuing your career, an impressive factor for employers.

Next, outline other important work experience. If you were a paralegal or a secretary, put it down; if you managed a shoe store, put it down. Though these jobs have nothing to do with Hollywood, they show off your level of experience and professionalism.

Education goes near the bottom and shouldn't include high school (unless you recently graduated and haven't gone to college). Focus only on college, grad school, conservatories, and special programs like writing schools or improv classes. Also, don't put in your GPA; no one cares.

Finally, list special skills that may help you in the job, such as computer knowledge, camera experience, editing skills, or foreign languages. You can also include intriguing professional factoids: volunteer work, awards and honors, and so on.

COVER LETTERS

If résumés are introductions to the "professional you," cover letters are introductions to the "personal you." This not only means you can infuse your letters with bits of charm and personality, it means you should customize them to whatever individuals or companies you're addressing them to.

Cover letters or cover e-mails should be as short as possible, and can be divided into three sections of no more than three or four sentences each.

Begin by stating what position you're applying for and how you heard of it. If you've been referred by someone, put this up front to separate you from stacks of anonymous applicants.

The second section explains why you're applying for this job: your passion, your unique experience, and why you outshine other candidates. "The 'why you would be good at it' is far more important than the rest," says Lifetime reality production coordinator Lisa Lenner. "Be more detailed than 'I'm a hard worker' or 'I type fast.' Say 'I've been watching reality TV religiously since it became huge, and [you produce my] favorite shows.' Be detailed about what you know and what you bring to the table."

End your letter with a short, upbeat closing—something like "I hope to hear from you soon," or "I look forward to meeting with you."

Here's a sample cover e-mail:

Dear Mr. Honcho,

I received your contact info from Amy Wrighter, who mentioned that you and Creative Studios were in the process of hiring a new development assistant, so I wanted to shoot you an e-mail to say hello and introduce myself.

I've been a fan of Creative Studios' work ever since Welcome to Stonehenge, the show that inspired me to go into television. So when I heard there may be an opening at Creative, I wasted no time in writing this e-mail. My goal has always been to work in TV development, and I only want to learn from the best.

I graduated last year from Hallowed Halls University, where I met Amy, and I'm currently working as a development intern at Shining Star Studios.

I've attached my résumé, but if you have any questions or need more info, please don't hesitate to ask. In the meantime, thank you for your consideration, and I hope to hear from you soon!

Sincerely,
Curt Newbie
Cell: 555-648-0812
E-mail: curtn@needajob.com

OTHER APPLICATION MATERIALS

In addition to a résumé and cover letter, some employers want **coverage** so they can evaluate script-reading and critical-thinking skills. Although many give you scripts to cover when you're applying for the job, others may expect you to have coverage on file that you can simply hand it to them.

Some writers and producers, especially in **alternative programming** (where there aren't always traditional writing samples) also use a **demo reel,** a DVD of their produced work, to help them get jobs. This could include clips of TV shows and movies they've written or produced, comedy sketches, short films or Internet content, even standup comedy clips.

FOLLOWING UP

After your initial application, be sure to follow up. If you've applied directly to the person who will be your boss, give them a week, then send an e-mail. If they don't have an answer, ask when you should check in again. Respect their schedule; if they tell you to wait two weeks, don't call sooner. If you're following up with an HR rep, you can probably be more aggressive.

"[When I applied for my first job], I sent my résumé to human resources departments at every major agency," says Schuler. "I called two to three times a week until I got in. And then I was offered mail-room positions at UTA and ICM." (Schuler ultimately accepted at UTA, worked his way up, and eventually became a manager at Levity Entertainment.)

Like Schuler, you'll eventually get a call for an interview. This could be as early as tomorrow, or as far away as a few weeks. Either way, the spotlight's on you: it's showtime.

PREPARING FOR A JOB INTERVIEW

Most applicants go through two rounds of interviews. That's because departing assistants often must hire their own replacements before moving on. So the first interview is with the assistant you'll be replacing; the second is with the boss.

Wherever you begin the interview process, do your research. Learn everything you can about the company, the people who work there, their successes, their failures.

"A lot of times, a simple Google News search will give you all the information you need: projects, deals, upcoming series the company is producing," says Endemol development executive C. J. Yu. "The worst thing you can do is go into an interview for, say, a reality company, and tell them you don't watch reality TV. I once had an interview at a production company . . . and I watched three seasons of their DVD collection. I'd never seen any of their shows, but I didn't want them to know that. Always be knowledgeable."

It's also important to know what's going on in the industry at large. Don't just know what the number-one TV show is—watch it. If your interview is on Wednesday, watch all the shows on Tuesday night. See the current hit movies—as well as non-hits. Listen to the week's top musical artists. Know today's top videos on YouTube and MySpace. Also, be able to articulate your opinion on films, records, and TV shows. This is part of how your future boss will evaluate you—even if you disagree. He's less concerned about whether or not you both agree on your reactions to the latest *Harry Potter* movie than about whether you can clearly express why you feel the way you do.

VITAL STATS YOU SHOULD ALWAYS KNOW

As a pop culture creator and purveyor, it's important to keep your finger on the pulse of what audiences are consuming. Here are some important facts and figures you can monitor to stay at the forefront of popular art and entertainment:

- the top TV series, their Nielsen numbers, and what's happening on each of them
- the latest box office reports
- artists topping the *Billboard* and iTunes charts
- books on the *New York Times* bestseller lists
- hot plays on Broadway and off-Broadway
- successful TV shows in England and Canada
- the most-watched Internet videos
- the most popular video games

DURING THE INTERVIEW

As mentioned, your first meeting will likely be with the current assistant. As a former assistant at Innovative Artists, Janelle Young knows what assistants look for when meeting potential replacements.

"The best way to impress another assistant," says Young, now a development assistant at the Littlefield Company, "is to be inquisitive about the position. Get as much information [as possible] about their routine and their experience at the job. That shows you're interested and, if given the position, will be wary of the do's and don'ts. The next day, send a thank-you card. It's cheesy, but it's appreciated."

Second interviews, which can happen the same day or the following week, are usually with the executive, agent, or producer you'll be working under, so—as with a first date—it's about discovering whether or not you can be partners.

Hollywood is "a performance-based industry," says Karen Jacobs, assistant to *Carpoolers* showrunner Marsh McCall, "so people want to see you 'perform.' How well do you speak? Can you hold your own when someone asks you a tough question? How do you look? In corporate America, [employers look at a résumé] and say, 'This kid went to . . . Harvard undergrad, he looks perfect for this job.' [But] in the entertainment industry . . . it's more based on emotion, gut instincts. It's more like: 'Did we connect?' "

Q & A: HOW TO NAVIGATE
A JOB INTERVIEW

"I'm dismayed at how many people stink at interviewing," says talent and literary manager Kara Welker. "I never understand why people come unprepared and dress poorly. No one expects you to don an Armani suit, but dress professionally and be well-groomed. Know about my company, me, even my clients . . . or what I've produced. We're all Google-able."

Fortunately, you are not going to have any of those problems, because we've brought together a panel of writers, executives, agents, and assistants to guide you through the minefield of your next (or first) Hollywood job interview.

Besides being up-to-date on what's happening in the industry, what else can I say to prove I'm qualified for the job?

"Name-drop if you can. It seems like it should be obnoxious, but it does prove that you know the names to drop, which is better than being completely clueless. It's utterly shameless, but invariably it's a conversation starter."

—Jennifer Godwin, associate editor, E! Online

Is there anything I should *never* say in an interview?

"Avoid negative anecdotes. This is a small town and industry. People know each other who you'd never imagine know each other, so [never] disparage a former employer or working relationship. If you worked for a boss who called you at 4:00 a.m. to pick up his dry-cleaning, save that story for people you're closest to. Focus on what you've learned. There's something to glean from every experience, whether you're an intern, a production assistant, a writers' assistant, a showrunners' assistant."

—Rick Muirragui, script coordinator, *Life*

continued

I secretly want to be a drama writer, but I'm interviewing for assistant jobs at agencies and production companies. I've heard it's unwise to tell interviewers what I really want to do, but I don't want to lie. What's the best path?

"If you're in an interview and someone asks what you aspire to, and you know the answer, you should definitely tell them. But there's a difference between that and announcing your dreams to your new boss on the first day. So if you get hired as a PA, shut up about your dreams and get everybody's lunch. After you've proven your value, then show people your script."

—Adam Chase, showrunner, *Friends*

I'm an ambitious person and have no intention of staying an assistant for long. Should I make this clear so they know I'm always looking?

"No one wants to hire someone who's there for the short term. Give the impression you're . . . someone who will be there for a substantial amount of time."

—C. J. Yu, manager of development, digital media, Endemol USA

After the interview, follow up with a handwritten, snail-mailed thank-you note. It may take a while to hear back, but don't cut off communication. If you haven't heard anything in another week, send an e-mail. And if you're not sure how much to follow up . . . *ask.* The employer may tell you to check in once a week; he may suggest not checking in for a month. Respect his wishes, and you'll soon get a call saying . . .

"You got the job!"

Congratulations! You have now officially crossed the threshold into the red-carpeted, gold-plated, star-studded world of professional Hollywood. Which means you'll soon have connections begging to read your scripts. A boss eager to send out your reel. Writers dying to hire you on their shows . . . Right?

Wrong.

You haven't been hired as a writer. You haven't been hired as a director. You haven't been hired as any kind of producer. (Of course, if you *have* been hired as a writer, director, or producer—my apologies. And if so, why the hell are you reading this book?! I need *you* to hire *me!*) So your first responsibility—and the best way to impress superiors—is to do the job you've been hired for.

"Sometimes in Hollywood, people forget jobs are jobs," says executive producer Adam Chase. "When you get hired for a job, it doesn't mean the person who hired you is going to read your script and get you an agent. It means you got hired to be a PA. So be the best PA you can be, and when you prove yourself to be a useful member of the company, then ask, 'Would you read something I wrote?' They'll be much more open to helping you, and it shows more respect for the people you're working for . . . that what they're doing is important."

Your actual duties will vary from boss to boss. Many bosses are patient and nurturing; others are abrasive and demanding. Some give assistants autonomy; others are meddling micromanagers. Regardless, it takes time to familiarize yourself with projects, learn important players, and develop a rapport with your boss . . . and this time will be smoother if you have thick skin.

"When I first got out here, I didn't know how to spell [then Paramount president] Sherry Lansing's name," says Terri Lubaroff, who went through ICM's agent training program before becoming senior VP of Humble Journey Films. "My boss literally threw a *Creative Directory* in my face and said, 'Memorize it. You'll be quizzed every Monday.' And she followed through. I went home crying for three weeks because I had no idea what I was doing."

Get used to taking work home at night. Every executive and assistant in television carts home piles of scripts, treatments, and development reports. You should also review your boss's phone sheets, calendars, and address books. Familiarize yourself with every aspect of his life. You may also find yourself doing higher-ups' personal tasks: picking up their kids, delivering private packages, making personal calls.

"You're going to do a lot that's not in the job description," says Lenner, and "you have to understand why you're doing it. You're doing it so you can get ahead in the business, so someone trusts you. You're doing it because your boss is busier than you, and you want him to be happy with his job and happy with you. So if you have to do something personal so business can move smoothly and he's not crabby every day, do it. That said, if you're uncomfortable with something, and it's really out of the ordinary, you should talk to someone."

As you settle into the job, you'll solidify your relationship with your boss. And as you become more comfortable juggling day-to-day duties, you'll start to hunger for additional responsibilities, like finding and pitching your own ideas.

MOVING AHEAD

No one expects to be an assistant forever. Yet moving too quickly can be as damaging as moving slowly. Though you may be eager to pitch new projects and develop new shows, your first goal is to please your superiors.

"Prove you're hardworking and reliable," suggests Mike Dunham, coordinator of digital entertainment strategy and operations at NBC Universal, "and once you get an indication your boss trusts you, then start offering up your own ideas."

The best way to earn your bosses' trust is to come to work early, leave late, and demonstrate "you're willing to work harder than you need to get the job done. That will get noticed by your bosses," Dunham says. "And hopefully it'll get noticed by people higher up who might put you in line to take that coordinator position."

ONE-ON-ONE WITH JOEL BEGLEITER, TV LITERARY AGENT, UTA

After clawing his way out of the mail room and up through the assistant ranks, Joel Begleiter is now one of the leading TV lit agents at United Talent Agency, one of the largest agencies in Hollywood. Here, Joel shares his rules for excelling as a Hollywood assistant:

- "Be the first one into the office, and the last one to leave."
- "Plan to work on the weekends. Whether that's reading, doing coverage, running errands, or simply forwarding the office phones to your cell, working in Hollywood is a seven-day-a-week job."
- "Be professional. Hollywood is a pretty informal industry, but let your boss be the one cursing and using slang on the phone. They've earned it, and you have not."
- "Make a point of networking with as many other assistants as you can. Set aside a few nights per week to grab a drink with people you meet on the phone."
- "If you don't understand something that your boss is discussing, ask! You'll be working very long hours for very little pay. It's your boss's job to mentor you, and he or she knows it!"

Most people spend a year or more in one assistant position before getting promoted or moving on. As your year's mark approaches, show signs you're ready for the next step. Offer opinions on scripts and cuts. Ask to sit in on meetings. Bring in your own pitches and writers.

When you finally feel you've proven yourself, schedule time to talk with your boss in person. Then explain what you'd like (a promotion) and why you think you deserve it.

"This is why it's important to have contributed," says Lenner, "so you can say, 'I've been reading all the scripts, watching all the cuts, taking my own notes, and listening to what you've been saying. I think I have a lot to contribute, and I want to know: is there room for growth in this company? Because I think it's time for me to move up or move on.'"

If there's no room for internal growth, let your boss know you need to start looking elsewhere. Don't look without telling him; even if you can't stay, a good relationship will serve you for years to come. And if you've been a good assistant, your boss can help you progress. Hollywood's a small town, and your boss can—and should—make phone calls or serve as a reference.

When you finally get that next job, leave your current role in good standing. Like the assistant before you, you may need to find your replacement or see important projects to completion. Do your best to cooperate. After all, in a short time, you won't be your boss's underling, you'll be a colleague needing to do business together.

HOW TO LOSE A JOB . . . AND SURVIVE UNTIL THE NEXT ONE

Hollywood is always a business of uncertainties. But there's one certainty everyone faces: at some point—whether you're an actor, writer, director, agent, executive, or producer—you will, probably more than once, be unemployed. Shows get canceled. Deals expire. Pilots don't get picked up. Even hit series go on hiatus. So "if you're the type of person who stresses about not having a job next year, or in a month," says writers' assistant David Wright (*Notes from the Underbelly, Malcolm in the Middle*), "this is probably the wrong business."

Here to offer tips on how to plan for and survive leaner times is Susan Marlowe, a CPA who specializes in entertainment-related topics, issues, and clients.

NOTE: Talk to your accountant before doing anything. These tips are simply advice; an experienced entertainment CPA will help figure out which are the best paths for you.

continued

Deposit 15–20 percent of each paycheck into a savings account.

"There's a difference for those just entering the business versus people who have been in it for a while. If you're just entering, you're starting at a lower pay scale, but you have to try and save a little. I would advise people who have been in the industry a while to save even more money."

Don't be afraid to go on unemployment.

"If you work on one job as a paid employee where taxes are taken out, you're normally eligible for unemployment . . . [so] if you need to do it, do it. It's a normal function of the industry . . . [people] go on unemployment till the next job comes up. During the time they're on unemployment, they're looking for the next job, so they have job-hunting expenses, like auditions."

Learn what's tax-deductible.

"One of the biggest mistakes people make is not realizing what might be deductible. The IRS allows people to deduct business expenses that are 'ordinary and necessary' in their trade or business. So if you're an actor, you need to buy books that have do with the entertainment industry, as well as scripts, plays, industry magazines. You may need to go to movies, rent movies, buy DVDs, go to plays, read plays, read about actors. Other things that are deductible are classes, a percentage of your telephone, a percentage of the car that you use to go to auditions. These expenses help you to do your job better. Wardrobe is deductible in the sense that it's not adaptable to street wear. Think of Liberace's costumes; those are the types of wardrobes that would be deductible."

Keep and organize your receipts.

"The best way to keep receipts is to know the list of categories that are deductible. An accountant who specializes in entertainment can give you a list. Keep envelopes and label them by categories, and just put your receipts in each envelope. It's archaic, but it works. At the end of the year, you add everything up and have your deductible expenses."

If you're a starving actor, ask your accountant if you're eligible for performing artists' special exemption, IRC 62 (b)(1) and (2).

"This is an odd little quirk in the law: if someone's adjusted gross income is $16,000 or less, and they have two or more W2s (with income of at least $200 from each employer), and total business deductions exceed 10 percent of income received from those services, then they're allowed to take their expenses as an adjustment to income. So if they make $15,000 and have three acting jobs all year, but have $3,000 in expenses, that $3,000 is deductible against the $15,000 they make. They don't have to itemize their deductions."

HOLLYWOOD JOB-HUNTING RESOURCES

And now, for one of the greatest entertainment job-hunting guides you're ever likely to find . . .

TRADES AND PUBLICATIONS' JOB SEARCH PAGES

Daily Variety—www.varietycareers.com

The Hollywood Reporter—www.hollywoodreporterjobs.com

Backstage—www.backstage.com

AdWeek and **MediaWeek**—www.mediaweekjobs.com

WEBSITES AND ONLINE RESOURCES

4 Entertainment Jobs—www.4entertainmentjobs.com

Aquent—www.aquent.com

Connecting Reality—connectingreality.com

Cynopsis—www.cynopsis.com

EntertainmentCareers.Net—www.entertainmentcareers.net

EntertainmentJobs.com—www.entertainmentjobs.com

FilmStaff.com—www.filmstaff.com

The Grapevine—www.grapevinejobs.com

Greenlight Jobs—greenlightjobs.com

The Hollywood Creative Directory—www.hcdonline.com

Jeff Gund's Info List—www.infolist.com

Mandy—www.mandy.com

Media Match—www.media-match.com

Planet Shark—www.planetsharkproductions.com

RealityStaff.com—www.realitystaff.com

Showbizjobs.com—www.showbizjobs.com

Streetlights—www.streetlights.org

EMPLOYMENT AGENCIES—EXECUTIVE AND ADMINISTRATIVE POSITIONS

Ad Personnel—www.adpersonnel.com

Brad Marks International—www.bradmarks.com

continued

The Comar Agency—www.comaragency.com

Executive Temps—executive-temps.com

The Friedman Agency—www.friedmanpersonnel.com

Star Personnel—www.starpersonnel.ca

Workplace Hollywood—www.workplacehollywood.org

EMPLOYMENT AGENCIES—PERSONAL AND DOMESTIC POSITIONS (PERSONAL ASSISTANTS, NANNIES, ETC.)

Christopher Baker Personal & Corporate Staffing—www.christopher
bakerstaffing.com

Elizabeth Rose Agency—www.elizabethroseagency.com

The Help Company—www.thehelpcompany.com

CORPORATE JOB SITES

CBS—cbscareers.com

Comcast—www.comcast.com/Corporate/About/Careers/careers.html

Disney—www.disneycareers.com

E! Entertainment—www.eentertainment.com/careers/categories

Fox—www.foxcareers.com

Liberty Media—www.libertymedia.com/careers/default.htm

MGM—www.mgm.com/employment.php

MTV—www.mtvcareers.com

NBC Universal—www.nbcunicareers.com

Scripps Networks Interactive—jobs.scripps.com

Sony—www.sony.com/SCA/jobs.shtml

Viacom—viacomcareers.com

Warner Bros.—www.wbjobs.com

AGENCY JOB SITES AND AGENT TRAINING PROGRAMS

Agency for the Performing Arts (APA)—www.apa-agency.com/jobs.php

Association of Talent Agents—www.agentassociation.com/frontdoor/
classifieds.cfm

Creative Artists Agency (CAA)—www.caa.com

International Creative Management (ICM)—e-mail: careers@icmtalent.com

Kaplan Stahler Gumer Braun Agency—www.ksgbagency.com

Paradigm—paradigmla.com/about/openposition

United Talent Agency (UTA) Training Program—www.unitedtalent.com/training/index.html

William Morris Agency—www.wma.com/0/careers/wmacareers

William Morris Training Program—www.wma.com/0/careers/agentcareers

26

Other Ways of Breaking into Hollywood

Sometimes traditional Hollywood paths don't work out. Maybe you can't move to New York or California. Maybe you can't find a job as an assistant. Perhaps you've spent your life in another field and—while you know the most sure-fire way to success is beginning at the bottom—you just can't bring yourself to start over. What then? Are you out of luck? Should you pack it in?

Of course not. Every year, countless people make it in Hollywood through inventive, unconventional channels. It makes it exponentially harder, but it can be done. Sam Greene sold *American Body Shop* to Comedy Central by shooting a spec pilot and sending it cold to the network. Rob McElhenney, Charlie Day, and Glenn Howerton sold *It's Always Sunny in Philadelphia* to FX after shooting a pilot on video for less than $200. In 2007, CBS hired Steven Tsapelas, Angel Acevedo, and Brian Amyot to adapt their YouTube series, *We Need Girlfriends,* into a pilot script (at the time, the eleven-episode series was pulling in up to 700,000 online viewers per episode). And while it's hard to advise somebody on how to be an anomaly, which all these examples are, this chapter explores some "back door" routes into successful TV careers.

GET A JOB AT A LOCAL TV STATION

Local stations are great places to begin learning both the business and the creative sides of producing television. They rarely do scripted series, but they produce daily newscasts, as well as unscripted programming. Chicago's

WLS-TV/Channel 7, an ABC O&O, produces *190 North,* a half-hour magazine program about local entertainment. Modesto, California's KAZV-14 broadcasts local interest shows like *Hometown Focus,* and Houston, Texas's KNWS aired homegrown sitcom *As for Me and My House.* You can even find local cable networks like the Yankees Entertainment and Sports Network (YES), which broadcasts games of the New York Yankees and the New Jersey Nets, or ComCast SportsNet (CSN), which includes several regional cable channels specializing in local sporting events. At these companies, and hundreds like them, you can often find hands-on opportunities it might take months or years to get at larger companies.

"The smaller you go, the more likely you'll find somebody to give you that first chance," says Lori Mitchell, an on-air VJ (video journalist) for WKRN, Nashville's ABC affiliate. "Start in smaller markets. People are much more forgiving there—you're not likely to lose your job if you make a mistake—then move your way up the ladder. Start in Bowling Green, then move to Nashville, then Philadelphia. You're moving around a lot, unfortunately, but that's how you get to the network or large city markets."

Local stations often offer internships and entry-level positions where newbies can learn to shoot, edit, schedule, and budget. They may not pay much (often $20,000–$25,000 per year, depending on the market), but you'll learn production and meet contacts to help you take the next step.

"You have to be in the business because you love it," says Mitchell, "not because you want to make money. You're going to work weird hours and long days . . . you won't have time to go out with friends or party or even go shopping. But get through those first couple years and it gets easier. It all pays off in the end."

PRODUCE A LOCAL TV SHOW

If you can't get to L.A. or New York, another great way to begin producing television is simply to start doing it yourself. Advertising exec Todd Walker and publicist Jean Golden, for instance, had dreamed of producing a TV show since they met in junior high. But living in Minnesota, they had little access to the entertainment industry. So, after years in separate careers, they put their heads together to figure out what untapped TV show territory they could address.

"We looked at the landscape and said, 'Martha Stewart owns living, Bob Vila owns home, *Queer Eye* was beginning to own style,' " says Walker. "We had a relationship with QVC and saw the number of budding inventors who were bringing them in new products. And we thought, 'How can we take this market and capitalize on it?' "

Thus, they landed upon *Million Dollar Idea,* a competition/elimination reality show in which amateur inventors battled for a shot to launch their products. The friends pitched their idea to Mike Smith at KSTP, Minneapolis–St. Paul's local ABC affiliate, who had already received pitches for over 200 new shows that year. But because Walker and Golden were both intimately acquainted with marketing new products and—as marketers and publicists—had access to the world of aspiring inventors (as well as corporate backers who played in that territory), Smith decided to give them a shot.

Walker and Golden met with "anyone and everyone who was in the industry locally," learning everything they could about how to produce a local TV show.

"We had to cast each show, direct each show, produce each show, and *be* in each show," says Walker. "We did everything from A to Z, and we were 100 percent responsible for what went on the air each week."

The show premiered in May 2003. And after three years of hard work and do-it-yourself stick-to-itiveness, *Million Dollar Idea* not only became a hit on local KSTP . . . it sold into **first-run syndication** in virtually every major market in America and was featured on *The Late Show with David Letterman, The Today Show,* and in *Time* magazine. (Learn more about first-run syndication in the text box on the following page.)

"With passion, drive, and determination," says Walker, "there are no geographic boundaries to fulfilling your dream of creating the next hit TV show. It's up to *you* . . . not New York, L.A., or any other city . . . but *you.*"

WORDS OF WISDOM FROM JEAN GOLDEN,
EXECUTIVE PRODUCER, *MILLION DOLLAR IDEA*

Selling a TV show is never easy, and no one knows this better than executive producer Jean Golden. Here, Jean offers some of the pavement-pounding secrets she discovered while setting up her first-run syndicated hit, *Million Dollar Idea.*

- **Research the people responsible for networks or stations you're targeting.** "Often, smaller cable networks have information on their websites as to how to submit a show idea."
- **Read the trades** to "see which executives are being interviewed and quoted on new programming for their networks." These are people you can try to meet and set meetings with.
- **When you call an exec at a network, station, or production company,** "don't leave a message if they're not in. Keep calling until you reach them live. Block out your phone number so they don't think you're a stalker. You may have to call a hundred times before you actually reach them. Call during off-hours, because that's when many executives are in their offices—early in the morning, over noon, early evening. Call rather than e-mail because they won't hang up if you call. And make it *brief*—you'll have thirty seconds or less to pitch your idea."

FROM OPRAH TO XENA: THE WORLD OF FIRST-RUN SYNDICATION

Remember in chapter 3, when we talked about **syndication,** the process of taking TV shows that have already aired on networks and reselling them to local stations? Well, imagine you took a new show and sold it to individual local stations *first,* bypassing networks altogether. As with traditional syndication, you would collect a license fee from each individual station, meaning you'd turn a hefty profit immediately, rather than waiting and hoping the show became a hit and lasted long enough to earn a backend. You'd still have to go to each station or station group individually (which isn't easy), and you'd have the added challenge of trying to sell a show no one had ever seen before, but if it worked, the profitability would be enormous.

The truth is, many people do this. It's exactly what Todd Walker and Jean Golden did with their *Million Dollar Idea* after it had been successful on Minneapolis–St. Paul's local KSTP. While more time-consuming and difficult than selling a preexisting hit, selling a new show into first-run syndication can be extremely lucrative. In fact, many conglomerates have divisions specializing solely in first-run syndication. Disney-ABC Domestic Television, for example, syndicates *Live with Regis and Kelly.* Warner Bros.' Domestic Television Distribution syndicates *The Tyra Banks Show* and *TMZ.com.*

Of course, the same rules that apply to second-run syndication apply to first-run syndication. Local stations still want **strips** (daily shows), and they still pay lower license fees than networks pay, so episodes must be produced with drastically less money. Many first-run syndicated shows have entire season

continued

budgets of $6.5 to $9 million—the average cost of three or four hours of a primetime series. Most are studio-bound, easily produceable programs like game shows (*Jeopardy*), court shows (*The People's Court*), and daytime talk shows (*The Oprah Winfrey Show*). Occasionally, companies produce low-budget scripted shows, such as *Xena: Warrior Princess, Tyler Perry's House of Payne,* and *Wizard's First Rule,* but these are rare.

One advantage to working in first-run syndication is that shows can be produced and sold by independent, non-L.A. or New York–based producers like Walker and Golden. Producers may partner with syndicators like Litton Entertainment and Debmar-Mercury, companies that specialize in selling first-run syndicated TV shows. They may also buy and sell projects at Las Vegas's annual NATPE (National Association of Television Program Executives [www.natpe.org]) Conference & Exhibition, where thousands of international network, studio, and production company execs and producers gather to network and buy or sell **multiplatform** projects (projects that exist on TV, the Internet, cell phones, etc.). While first-run syndication isn't necessarily an *easier* path than TV's traditional network-studio route, it's sometimes more open to creators and producers living outside the Hollywood bubble.

WORK FOR A LOCAL PRODUCTION COMPANY

Most cities, even small ones, have production companies specializing in local commercials, TV or online content, even wedding videos. Bigger cities may have more sophisticated companies doing big-budget industrial videos, short films, and TV specials.

"Starting out with a small company, you're going to get experience," says Addie Rosenthal, president of Blind Squirrels Production Group, a Cincinnati-based company specializing in primetime specials for local and regional programming (*Tradition, One Day,* the *Dreambuilder* film series). "In this industry, more than many others, experience is what counts. It's not book-learning, it's not technology, it's actually doing it."

Because many local production companies are small, interns, assistants, and PAs have a chance to be much more hands-on and actually contribute to projects.

"It's one step from the bottom to the top of the company," says Emmy-winning producer and Blind Squirrels founder Jim Friedman. "You can sit in on the highest-level meetings, but also be on location, in the edit bay, on the set. When you get out [to Hollywood], you'll just be in one department."

Many successful non-L.A. or New York–based production companies have strong connections to their East Coast and West Coast counterparts. Blind Squrrels, for instance, has worked with Drew Carey, Ann Donahue, and Blair Underwood.

"Several of our interns—camera people, lighting, makeup, writers— have gone on to major markets," says Rosenthal, "or stayed here and made a hell of a livelihood in a midsize market."

FIND A JOB IN A TV-RELATED FIELD

If you can't get a position at an actual station or production company, seek out other media fields. Find a job at a radio station, newspaper, or magazine where you can flex creative muscles, watch business decisions being made, and understand how the media interacts with advertisers and audiences.

You can also try marketing and advertising firms, which communicate regularly with TV execs and provide creative opportunities for writers and producers. In 2002, CBS picked up *Baby Bob,* a comedy based on a series of freeInternet.com commercials made by Siltanen/Keehn Advertising. Five years later, ABC ordered *Cavemen,* a half-hour based on The Martin Agency's famous Geico ads. (The pilot was even written by Joe Lawson, a Martin Agency copywriter in Richmond, Virginia.)

Most cities also have local talent agencies. Some, like San Francisco's Stars Agency, provide models for print ads; others, like Boston's Dynasty Models & Talent, provide actors for TV commercials; and some, like Aria Talent in Chicago, specialize in performers for radio and theater spots. Either way, you'll make valuable contacts and get a sense of how the industry runs.

Of course, maybe none of these ideas floats your boat. Maybe you have no interest in sneaking in the back door; you want to start producing content that can get spotted *now*—even if you're nowhere near Hollywood. No problem. Although it's still difficult to get "discovered" outside of New York or California, new technologies and opportunities make it easier. More important, it's essential for artists of all kinds to keep pumping out material, and you should take advantage of every occasion to get your work before audiences. Here are some arenas that often attract TV agents, producers, and execs looking for new talent:

STAND-UP, SKETCH, AND IMPROV

Many of TV's greatest stars hail from live comedy: Jerry Seinfeld, Steve Carell, Lucille Ball. But writers also come from performance backgrounds. *Carpoolers* creator Bruce McCulloch began as a sketch performer with The Kids in the Hall. *Rules of Engagement* creator Tom Hertz began as a stand-up. So did *Everybody Loves Raymond* EP Steve Skrovan.

"Improv classes . . . like The Groundlings and Second City . . .[teach you] to think on your feet," says *Life* writer Wendy Calhoun. "Being in the writers' room is like improv. You have to get up, say what you're thinking, and riff. Improv is great for that. It's also great for teaching you how to do dialogue on the fly. It opens you up out of your shell. Writers get stuck behind their computers, and we forget that what we're putting together has a life of its own afterward. So every writer needs some sort of performance experience."

Stand-up and sketch also give you great contacts. Comedy clubs like The Improv and The Laugh Factory in L.A., and The Cellar and Upright Citizens Brigade in New York, are popular watering holes for people keeping their fingers on the pulse of America's comedy scene.

"People doing stand-up are generally either actors or writers, or some combination," says writer/producer Lesley Wake-Webster (*Notes from the Underbelly, Kitchen Confidential*). "So you meet people who—five or ten years down the road—you'll see in writers' rooms or cast in something you wrote. You hook into a network of people all in the same business, and that's a positive thing."

TV producers, agents, and execs also scour many of the big comedy festivals, like Montreals's Just for Laughs, looking for fresh talent. Festivals often boast a mix of mediums, genres, and performers, from stand-ups and plays to short films and features.

GREAT COMEDY CLUBS ACROSS THE COUNTRY

LOS ANGELES

The Comedy Store (www.thecomedystore.com), 8433 Sunset Blvd., Los Angeles, CA 90069, 323-651-2583

The Comedy Union (www.comedyunion.com), 5040 W. Pico Blvd., Los Angeles, CA 90019, 323-934-9300

The Groundlings (www.groundlings.com), 7307 Melrose Avenue, Los Angeles, CA 90046, 323-934-4747

The Improv (www.improv2.com), 8162 Melrose Avenue, Los Angeles, CA 90046, 323-651-2583 (also locations nationwide: New York, Houston, Chicago, Pittsburgh, etc.)

The Laugh Factory (www.laughfactory.com), 8001 Sunset Blvd., Hollywood, CA 90046, 323-848-2800

Upright Citizens Brigade (www.ucbtheatre.com), 5919 Franklin Ave., Los Angeles, CA 90028, 323-908-8702

NEW YORK

Caroline's (www.carolines.com), 1626 Broadway, New York, NY 10019, 212-757-4100

The Comedy Cellar (www.comedycellar.com), 117 Macdougal Street, New York, NY 10012, 212-254-3480

The Comic Strip Live (www.comicstriplive.com), 1568 Second Ave., New York, NY 10028, 212-861-9386

The Gotham (www.gothamcomedyclub.com), 208 W. 23rd Street, New York, NY 10011 212-367-9000

The Laugh Factory (www.laughfactory.com), 303 West 42nd Street, New York, NY 10036, 212-586-7829

Pianos (www.pianosnyc.com), 158 Ludlow Street, New York, NY 10002, 212-505-3733

The People's Improv Theater (The PIT) (www.thepit-nyc.com), 154 W. 29th Street, New York, NY 10001, 212-563-7488

Rififi (rififinyc.com), 332 E. 11th Street, New York, NY 10003, 212-677-1027

Upright Citizens Brigade (www.ucbtheatre.com), 307 W. 26th Street, New York, NY 10001, 212-366-9176

continued

OTHER GREAT CLUBS

The Comedy Works (www.comedyworks.com), 1226 15th Street, Denver, CO 80202, 303-595-3637

The Second City (www.secondcity.com), 1616 N. Wells Street, Chicago, IL 60614, 312-664-4032

Zanies (www.zanies.com), locations in Nashville, TN, and Chicago, Vernon Hills, and St. Charles, IL

POPULAR COMEDY FESTIVALS AROUND THE WORLD

Edinburgh Festival Fringe (www.edfringe.com). The world's largest arts festival, open to all performers—theater, stand-up, sketch, improv, even dance.

Just for Laughs Festival (www.justforlaughs.ca), Montreal, Quebec, Canada. Where Hollywood finds fresh comedy talent, from stand-ups and sketch groups to short films and features.

Melbourne International Comedy Festival (www.comedyfestival.com.au). Third-biggest comedy fest in the world; often attracts American agents, managers, and producers.

New York Comedy Festival (www.nycomedyfestival.com). Focuses more on big names that draw crowds rather than fresh faces drawing Hollywood scouts.

San Francisco Sketchfest (sketchfest.com). A top festival for sketch, variety, and alternative comedy.

Sketchfest NYC (www.sketchfestnyc.com). Another leading sketch and variety festival.

THEATER

TV execs, unfortunately, aren't usually big theater-goers—which is a shame, because America has a lot of great theater. Nevertheless, if you write, produce, or direct a play that gets good buzz, you can attract the eyeballs of the industry. Pulitzer Prize nominee Jon Robin Baitz had written numerous plays, including Broadway's 2001 *Hedda Gabler* adaptation and Drama Desk nominees *The Film Society* and *Three Hotels*, before writing on *The West Wing* and *Alias* and eventually creating *Brothers & Sisters* for ABC. Bridget Carpenter had had plays produced (*Trepidation Nation, Hurry!*) at Minneapolis's prestigious Guthrie Theater and Kentucky's Humana Festival before staffing on *Dead Like Me* and *Friday Night Lights.* And L.A. stage director Matt Shakman's acclaimed Black Dahlia Theatre production of *Orson's Shadow* landed him his first TV directing gig, directing an episode of ABC's *Once & Again.*

"When I'm developing and producing a new play, I have a close collaboration with the playwright that's similar to a pilot director working with a writer," says Shakman, who now directs hit shows like *House* and *Everybody Hates Chris* while still serving as the Black Dahlia's artistic director. "You're developing something from the beginning, helping establish a world, casting all your performers as opposed to just your guest cast. You're putting something together from beginning to end, which is a satisfying process, because in television you're not able to have that impact. When I come to a television set, I am, hopefully, more supple than I might have been if I only did television."

Of course, even if your play doesn't immediately land you a successful TV career, it still strengthens your writing, gives you production experience, and helps you meet directors, actors, designers, and producers.

"I wouldn't say working in theater is a great way to build a career in another medium," says Shakman, "but it certainly can be a great way to build a community of artists, and that circle can rise together. You meet a bunch of writers, people start having success here or there, hopefully they'll reach out and help you as well. That's what happens when you have a community of friends who respect each other's work."

MAKE A MOVIE

Okay, sure—making a movie is easier said than done. But in an age where top-quality cameras and professional editing software are fairly inexpensive, making a film, whether it's a short or a feature, has never been easier. Also, television often mines the world of features for viable TV ideas. *Friday Night Lights* and *Stargate SG-1* were obviously based on big studio blockbusters, but TV execs also comb through the ranks of shorts and indie films. In 2006, MTV's Logo announced their first scripted series, *Exes and Ohs,* based on Michelle Paradise and Lee Friedlander's award-winning short, *The Ten Rules: A Lesbian Survival Guide.* And CBS's 2003 sitcom *My Big Fat Greek Life* was based on Nia Vardalos's independent comedy, *My Big Fat Greek Wedding.*

The toughest part, of course, isn't actually making the film; it's getting it seen by the right people. Fortunately, America's full of film festivals, from massive industry hangouts like Sundance to local celebrations like the Wisconsin Film Festival. And although premiering your film at Pennsylvania's Algonquin Indiefest may not attract the attention of network presidents, it certainly gives you good press, street cred, and access to other artists and filmmakers. Find film festivals near you at websites like FilmFestivals.com, Inside Film Magazine (www.insidefilm.com), or Yahoo!'s film fest directory.

You can also post short films on websites like YouTube, FunnyorDie, MySpace, Vimeo, and Metacafe. Twenty-year-old Brooke Brodack signed a TV development deal with Carson Daly Productions after Daly saw her online portfolio of shorts and sketches. And twenty-one-year-old college dropout and filmmaker David Lehre earned a $300,000 pilot deal with FOX after posting his eleven-minute *MySpace: The Movie.*

"The number-one way people are blowing up in comedy today," says Levity Entertainment manager Matt Schuler, "is by making a funny short film and [having it blow up] on the Internet. A big MySpace presence, or lots of hits on YouTube, gets more attention than almost anything else in the comedy business."

For lists of online distribution sites, check out the appendix or the text box on pages 279–280.

TV FESTIVALS AND CONFERENCES

TV festivals and conferences haven't taken off like film and comedy fests, but some are gaining traction. The NATPE Conference & Exhibition (www.natpe.org), which we discussed in the sidebar on pages 363–364, was a longtime leader, but in 2008 converted itself into a new-media and multiplatform conference.

A newcomer to the festival/conference circuit is the New York Television Festival (www.newyorktelevisionfestival.com), which began in 2005 as a way to connect independent artists with executives, agents, producers, and fans. Each fall, the festival hosts parties, panels, premieres, and the Independent Pilot Competition, which allows budding writers and directors to showcase work for industry buyers. At the 2005 festival, A&E picked up the improv comedy pilot *Criss-Cross,* and Versus purchased *Off the Hook,* a docu-series about deep-sea fishermen. The next year, *Split the Difference,* a scripted pilot from Mary Egan Callahan, Joe Narciso, and Bruce Hurwitt, found a home at NBC Universal Television Studios (now Universal Media Studios).

A quick Google search will uncover other TV festivals, like L.A.'s Independent TV Festival (www.itvfest.org), as well as international celebrations, like Canada's Banff World Television Festival (www.bwtvf.com) and the Edinburgh International Television Festival (www.mgeitf.co.uk).

WRITING PROGRAMS AND CONTESTS

In the cutthroat world of TV staffing, network and studios' writing and diversity programs (see the sidebar on page 192) are terrific ways to get noticed and break in. But they're also incredibly competitive, and acceptance is a roll of the dice. Although a quick Internet search will reveal scores of writing contests, few—if any—are monitored by people in the TV industry. My advice: apply to these contests at your own risk, and while any win or acknowledgment can bolster your résumé, most aren't viable ways to an actual TV writing job. Still, check out the box below for a handful of legit contests. And by "legit," I don't mean they'll get you a job; I just mean they're reliable places that won't rip you off.

TV WRITING CONTESTS

Austin Film Festival Screenplay & Teleplay Competition—www.austin filmfestival.com

Creative Screenwriting's AAA (Access, Acclaim, Achievement) Screenwriting Contest—www.creativescreenwriting.com/aaa/index.html

Filmaka/FX Competition—www.filmaka.com

People's Pilot Competition—www.tvwriter.com/contests/peoples/about.htm

Scriptapalooza International TV Writing Competition—www.scriptapalooza .com

Slamdance Teleplay Competition—www.slamdance.com

Spec Scriptacular—www.tvwriter.com/contests/spec/index.htm

Writer's Digest Annual Writing Competition—www.writersdigest.com/ competitions

WRITE SOMETHING ELSE

If none of these routes work, there's only one thing left to do: *write something else.* Follow in the footsteps of Tucker Max or Jeremy Blachman, whose blogs (www.tuckermax.com and The Anonymous Lawyer, anonymouslawyer .blogspot.com, respectively) were developed as pilots at Comedy Central and NBC. Write a graphic novel like *The Pro, Six,* or *Nobody,* which were adapted into pilots for Spike, FOX, and ABC Family. Publish a nonfiction book, like reincarnation expert Brian Weiss's *Many Lives, Many Masters* or Harvard professor Jerome Groopman's *The Anatomy of Hope: How People Prevail in the Face of Illness,* which were transformed into drama pilots at CBS and HBO.

"Don't be afraid to try different forms: plays, screenplays, short stories, novels, webisodes," says *Boston Legal* co-producer Sanford Golden. "And read everything you can: other people's scripts, books on form, writer biographies, etcetera. Take classes, join a writers' group, get actors to do readings of what you've written. Write that screenplay you always wanted to write, finish it and move on. Someday, something will happen. You'll sell something you've written, someone will hire you to write something, or you'll wake up and realize you have a choice: if you want to keep writing, you're going to have to give up something else—a house, a job, a marriage. And you'll need to measure what's most important. If it's writing, the choice is made. If not, then congratulations: you have a life."

Ultimately, Hollywood is looking for one thing: writers who see the world in unique ways. So if the best way to showcase your vision is in a comic book or a novel or a series of sketches—write that. It may not be the most direct path to Hollywood, but it'll do something more valuable: *make you a better writer.*

And at the end of the day, that's why you're here.

Because being an employable writer is not about massive ratings. It's not about overall deals. It's not about syndication. It's about being the best writer you can possibly be—then getting even better. And the only way to do that is by continuing to put pen to paper, fingers to keyboard, and letting your deepest, darkest thoughts drain into the words. Finding your own unique voice and using it to show the world what's inside. And then doing it again. And again. And again.

Now, *that's* good television.

Glossary

A-STORY The main plot of a TV episode.

ABBY SINGER The second-to-last shot of the day.

ABOVE-THE-LINE "Creative" employees and artists: writers, directors, actors, hosts, etc.

ACQUISITION A second-run TV program or movie purchased for reuse.

AD SALES The department of a network charged with selling and maintaining ad space within TV shows.

AFFILIATE A privately owned TV station that aligns itself with a broadcast network.

AFFILIATE REVENUE License fees paid by cable service providers to cable networks in exchange for programming.

AGENT A representative authorized by a client to procure work and negotiate contracts.

ALTERNATIVE PROGRAMMING The process of developing TV programs that aren't traditionally scripted comedies or dramas (reality shows, talk shows, sketch shows, game shows, etc.); also, the department of a network or studio responsible for developing unscripted programming.

ANALOG SIGNAL Televised data (picture and sound) that are converted to actual radio waves and transmitted from a broadcaster to a receiver, then converted back into sound and picture.

ASSISTANT DIRECTOR (*AKA* AD *OR* 1ST AD) The below-the-line stagehand responsible for overseeing the set during shooting.

ATTACHMENT Elements added to a project to make it more attractive to buyers: showrunners, stars, directors, etc.

AUTOMATIC DIALOGUE REPLACEMENT (ADR) The process of rerecording specific lines of dialogue; also known as "looping."

B-STORY The primary subplot of a TV episode.

BABY WRITER A TV writer who has not yet been staffed or hired on an actual show.

BACK NINE The final nine episodes of a TV series' full twenty-two-episode season.

BACKEND Revenue generated after, or in addition to, a series' network run; usually includes syndication, home video, Internet distribution, etc.

BARTER TIME Advertising time used instead of money as compensation for a TV show's syndication rights.

BASE CAMP A meeting and preparation location for a TV crew shooting on location.

BEAT A single piece of story information.

BEAT OUT To outline a scene, story, or entire TV episode.

BELOW-THE-LINE "Technical" employees: line producers, costume designers, cameramen, etc.

BLIND SCRIPT A development deal contracting a writer to develop and write an as-yet-undetermined TV project.

BLOCK A group of thematically or demographically related TV shows; also, to choreograph actors' or cameras' on-stage movements.

BOOKEND An ad spot on either side of a commercial break, often one of the most valuable spots.

BRANDED ENTERTAINMENT Original programming, usually on the Internet, designed to promote a specific brand or product.

BREAK A BABY To get a baby writer his or her first writing job.

BREAK A STORY To beat out, or outline, a story.

BREAKDOWN A description of a TV show's characters, used to inform actors and talent agents about available acting opportunities; also, in soap opera writing, a detailed story outline of an actual episode.

BREAKDOWN WRITER A daytime soap opera writer charged with writing highly detailed breakdowns, or outlines, of full episodes.

BROADCAST To transmit TV content as radio signals over airwaves.

BUG A graphic image used for promotional purposes. Bugs often appear in corners of the TV screen to remind audiences what network they're watching.

BUMPER A short on-air promotional spot leading into or out of a commercial break.

BURN OFF To move episodes of a TV series to a poor time slot in order to use them up without officially canceling the show.

CABLE PROVIDER (*AKA* CABLE OPERATOR) A company that owns, installs, and allows access to wires delivering TV content to consumers' television sets (Time Warner, Comcast, Cablevision, etc.).

CALL SHEET A document distributed to a production crew detailing a workday's schedule, location, driving directions, and call times.

CALL TIME The designated arrival time for members of a TV shoot's cast and crew.

CAMERA BLOCKING The process of choreographing camera movements to film a TV show.

CAST-CONTINGENT A pilot that must hire an approvable cast before being greenlighted for production.

CABLE To transmit radio signals carrying TV content over wires (rather than radio waves), which customers pay to access.

CHARACTER-DRIVEN A story whose stories spring from character interactions and relationships, à la *Grey's Anatomy, The West Wing,* etc.

CO-EXECUTIVE PRODUCER The second-highest title for a writer or producer on the staff of a TV show, just behind executive producer.

COMPETITIVE REPORT A development report tracking and detailing projects at other companies.

CONSULTING PRODUCER Upper-level writers who aren't necessarily part of a TV show's regular staff.

CONTINUITY Story and visual consistency within an episode (i.e., a script supervisor monitors continuity to make sure scenic elements are logical and consistent from one shot to the next).

CONVERGENCE The ultimate union of TV and the Internet into a single medium.

CO-PRODUCER In scripted television, usually a title for a mid-level writer.

COUNTERPROGRAM A TV scheduling strategy in which networks air content to attract audiences not being serviced by other networks.

COVERAGE Individual shots focusing on specific parts or people in a filmed scene; also, a report synopsizing a movie, book, or TV script; also, a "book report" detailing a reader's reaction to script, treatment, or project.

CPC (COST PER CLICK) A unit measuring the price of online advertisements based on how many people click the ads.

CPM (COST PER MILLE) A unit measuring the price of an advertisement on either TV or the Internet based on how many thousands of people watch it.

CRAFT SERVICES An on-stage department responsible for cleaning the stage and providing refreshments.

CREDITS A writer's or producer's résumé of projects; also, the list of a TV show's employees, usually scrolled on-screen at the beginning or end of a program.

CURRENT PROGRAMMING The division of a network or studio that oversees and maintains TV shows already on the air.

D5 A popular digital video format invented by Panasonic.

DAILIES During principal photography, daily video compilations of all footage shot the previous day.

DAYPART Groups of hours dividing the day's TV schedule, based on demographics watching television during those times.

DEFICIT FINANCE A system of funding a TV show in which one company covers a show's excess budget in order to maintain ownership of the property.

DEMO REEL A compilation of video clips used to showcase the on-air work of an actor, director, producer, or host.

DERIVATIVE CONTENT Online shows based on preexisting properties.

DESIGNATED MARKET AREA (DMA) A term coined by Nielsen Media Research to refer to specific U.S. media markets.

DESTINATION PROGRAMMING TV shows or series that air only in specific slots on a network's schedule, meaning audiences can watch them only at that specific time.

DEVELOPMENT DEAL A contract in which a writer or producer agrees to develop or write a certain number of projects for a studio or production company. Also, a talent deal in which a studio or production company develops a new project for a particular performer.

DEVELOPMENT REPORT A chart detailing TV scripts, pilots, and projects in development, either internally or at rival companies.

DEVELOPMENT SLATE A roster of a network, studio, or production company's current projects.

DIGITAL MEDIA Any distribution platform using digital technology, usually including downloads, streams, or video-on-demand.

DIGITAL SIGNAL Television information that's translated into bits of computerized data (rather than radio waves) and transmitted from a broadcaster to a receiver, where the receiver reconstructs the original sound and picture.

DIGITAL VIDEO RECORDER (DVR) A machine allowing users to record video content to a hard drive or other device.

DIGITIZE The process of uploading high-definition video into a computer at lower resolution.

DIRECTOR An above-the-line artist responsible for translating a script into images, establishing a TV show's visual style, and helping actors develop characters.

DIRECTOR'S CUT The second cut of a TV episode, compiled by the director and editor.

DUB HOUSE A facility that creates copies, or dubs, of video and audio media.

EDIT DECISION LIST (EDL) An electronic list of an episode's audio or visual cues and cuts.

EDITOR'S CUT The first cut of a TV episode, compiled solely by the editor.

EFFECTS HOUSE A company that designs and implements visual effects.

ELECTRONIC SELL-THROUGH (EST) The ability to buy video or audio content that can be kept on a hard drive.

EPISODIC Pertaining to any television program whose story and characters continue from episode to episode (almost any traditional series with multiple episodes is considered "episodic"); also, an on-air promotional spot that teases upcoming episodes of a particular series.

EVENT DRAMA A TV series whose stories revolve around a single event, like *Lost*'s plane crash or *Jericho*'s bombings.

EXECUTIVE PRODUCER The highest producer credit in television.

EXECUTIVE STORY EDITOR In scripted television, usually a title for a low-level writer.

FIRST-LOOK A development deal in which a studio contracts a writer, producer, or production company to give the studio first dibs on anything the writer/producer creates.

FIRST-RUN SYNDICATION To bypass broadcast or cable networks and sell original content directly to individual TV stations.

FLIGHTING The series of weeks or programs in which a particular TV advertisement airs.

FORCE MAJEURE A contractual clause allowing a party to terminate a legal agreement due to an unforeseen event or "act of God."

FORMAT The unique architecture of a specific TV concept (i.e., the format of *Law & Order* involves cops solving a crime in the show's first half and lawyers prosecuting it in the second. The format of *American Idol* involves singing contestants being eliminated each week until one winner remains.).

FORMAT-DRIVEN TV shows whose episodes find conflict by recycling story-generating situations. Game shows like *Wheel of Fortune* rely on the same games each episode; procedurals like *CSI: New York* rely on crimes and crime-solving techniques.

FORMAT RIGHTS The legal ability to produce, or reproduce, a specific television concept.

FRANCHISE A literary device allowing a TV show to generate an endless number of organic stories.

FREELANCE EPISODE An episode of a TV show not written by the regular staff.

FULL PILOT A pilot that has been given an order for a full-length, broadcast-quality production.

GIVE-BACK A refund of money given to an advertiser when ad space in a certain program has been canceled or fails to meet expectations.

GRID A daily, weekly, or yearly chart used by TV schedulers to strategize and organize a network's airtime.

HANDLER A representative who handles the professional and legal needs of his of her clients. Most handlers are agents, managers, lawyers, or publicists.

HEADEND A cable provider's regional hub, where television content is received via satellite before being transmitted as light pulses via fiberoptic wires to nodes and televisions.

HEAD WRITER The top writer on a daytime soap opera staff.

HIGH-DEFINITION A digital broadcast television format with much greater resolution than standard television broadcasts. High-def is different from mere digital television; traditional TV sets can't receive a high-def signal, even with a digital converter box.

HIP POCKET To unofficially represent a writer, director, actor, etc.; to help them without making them an official client.

HOLDING DEAL A talent deal made in hopes of casting a performer into a show, but without the intention of developing a show specifically for that performer.

HORIZONTAL PROGRAMMING A TV scheduling strategy in which airtime is filled with destination programming, forcing viewers to tune in at specific times.

HUT LEVELS A percentage of "Homes Using Television" during a specific measurement period.

IF-COME A development deal in which a writer partners with a studio or production company on a particular project, but only gets paid if the company sells the project to a distributor.

IN THE FIELD Shooting on location.

INVENTORY A network's stock of available ad time.

LAYBACK The process of synchronizing a TV episode's visual and audio elements into the final version.

LEAD-IN A TV show preceding another show.

LEAD-OUT A TV show following another show.

LEAN-BACK Entertainment that allows audiences to have a passive, noninteractive experience.

LEAN-FORWARD Entertainment that allows audiences to interact with content.

LEAVE-BEHIND A document left with potential buyers as a refresher after a pitch.

LEGS A show's sustainability.

LICENSE FEE A fee paid to temporarily acquire or distribute TV content.

LINE CUT A cut of a sitcom compiled live as it's being performed and taped.

LINE PRODUCER A below-the-line employee who oversees a TV pilot or series' physical production.

LOCK PICTURE To agree not to change any more of an edited cut.

LOGLINE A one-sentence distillation of a story's premise.

LOGGER In reality TV, a low-level employee who transcribes filmed footage into a script to be used by producers.

LONGFORM TV movies or miniseries.

LONGFORM CONTRACT An official, full-length legal contract.

LOOPING See Automatic Dialogue Replacement.

LORE See Mythology.

MAKE-GOOD A reparation, usually free ad space, given to an advertiser who has purchased a network ad spot that fails to meet expectations.

MANAGER A representative hired by clients to offer career advice, make introductions, and help facilitate work opportunities.

MARKET A geographic region where the population receives the same TV and/or radio broadcasts.

MARTINI The final shot of the day.

MASTER A wide shot covering an entire scene.

MEDIA BUYER A middleman, usually representing multiple advertisers, who negotiates contracts and advertising arrangements between advertisers and ad sellers.

MEDIA CONGLOMERATE A corporation comprised of smaller companies and holdings; media conglomerates usually consist of many entertainment- and media-related subsidiaries.

MOBISODE An episode of a series created specifically for cell phones or mobile devices.

MULTICAMERA A style of shooting in which actors perform on a soundstage while cameras, placed around the stage's perimeter, film the action. Multicams typically have live audiences and laugh tracks.

MULTIPLATFORM Projects with components existing in more than one medium; i.e., a TV component, an Internet component, a mobile phone component.

MYTHOLOGY A TV series' narrative backstory and history, the internal story-world created by the writers.

NETWORK A company responsible for distributing television content.

NETWORK COMPENSATION ("NETWORK COMP") A fee paid by a broadcast network to local affiliates in exchange for affiliates airing that network's content.

NETWORK CUT The cut of a TV episode that is delivered to network executives.

NETWORK DRAFT The draft of a script that is delivered to network executives.

NETWORK TEST The final stage of auditions, in which actors read for TV network executives.

NEW MEDIA See Digital Media.

NODE In the cable TV delivery process, neighborhood devices used to convert light pulses received from cable headends into electronic signals, which are delivered to consumers' TV sets via coaxial cable.

OFF-BOOK Able to be performed without relying on a script or book (i.e., "The actor had memorized all her lines and was completely off-book").

OFFLINE EDITING The stage of editing in which a TV episode is constructed using low-resolution, digitized footage.

ON-BOOK Unable to be performed without looking at a script or book; the opposite of off-book.

ON THE BUBBLE A term referring to a show whose survival is uncertain.

ONE-OFF A one-time TV program or event.

ONE-SHEET (*AKA* ONE-LINER) During principal photography, a list of each day's scenes and shots in the order they'll be filmed.

ONLINE EDITING The stage of editing in which a high-resolution version of a TV episode is constructed using original high-resolution footage.

OPTION A privilege, secured by paying an upfront fee, allowing the buyer to execute a transaction within a specified time frame and agreed-upon terms. An advertiser, for instance, may have an option to keep or back out of acquired ad spots. A producer may acquire an option on a script or project.

OUTPUT A tape of the final offline edit of a TV episode.

OUTPUT DEAL A contract in which a foreign distributor agrees to buy a certain number of a TV studio's productions, even before seeing the shows.

OVERALL DEAL A development deal in which a studio contracts a writer, producer, or production company to create content exclusively for its company for a specific amount of time.

OWNED-AND-OPERATED (O&O) A local TV station owned and controlled by one of the major broadcast networks (ABC, CBS, NBC, FOX, CW, MyNetworkTV).

PACKAGE To combine elements of a TV project to make it more sellable; also, the combined bundle of those elements.

PARTICIPATION ADVERTISING A method of selling ad space in which multiple advertisers buy space in one product, such as a magazine or TV program.

PARTICIPATION POINTS (*AKA JUST* "POINTS") The one hundred points into which the backend of a TV show is divided. Points are split between the studio, production company, showrunner, and anyone else allowed to partake in the show's profits.

PAY-OR-PLAY A development deal in which a writer is hired by a studio or production company to work on a project and gets paid whether the project sells or not.

PENALTY A fine paid by a TV network to a studio if the network fails to order a promised project or number of episodes.

PERSONALITY-DRIVEN See Talent-Driven.

PICKUP Scenes or shots that are refilmed after a multicamera sitcom's live taping.

PICK UP THE OPTION To choose to exercise one's option; in TV, usually referring to a showrunner's decision to keep a particular writer on staff.

PILOT A sample episode of a new TV show, used to convince networks to "pick up," or buy, the entire series.

POD A group of commercials, or commercial break; also, short for Production Overall Deal.

POD DEAL ("PRODUCTION OVERALL DEAL") An overall deal specifically for a production company, not an individual writer or producer.

PODCAST A digital audio or video show distributed online for use on portable media players; to create and distribute a podcast.

POP-UP MESSAGING Text or graphic images that appear on a TV screen to promote specific shows, events, or the network brand.

PORTAL An online distribution site.

PREMISE A TV series' most basic, overarching story.

PREMIUM CABLE NETWORK Subscription-based cable networks whose revenue comes solely from subscriber fees rather than advertising.

PRE-READ The first stage of auditions, during which actors read only for the casting director.

PRESENTATION ("PILOT PRESENTATION") A low-budget, often truncated, pilot.

PRESHOOT In a sitcom, scenes or shots that are filmed before the arrival of a live audience.

PRE-TABLE An "unofficial" table read, usually consisting only of a show's actors, director, and writer, and occurring shortly before the official table read.

PRIMETIME The daypart between 8–11 p.m. (PST) when the largest number of viewers watch television.

PRINCIPAL PHOTOGRAPHY (*AKA* PRODUCTION) The actual filming of a TV pilot or episode.

PROCEDURAL A story in which characters follow a specific procedure to get them through the story. Mysteries are often procedurals, as detectives follow a set of clues until they close the case and complete the story.

PRODUCER In scripted television, usually a title for a line producer or mid-level writer.

PRODUCERS' SESSION The second stage of auditions, during which actors read for a TV show's producers.

PRODUCER'S CUT The third cut of a TV episode, compiled by the writer, producers, director, and editor.

PRODUCT INTEGRATION A method of promotion in which an advertiser pays to have its brand or product woven organically into a story or TV episode.

PRODUCTION COMPANY A professional organization responsible for the creative development of a TV or an Internet program.

PRODUCTION DESIGNER A below-the-line artist who supervises a TV show's art department and oversees the show's visual design.

PRODUCTION DRAFT The draft of a TV script given to the production crew to begin prepping and shooting.

PUNCH UP To rewrite or improve a script.

PUT PILOT A pilot that a network has promised to produce by attaching a penalty (paid to the project's studio) if it reneges.

RATING In Nielsen Media Research's widely used audience measurement system, ratings (as opposed to shares) calculate the percentage of homes or individuals watching a specific show at a specific time, based on the total number of households that own TV sets—whether those TVs are currently turned on or not. As of August 2007, one ratings point equals about 1,128,000 households (with each household averaging 2.7 viewers).

RECURRING Actors or characters who aren't usually contracted to a specific number of episodes but are continually brought back to a TV show.

REGULAR An actor or character contracted to appear in a certain number of a TV series' episodes; usually the show's main characters.

REPURPOSE To reuse television content.

RESIDUALS Additional payments to a writer, producer, actor, or director for reusing material that artist helped create.

RERUN A repeat of a particular TV episode; also, to air repeats.

REVERSE COMPENSATION ("REVERSE COMP") A fee paid by local affiliates to a broadcast network in exchange for being provided with TV content.

ROLLING CALLS The process where one person, usually an assistant, connects two other people over the phone (often the assistant's boss and a third party). The assistant then stays on the phone so when the call's over, he or she can connect their boss to another call. This allows the boss to make several phone calls without hanging up or dialing.

RUN A TV show's specific cycle of airing. A series' first airing on a network is its "network run," or "broadcast run"; its subsequent airing in syndication is its "second run," etc.

RUN-THROUGH A scaled-down performance of a TV show, taking place a few days before the actual filming, in order to get notes and suggestions from producers and executives.

SAMPLE SPEC An episode of a currently airing TV show used by television writers as a calling card to get hired.

SCATTER MARKET Ad inventory remaining after networks' upfront buying season; scatter market inventory is usually bought and sold on an à la carte basis.

SCRIPT COMMITMENT A development deal contracting a writer to develop and write one particular project.

SCRIPT COORDINATOR Support for a TV show's writing staff, usually responsible for tracking script changes, archiving scripts and paperwork, distributing drafts, etc.

SCRIPT READER Freelance employee hired to read scripts and write coverage.

SCRIPT WRITER A daytime soap-opera writer who writes a full script based on a breakdown writer's detailed outline.

SCRIPTED Television programming using a traditional script: comedy, drama, sketch, etc.

SECOND-RUN SYNDICATION (*AKA* OFF-NET SYNDICATION) The process of selling to individual local stations and/or cable channels a TV show that has already aired.

SECOND TEAM The group of stand-ins used to help stagehands light and prep a scene for shooting when the actual actors are unavailable.

SEPARATED RIGHTS An artist's ownership in continuations, remakes, sequels, or adaptations of a particular work.

SERIALIZED A story told over several installments or episodes.

SERIES COMMITMENT A promise, made by a network to a studio (usually backed up with a penalty), to greenlight and air a specific TV project.

SERIES SEQUEL PAYMENTS Fees paid to TV show creators for every produced episode of their series.

SET-TOP BOX An external piece of hardware that transfers content from one device (like a computer) to a television.

SHARE In Nielsen Media Research's audience measurement system, shares (as opposed to ratings) measure the percentage of households or individuals watching a certain show at a certain time, based on the total number of homes that own TV sets and actually have them *turned on* at that specific time.

SHOOTING DRAFT See Production Draft.

SHORTFORM TV or online content that is shorter than TV's usual hour or half-hour programming.

SHOTLIST A director's list of specific shots needed for each scene.

SHOWRUNNER A show's head writer or producer, overseeing everything from writing and storytelling to props and set design.

SIDES Pages of a script read by an actor during auditions.

SINGLE-CAMERA A style of shooting in which one primary camera is used, giving a TV show a look similar to a movie.

SINGLE-LEAD A TV series whose stories revolve mainly around one particular character (*Eli Stone, The New Adventures of Old Christine*).

SIZZLE REEL A short video introducing a reality show's characters and format; a teaser video to help sell a reality show.

SNIPE A larger version of a bug, or graphic image used for promotion. Snipes can sometimes take up to a third of the television screen.

SOAP OPERA (*AKA* SOAP) A highly serialized series that derives stories and conflicts from character interaction (*Days of Our Lives, Beverly Hills 90210*).

SPEC PILOT A pilot written without being first bought and developed by a network or studio.

SPEC SCRIPT A script, either a pilot or an episode of a show already on air, that's written without being commissioned first by a network or studio.

SPECIALS One-time programs such as the Academy Awards or CBS's Celine Dion concert special, *That's Just the Woman in Me.*

SPOT In postproduction, to watch a TV episode and evaluate its sound elements: music, dialogue, sound effects, etc.

STAFF WRITER The title for the lowest-level writer on a TV show's staff.

STAND-ALONE An episode of television where a close-ended story begins and ends in the same episode.

STATION A local studio that broadcasts TV or radio content to a specific region or market.

STATION GROUP A company owning and controlling multiple TV stations.

STORING AND FORWARDING The process of transmitting content to a digital storage device.

STORY EDITOR A title for a low-level writer.

STORY PRODUCER Storytellers on a reality show; reality TV's version of writers.

STREAM Digital or online content received by the consumer as it's being provided by the distributor. Unlike a download, the material is never stored on the consumer's hard drive.

STRIKE To deconstruct the set of a TV show.

STRIP To air a show on a daily basis.

STRUCTURE The architecture of a TV series' storytelling mechanism. Most shows tell either stand-alone stories or serialized stories.

STUDIO A company responsible for financing, developing, and producing TV content for networks and distributors.

STUDIO CUT The cut of a TV episode delivered to studio executives.

STUDIO DRAFT The draft of a script sent to the show's studio executives.

STUDIO TEST The stage of auditions during which actors read for studio executives.

STUNT A sensational event or TV special used to draw large audiences.

STUNT CASTING Hiring high-profile guest stars to lure audiences.

SUPERVISING PRODUCER In scripted television, an experienced mid-level writer. In nonscripted television, an upper-level producer who deals with both story and management.

SWEEPS Quarterly periods in which Nielsen Media Research monitors viewing habits of larger-than-normal swaths of the TV audience.

SYNDICATE To sell TV content directly to individual local stations and/or cable channels.

TABLE READ A meeting in which a TV show's actors read aloud the show's script for an audience of producers, writers, and executives.

TALENT Usually refers to on-air artists such as hosts, actors, or other performers. "Talent" occasionally refers to all artists, however, including directors and writers. Also, the department of a network, studio, or production company responsible for casting.

TALENT DEAL A contract made between a performer and a network, studio, or production company, binding the performer to that company for a specified amount of time.

TALENT-DRIVEN A TV series developed around a particular performer (*Everybody Loves Raymond, Cosby, The Oprah Winfrey Show,* etc.).

TECH SCOUT The process of surveying a shooting location for technical issues.

TELECINE The process of transferring photographic film to high-definition video.

TELENOVELA Limited-run, highly serialized TV programs that usually run over one hundred episodes. Telenovelas have been most popular in Spanish-speaking countries, where programs like Colombia's *Betty la fea (Ugly Betty)* have gone on to massive international success.

TELEPLAY A script for a TV episode.

TENTPOLE A high-profile TV program or series around which other programming is based or scheduled.

THRUST A document laying out the direction of a daytime soap's story over the next two weeks.

TIME-SHIFT To record or download TV or online content in order to watch it on one's own schedule.

TITLE HOUSE A company that designs shows' opening credits and title sequences.

TONE MEETING In single-camera television, a meeting between the director and writer to discuss the style, feel, and tone of a particular episode.

TRACKING BOARD An online information forum where users find, post, and swap information about companies' development slates.

TRADITIONAL CABLE NETWORK A cable network that generates revenue from both subscription fees and advertising sales.

TUNE-IN An on-air promotional spot directing viewers to one particular program or event.

TURNAROUND A predetermined set of nonworking hours that production crew members must receive before beginning another workday.

UNIT PRODUCTION MANAGER (UPM) The line producer's second-in-command, helping to oversee a TV show's physical production issues such as renting equipment and maintaining a budget.

UNSCRIPTED Television programming not using a traditional script (talk, reality, game shows).

UPFRONT BUYING SEASON A period, usually preceding the new TV season, when networks sell future ad space at a reduced cost.

UPFRONT PRESENTATIONS (*AKA* UPFRONT ANNOUNCEMENTS) Gala affairs in which broadcast networks announce new and returning series to advertisers in hopes of generating early ad support.

VANITIES Production departments dealing with hair, makeup, or wardrobe.

VERTICAL PROGRAMMING A TV scheduling strategy that schedules the same shows at many different times on the schedule, hoping that audiences may tune in randomly, but once they do, they'll be hooked.

VIDEO-ON-DEMAND (VOD) A system allowing viewers to select and watch, either via downloads or streams, video content over an interactive TV or Internet connection.

VIDEO VILLAGE During a TV shoot, a portable grouping of TV monitors connected to cameras, allowing production staff and crew to see what the cameras see.

VLOG Short for "video blog," an online journal of video posts.

VOICE (*AKA* POINT-OF-VIEW) The unique quality of how a writer or artist "sees the world," then articulates that vision into his or her work.

VOLUME DEAL See Output Deal.

WALLPAPER To fill airtime with repeats of the same episodes or series, to make them ubiquitous.

WEBISODE An episode of a series created specifically for the Internet.

WORK-FOR-HIRE A deal in which a company hires an employee (often a writer or producer) to work on a project without giving them ownership in the product.

WRITERS' ASSISTANT An assistant responsible for supporting the writing staff of a TV show: taking notes, researching stories, typing outlines, etc.

WRITER'S DRAFT The first draft of a writer's script to be shared with the rest of the writing staff.

WRITERS' ROOM The writing staff of a television series; also, the actual room in which the writing staff works.

Throughout this book, we've given you many resources to help you on your path to television domination: books, websites, software, etc. But just when you thought we couldn't give you any more helpful tools . . . here we are again, with an entire appendix of secret weapons to help you climb the television ladder. (Seriously: I expect a mention in your Emmy speech.) I've organized the appendix into the following topics:

- Staying Informed—Trades, Periodicals, and News Sources
- Organizations and Associations
  - Labor unions
  - Museums, professional organizations, and trade associations
  - Networking, support, and community-building
- Writing Programs, Classes, and Fellowships
- Research and Tracking Boards
- Reading About Writing and Writers
  - Books
  - Magazines
  - Blogs and websites
- News Schmewz! Gossip, Commentary, and Other Fun (but Oh-So-Important) Stuff
- Podcasts
- Theater
- Extra Reading (and Viewing)

STAYING INFORMED—TRADES, PERIODICALS AND NEWS SOURCES

The entertainment industry is full of news sources—news for TV, news for film, news for actors, producers, gaffers, and grips. There are so many news sources, in fact, it's often hard to tell the difference or which are any good. So here's a list of some of the industry's most popular (and trusted) news sources: trades, magazines, websites, blogs. And to help you further, I've organized them according to my personal favorites. (Feel free to disagree, of course; these are just the ones I find most helpful.)

Good

Ain't It Cool News (www.aintitcoolnews.com): Film and TV news/rumors site focusing on sci-fi, fantasy, and horror projects.

Box Office Mojo (www.boxofficemojo.com): In-depth movie box office data.

Cable U (www.cableu.tv): Subscription-only service offering analyses of cable performances and trends.

Deadline Hollywood Daily (www.deadlinehollywooddaily.com): Industry reporter Nikki Finke's blog; one of the best places to go for high-profile breaking news stories.

The Futon Critic (www.thefutoncritic.com): Television news, as well as projects in development (both current and archived).

Hollywood Wiretap (www.hollywoodwiretap.com): Aggregate of Hollywood gossip and hard news, with links to original sources.

Nielsen Media Research (www.nielsenmedia.com): TV ratings data, as well as TV news and tracking technology developments.

Programming Insider (pifeedback.com): *MediaWeek*'s senior TV editor shares news, Nielsen ratings, and analyses of the TV industry.

TV Guide (www.tvguide.com): Online regional TV schedules; plus, TV and pop-culture news, gossip, and commentary.

TVNewser (www.mediabistro.com/tvnewser): News about the world of TV news.

TVTattle (www.tvtattle.com): Mixture of TV news and criticism.

Zap2It (www.zap2it.com): Covers TV and film news, plus TV schedules, ratings, and reviews.

Better

Broadcasting & Cable (www.broadcastingcable.com): Coverage of all aspects of the TV industry: programming, financial, technological, regulatory, etc.

MediaWeek (www.mediaweek.com): News and analysis of all forms of mass media: TV, radio, digital media, newspapers, etc.

Multichannel News (www.multichannel.com): Weekly trade paper about the cable TV world.

Television Week (www.tvweek.com): Coverage specifically of the TV industry.

Best

Cynopsis (www.cynopsis.com): Focuses specifically on news updates in TV and digital media; also includes a podcast and daily e-mail newsletters.

Hollywood Reporter (www.hollywoodreporter.com): One of the entertainment industry's top two trade papers.

Variety (www.variety.com): One of the entertainment industry's top two trade papers.

ORGANIZATIONS AND ASSOCIATIONS

Labor Unions

American Federation of Television & Radio Artists (www.aftra.org): Represents actors in TV, film, and commercials, as well as news reporters, singers, voice-over artists, dancers, etc.

Directors Guild (www.dga.org): Represents TV and film directors.

International Alliance of Theatrical Stage Employees (IATSE) (www.iatse-intl.org): Represents TV and film stagehands.

Motion Picture Editors Guild (www.editorsguild.com): Represents editors and postproduction artists in TV and film.

SAG (www.sag.org): Represents TV and film actors and performers.

Writers Guild of America, East (www.wgaeast.org): Represents East Coast TV, film, news, and radio writers.

Writers Guild of America, West (www.wga.org): Represents California TV, film, news, and radio writers.

Museums, Professional Organizations, and Trade Associations

Academy of Television Arts & Sciences (www.emmys.tv): Home to the primetime Emmys, Los Angeles Emmys, and the Television Hall of Fame.

Museum of Broadcast Communications (www.museum.tv): Located in Chicago, the "premiere broadcast museum in America and home to the only National Radio Hall of Fame"; don't miss their incredible on-line Encyclopedia of Television (www.museum.tv/archives/etv/).

Museum of the Moving Image (www.movingimage.us): New York museum dedicated to collecting and protecting artifacts related to TV, film, and digital media.

National Academy of Television Arts & Sciences (www.emmyonline .org): Nonprofit "dedicated to the advancement and promotion of artistic, educational, and technical achievements within the television industry." Also, home of Emmys for News, Sports, Daytime, Public Service, and Technology.

National Association of Broadcasters (www.nab.org): Trade organization representing local TV and radio stations; also hosts the annual NAB Show convention.

National Association of Television Program Executives (NATPE) (www.natpe.org): Organization providing information and networking opportunities in the world of TV programming.

National Cable & Telecommunications Association (www.ncta.com): Trade association for the American cable industry.

The Paley Center for Media (www.paleycenter.org): With centers in New York and L.A., a leader in ongoing dialogues about the "cultural, creative, and social significance of television, radio, and emerging platforms." Also, home to the outstanding annual Paleyfest.

Producers Guild of America (www.producersguild.org/pg): A trade association representing TV, film, and digital media producers.

Writers Guild Foundation (www.wgfoundation.org): Nonprofit organization designed to "preserve and promote excellence" in TV and film writing; the Foundation also operates the Writers Guild Foundation Shavelson-Webb Library, which houses a massive collection of TV scripts and screenplays available to the public for in-house reading.

Networking, Support, and Community-Building

Association of Celebrity Personal Assistants (www.acpa-la.com): Support organization for L.A.-based personal assistants.

Connecting Reality (www.connectingreality.com): Organization for reality TV artists and employees; includes networking events, a job board, online forums, etc.

Hollywood Hill (www.hhill.org): Social change and activism organization for Hollywood professionals.

Hollywood Radio & Television Society (www.hrts.org): Nonprofit networking and educational organization comprised of West Coast TV execs and producers.

The Jewish Federation (www.jewishla.org): L.A.'s largest Jewish nonprofit includes its high-profile Entertainment Division, which provides members with social projects and networking opportunities.

Junior Hollywood Radio & Television Society (www.jhrts.com): The "junior" branch of the Hollywood Radio & Television Society, geared toward junior executives, agents, assistants, and coordinators.

mediabistro.com (www.mediabistro.com): Organization for professionals working in all branches of media, including TV, publishing, digital media, radio, film, advertising, public relations, and more.

Next Gen Femmes (www.nextgenfemmes.com): Community-building organization dedicated to young women working in entertainment.

New York Celebrity Assistants (www.nycelebrityassistants.org): Support organization for L.A.-based personal assistants.

Organization of Black Screenwriters (www.obswriter.com): Networking and support organization for African American TV and film writers; includes writers groups, workshops, seminars, and contests.

Women in Film (www.wif.org): Organization dedicated to empowering women working in media and entertainment, including offering internship and mentoring programs.

WRITING PROGRAMS, CLASSES, AND FELLOWSHIPS

CBS Diversity Institute: Writers Program—www.cbscorporation.com/diversity/cbs_network/index.php

Disney Fellowship—abctalentdevelopment.com/programs_writers.htm

FOX Writers Initiative—www.fox.com/diversity/creative/writer_initiative.htm

Groundlings—www.groundlings.com

Improv Olympic—www.iowest.com, chicago.ioimprov.com

mediabistro.com—www.mediabistro.com

NBC: Writers on the Verge—www.diversecitynbc.com

Nickelodeon Writing Fellowship—www.nickwriting.com

The People's Improv Theater (PIT)—www.thepit-nyc.com/classes.html

Robert McKee's Story Seminar—mckeestory.com

Second City—www.secondcity.com

Sherwood Oaks Experimental College—www.sherwoodoakscollege.com

Steve Kaplan's Comedy Intensive—www.kaplancomedy.com

UCLA Extension—www.uclaextension.edu

Upright Citizens Brigade—www.ucbtheatre.com

Warner Bros. Writing Program—www2.warnerbros.com/writersworkshop

RESEARCH AND TRACKING BOARDS

Hollywood Creative Directory (www.hcdonline.com): Periodically published "phone books" to the industry, including titles, credits, and contact info.

IMDB (www.imdb.com): Database of detailed production info and business data for TV shows and movies.

ShowbizData (www.showbizdata.com): Aggregates film and TV news, as well as box office data and films in development and production.

Studio System (studiosystem.com): Subscription-based website providing contact info, project tracking data, business updates, etc.

TrackingB (www.trackingb.com): Subscription-only tracking board.

TVbytheNumbers (www.tvbythenumbers.com): Daily Nielsen TV ratings, analysis, and commentary.

TV.com (www.tv.com): Database of current and old TV shows, including crew lists and episodes guides.

TVTracker & FilmTracker (www.tvtracker.com, www.filmtracker.com): Subscription-only TV and film tracking boards.

Who Represents (www.WhoRepresents.com): Subscription-based system providing detailed representation info for Hollywood talent.

READING ABOUT WRITING AND WRITERS

Books

Created By: Inside the Minds of TV's Top Show Creators, by Steven Prigge

On Writing, by Stephen King

The Showrunners, by David Wild

TV Creators: Conversations with America's Top Producers of Television Drama, by James L. Longworth

The Writer Got Screwed (but didn't have to): A Guide to the Legal and Business Practices of Writing for the Entertainment Industry, by Brooke A. Wharton

Magazines

Creative Screenwriting—www.creativescreenwriting.com

Script—www.scriptmag.com

Written By—www.wga.org/writtenby/writtenby.aspx

Writers Digest—www.writersdigest.com

Blogs and Websites

The Artful Writer (http://artfulwriter.com): Screenwriter Craig Mazin (*Scary Movie 3, Superhero Movie*).

By Ken Levine (kenlevine.blogspot.com): TV writer Ken Levine (*Cheers, Frasier*).

Complications Ensue (complicationsensue.blogspot.com): Canadian TV writer Alex Epstein (*Galidor, Charlie Jade*).

Jane Espenson.com (www.janeespenson.com): TV writer Jane Espenson (*Buffy the Vampire Slayer, Battlestar Galactica*).

JohnAugust.com (www.johnaugust.com): "A ton of useful information on screenwriting" from the writer of *Corpse Bride* and *Charlie and the Chocolate Factory.*

Kung Fu Monkey (kfmonkey.blogspot.com): Film and TV writer John Rogers (*Cosby, Leverage, Transformers*).

News From Me (www.newsfromme.com): Veteran TV writer Mark Evanier.

Script Notes (www.writersdigest.com/scriptnotes): Yours truly, Chad Gervich.

TVWriter.com (www.tvwriter.com): TV veteran Larry Brody (*Mike Hammer, The Fall Guy, Police Story*).

What It's Like: The Real World of Television, According to Lisa Klink (Lisaklink.com): Film and TV writer Lisa Klink (*Roswell, Martial Law, Painkiller Jane*).

NEWS SCHMEWZ! GOSSIP, COMMENTARY, AND OTHER FUN (BUT OH-SO-IMPORTANT) STUFF

Defamer (defamer.com): L.A.-based TV, film, and pop-culture news and gossip.

E! Online (www.eonline.com): Entertainment and celebrity news and gossip.

FishbowlLA (www.fishbowlla.com): Breaking news about L.A. media—with an attitude.

FishbowlNY (www.fishbowlny.com): Breaking New York media news.

Gawker (gawker.com): New York's most ruthless source for "media gossip and pop culture round the clock."

The Huffington Post (www.huffingtonpost.com): Arianna Huffington and Ken Lerer's site of news, media, and cultural commentary.

The Industry.LA (www.theindustry.la): Invite/referral-only service providing updates on industry events, job openings, etc.

Lost Remote (lostremote.com): TV news and commentary.

The Mayor of Television (www.insidesocal.com/tv): TV and film critic David Kronke's blog on the state of television.

Past Deadline (www.pastdeadline.com): Ray Richmond, critic and columnist for *The Hollywood Reporter,* analyzes the entertainment industry.

Perez Hilton (perezhilton.com): Juicy celeb gossip with attitude. This definitely isn't "news," but everybody talks about it.

Planet Shark (www.planetsharkproductions.com): Production company that also publishes a website promoting industry events, jobs, casting calls, and news.

Previously On . . . (www.previouslyontv.com): Current and extensive libraries of episode guides and recaps of current TV shows.

The Superficial (www.thesuperficial.com): Anticlown Media's acclaimed site of celebrity news and gossip.

Television Without Pity (www.televisionwithoutpity.com): Some of the best (and snarkiest) recaps of current TV episodes.

TMZ (www.tmz.com): Like Perez Hilton, a go-to spot for celeb gossip and videos.

Trend Central (www.trendcentral.com): The Intelligence Group's free website and e-mail monitoring hot trends in entertainment, technology, fashion, and lifestyles.

TV Decoder (tvdecoder.blogs.nytimes.com): *New York Times* media reporter Brian Steller's blog covering "what's on, who's watching, and why it matters."

TV Guide.com (www.tvguide.com): National TV schedules and news.

Valleywag (valleywag.com): Witty news and gossip from Silicon Valley.

Videogum (videogum.com): Scott Lapatire's companion blog to Stereogum, but covering TV, web videos, film, and on-screen entertainment.

PODCASTS

For people on the go, podcasts are a great way to take your news or entertainment with you . . . whenever or wherever you're going. Podcasts are downloadable, streamable, portable, and—usually—totally free. Here are some of my favorite podcasts for and about writing and television.

Creative Screenwriting Magazine (www.creativescreenwriting.com): Interviews with Hollywood's top TV and film writers.

Cynopsis: In Your Ear (www.cynopsis.com): Audio and video versions of Cynopsis's daily TV news updates.

KCRW's The Business (www.kcrw.com/etc/programs/tb): Claude Brodesser-Akner's weekly half-hour look at the business machinations of Hollywood.

KCRW's Martini Shot (www.kcrw.com/etc/programs/ma): TV writer Rob Long's weekly five-minute take on the inner workings of Hollywood.

Programming Insider (marcberman.tv/podcast): *MediaWeek*'s senior editor Marc Berman's audio podcast sharing TV news, ratings, and analyses.

THEATER

I know I said TV execs don't see much theater, and it's true. But that doesn't mean there's not good theater out there, and finding it is a great way to see inspiring art, meet talented artists, and get your own work in front of audiences. Here are some of my favorite L.A. theaters and sketch groups supporting new work and—sometimes—attracting industry eyes. (Also check out the list of comedy and sketch clubs on pages 367–368—they're other great places to see interesting live work.)

The Actors Gang—www.theactorsgang.com

Black Dahlia—www.thedahlia.com

Comedy Central Stage—www.comedycentral.com/comedians/ccstage

Evidence Room—evidenceroomtheater.com

Groundlings—www.groundlings.com

Odyssey—www.odysseytheatre.com

Second City—www.secondcity.com

Upright Citizens Brigade—www.ucbtheatre.com

EXTRA READING (AND VIEWING)

Books

The Agency: William Morris and the Hidden History of Showbusiness, by Frank Rich

The Business of Television, by Howard J. Blumenthal

The Complete Directory to Prime Time Network and Cable TV Shows, 1946–Present, by Tim Brooks and Earle F. Marsh

Desperate Networks, by Bill Carter

It's All Your Fault: How to Make It as a Hollywood Assistant, by Bill Robinson and Ceridwen Morris

Jump In: Even If You Don't Know How to Swim, by Mark Burnett

The Last Lone Inventor: A Tale of Genius, Deceit, and the Birth of Television, by Evan I. Schwartz (also check out Aaron Sorkin's stage play, *The Farnsworth Invention,* which is not related to this book, but tells the story of TV inventor Philo Farnsworth in classic Sorkin style)

The Late Shift, by Bill Carter (was also turned into a movie, directed by Betty Thomas)

The Mailroom: Hollywood History from the Bottom Up, by David Rensin

Show Runner: Producing Variety & Talk Shows for Television, by Steve Clements

Television Disrupted: The Transition from Network to Networked TV, by Shelly Palmer

Where Did I Go Right?: You're No One in Hollywood Unless Someone Wants You Dead, by Bernie Brillstein

Periodicals

Backstage (www.backstage.com): TV and film news and casting information for actors and performers.

Below the Line (www.btlnews.com): Newspaper geared toward below-the-line and postproduction workers.

DGA Monthly (www.dga.org/news/current/mag_current.php3): Official print magazine of the Directors Guild of America.

Emmy (www.emmys.tv/emmymag): Official print magazine of the Academy of Television Arts & Sciences.

Movies and TV

Want to see the television industry in action? Can't get to Los Angeles? These TV series and films offer varying depictions of how television works (and, with the PBS documentaries, how it came to be). If you're not actually watching how Hollywood works firsthand, these may be the next best thing.

30 Rock (NBC TV series), created by Tina Fey (Broadway Video, Universal Media Studios: 2006–present).

Californication (Showtime TV series), created by Tom Kapinos (Showtime: 2007–present).

The Comeback (HBO TV series), created by Lisa Kudrow and Michael
   Patrick King (Warner Bros. Television, Home Box Office: 2005).

The Larry Sanders Show (HBO TV series), created by Dennis Klein and
   Garry Shandling (Columbia Pictures Television, Brillstein-Grey Entertainment, Home Box Office: 1992–1998).

Network (Movie), produced by Howard Gottfried, directed by Sidney
   Lumet, written by Paddy Chayefsky; starring: Faye Dunaway, William
   Holden, Peter Finch (MGM, United Artists: 1976).

Sports Night (ABC TV series), created by Aaron Sorkin (Touchstone Television, Imagine Television: 1998–2000).

The TV Set (Movie), produced by Jake Kasdan and Aaron Ryder, written
   and directed by Jake Kasdan; starring: David Duchovny, Sigourney
   Weaver (2006).

Pioneers of Primetime (PBS documentary special), produced by Steven J.
   Boettcher (Public Broadcasting Service: 1995).

Pioneers of Television (PBS documentary miniseries), produced by
   Steven J. Boettcher and Michael J. Trinklein (Boettcher/Trinklein Productions: 2008).

Studio 60 on the Sunset Strip (NBC TV series), created by Aaron Sorkin
   (Warner Bros. Television: 2006–2007).

Acknowledgments

Now that we've come to the end, I can safely tell you the secret I've been keeping this entire time: *I didn't write this book myself.* Every word on these pages exists thanks to the support, encouragement, hard work, and friendship of a massive list of people. I wish I could fit their names on the cover, but I can't. So do me a favor: read these final paragraphs and give a bit of thanks to the people here. Everything you learned is because of them.

First, three people without whom this book would not exist. Taffy Brodesser-Akner has championed this project—and me—since day one. I have never met someone who's as able as she is to make the impossible happen. She's an incredible ally, a great writer, a terrific friend. Next: Lindsay Orman, whose laser-sharp notes and insight have made the book infinitely better . . . and me a stronger writer. She doesn't know it yet, but from now on I'm asking her for notes on *everything* . . . my next book, my next TV show, the chicken recipe I'm making for dinner tonight. And of course: Laurel Touby . . . the genius behind mediabistro.com, whose vision and enthusiasm are nothing short of miraculous.

An incredible thank-you goes to Warren Littlefield. Every once in a while, you meet someone whose guidance, support, and friendship changes the course of your life. Warren fulfilled his mentor duties years ago . . . and continues to be the best mentor I've ever known. Also, he owes me a Porsche.

A huge note of gratitude for Lindsay Howard, who has truly earned her title of "most bad-ass, motherfucking, take-no-shit agent in town." Her tireless belief in me is both flattering and humbling, and I hope I can soon repay the favor by making her insanely, disgustingly rich. Of course, right there alongside her: Alan Moore, who is—without a doubt—going to rule reality television someday. Also, thanks to Hayden Meyer for all his help and hard work, and the tireless efforts of Dan Abrams, John Seitzer, and Colin Whitman.

To all the people at mediabistro.com who have helped in so many ways:

Chris Ariens, Amanda Barrett, Erin Berkery, Shao Chen, Seamus Condron, Megan Diamondstein, Rachel Edelman, Jessica Eule, Stefanie Flaxman, Rebecca Fox, Amy Hauck, Brie O'Reilly, Mara Piazza, Carmen Scheidel, and Michelle Yates.

This book would not have been possible without days upon days of interviews, favors, and referrals. I'd like to thank a handful of people who went above and beyond the call of duty, giving me way more time and energy than I had any right to expect. Special thanks to Sara Auspitz, Andy Bourne, Mark Burley, Adam Chase, Cindy Chupack, Allison Cooper, Rob Corn, Cara Coslow, Tony Cowley, Jane Espenson, Drew Goddard, Allison Gibson, Richard Hatem, Rich Hull, Karen Jacobs, Eric Kim, Aaron Korsh, Barry Kotler, Patty Mann, Jeff Melvoin, Rick Muirragui, Mark Ovitz, Paul Rabwin, Lesley Wake-Webster, Kara Welker, Scott Wallace, Aury Wallington, David Wright, and Jill Young.

And to the heart and soul of this book, everyone who allowed me to pick their brains, use their genius, and learn from their knowledge and experiences: an enormous, heartfelt THANK-YOU. These are the true authors of *Small Screen, Big Picture:* Rachel Abarbanell, Anya Adams, Will Akers, Chris Alexander, David Armour, Janae Bakken, Char Beales, Preston Beckman, Joel Begleiter, Michael Benson, Felicity Blunt, Joan Boorstein, Yvette Lee Bowser, Tully Bragg, Claude Brodesser-Akner, Harold Brook, Kate Burns, David Bushman, Wendy Calhoun, Sal Calleros, Eric Cardinal, Bill Carroll, Antonia Coffman, Kyle Crafton, Diana Cronan, Jim Delisle, Emily Dennis, Jocelyn Diaz, Kelly Drinan, Mike Dunham, Joe Earley, Michael Egan, Ari Eisner, Loren Elkins, Joke Fincioen, Jim Friedman, Elise Friemuth, Alexandra Gaines, Lainie Gallers, Rafael Garcia, Zig Gauthier, Bruce Gellman, Rochelle Gerson, Curt Gervich, Dave Gervich, Sue Gervich, Sam Girgus, Jen Godwin, Jean Golden, Sanford Golden, Jen Good, Erin Gough-Wehrenberg, Tracy Grant, Scott Grogin, Craig Harrison, Dan Harrison, Chris Henze, Joe Hipps, Jim Holbrook, Lee Horvitz, Daniel Hsia, Angela Iuorno, Laura James, Al Jean, Andrew Johnson, Scott Kamler, Alexa Kent, Curt King, Aaron Kogan, Amanda Kogan, Kate Korsh, Brad Kreisberg, Correne Kristiansen, Jackie Kulesza, Lisa Lenner, Stuart Levine, Scott Levy, Rich Licata, Jack Loftus, Steve Love, Terri Lubaroff, Oliver Luckett, Gabriel Marano, Marsh McCall, Patrick McClenahan, Lisa McDivitt, Biagio Messina, Gaurav Misra, Gregg Mitchell, Lori Mitchell, Sahar Moridani,

Paul Nawrocki, Mike Nelson, Molly Newman, Graham Nolan, Sean O'Boyle, Chris Parnell, Donald Passman, Karen Pedersen, Jerry Petry, Jon Piebenga, Jason Pinter, Kevin Plunkett, Marla Provencio, Ryan Quigley, Cathy Rasenberger, Suhail Rizvi, Ann Lewis Roberts, Melissa Rosenberg, Addie Rosenthal, Karine Rosenthal, Rich Rosenthal, Melissa Sadoff, Andrew Saunders, Joe Schlosser, Matt Schuler, Beth Schwartz, Kenny Schwartz, Mike Schwartz, Melissa Scrivner, Bryan Seabury, Jenna Seiden, Matt Shakman, Jim Sharp, Elizabeth Sheinkman, Dana Shelburne, Matt Short, Rebecca Short, Chris Silbermann, Ted Sinclair, Sarah Singer, Charles Slocum, Mike Smith, Brian Stampnitsky, Charlie Stickney, Angie Strobl, Lorrie Sullenberger, Lance Taylor, Amanda Tracey, Craig Turk, Michael Valeo, Todd Walker, Jon Wax, A. J. Webster, Dann Webster, Jon Weisman, Danielle Weinstock, Matt Weitzman, Chris Whitesell, Tracy Wilcoxen, Brad Wollack, Karen Wyscarver, Curtis Yomtob, Paul Young, C. J. Yu, Marlene Zakovich, and Monika Zielinska.

Most important, thanks to my parents, who only let me watch an hour of TV a day so I'd appreciate reading more. It backfired.

And thanks to Kelly, who spent a year sleeping alone and talking me off cliffs. I love you.

Index

A&M Records, 22
A&E channel, 23, 25, 245, 370–71
A-side, 210
A-story, 105, 106, 189
Abarbanell, Rachel, 329
Abby Singer, 160
ABC: advertising on, 179, 180, 181,
    182–83, 185; affiliates of, 361, 362; and
    cable, 247, 248; cancellations at, 230,
    236, 238; and comparison of broadcast
    and cable networks, 242, 248; and deals,
    129; development at, 75, 76, 81, 82, 91,
    137–38; and differences between studios
    and production companies, 75, 76; and
    digital media, 268, 271, 273–74; Family
    channel of, 91, 372; Hatem's pilot for,
    176–78; hiring at, 365; and industry
    structure, 19, 20–21, 22, 23, 25, 28, 29,
    30–31, 35, 36; interns at, 341; market-
    ing at, 228; and packaging, 311; pickups
    by, 175; and pilot season, 88; and
    pitches, 118, 121; production company
    deals with, 20, 43; programming on,
    60–62, 64, 71; ratings of, 34; and reality
    TV, 250, 252; and recipe for TV shows,
    100, 104; reruns on, 245; soap operas
    on, 218; and syndication and backend,
    51, 53, 54; Television Studio of, 35; and
    upfronts, 179, 180, 181, 182–83, 185;
    and WGA Strike, 13, 44, 252; writers'
    room at, 203. *See also* Touchstone;
    specific person
Abrams, J. J., 40, 41, 54, 96, 309
Academy Awards, 13
accounting department, 163
Accustream Media Research, 282–83
Acevedo, Angel, 360
acquisitions, and cable networks, 244
actors: contracts for, 75; and development
    season, 84; and digital media, 284; im-
    pact of WGA Strike on, 284; and post-

production, 172; and premiere, 230; and
    preproduction, 142–43, 144, 146, 149,
    150, 151, 152–55; and production, 222,
    223, 224; representation for, 308–9,
    310; residuals for, 47; and shooting, 156,
    157, 158, 159; talent deals with, 84;
    unions for, 156; and upfronts, 178
Adams, Anya, 219
advertising: and backends/syndication, 49,
    56; on broadcast television, 28, 178,
    179, 180–81, 182, 186, 242, 248, 249,
    283; on cable, 178, 180, 242, 243, 244,
    248, 249; and cancellations, 237;
    changes in, 184–86; cost of, 183, 184;
    and differences between studios and pro-
    duction departments, 75; and digital
    media, 270, 271, 272, 283, 284; foreign,
    180; and industry structure, 30, 32, 33,
    37; and networks, 270; online, 178; par-
    ticipation, 184; and pilot season, 87; and
    production, 225; and programming, 61,
    62, 65, 67, 73, 74; and ratings, 67; and
    reality TV, 253, 254; and soap operas,
    216; and staying on the air, 229, 231;
    and upfronts, 178–86; and WGA Strike
    of 2007–2008, 11, 14, 85; and what ad-
    vertisers don't choose, 184. *See also* mar-
    keting; publicity; *specific organization*
affiliates, 29, 67, 68, 179, 225, 229, 243,
    244, 266
Agency for the Performing Arts (APA), 307,
    310, 330, 332, 334, 358
agents/agencies: above-the-line, 309–10;
    agenting, 318; assistants at, 333–34, 335;
    attracting, 315–17; below-the-line, 309,
    310; and contracts/deals, 124, 125, 130,
    146; employment, 357–58; green room
    of, 162; and hiring staff, 191–92,
    198–99, 200-201; and job sites and train-
    ing programs, 358; keeping, 317–19; lev-
    els of, 310–11; and pitches, 117, 120;

ABOUT THE AUTHOR

Chad Gervich is a television producer, published author, and award-winning playwright. After spending almost five years as a development executive with the Littlefield Company, former NBC president Warren Littlefield's production company, Chad developed and produced the Style network's hit comedy/reality series, *Foody Call*. He then went on to executive produce *Celebrity Drive-By*, a talk show pilot for E! Entertainment, and *The Witches of Orange County*, a docu-series with the Weinstein Company. Chad has also written and produced for *Reality Binge* on Fox Reality Channel and *Wig Out*, an online sitcom for Warner Bros., as well as developing *Dirty Laundry*, an Internet soap for Fox TV Studios. In addition, he created and produced *Morning Call Time*, the only news podcast geared specifically to the entertainment industry. Chad has also worked in production on such shows as *Malcolm in the Middle* (FOX), *Girls Club* (FOX), and *Star Search* (CBS). His plays have been produced across the country, and his writing frequently appears in *Daily Variety*, *Fade In*, *Moving Pictures*, *Writer's Digest*, and *Orange Coast*, as well as several other nationally available books and magazines. Chad is also the regular blogger for *Script Notes*, *Writer's Digest* magazine's screenwriting blog. You can contact Chad directly and learn more about writing and producing television at www.chadgervich.com.

mediabistro.com was founded by Laurel Touby more than a decade ago, and has since become the country's largest online destination for media professionals.

Also from mediabistro.com

Write Your Own Check

GET A FREELANCE LIFE
mediabistro.com's Insider
Guide to Freelance Writing
$14.00 paper (Canada: $21.00)
978-0-307-23803-0

Considering a career in freelance writing? Already a free-lancer but seeking practical, solid advice on the basics of the business? *Get a Freelance Life* is the complete guide to all aspects of a freelance writing career, straight from the creators of mediabistro.com—the nation's most connected, authoritative source for media professionals.

Available from Three Rivers Press wherever books are sold.
www.crownpublishing.com